In Love in War and Peace

First published in 2002 by Fortingall Publications Ltd in Association with Pedigree Books Ltd,
The Old Rectory, Matford Lane, Exeter EX2 4PS

ISBN No. 1904329004

©Fortingall Publications Ltd (Company No.2816254) 2000

All rights reserved. No part of this publication may be reproduced, stored in or introduced into a retrieval system, or transmitted, in any form, or by any means (electronic, mechanical, photocopying, recording or otherwise) without the prior written permission of the publisher. Any person who does any unauthorized act in relation to this publication may be liable to criminal prosecution and civil claims for damages.

A CIP Catalogue record for this book is available from the British Library.

Typeset by Scriveners, Totnes, Devon TQ9 5XT
Printed in Spain by Artes Gráficas Elkar, S. Coop by arrangement with Associated Agencies Ltd, Oxford

In Love in War and Peace

My Life
1926-1948

by Mavis Fortingall

This book is dedicated to:

Lieutenant David McBain
1923-1944

The architectural student from Victoria, British Columbia, who gave his life on 6th June 1944 when the Canadian forces landed at Juno Beach, Normandy, so that British family of nations should no longer be threatened by German dominion and the occupied nations of Europe should regain their freedom.

David and I were married on 14th November 1943.

LIST OF ILLUSTRATIONS

1. The Village of Fortingall, Perthshire

2. Hornton Street, Kensington - Mum's home as a girl

3. "Only a Frenchman could have designed this car", The Big Pre-War Citroen (The Maigret Car)

4. (i) Quai de Bergues - in the early years of the 20th century with the Hotel in the background
   (ii) Hotel Les Bergues, Geneva, as it is today

5. (i) Taking Aim - This girl (not me) knew she wasn't going to enjoy the next few minutes of her life
   (ii) 'Give the Boys a Treat'

6. (i) Victoria, British Columbia, (David's home town)
   (ii) Canadian troops landing on the Eastern Sector of Juno Beach on 6th June 1944

7. (i) St. Hilda's College, Oxford (my College)
   (ii) The Cherwell, a view from St. Hilda's

8. Two pen and ink drawings of BNC (John's College) made in 1917 by an earlier wartime pilot, Lt. Lawrence Gilling-Smith who had rooms in BNC while attending a short course
   (i) BNC and the Radcliffe Camera
   (ii) BNC and St Mary's, the University Church

CONTENTS

List of Illustrations		vi
Acknowledgments and Apologies		ix
Who's Who (including genealogical tables)		xiii
1.	Prologue - who I am and why I have written this book	19
2.	My Pedigree	27
3.	Dad and Mum	43
4.	My Early Childhood	61
5.	Politics and War	79
6.	The Four Musketeers	101
7.	Cultural Awakening	111
8.	A Different Kind of Education	123
9.	"Three of the Best for Boadie"	129
10.	Jacko - The Imperfect Enjoyment	147
11.	Jean's Life in the Wrens	153
12.	'Give the Boys a Treat'	157
13.	1942-3 Academic Success But My Uninhibited 'Lecture' Lands Me in Trouble	167
14.	School Farm Camp 1943	189
15.	Annus Mirabilis	197
16.	Marriage	201
17.	Christmas Leave 1943	217
18.	Mum's Problems and Mine	229
19.	In Memoriam - David McBain and Dick Squires	239
20.	Victory Celebrations 1945 - But Dad's Plane is Reported Missing	251
21.	Oxford - Michaelmas 1945	257
22.	Rehabilitation	267
23.	My New Life - An Emotional and Spiritual Odyssey	279
24.	Epilogue - The Testament of Boadie Business Life On Lovers and Mistresses Distortion of History The Spiritual/Religious Dimension of My Life Insidious Collectivism Envoi	299

ACKNOWLEDGMENTS AND APOLOGIES

I acknowledge first and foremostly the 56 years (54 of them as husband and wife) of love, emotional and spiritual support of my second husband John, who has provided the tranquillity necessary for me to recollect the tragic events and emotions as well as the months of unequalled joy of the war days in the form this book has taken. Had my later life taken a different path my recollections of those turbulent years might have been tinged with a bitterness that I hope you will not find in what you read here. In my later business life John has been such a wonderful support that many of our friends refer to him as 'Mr. Thatcher'. Whilst we both have a tremendous regard for both Mr. and Mrs. Thatcher may I hasten to add that I have never had any pretensions to being a person anywhere near Mrs. Thatcher's league table. John has also been remarkably patient during the long period whilst this book has been in the making. No doubt he hoped that my 'official' retirement would give me more leisure, but like most husbands he has had to learn that women, while they are sound in mind and body never retire but merely change their jobs.

I must also thank my Granddaughter Jennie, who has not only been the main driving force in getting me to turn my story into a book, but who has also acted as my 'interpreter', telling me what I needed to explain in terms of words and background information that I would have to include if parts of this book are to be clearly understood by readers of her generation. It was Jennie who suggested the title and throughout had an intuitive feel for the common thread that runs through so many of our lives regardless of the period in which we live them.

If at times you think I have devoted too many pages to the way I thought and felt as a teenager and our trials and tribulations of amorous dalliance in the pre-pill days, it is because Jennie has convinced me that this has helped her to understand and identify with her grandmother's generation. Jennie, as a seventeen year old, had her own sad story, and the mutual understanding that resulted convinced us both (if we needed convincing) that while the aspirations and bodily yearnings of teenage girls change little if at all from generation to generation, we can be helped or seriously hindered by the clothes we wear and the fashionable attitudes of the adult worlds to which we all have to adapt.

I must also acknowledge the help of Dryden Gilling-Smith, who in addition to being the confidential pension adviser to my Company and family for the past 25 years has taken on the job of business manager for this project and with it the role of advisory editor. Having decided for the reasons given in Chapter 1 that I want this book to be anonymous, I needed an intermediary in whom I had confidence to deal with lawyers, publishers, etc.

I also wish to acknowledge the very considerable help I have had from Jo Barker and Lynn Murphy who have succeeded in producing the text of this book from the vast number of garbled second-hand tapes, revising and editing the text and making many useful suggestions.

I am particularly grateful to the actress and model Tonia Chown, to Gary Reece and to the photographer Howard Bartrop for the loving care they have shown in recreating, with the all important help of the Rev. Michael Beer, the memorable moment on Sunday 14th November 1943 when David and I stood before the altar in Bishop Wantock Church. This is the picture which the publishers have used for the cover of this book. I am also grateful to Tonia and Howard for the patience they have shown in recreating some of the not so reputable escapades in my early life as I have described them in some of the chapters which I hope you will enjoy reading. I am full of admiration for Howard's patience in braving the winter elements in Kensington until he could find a day when the warm afternoon sun could convey something of the warm friendly atmosphere which Mum associated with what was home to her until she married Dad when she was 21 and to which she returned in her years of retirement.

I am grateful also to Steve Acheson, archaeologist to the Government of British Colombia, and a fellow member of the Oxford Society for providing me with the photo of Victoria, David's home town, the most English part of Canada, where one even finds red double-decker buses. Nigel Lumsden, a professional photographer from Aberfeldy has kindly provided me with the photo of the beautiful village of Fortingall in Perthshire from which Dad's family originally hailed in the 18th Century. Eileen Roberts of the Development Office, St. Hilda's Oxford has been kind enough to provide two photos of my college which was a haven of peace in 1945-48 after the turbulent war years when I was still trying to come to terms with my loss of David.

I wish to thank the staff of the Photographic Archive Department of the Imperial War Museum for their assistance in helping me to locate a photo of Canadian troops landing on Juno Beach on 6th June 1944 and for permission to use an adaptation of photo number MH4505 as an illustration and in an adapted form on the dust jacket/cover.

My thanks and appreciation to many of the people who have provided vital help and support at critical stages in my life have been given at the appropriate places in the text. Sadly for me (but not I hope for them) most of them, like Mum, Father Wakehurst, and Mrs. Rainham, have long since (of this I am more certain than of anything else) been received into the Kingdom of Heaven and I can only hope that I shall one day have the joy of meeting them again.

I apologise in advance to readers who may spot errors in my recollection of historical events. I am not a professional historian, but since my childhood I have always taken an interest in international affairs and as my memory for the events that would have taken place in my own lifetime has been reasonably good, I have tended to be lazy about double-checking. I also remember the events that took place during the lives of my parents as if they had taken place in my own life. They were constant subjects of discussion in my childhood and they were as real to me as if I had heard about them on radio news bulletins. Ford Madox Ford in his History of Our Own Times described the way we each of us build an historical picture of our own time that starts in the world we hear our parents talking about as we grow up.

Because I was fortunate enough to have parents and teachers who enabled me at an early age to acquire a familiarity with the story of Odysseus and many of the wonderful Bible stories, they too have remained in my memory as part of the real world in which I grew up and if a reliance on my memory has any errors I must crave your indulgence. Because William Tyndale, who was burnt at the stake for translating the Bible into an English that could be 'understood by the ploughboy' has been one of my heroes since my Oxford days and because his translation is one of the most beautiful books in the English language, in my view superior in many places to the committee version produced 80 years later for King James, it is the Tyndale rendering of the Lazarus story that has remained in my mind as the second lesson in the memorial service to David (Chapter 19) rather than that of the Authorised Version which was more likely to have been in use in the College chapel.

For those of you whose sensibilities are offended by the inclusion in Chapter 14 of what are now euphemistically referred to as 'four letter words' I can only say that I refuse to bowdlerise Peggy, who, as a member of the Women's Land Army, not only did a wonderful job helping to ensure the food supply of our country during the war years but also succeeded in shaking into a bunch of teenage girls more practical awareness and good sense on sex matters than most teachers (judging by the results) are able to achieve today. In passing I would ask you to differentiate between the monotonous repetition of these words used as empty expletives (which is what irritates most of us) and the literal sense in which Peggy used these words which have remained in use for at least 1200 years (they were in common usage in the time of Alfred the Great who as a hard-boiled war veteran would have certainly used them himself) and probably for 1500 years or longer.

I hope Welsh readers will not be upset by the fact that I cite both great-uncle Henry and Dad talking of Lloyd George as a 'Welsh bounder'. In recent years we have allowed ourselves to be collectivised to the point where people mistakenly assume an adjective such as Scots, Irish, Welsh (or any other collectivist identification label) to be the operative word rather than the noun which it qualifies. We even had an absurd case of a man claiming 'racial harassment' against a fellow golfer who described him as 'a dirty Irish bastard'. Surprisingly the plaintiff didn't seem the least bit concerned by the need to prove that he was legitimate. 'Bounder', though an out of date term, would be a more appropriate word on such occasions than 'bastard'. I know that great-uncle Henry adored his mother, who was Welsh, and Dad too adored her as the grandmother who had brought him up after the death of his mother when he was only six. In other words, to my parents' and grandparents' generation (and in most of my own lifetime) people were not in the habit of using national appellations in the emotionally nutty way that they currently seem to be interpreted. If Lloyd George was a 'bounder' who happened to be Welsh, any reference to his Welshness would be construed as incidental information about Lloyd George and not as an adverse comment on Wales or the Welsh people. He might even have been referred to as a 'Liberal bounder' but for the fact that most Liberals regarded him as something of a Judas.

When it comes, however, to my occasional throw-away line criticisms of the anti-hunting lobby, the anti-fur coat lobby or lunatic fringe feminists who promote the use of bad grammar (using 'their' instead of 'his' to refer to a singular subject), I offer no apologies. On the contrary, it is those who in Hitlerian style indulge in fanatical attacks against the freedom of English men and women to pursue a traditional sport with all its pageantry or to wear clothes of their choice that owe an apology to the memory of those who gave their lives in the cause of individual freedom.

As for the lunatic fringe feminists whose self publicist ambitions have brought nothing but ridicule and contempt to the cause to which my great-grandmother Catherine devoted her life - convincing the men, who at that time had the power to admit or refuse women entry into the professions and universities, that her cause was just and right and should be taken seriously - the perpetrators of such childish pranks are the people who should be putting on sack-cloth and doing penance for bringing into disrepute a cause for which many women of my great-grandmother's generation laboured so tirelessly and selflessly - these latter day feminist nutters deserve no apology from me.

WHO'S WHO

A considerable number of people are inevitably mentioned in the course of my life story. Whenever I read a biography, history or novel, I find it exasperating when I have to keep flicking through previous chapters to find out who somebody is that I am supposed to have remembered. In this book I have included a Who's Who so that you only need to keep a bookmark in one place when you have to turn back. I have not bothered to include people who appear only once, such as Phyllis Henderson in Chapter 10. In some chapters I have preferred to indulge in repetition even though this may irritate some readers. For example, I have explained both in Chapters 8 and 9 that Alec Horsman was the College Music master and that Mildred Pearce had a crush on him.

I have also adopted an unconventional approach to indexing. For example, if I generally refer to someone by his or her Christian name or nickname, that is what I use here. Thus you should look up Liz for Elizabeth Gundry, Mildred for Mildred Pierce and Jacko appears simply as Jacko. I have had to invent names for some people just as I had to invent Tawchester for the Cathedral City in which I grew up in order to maintain my anonymity. In many cases it is not necessary to invent two names if only one is needed, so that I refer to my late father-in-law simply as Hugh. People holding senior positions such as Dr. Wilding, the Dean of Tawchester, and Miss Blantyre, my High School Headmistress, are referred to by their surnames.

With all general rules there have to be exceptions. For example, the Squires family are mentioned so many times that I don't think any reader is going to have difficulty remembering who any of them are, so I have listed them all under their family name.

As regards my own family, the easiest way to explain relationships to one's forebears is to draw up family trees which are included in this Who's Who as genealogical tables 1, 2 and 3. To keep the number of names in this Who's Who to a minimum I have not included members of my own family who appear in the genealogical tables, but again I have made two exceptions. Firstly there is my maternal-maternal-great-grandmother Henriette de Roncesvalles, who appears in a number of chapters under the name Arrière, or occasionally as Madame la Baronne. I have also included my maternal-paternal-great-grandmother, Catherine Johnston, the woman who did so much to bring higher and professional education within the reach of women, and was called Catherine the Great by my Oxford tutor and Grandma by Mum.

I have been able to leave a number of names unchanged. Sadly my Oxford friend, Clifford Dobb, who did so much to help me find my way around Bodley, died some years ago, so no-one is going to start troubling him with questions in order to ferret out who I might be and those who have joined him in Paradise will presumably know without being told, if they are interested in such matters.

You may not approve of my system, but I hope you will agree that it does have a certain practical utility in the kind of book I hope you will read and enjoy with minimal irritation.

I have put a number in brackets after each name to indicate the chapter where the person is first mentioned:

Angus (23)	My sister Jean's husband
Arrière (2)	Sometimes referred to as Madame la Baronne, my maternal-maternal-great-grandmother Henriette de Roncesvalles
Miss Blantyre (15)	High School Headmistress in the years when I was a pupil
'Catherine the Great' (2)	Catherine Johnston, my other maternal-paternal-great-grandmother, occasionally referred to by Mum as Grandma and given the name Catherine the Great by my Oxford tutor Helen Gardner
Uncle Charles (2)	Aunt Bea's husband who gave Jean away at her wedding and me at my second wedding to John
Clifford Dobb (5)	A friend of my Oxford years who provided invaluable guidance on finding books in the Bodley catalogue and in other libraries
Alice Draper (14)	Mum's Newnham friend who was Head of English in a leading Independent Girls' School
Captain Ferrers (13)	'Old Ferret' Senior College History master who taught me in the Sixth Form, Gallipoli veteran
Dame Helen Gardner (21)	My tutor at St. Hilda's
Dr. Hanscombe (5)	Appointed College Head Master in 1938
Uncle Henry (2)	Dad's Uncle, Dean of Tawchester until 1935
Alec Horsman (8)	College Music master
Hugh (23)	John's father who founded the company which I later joined and where I worked until my retirement
Jacko (8)	My College boyfriend
June (Barnes) (22)	Jacko's one-time girlfriend who became my life-long friend and 'wardrobe mistress'

WHO'S WHO

Liz (6)	Elizabeth Gundry, one of the Four Musketeers
Maureen O'Hagan (6)	One of the Four Musketeers
Mildred (8)	High School Gym mistress
Tante Nicole (3)	One of Mum's cousins with whom we maintained close links throughout her life
Peggy (Johnson) (14)	Ex-ATS, member of the Women's Land Army who was in charge of the High School Summer Farm Camps which I attended
Mrs. Sylvia Rainham (6)	My High School English mistress who was also my guide, philosopher and friend at a critical period in my life
The Squires (4)	Apart from being long-standing family friends of my parents, a number of them were involved in many episodes of my life. To complete this, I list them all below: Walford - College Second Master Milly (Mrs. Millicent Squires) - apart from doing a good deal of Walford's job and being Mum's closest friend, she was a member of the High School Governing Body Dick (born 1917) - Captain in the Parachute Regiment, killed at Arnhem Janet - Dick's wife Helen (born 1920) Michael (born 1924) Louise (born 1926) - one of the Four Musketeers who has remained my life-long friend
Gerald Wakehurst (3)	Father Wakehurst, Perpetual Curate of Bishop Wantock, the family friend to whom I owe more than to anyone outside my family
Dr. and Mrs. Wilding (5)	Dean of Tawchester 1935 - 1947, Chairman of the Governors of both the College and High School

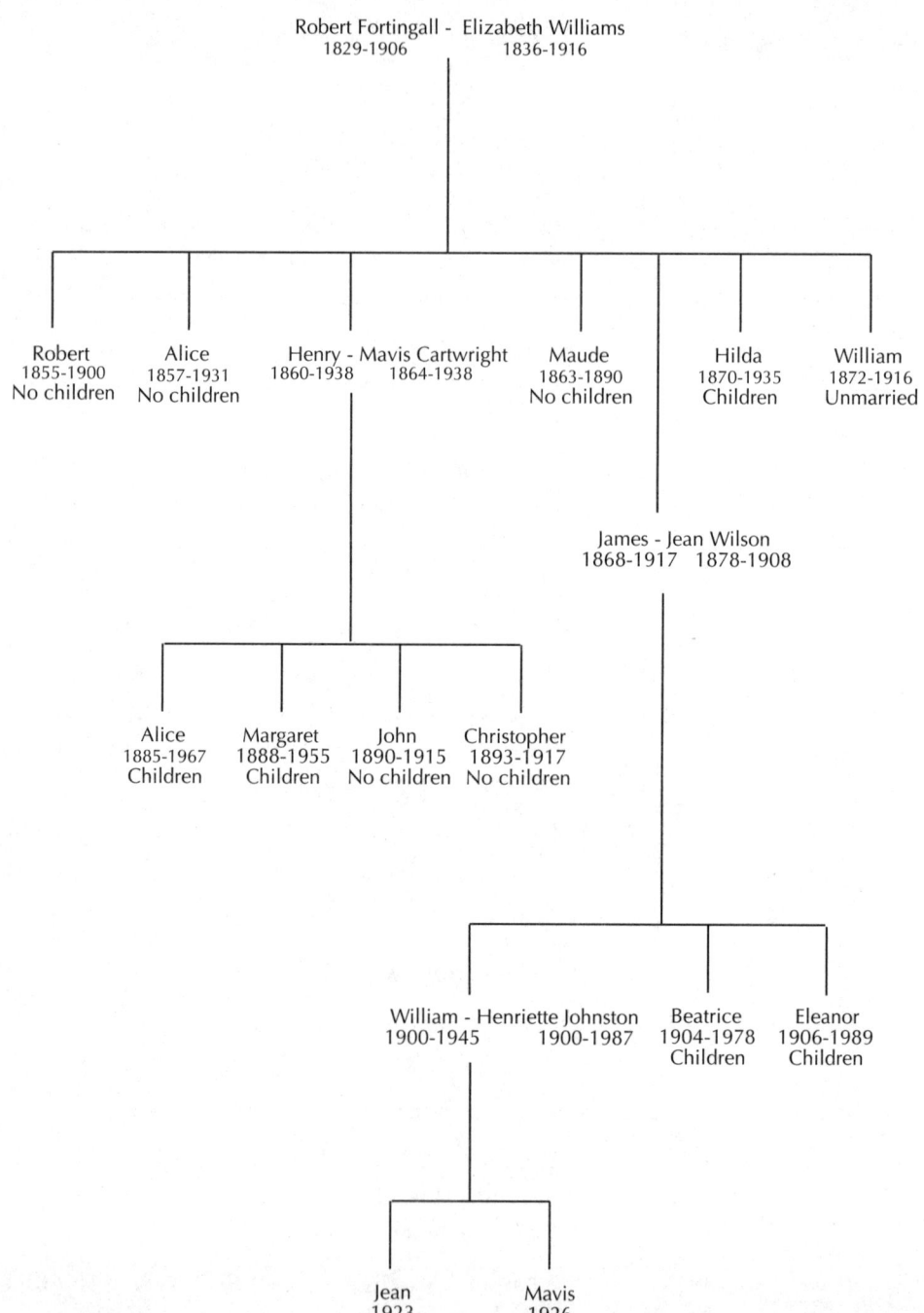

Table 1. The Fortingalls

WHO'S WHO

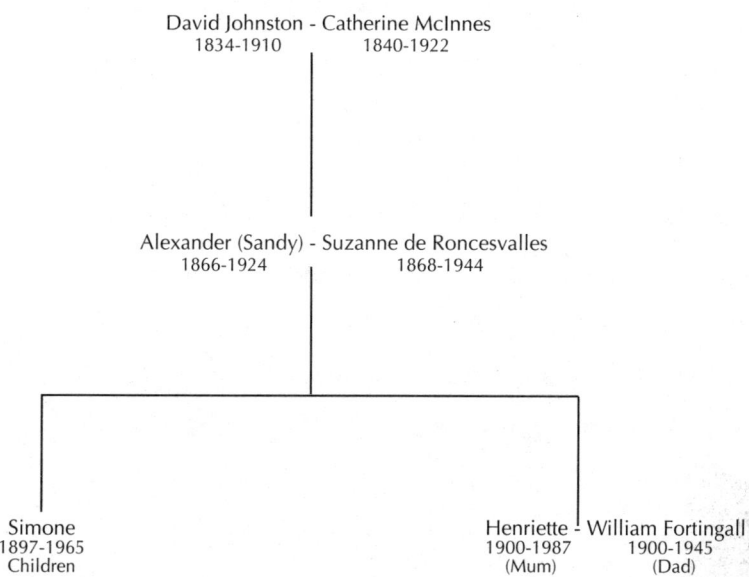

Table 2. The Johnstons (Mum's Father's Family)

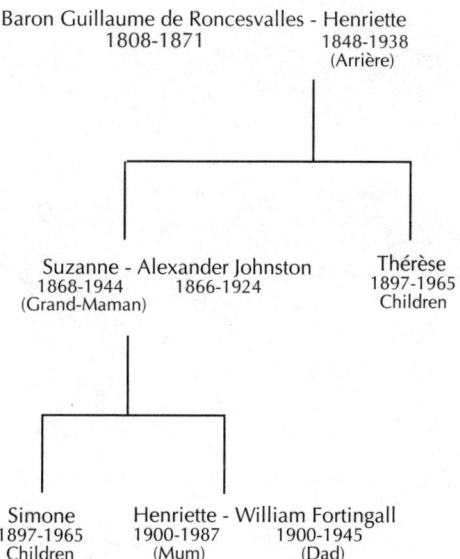

Table 3. Mum's French Maternal Ancestry

CHAPTER 1

PROLOGUE
Who I am and why I have written this book

I was born on 16 June 1926, the same year as the Queen. Four years after my tragic loss of David in the 1944 Normandy landings, I remarried and my second husband, John, and I have been granted over fifty wonderful years together in the peaceful conditions which both David and John fought so hard to bring to our country. I have borne him four children who, thanks be to God, were all born sound in mind and body (though I worried and prayed unceasingly before each birth), have 10 grandchildren and am currently expecting (or rather one of my granddaughters is expecting) my first great-grandchild. For much of my life I have been running a company founded by my late father-in-law and which one of my sons and two of my grandsons are continuing to run very successfully, although I still have a seat on the Board.

As you can see I have not been idle.

But this book is not about my life since my second marriage in June 1948, except for certain snippets that I have included to give younger readers a better perspective and understanding of some of the thought habits and attitudes of mind that were current sixty or so years ago, but which we can no longer take for granted.

When I talk to my friends or my family about events of the war years they sit spellbound as if I were the storyteller in the Arabian Nights. When I read the biographies of the great men and women who played an important part in the events of those times, I read little or nothing about everyday life as we lived it. When I read sociological studies by contemporaries of my grandchildren that say what 'people' thought and did at the time, I grit my teeth at the lack of precise knowledge and the tendency to bulk individual people together as block units.

The posters that we saw in our streets and railway stations used to proclaim such slogans as "lend to defend the right to be free" or "I may detest what that man says but I am prepared to die for his right to say it". I feel that a lot of important truths have been allowed to slip through the fingers of the people who are supposed to be the guardians of our democracy, and that we as a nation have become more dictatorial (more like Hitler), less tolerant of individual opinions and idiosyncrasies. As a nation, our aim was to defend the rights of individuals to express their individual views on any subject without fear of being put in a concentration camp. We were a nation of free-thinking individuals and not a collective mishmash.

So many of the people with whom these basic beliefs were shared are no longer in the land of the living (every day the Times obituary column bears witness to this) that

I now tend to feel a beleaguered loner so that if I do not put some of my thoughts and memories to paper they will disappear without trace.

As a High School girl in an English Cathedral City, far enough from London and the south coast to escape German bombs and rockets (although my mother and I spent some anxious night hours in our domestic air-raid shelter when the sirens went, either in error or when an unidentified plane had been picked up by radar or the Observer Corps), I did not suffer as those in the forces or in bombed cities. But apart from obvious things such as food rationing and clothes rationing (from which well-dressed women suffered much more than men, unless like my mother they had cupboards and wardrobes full of little worn clothes from days gone by), the war affected our lives in many fundamental ways.

Most of my friends were being brought up single handed by their mothers who were usually doing full-time jobs because their fathers were away on active service. I suppose they differed from many of today's single parent families in sensing the warmth and affection, often increased by absence, of the man to whom they wrote letters once or twice a week and who occasionally appeared on leave. There were girls whose fathers had been taken prisoners in the last days before Dunkirk and who were thus absent in prisoner of war camps for the whole of the war.

My father, who had been too young to serve in World War I, had obtained the rank of Captain in the Territorial Army before the war and therefore left us to join his unit shortly before the war started, when he and everyone in his circle knew, or said they knew, that war was imminent. He insisted that we girls (my sister and myself) must remember to carry our gas masks everywhere. I learned to move quickly down to the air-raid shelter, with enough warm clothes, as soon as we heard the siren. He had only one or two home leaves, including the joy of Christmas 1939, before he was posted to Egypt, to General Wavell's army, which gave us our first success in the war against the Italians in Libya. It proved a short-lived success, although it brought names such as Bardia and Tobruk into our memories, as well as Geography lessons. After that Dad moved to India with General Wavell and, in the final phase of the war against Japan, he rose to the rank of Brigadier serving on Mountbatten's staff at SEAC (South East Asia Command) in Ceylon (now called Sri Lanka). Mountbatten's No. 2 was Stilwell, the most senior US General at the time, known to his troops as Vinegar Joe.

Most of what Mum and I had learned about his later war years, we learned from some of his fellow officers when they came to see us many years later. Although Dad survived long enough to learn the good news of victory in the West, the plane in which he was travelling on a liaison mission in the Pacific area never arrived at its destination. No-one knew whether it had been shot down by Japs or merely suffered engine failure or some other defect. Even with the vast improvements in aviation technology and safety in the air since 1945 we frequently read of unexplained air disasters. The risks of such mishaps were much greater in the war years, but you rarely read about flying accidents in the newspapers unless an important person was involved, as when the Duke of Kent's father was killed when his plane crashed into the side of a hill in Scotland.

When I last saw my father I was only a girl of 13 and although he has remained permanently in my mind as a towering presence, much of what I know about him is based on what I learned in adult life from Mum, with whom I had a wonderful rapport for the rest of her life.

Like many men with tremendous mental and physical energy (and many women for that matter) he also had powerful bodily appetites and brought moments of happiness to a number of ladies (as they were then called) as well as Mum, but she had no grudges. I know that after his death she made no secret (to me at any rate) of her admiration of his prowess as an amorist, and knowing Mum as I do I think she felt the same way at the time these things were happening.

This knowledge has made a tremendous contribution to my own happiness in later life. If I had not known this I am sure I would have felt guilty about some of my peccadilloes, however discreet and secret I managed to keep them. I should have thought of him looking down from on high with stern disapproval, tinged with sadness at the thought of one of his daughters going astray and this would have hurt. Instead I have always thought of him chuckling impishly and giving me a conspiratorial tap on the rump saying "Go it, old girl. You are a true Fortingall." So I have never thought of these peccadilloes as sins. On the contrary, if I have given something to the men concerned in exchange for what they have given me, I believe I have been bestowing some of the gifts God has given me for that purpose. You may disapprove of my theology, but I am writing this to tell you something of myself and not to argue my cause with Saint Peter, which I will have to do when I am down on my knees on that fateful day.

The war also meant that my elder sister Jean, (we were a two - girl family with no brothers) left home to join the Womens' Royal Naval Service (the Wrens) in the Autumn of 1940 when she was 17. She had done brilliantly in "Higher Cert." (Higher School Certificate, the exam we all took at the end of two years in the Upper Sixth if we were good enough - in the days before they invented 'A' levels), and as the daughter of a Newnham girl (Mum) she was expected to go to Cambridge.

But Jean was a patriot and in the dark days after the defeat of France in 1940 when Britain stood alone, the Battle of Britain spirit pervaded every home and school in the country. This was certainly my memory of those homes and schools that I knew. Later generations may only have seen the funny side in television films such as Dad's Army, but we saw ourselves in deadly earnest.

In addition, Jean hero-worshiped her great-uncle, Captain William Fortingall, who went down with his ship at the battle of Jutland in 1916. She saw him as the equivalent of Nelson in our own family and used to listen spellbound (we both did but Jean was older and understood more) to the many stories that Dad used to tell us in pre-war days of his memories from the yarns that Uncle William had told him. Uncle William, who was a bachelor, often spent shore leave with his brother (Dad's father), and Dad as a schoolboy used to go for long walks with him.

These tales spurred Jean into an enthusiastic search for any history books on naval battles of the past. The navy for her had always been the Senior Service. She wore her uniform with pride, none greater than on the day she became an Officer, although in those days Wrens did not serve at sea.

The happiest day in her life was when, after the end of the war she married, as the second wife, a naval Captain with a distinguished record. He was promoted to Admiral and finished his career in a series of overseas diplomatic and defence liaison posts around the world where she, too, played a distinguished role, and though she has been a widow for some years (her husband was many years older) she is still, as Lady Jean, playing a lead role in many voluntary bodies. I am sure both Dad and the ghost of great-uncle William are proud of her.

So Mum and I were alone in the house for most of the war, although Jean came home on leave from time to time. We no longer had a live-in maid because every able-bodied man and woman was expected to be doing work of national importance and the maid we had known for some years left to join the Women's Land Army. Mum found what was known as a "treasure" whose rheumatism made most of her movements painful, but who managed to "do for us" two or three mornings a week.

Dad, who was the senior partner in a firm of solicitors which, thanks to him, was handling virtually all the property transactions for the diocese, the College (a leading English Public School) and the High School (my school) and a lot more, had suggested some time before the war had started that Mum might be able to help in the firm's accounts department. Whilst Dad, as a financial expert in his own right, had a tight grip on the firm's finances and cashflow (although I don't think the term was invented at that time) he was worried that a number of his partners were not "mathematically minded" and would not feel it was part of their professional role to become involved in such ordinary housekeeping matters.

What started for Mum as a part-time job rapidly became a full-time job and she became the firm's business manager. She had the mystique of being a Cambridge Mathematician but, as she never ceased to point out (to me at any rate), she had learned all the arithmetic she needed for this job before she went to her senior school. It was before the days of calculators and computers. Mum had the gift of being able to run her eye down a column of figures and see if the total was correct before most of her colleagues had added up the first two or three numbers. She often worked late into the evenings and on Saturdays.

We ate very simply and I did my share of housekeeping, shopping and cooking. There were no more of the lively pre-war dinner parties that she and Dad used to host. As children we used to hear the animated conversation from the dining room but daren't show ourselves for fear of Dad's stern rebuke, and more to the point, fear of what would happen to our behinds the next evening.

Without the war I would never had experienced the most wonderful first love that any 17 year old girl could dream of and a memory that has remained sacred for the rest of my life. David was a young Canadian officer trainee from Victoria, British Colombia, the most English part of Canada. His father had been recruited in Scotland before World War I by what was then the Canadian Bank of Commerce. David was about to start university when he had volunteered. He had had the chance to apply for a commission and he was posted to a training unit at a camp about 10 miles from our city.

Although the war brought David to me (I would never have met him had there not been the war), the war also took him away from me. David was killed in the Normandy landings in June 1944, barely seven months after our first tryst. It was the end of the world for me.

The war did not, therefore, leave us untouched, even if we were not subjected to the daily bombings of the Luftwaffe or the later attacks of V1s and V2s. My loss was (in retrospect) much less in practical terms than that of all the women with young children who had lost their husbands and had to cope. I hope and believe that my own experience helped me to provide whatever support Mum needed just over a year later when she learned that Dad would not return. She was devastated. We sat and held hands for a long time as daylight faded. We knew that we were more to each other than mother and daughter. We would have to survive in a new and different world, that was supposed to be the brave new world of the propagandists, but we both knew a lot better.

I have mentioned these important happenings at time one to ensure that you do not start with the impression that the war passed us by and that life as a schoolgirl during the war was no different from life as a schoolgirl today, or in any period of history in the last 150 years, more or less.

Every generation talks of itself as being "sexually liberated". I doubt it. We did as much and possibly more. There is no way of knowing.

People talk about improved sex education in schools, but the increased number of teenage pregnancies and single mothers makes me wonder. We didn't have the Pill in those days, but every young woman who knew what she was about carried at least six condoms in her handbag and if she was actively involved with a man, or men, carried a lot more. They were not to be found displayed in different shapes and sizes in chemist shops as they are today, so you had to lay in a stock (it was sent to you by mail order in plain coloured envelopes) if you didn't want to get pregnant and none of us did.

There were a lot of conventions and behaviour that may look fuddy-duddy today, but they didn't constrain us in the way that some people may think.

I cannot believe that girls in their teens, or women of any age up to my age and beyond, had different bodily needs in any period of history. Some of us have greater needs than others. Some are more hungry for food. I once had a friend whose husband had left her (or she may have thrown him out) who used to get up in the morning and think of nothing except what she was going to cook herself for lunch and she was a very good cook. She ate that lunch many times in her imagination before she ate the real lunch, but it kept her from thinking of disagreeable things and after lunch she did the same until she ate the dinner that she had cooked with the same anticipation. To me a close human contact with the men in my life has been important from the moment of its first stirrings when I didn't know quite what I wanted and it's still there now.

Don't kid yourself that it goes away at the menopause, or 60 or 70. It may not go away at 80, but I'm not there yet. For the past seven years my husband has suffered from high blood pressure. He has had to take a morning and evening dosage of tablets with names like Adelat Retard, Ramipril, Trandolapril, in order to keep his pressure down to something like 170/95, and even this is considered too high, but at least I still have him with me which is more important than what I want him to do to me. The side-effect of all this medication is that the blood pressure in one small, but all important, part of his anatomy seems to be permanently zero and, in the old nautical language, there is no more chance of his ever being able to get his end in.

He, poor man, is as devastated as I am. His desire is as great as ever it was. He has more time and leisure than ever he had. He does everything to me with every other part of his body that any woman could possibly want, but he can't do what both of us want. I won't let him try Viagra because I would worry about how it would mix with all the blood pressure drugs and, in any case, I want John alive for a few more years even more than my body wants what it wants.

Having reached the topic that causes the greatest difficulty with any biographer, including an autobiographer, I should perhaps make the sort of warning noises that will act as a guide to people who may not want to read any further. If I don't include the earthy bits about myself my life story will lack balance. Younger readers will think I am a prig. In any case, why bother to use a fictitious name unless I am going to tell it as it was.

Our generation did all sorts of things our parents might have disapproved of and they did the same vis-à-vis their parents. In the war years we were perhaps more relaxed because the ruling philosophy was 'give the boys a treat - they deserve it'. When the men who were fighting and dying for us were home on leave or had a night out it was tacitly accepted that the girls would give them what they wanted and were doing their bit for the war effort. The most important thing was not to get pregnant. A lot of girls, nevertheless, followed the safety first 'everything but' route, which meant that we didn't object to getting fondled when the lights were turned out during a dance, or when we were seen home by someone we had met for the first time on the dance floor, but no more.

Language has also changed enormously. For example, the words "girlfriend" and "boyfriend" now have totally different meanings. It was normal for an attractive girl to have lots of boyfriends, each of whom would stand a chance of taking her out to a dance or to a film. The term merely meant an escort for the evening and a man would likewise have a girlfriend on the camp where he was stationed, another to take out when he was home on leave, another at his College, etc. - a far cry from the current usage as a sleeping partner or whatever.

Women were perfectly familiar with the uncouth four-letter words that seemed to constitute the sole vocabulary of army Sergeant Majors or men who came to repair burst pipes, but we didn't use them in polite conversation. I remember feeling very ill at ease when one of my grandsons and his wife invited me to dinner and they cursed and swore at each other, using nothing but the 'f' word for most of the evening, although their marriage seems perfectly stable and all I was listening to was what they regarded as normal conversation.

If one is to believe the newspapers, the present generation gets all het up at the idea of a man having a mistress, or possibly two or more. We had inherited from our parents' generation a familiarity with the way the late King Edward VII (Edward the Caresser as he was nicknamed) had loads of mistresses and so did the World War I Prime Minister, Lloyd George. It was taken for granted that if a man had enough money and power to attract someone willing to be his mistress, then he would do so, but if he was a man of the world he would keep quiet about it and so would the mistress. The last thing she would dream of doing would be to sell her story to a Sunday newspaper because she would have the sense to know that it would be the kiss of death. Where could she possibly hope to find another lover when the present one got bored with her if she went around making waves.

What was regarded as unforgivable was a man who abandoned his wife and family to take up with another woman. Robin Cook, for example, would have been pilloried for leaving his wife for another woman, whilst it would have been regarded as perfectly normal and socially acceptable to keep a floozy in his London flat during the week, given that his wife lived in Edinburgh. The same would have been true of Cecil Parkinson. These changes in moral attitudes and usage of words should be borne in mind when you read what I have to say about my early life. You may disapprove of quite a lot that I did, but so be it.

In places I have felt it appropriate to use the language in which I thought when I was a schoolgirl and which we used to each other. Those of us who wanted to feel daring tended to copy the words used by the more cheeky College boys. Many of us dreamed of being 'mounted' by someone like Errol Flynn, a film star of the day whom we probably would have disliked had we met him. I make no apology for all the uncouth four-letter words used by Peggy, the Landgirl who was in charge of us on a school Summer holiday Farm Camp. I think she did a great job of work and if there were a few more people like her around who could explain certain things in the clear, blunt terms she used there would be a lot fewer unwanted teenage pregnancies today.

Many readers may be disappointed at my failure to describe in detail a lot of intimate bedroom scenes. That would have been fun, but it would be a different sort of book. The puritans among you (if there are any left) may be shocked by what I do say and again I make no apology. There were certain defining moments in my life, particularly during the very short and intense time I had with my first husband, that are so important to me that a key part of my life story would be missing if I left them out. There have been pleasant moments with other men in later life that have not brought any harm to their families or my family. At worst they can be treated as peccadilloes, but I do not regret them. They have all been with men who have brought something worthwhile into my life and I hope I have brought something into theirs.

When I talked to my life-long friend, Louise, about writing my life story she jocularly remarked, "If you start putting personal bits in you'll be taken for a female Alan Clark." This is, of course, the exaggeration of a best friend because I could never be in his league table, but it provides sound reason for using a nom-de-plume. If what I have to say is worth reading, it doesn't matter who I am. People enjoy the diaries of Samuel Pepys because they give an insight into his time and the fact that he tells the naughty bits means we think of him as human and like ourselves.

However heroic many of my contemporaries were, we were also ordinary, earthy human beings.

There is a further reason for anonymity. There has, in recent years, been a growing propensity amongst certain biographers to behave like gossip column writers and to divert attention from their subject's important work to speculation (often ill-founded), about their subject's private life. I have taken considerable trouble to select and comment on a period of my life that I believe will be helpful to future generations who wish to understand the way many of us thought, felt and reacted to the momentous events that future generations cannot ignore. Other historians have written about the people who played a major part in causing these events and in preventing the wrong outcome. My endeavour has been to present these events as seen by an ordinary person, who was, nevertheless, fortunate enough to live amongst educated and thinking people who were seriously trying to understand what was going on.

I want to be the final arbiter of what I include and, by choosing to remain anonymous and to make selected changes in the names of certain key people, I have been able to give an accurate picture without offending anyone - except, of course, the people who may be offended by some of my political opinions. But I was brought up in the traditional English manner where differences of opinion did not give offence, although they might be the subject of heated debate. It was for this purpose that we developed a parliamentary system that has been copied (successfully or otherwise) by many other countries, even though it now seems to be sadly degenerating into something of a Punch and Judy show.

What I feel is important is to show that, whilst some things change between generations (we now have air travel, improved medication, the Pill and computers), there remain certain underlying patterns of human life that do not change.

Later in this book I quote Ezra Pound's comment in the Spirit of Romance that a book written in any period of history becomes literature if it can be read and enjoyed by people of many different generations - 'where our grandfathers' great-grandfathers are our contemporaries...' I make no claim to writing literature, but I like to feel that amongst the events I describe, readers of other generations than my own will wish to accept the hand of human warmth and support that I am holding out to people of like mind and kindred spirit wherever they are.

CHAPTER 2

MY PEDIGREE

I have often been puzzled by the fact that while the English attach tremendous importance to the pedigrees of the dogs and horses in which they invest, they try, in the current generation, to pretend that when it comes to human beings pedigree has little or no importance. This was not always so. In Old English literature such as Beowulf, a person's lineage was the most important factor in presenting his credentials. Even in the 18th Century the upper classes had their wives chosen for them in the hope of breeding the right sort of heirs. The men had (and Boswell may be a typical example) plenty of opportunity to satisfy their bodily needs in other ways, possibly in places like Mrs. Cole's establishment, where Fanny Hill spent part of her professional career.

My ancestors have always been important to me. Admittedly I have tended to pick and choose the ones that interest me. In any case, there are quite a number of whom I know little or nothing. Unfortunately I didn't start the serious business of trying to draw up a family tree until most of the people who might have helped me had long since ceased to exist.

There are many ways in which a knowledge of one's ancestors can help one in life. You can say to yourself that "if my great-grandmother could do it, then so can I". On my mother's side I am descended from two remarkable great-grandmothers. They each achieved a tremendous amount in spite of overwhelming odds and if I could boast one-tenth of the achievements of either I would feel that I had accomplished something worthwhile in the course of my life. They were totally different from each other and totally different from Dad's family, with whom I shall be dealing first.

As you can tell from my name, Fortingall, Dad's family originally came from Scotland. I like to think they originated in a lovely little village called Fortingall in Perthshire, a short walk north of Fearnan on the northern shore of Loch Tay. From Fortingall one can walk for miles up the beautiful wooded valley known as Glen Lyon and see what is supposed to be Rob Roy's Leap when he was reputed to have escaped from pursuers by jumping across a dangerous gorge without falling into the torrent below.

Unfortunately, there are no gravestones or church records in or near Fortingall where the founder of our dynasty was supposed to have been born and bred before he set off to seek his fortune in England in the latter part of the 18th Century. It is possible that he only took the name Fortingall when he left the place of his birth to travel to the country which was, at that time, the land of opportunity for many Scotsmen.

It used to be said that the best thing that came out of Scotland was the road to England and in the 18th Century this was certainly the case. There was no talk of Scottish nationalism in those days. Living standards in England were higher than in any known part of the world. England possessed the thirteen North American colonies that were later to become the United States and until the act of union between England and Scotland in 1707, the Scots, as inhabitants of a separate country, were not allowed to trade with England's colonies.

I can only presume that the founder of our family walked to England. I would love to know how he managed to find his way, what prompted him to set out on his journey, what he carried with him, how he fed himself on his way and why he chose to direct his steps towards Liverpool, which was at that time one of the most important trading cities in England.

One of the reasons that people like that were able to succeed in later life must surely be the sheer strength of purpose and courage of those who set out on such journeys. In my Oxford days I was very friendly with a man whose grandfather had arrived in England penniless from what is now Lithuania (it was then part of Russia). His grandmother had come from Poland (at that time also part of Russia) on an equally precarious journey. Their children and grandchildren built successful careers in England (some in business and some in the professions). He and I both thought and still think of ourselves as one hundred percent English. I never thought of myself as Scots and he never thought of himself as Lithuanian or Russian, or whatever. He happened to be of the Jewish faith, but in those days being Jewish was regarded as a religion just as being Catholic or Methodist. I am sure he would have been very angry if anyone had referred to his family as being part of an 'ethnic minority', just as Dad's family would have been incensed if someone had put them in a box designated as a Scots ethnic minority, or referred to them as being of Scots race.

The strength of England during our most successful period of history (the 18th Century) was to attract talented people from many countries in the world (the French Huguenots for example) who wanted to live in England and become English because England was a land of opportunity, and it didn't matter where you came from. What was important was what you brought to the table. This was still the case in the late 19th Century when my friend's grandparents came here from Lithuania and Poland, although by then we were already in decline.

I stress this background because, until relatively recently, nobody tried to collectivise different groups of English and refer to them as being of this race, or that race. Our strength was that we were not a collectivist state but a country of relatively free-thinking individuals. Because of his Scottish name Dad, of course, enjoyed attending the Burns dinner, but he would have got equal pleasure singing the Men of Harlech in honour of one or two of our Welsh ancestors. Dad was a clubbable bon viveur and he was always welcome in such gatherings. Dad would surely have referred to his Scots, Welsh, Irish and any other ancestors as part of his pedigree, a word that has nothing to do with race and was, in fact, the word used by my Oxford friend to describe his Lithuanian and Polish origins.

By the time our family records started, the Fortingalls had built up a substantial fortune and had ambitions to move up the social scale and be accepted as part of the English squirearchy.

My great-grandfather (Robert Fortingall 1829-1906) was the grand old man of the dynasty as we know it, although I suspect he got most of his money from his father. He married a wealthy lady, Elizabeth Williams, and acquired a pleasant country seat and estate in Shropshire where he did his best to follow the conventional pattern of life of an English country gentleman. This was probably a mistake. Britain's success as a nation depended on trade and the 19th Century propensity of people who had made money in trade to believe that trade was somehow inferior to life as a country gentleman had disastrous consequences. The business world lost a lot of talented people and this must have undermined our commercial position as a nation that was already in decline by the late 19th Century.

The Scots and Welsh origins of Robert Fortingall and his wife, Elizabeth, may have had some part in the academic achievements of their family. Both the Scots and the Welsh traditionally attached more importance to education as a means of advancement than the proverbial native English. At any rate this appeared to be the case in the 19th Century.

Great-grandfather Fortingall had three daughters and four sons. The three daughters all made 'good' marriages which, by the standards of the time, meant that their husbands had good jobs and no doubt some family money as well. Whether they were good in today's sense of being loving and satisfactory personal relationships I know not. In those days people didn't talk in public about such matters.

As a boy Dad was, I believe, quite friendly with some of the cousins in the families of his aunts, but, by the time I was old enough to take an interest in my wider family, Dad was away and wartime upheavals (when so many people had to move away from their old homes) meant that our family Christmas card address list wouldn't have been all that use to me. In any case I had other preoccupations.

I've provided a Fortingall family tree (see Table 1, Who's Who) which gives you a who was who and when he or she lived, which is the easiest way to give you an overview. As you can see, the four sons of great-grandfather Fortingall all had distinguished careers, though sadly he put none of them into business.

In accordance with great-grandfather's perception of best English practice he had decided that his eldest son, Robert, would inherit the estates and enter Parliament in the hope that he might have a distinguished ministerial career and finish up as Sir Robert. In those days being an MP was an unpaid, voluntary job so you had to have a private income to be in the running and he probably had to spend a good deal of money at each election.

Robert was a Tory back-bencher who, from all accounts, had acquired a good working knowledge of international trade matters and foreign affairs, but he wasn't in the same league as the young George Nathaniel Curzon who was a junior minister and handled foreign affairs in the House of Commons in the government of Lord Salisbury who, as Prime Minister, chose to be his own foreign minister.

Robert unfortunately died of a failed appendix operation in 1900 at the age of 45. It was still a risky operation and two years later Edward VII was being congratulated on being a pioneer in agreeing to undergo such an operation. As he would probably have died had he not undergone the operation I don't see why he should be congratulated for taking a chance that enabled him to live for another eight years. It would be reasonable to assume that 'Le bon roi Edouard' (as my French great-grandmother called him) had access to a higher level of surgical capability than my great-uncle Robert.

Although he had been married for nearly 25 years he had not produced (or rather his wife had not produced) any heirs or heiresses. At the time people would no doubt have described his poor wife as 'barren'. Fertility treatment as we know it today did not exist. We now know that some fifty percent of the cases of infertility in couples result from a defect in the male sperm or in the way it is delivered. If we are charitable we ought to spare a thought for the millions of women throughout recorded history who have suffered unjustly as a result of some medical defect in the men to whom they were married.

The next in line of succession to the Fortingall estate was great-uncle Henry. His name will appear in a number of future chapters. He lived until 1938 (when I was 12) and so he is the only one of Dad's three uncles whom I ever met. He had a major influence on my parents' lives and hence on the lives of my sister, Jean, and myself. He was a man who combined academic ability, a shrewd business sense, shrewder judgment of human beings and great personal charm, particularly where the ladies were concerned. As the second son of a landed family he would have been destined for the Church where he would no doubt have been able to benefit from the patronage of his father or elder brother in terms of appointment to the 'living' i.e. as parish priest of the church on the Fortingall estates. To please his father he took Holy Orders after he had gained a first at Cambridge.

In the event he became a schoolmaster in one of the best known English Public Schools, was promoted to housemaster and married the Headmaster's daughter, Mavis Cartwright, after whom I was presumably named. She came of a well-heeled family with aristocratic connections, so Henry had obviously married 'well' by the standard of the times. I would hazard a guess that Henry and Mavis also had a very successful marriage by present day standards. Whilst a child of 10 or 11 (as I then was) may not have much skill in judging such matters, there was something loving and kindly about both of them in the way they treated each other and this seemed to radiate warmth and affection to those around them. A child has a sixth sense of such matters, or at any rate I did.

Henry's decision to take Holy Orders had proved a good investment, first in enabling him to achieve the position of Headmaster in a school where Church of England tradition had usually required the incumbent to wear his collar the wrong way round, and secondly, in his appointment (on retirement from the school) to the position of Dean of Tawchester, as we shall call the Cathedral City where I grew up to avoid embarrassment to any of the inhabitants who may have been around in the years when I was growing up and doing mischief in their midst.

Henry, however, suffered more than most in the mass slaughter of World War I. He had four children, Alice, Margaret, John and Christopher. John (born 1890) was killed in the Gallipoli landings in 1915 and Christopher at Passchendaele in 1917. The only surviving Fortingall in the male line of succession was his nephew, Dad, who was 18 when the war ended, and whom Uncle Henry took under his wing as if he had been an adopted son.

Dad's father, James, the third son of great-grandfather Fortingall was born in 1868. His father had made up his mind at an early stage that young James would not follow Henry to Pembroke College, Cambridge but instead be sent to Sandhurst in the expectation that he would bring honour to the family by pursuing a successful military career. As a result, Dad hardly knew his father. In later life I learned from Mum that Uncle Henry had been highly critical of this decision. He was reported to have said that James had the ability to go to Cambridge and wanted to go to Cambridge like Henry, but had no choice.

By all accounts James was too intelligent for the peace-time British army of the late nineteenth and early twentieth centuries. In World War I Hindenberg is quoted by Alan Clark as saying that the British army fought like lions but was led by donkeys and the disastrous way in which the top brass of the British army handled first the Boer War and then the trench warfare of 1914 - 18 bears this out.

Although James fought with distinction, first in the campaign led by Kitchener in 1896 to recapture Khartoum and then in South Africa during the Boer War, he never achieved a higher rank than Major and retired (at Henry's suggestion) in 1913 when he was 45, with the intention of managing the family estates but was recalled on the outbreak of war in 1914. As he had made a serious effort to learn some Arabic during his years of service in Egypt and the Sudan, he was surprisingly posted to the army that was attempting to advance up the Tigris and Euphrates in the area we now call Iraq and which was then known as Mesopotamia and part of Turkey. He survived the disastrous 1915 expedition to Kut but died either from an infected wound or from some disease or food poisoning in the final stages of General Maude's successful campaign to capture Baghdad in the early months of 1917.

In 1898 on a home posting after the successful capture of Khartoum, James had, at the age of 30, married Jean Watson, a girl ten years younger, and by the time Dad was born (their firstborn) in November 1900, James was serving in South Africa. Jean died in childbirth in 1908, having given birth to Aunt Beatrice in 1904 and Aunt Eleanor in 1906. For virtually all her marriage Jean and her children had lived in Shropshire with her in-laws. Great-grandfather Fortingall died in 1906, but his widow, Elizabeth, survived until 1916 when she died at the age of 80. After Jean's (my grandmother's) death she had made herself responsible for the upbringing of James' children.

Dad always revered his mother as a saintly woman and he named his own firstborn child (my elder sister) Jean after his mother. As far as I can judge from old black and white photos in the family album, the grandmother whom I never knew does have a pure and serene appearance, perhaps tinged with an air of sadness and resignation. My sister, Jean, who is also fair-haired (I have always been dark-haired) does in her appearance have certain points of resemblance to her grandmother, although I always think of Jean as having a tough, hard-boiled expression, but then I have known Jean all my life and inevitably tend to read character traits into her features.

I never, therefore, knew either of my Fortingall grandparents. Dad was particularly attached to his sister, Beatrice, who used to stay with us with her husband, Charles, and children (who were much younger than Jean and me) before the war and who used to invite us to stay with them in Putney when we were in London, which we did most Summers when we were travelling to or returning from France. Uncle Charles was the man who after the war 'gave Jean away' at her wedding and in 1948 gave me away when I married John.

The youngest of the four brothers was William, who was born in 1872 and sent to Dartmouth when he was a boy of about 14 in the hope that he would become a successful naval officer. He did and as a Captain in command of one of the cruisers in Admiral Beatty's battle cruiser fleet he went down with his ship when it was sunk in the Battle of Jutland in 1916.

Had William survived the Battle of Jutland he would, according to Uncle Henry, have been promoted to Admiral.

William never married. He used to spend his shore leaves in the family home. He appeared to have a soft spot for Dad, who was not only his nephew but his godson, who had been called William after him. He used to go for long country walks with Dad. Like most sea-salts of that day and age he had an endless fund of stories to tell of his adventures in various parts of the world where he had served. Many of these stories were remembered by Dad and told to Jean and me, either as bedtime stories or on train journeys when we were children.

My sister, Jean, grew up to worship Uncle William as the naval hero of the family, our own Nelson, and when she joined the Wrens in 1940 it was to follow in Uncle William's footsteps. A splendid photo of him in his Captain's uniform was hung, together with a photograph of grandfather James (also in uniform) in our entrance hall. It immediately attracted the attention of all our guests as they came in. When Dad left to join his unit at the beginning of the war, Mum rearranged the entrance hall so that a large picture of Dad in uniform took pride of place between the photos of James and Uncle William. The three pictures show a remarkable family resemblance on which nearly everyone commented. They all had distinguished war records and died for their country.

When Dad's military transport plane went missing in 1945 there were no more Fortingalls in the male line of succession. When I married David in 1943 I didn't change my name to McBain because I didn't want to embarrass the school and wanted them to go on treating me as a perfectly normal Sixth Form pupil. When I first started work as an odd-job woman in the accounts department of my father-in-law's firm I decided to revert to the name of Fortingall in order to remain anonymous. I was anxious not to be given special treatment as the boss's daughter-in-law and I think it was some years before anyone knew. When I eventually moved up the ladder and

MY PEDIGREE

joined the Board I was extremely glad that I had retained my family name for business purposes. It is now a fairly widespread practice for women in the professions and business to keep their original names, but in the 1950s it was unusual. I, therefore, think of myself as the last of the Fortingalls. Although Dad was obviously sad at being unable to have a son, I hope that when he looks down on me he will give me credit for trying to do my best to keep the family flag flying for another half-century.

Sadly, the fate of the Fortingall family has been replicated in the fate of many similar families who formed the backbone of the British Empire and who were largely wiped out in two world wars. Many families suffered greater losses than ours. If I have a criticism it is that such families tended to be too conventional and this applies particularly to great-grandfather Robert Fortingall who appears to have been driven by the wish to be accepted as part of the English Great and Good. The commercial strength of England which had succeeded in recruiting and mobilising the talents of the Scots, Welsh, Irish and other immigrants was based on being unconventional and entrepreneurial. Without a commercial empire people like Pitt the Younger would never have had the money to subsidise all the other countries in Europe in the wars against Napoleon and we would never have built a political empire.

I remember reading a marvellous book by Brooks Adams, a member of the Adams family that had produced two presidents of the United States, called the Law of Civilisation and Decay, which described how great Empires declined because they turned into bureaucracies staffed by second-rate conventional people who failed to promote or utilise the unconventional and talented type of person who had built these Empires in the first place. I have seen this happening again and again in large British companies.

For all his talents, great-grandfather Fortingall was misguided in trying to direct his sons into careers that ordinary, uninteresting, unimaginative people regarded as much more prestigious than trade or industry. In contrast, Mum's family contained a number of fascinating people who were highly unconventional pioneers and were not afraid to be in a minority of one. The other interesting thing about Mum's family is that it was the women, rather than the men, who played the key roles, in particular my two maternal great-grandmothers of whom more anon.

Mum's name before marriage was Henriette Johnston. Her father's family were mainly of Scots descent (yet more Scots blood in my arteries!) and her mother's family of French descent.

To begin with the Scots: Mum's grandfather, David Johnston (1834-1910), was a Scots doctor who trained in Glasgow and bought himself a third-class, single rail ticket to London, where he was able to find employment as an assistant in a fast-growing practice being built up by two fellow Glaswegians to whom he had, in fact, had a letter of introduction before he invested in a rail ticket. He had only been offered a job on an "on approval" basis but he was sufficiently confident to believe that he would satisfy the "on approval" tests, which he did.

His father had been the Headmaster of a school in a village which was fast turning into an industrial suburb. Being Headmaster probably meant that he was the only teacher, although he may have been assisted by what were then known as "pupil teachers". The schoolmaster, like many Scots of similar ilk, would have done his best to push each of his children forward to improve their positions in whatever manner was available to them.

David Johnston was a man of vision as well as ambition and once he had taken his job in Kensington in his stride, he was clearly not content to see his future as a life of saying "hold out your tongue and say ah" and prescribing caster oil. He was interested in public health. His mother, one of his brothers and one of his sisters had died in the cholera epidemic that had decimated the population of the village where his father's school was situated. Theories were being propounded about the deaths following the line of a drain and of cholera being brought by the workmen who were building the railway.

Once he had settled down in London and felt reasonably secure in his job he started attending public lectures on subjects that interested him. He was articulate and could, therefore, make his views known in any subsequent discussion. As he usually prefaced his remarks with a statement to the effect that he was concerned, as a doctor, with the effects of public health measures on the lives of his then patients, the non-medical members of the audience would immediately sit up and take notice. The other medics would no doubt perceive him as a competitor, unless they were practising in a different part of London.

On one of these occasions a medical journalist and writer was in the audience and was impressed, not only by what he said but the way he said it. Catherine McInnes was the journalist, who was later to become my great-grandmother.

Catherine McInnes is one of the most remarkable women that I could ever have wished to know. I couldn't hold a candle to her, neither could any of the women who write or speak about women's lib. Catherine was concerned with substance, not candy floss.

Catherine McInnes was yet another Scot, the daughter of a Scots doctor who had not emigrated to England. She had an older brother and a younger brother, both of whom studied medicine in Glasgow and became doctors. She wanted to be a doctor, but women were not at that time accepted as medical students. She could have given up but she didn't. She studied her older brother's text books and when her younger brother started medical school, she worked her way systematically through his course, demanding to see all his lecture notes and no doubt belabouring him when the notes were not clear or complete. I wouldn't have wanted to have been her younger brother.

She had decided that if she couldn't be a doctor, she would be a medical writer and this meant coming to London. How she managed to persuade her parents to give her the money for her train fare to London says a lot for her powers of persuasion. Given the reputation of London in those days as a sink of iniquity and white slavery, the poor parents must have been worried stiff about the fate that awaited their daughter. But her determination and charisma must have carried the day. I can think of no other plausible explanation.

She worked at slave labour rates writing the bulk of a medical magazine and then she got a break. She wrote a novel that sold. The second half of the 19th Century was the great romance period for fiction writers. She was not in the class of Hardy or Meredith, but her "three decker" (i.e. three volume) novels captured the spirit of the times and generated revenue for the publisher and herself.

Most of them were social reformist novels about people like herself. They tended to be pitched a little bit further up the social scale, but the theme was fairly constant. There would be a heroine who would inherit a vast fortune. She would take her inheritance seriously and go and visit the towns and villages where she had become a major proprietor and start spending her money reforming the drainage system, the education system, the schools, hospitals and so on. This caught the reforming spirit of the time, so she was not only commercially successful but popular in intellectual circles. She wrote well.

David Johnston's enthusiasm for practical and sensible measures to improve public health impressed her. He was a fellow Scot. He was a doctor and when she met him, she liked him and respected him. The feelings were mutual and in due course they married. They became a very powerful partnership. David finished his career in glory in one of the newly created positions of Medical Officer for Health and for many years they both enjoyed a respected position amongst writers, thinkers, reformers and politicians.

Whilst Catherine was obviously interested in public health, she was also interested in education for women and was active in various campaigns to persuade universities to accept women students. It was the period when Oxford, Cambridge, many other universities and medical schools were beginning to open their doors to women undergraduates. Whatever influence Catherine had on this process I know not, but I would be surprised if it was not significant. She was not a raucous heckler from the floor, but a consummate strategist and diplomatist. She knew how to say the right things to the right people at the right time and in the right way to get things done.

From all accounts she had a soft spot for Mum as the granddaughter (in fact her youngest) who was determined to make the most of her educational opportunities. When Mum gained a scholarship in Mathematics to Newnham College, Cambridge in 1918, Catherine was over the moon. She was 78 and walked with a stick, but she was Mum's most frequent visitor. She was awarded an honorary degree shortly after her eightieth birthday in 1920 for her services to women's education, a day that Mum used to describe as one of the most moving moments in her life. Here was this grand old lady, slightly stooped and walking with a stick, with a powerful look in her eye that wouldn't take no for an answer, with her great dignity and determination of manner, being given a tumultuous welcome and being written about in the national newspapers. As Mum put it:

"I felt quite small. I suddenly realised I was the granddaughter of someone important. Rather than thinking of myself as the bright hope of the family who had achieved great things, I started saying 'I'd better pull my socks up if I am going to live up to my grandmother's standards'."

And that's the way I've always felt, but even more so.

Catherine's interests were not limited to public health and women's education. She was sought after by people like the Pankhursts (of the suffragette movement) and the Webbs (socialists). From what Mum said Catherine was highly sceptical of both these political sets and used to say:

"I can't see what use it's going to be to any women being able to vote for Mr. Balfour or Mr. Asquith (the two political leaders in Edwardian times). I wouldn't vote for either of them and nothing that either of them is likely to do could conceivably have any practical effect on opportunities for women. If whoever wins is going to do something stupid there is nothing that my vote will do to stop it. The only important thing for women is to achieve financial independence, which means they must be able to become doctors, solicitors, barristers or members of any other profession if they are able to do so."

The fact that women at the end of the 20th Century have been able to achieve such positions, and that we now take this for granted, owes more than a little to people with the vision and determination of my great-grandmother.

But even in her 60s and 70s Catherine was still fighting battles that were causing outrage. By then she had taken up the cause of contraception for women. The development of vulcanised rubber in the 1860s had brought contraception within the reach of the upper classes who had taken the trouble to become knowledgeable in such matters. I have it on good authority that there were earlier, more rudimentary, methods that worked but I know not how.

What my great-grandmother and many of her friends such as Marie Stopes set out to achieve was to bring the benefits of this technology to the rest of the population and it was an uphill task. It still is an uphill task in certain countries of the world. Even in Britain today, the large number of unwanted teenage pregnancies is evidence of the fact that a big job remains to be done. If she was still alive my great-grandmother would probably say that we had fallen down because we have abandoned education as a social objective, in the sense that people of her ilk understood the word education. Education, in her book, was teaching people to aspire to lift themselves up on an individual basis, not to remain as part of the herd.

To the end of her life Catherine never let go. She had put the award of an honourary degree at risk by choosing late in life to make cause for what was then a highly controversial subject, in fact an almost unmentionable subject in polite circles, but she didn't give a damn. She would be polite, diplomatic and amiable as the situation might require, but she would never compromise on what she regarded as points of principle. If she hadn't been awarded an honourary degree she wouldn't have minded. There are not many people like Catherine. During my life I have only met a very small number, and I don't think any with quite the strength of character and achievement record that Mum has described to me. People like that are truly the salt of the earth.

David and Catherine's son, Alexander (Sandy) was born in 1866 and followed in his father's footsteps by qualifying as a doctor. One career analyst told me that more doctors follow in their father's footsteps than people of any other profession because traditionally a doctor's office was his home (I am speaking of the old style GP). This has its disadvantages. There tends to be a lot of backstairs intrigue in the hospital world, which means that mediocre doctors appear to be able to get on because of parental pulls, what the French call 'piston'. Be that as it may, young Sandy Johnston enjoyed a much better start in life than his father. He was educated at St. Paul's School and sent to Cambridge, unlike the sons of a lot of Scots doctors who were sent back to their father's alma mater.

Sandy was quite happy to work in general practice in Kensington where he had a lot of well-heeled patients and in due course met and married a very attractive French lady, Suzanne de Roncesvalles, the daughter of a deceased member of the French nobility whose widow had settled in South Kensington, which had been a French enclave since the time of the French Revolution, and still is.

Her mother, Madame la Baronne, was a most formidable lady and the most worrying moment in Sandy's not very eventful life was standing in the hall of her mansion, preparing for the interview at which he intended to ask her daughter's hand in marriage. He knew that Suzanne was on side because she had in fact done all the coaching in the hope that he would say the right things in the right way to her mother. The important thing was that he succeeded, so the 'auld alliance' of medieval times between France and Scotland enjoyed a new lease of life in Kensington which produced two little girls, the younger of whom was my mother who was born in 1900 (see Table 2, Who's Who). Sandy, who was my maternal grandfather, died in 1924 so I never knew him, although Suzanne survived until 1944. She was the only grandparent that I ever knew, but because she had moved back to France with her mother in 1925, we lost contact from 1939 onwards. She was in France, and England was cut off because of the war.

This brings me to the last and most formidable of my ancestors, Madame la Baronne (see Table 3, Who's Who). Although she was born in 1848, she lived until she had passed her ninetieth birthday in 1938 and I remember her well because from the age of four onwards I can recall the wonderful Summers that I spent at her chateau home near La Tour du Pin until the Summer of 1938. I shall, in a later chapter, describe her as she appeared to me in the 1930s. She was still a very upright, regal and elegant woman, but at the same time remarkably relaxed and friendly to me as one of her many great-grandchildren. I am concerned here to sketch something of her early life, or what we know of it which is not much.

We know that she came from somewhere near La Tour du Pin because this is what she told everybody and gave as her reason for settling there in 1925, when she decided to leave London and go back to the land of her birth. This was after her daughter, Suzanne, had in 1924 been left a widow and had agreed to go with her. It was the year that Winston Churchill, as Chancellor of the Exchequer, had put the pound back on the gold standard so that her sterling and dollar investments would buy her a lot more if her living expenses were in French francs, than if they were in English pounds.

Her origins are shrouded in mystery, possibly of her own making. One of the many legends about her is that, as a young peasant girl she took advantage of the coming of railways to make her way to Paris, where she found work in one of the more up-market brothels and succeeded in persuading one of the satisfied customers to marry her.

Another legend is that she was conceived on the wrong side of the sheet by some French aristocrat who had taken a fancy to a pretty chambermaid. Personally I don't think that the claim of French aristocratic connections would add any value to her pedigree. She was what she was. I have never had a particularly high opinion of the latter day French aristocracy. By all accounts they were a pretty effete bunch. Instead of running their estates they spent their time toadying around the royal court, making lecherous grabs at chambermaids and peasant girls, leaving it to lackeys and other hangers-on to serve their wives and produce heirs to their estates.

What we do know is that Henriette by the age of eighteen had found her way to Paris and succeeded in becoming the favourite mistress of a certain Baron Guillaume de Roncesvalles. Possibly she prevailed on a local lover from La Tour du Pin to take her to Paris and set her up in a flat, from where she was able to trade up. One can only assume that she was an outstandingly beautiful girl, had great sex appeal, was superb in bed and knew how to take maximum advantage of every opportunity. When she discovered that her titled lover was a widower she succeeded in getting him to marry her, although she was forty years his junior (he was born in 1808) and she bore him two daughters, Suzanne, my grandmother, in 1868 and Thérèse in 1870. She must, from an early age, have possessed the talents of a leading lady who could immediately play the part of Madame la Baronne and impress his guests, not only by her beauty, but by her regal manner.

The Baron du Roncesvalles was no common or garden French aristocrat. He had been one of the self-made social climbers of Napoleon III's empire. In essence he was a business man who made money in a time of great commercial expansion, rather than frittering it away. He had good commercial connections with a number of British merchant banks which had provided him with finance for a number of his commercial projects. He was anxious to raise finance for a major new enterprise and so he travelled to London in style with his new wife. It would have been surprising for any man of his age not to have enjoyed basking in the admiration (or jealousy) of all the men of similar age at his good fortune in persuading someone of Henriette's beauty and sex appeal to be his wife. Whatever her origins, I am sure that she already behaved as if she were to the manor born.

I don't wish to disparage my great-grandfather. I often boast of the fact that one of my great-grandfathers was born in 1808. I admire his perspicacity in identifying Henriette as a woman quite out of the ordinary and worthy to be his wife. There is no reason why, even with that age gap, there should not have been a strong emotional bond between them. I like to think that there was. She certainly served his memory well and not only her descendants, but many of the people she brought into her service benefited from the fortune he had gathered and which she succeeded in increasing and multiplying so successfully. I cannot image her as the sort of grasping woman who would have spent her time trying to cajole diamond tiaras and expensive jewellery out of him. She was the sort of person who would concentrate her mind on substance rather than candy floss. There was no reason why his fortune should not in due course become hers, so why fritter it away?

She had a remarkable capacity to absorb whatever she needed to know. During her years of marriage she had made it her business to understand what he was trying to do. She had quickly assimilated the English that she needed to know to get by and from all accounts she charmed every important Englishman she met. I have no authority for this statement except that of my grandmother, who was two years old at the time, but it is in character and I have no reason to disbelieve it.

When the war broke out between France and Prussia in 1870 most Frenchmen thought that Napoleon III's army would teach these upstart little Prussians a lesson in a matter of weeks, just as the great Napoleon Bonaparte had taught them a lesson at Jena. But the Baron was intelligent enough to know that a war situation meant a halt to his current project. He would probably have gone back to France with his wife and two year old child, but Henriette must have had some kind of gut feel and persuaded him to let her stay, probably arguing that he would be back in a few weeks, when the Prussians had been given a good hiding. Anyway, she stayed with my grandmother and the Baron went back to Paris.

Whether he was assassinated by some would-be revolutionary or died of heart failure no-one knows. Henriette remained installed in London in a temporarily rented house and had become a highly desirable 'heiress' in her own right, but this was before the Married Women's Property Act of 1882 and she had no intention of handing over her newly acquired wealth to anyone else so she never remarried, although she established a long-standing relationship with a director of Barings who acted as her impresario, turned her into a financial expert in her own right (she must been one of the fastest learners ever), arranged for her to be presented at court, both in the reigns of Queen Victoria and Edward VII, organised a number of journeys to the US, on one of which (in the early years of the 20th Century) he arranged for her to visit the White House and shake hands with Theodore Roosevelt.

She had thought of returning to Paris in the mid 1870s after the turmoil of defeat and revolution had passed safely into history, but decided that life was no longer the same without the imperial splendour of Napoleon III who was now living in exile in England. She had developed a taste for London which she saw as the centre of the world (this was when we were at the peak of our imperial power) and she was never happier than what she referred to as the golden days of Le Bon Roi Edouard. She had a Paris house for business visits but acquired or built a villa in the small peninsula of St. Jean-cap-Ferrat where she would spend the Winter months. We had a wonderful Summer holiday there in 1939 just before the war, where Jean and I enjoyed swimming from our private beach. In the 19th Century and early 20th Century the French Riviera had been largely colonised as a Winter resort by the English leisured classes who thought of it as too hot to go in Summer.

It was only after the death of Suzanne's husband (my maternal grandfather) in 1924 that Henriette had decided that London was no longer the place that it had once been and she decided to return to the land of her birth, now that she could take her daughter, Suzanne (my grandmother) with her. But they didn't return to Paris. She went to modernise a large country house near the place where she was born in the beautiful countryside near La Tour du Pin, which I shall describe more fully in the chapter on my childhood.

Her younger daughter, Thérèse, who had been brought to London as a baby had, as a pretty nineteen year old, been courted by a handsome naval attaché at the French Embassy who married her and gave her a large family, who in turn produced hordes of grandchildren. I was never able to keep track of all of them. I merely remember staying regularly with one family whenever we passed through Paris. This was the family of Mum's cousin, whom we called Tante Nicole. There used to be a lot of children that were invited to spend the long, two months Summer holidays at the chateau during the years between 1930 and 1938 when my sister, Jean, and I were also invited, enabling Mum and Dad to have a holiday on their own at the St. Jean-cap-Ferrat villa. I shall say more about the final years of Henriette's life, and about some of her other great-grandchildren when I come to deal with my own childhood.

Suffice it to say at this stage that Henriette was one of the most remarkable people that I could have wished to find amongst my ancestors. She had a true spark of genius combined with a dominating presence. She made maximum use of all the talents that God gave her, including her physical beauty and desirability as a lover, in addition to her remarkable intelligence and the shrewdness with which she judged people. She was a shrewd investor who understood the impact of politics, wars and social changes on the economies of the countries in which she invested. She used her money wisely, contributing to the happiness of many of her descendants and also many of the people who worked for her.

However imposing and regal her manner might appear from a distance, she could put people at ease because she had an instant feel for the way other people's minds worked. She could talk to all her great-grandchildren as if she were one of them. For me as a child she seemed like a wonderful fairy godmother and I treasure her memory, not only for its own sake, but as a personal link with a long lost period of history, conjuring up vistas of both the wonderful renaissance of France in the great days of Napoleon III and of England at the height of its imperial splendour and of the 'golden days of Good King Edward the Caresser'.

So you can see why my pedigree is important to me and why it may be of interest to my readers. I like to feel that I have inherited something of the Fortingall integrity and reliability, something of the crusading zeal of Catherine McInnes and something of Henriette's versatility. I may not have inherited her radiant beauty and regal manner, but I like to think that I share with her the capacity to be open and uninhibited about my enjoyment of the earthly pleasures that I believe were given to us to enjoy.

Finally, I think one's ancestors can play a useful part in one's own life. There have often been periods when I felt down and wanted to give up on whatever I happened to be doing because the going was tough and then I have thought of Dad, Catherine or Henriette looking down on me and saying "Pull yourself together, girl. You can do better than that." and it often works. It is easy to feel that the Almighty has more important things to do than becoming involved in one's minor day to day problems, but with one's ancestors it can be different. One assumes, possibly incorrectly, that they may have time on their hands to take an interest in their descendants, just as I do my best to help my children and grandchildren. I am not asking you to accept my theology. If it has helped me, that is all that matters.

CHAPTER 3

DAD AND MUM

Dad and Mum were born within a month of each other in 1900, Mum on 21st October and Dad on 6th November. Their childhood and teenage lives, however, were totally different.

Mum grew up in what was then a fashionable part of Kensington and was no doubt exercised daily in Kensington Gardens. She did not, as many upper class girls of the time, spend any time riding in Rotten Row. This may have been because of the war and also because the family were not typically English. Her Scots father was a serious person who worked hard and conscientiously as a GP and her French mother was much more interested in cultural and social activities. Mum was of a serious disposition and, although she no doubt enjoyed her own type of fun and games, that wasn't a side of her life that she used to talk about in later years. I know nothing about her teenage flirtations (if there were any) and I don't think I differ in this respect from the majority of other women.

As far as I can gather, Mum was studious from an early age. She was sent to St. Paul's Girls School. Even at her junior school she was recognised as a gifted child with a remarkable head for figures. She could do the most complex calculations in her head far quicker than most people can nowadays do them with the aid of pocket calculators or computers. Even in her mid 80s, when Mum was staying with us and helping with the week's shopping, she would tot up in her head all the items we bought as we filled up a massive trolley, carry on talking about other things whilst she was doing it, and when we got to the till she would immediately spot if there was an error in the total - and she was always right, unless something hadn't been properly priced on the shelves or the store had made some similar error.

Fortunately she had good teachers who were keen to stretch her capabilities and to set her sights high rather than low. The period of the 1914-18 war was one where women were doing many jobs that had hitherto been done by men and this may have helped in creating a more favourable climate of opinion during the four critical years of Mum's higher education, but I don't think this would have made much difference to someone like Mum. Where she had decided to go she would go. What was important was the guidance she had from the lady who had persuaded her to set her sights on getting a place at Newnham.

The senior Maths teacher had not been able to go to Cambridge herself because her parent's didn't have the money, and in any case hadn't regarded women's education as all that important.

In her family of course Mum had tremendous encouragement. Catherine, Mum's paternal grandmother, wanted girls to set their sights on becoming doctors, dentists, scientists, engineers. Maths came sufficiently close to this cluster of subjects to be given a welcome. In any case, Catherine was not the sort of person to try and influence anyone else's choice of subject.

Arrière was even more enthusiastic. I suspect that Mum inherited her skill in mental arithmetic from her maternal grandmother who had managed her own finances so successfully. She used to say to Mum that nobody could succeed in finance without a good head for figures, and with a Cambridge degree Mum could aspire in due course to a seat on the Board of Barings. Arrière still had the contacts there to get her a job when she had a degree. But Arrière insisted again and again that success could be achieved in finance only if you were a good all-rounder. By this she didn't mean being good on the hockey pitch, or good at playing the piano, but that you had to understand people and what made them tick. A knowledge of history could be useful as long as you didn't believe the rubbish they put in history books (she was always joking about the ignorant way in which Napoleon III's 21 years of government was presented both in England and France).

Fortunately Mum was at a school which provided a much better education in the sense that she could develop her own individual powers of judgment, to question the assumptions that other people would take for granted, to argue her case and not to be perturbed if she were in a minority of one. Many schools, and certainly the French State Education system both then and now are dictatorial in the sense that they present what is perceived as the orthodox view as the only acceptable view and educational advancement means learning to mug up a mish-mash of the current dogmas of the decade in the way communist youth in Russia was compelled to learn by rote the pernicious doctrines of Marx and Lenin.

Mum had a home where she learnt a tremendous amount that had nothing to do with formal education.

Although she was living in England, she grew up in what was essentially a French household. Although her mother (Suzanne) had also grown up in London, she was very much a French thinking as well as a French speaking individual and many of her childhood friends were from the French community in South Kensington.

A girl growing up in a French middle class household, no matter what her career prospects, had to learn to be a good 'Maitresse de Maison', which meant not only learning how to cook but how to budget for a household. In an age where middle class people usually had kitchen maids, lady's maids, cooks and bottle-washers, this training would include learning how to cope with all the wiles and ruses of the servants who would try to diddle you.

Mum used to say that when she was 14 and 15 she used to be put in charge of the household for a whole week, possibly a fortnight at a time (during the school holidays), left to make her own mistakes, and her mother wouldn't interfere unless she was asked for advice. Many women have told me they could never survive for long in a kitchen with their mothers because their mothers would always interfere on relatively trivial matters. I suppose I had a similar training to Mum, but it was different because during the war I was just left to cope, and in any case there were only two of us. Mum had learnt at an early age how to plan and organise dinner parties where there might be 10 or 12 people sitting around a table. There was no flap or panic. The food would be excellent as it was in the marvellous dinner parties which she used to give for Dad in the 1930s where he would hold forth on the ineptitudes and imbecilities of the politicians who were going to land us in another war for which we were totally unprepared.

Suzanne (her mother) was an artistic and literary person. She was also an excellent pianist. In the days before wireless, gramophones, etc. the only way in which a child could become familiar with music was if someone in the family could play the piano. This meant that scores of unmusical children were sent to learn The Bluebells of Scotland so that they could come home and do their best to put other members of their families off whatever masterpieces they were currently trying to massacre, but if there was a good pianist in the family a child with an ear for music could learn a lot.

Mum and her sister had piano lessons, but Mum used to say that she never had the time to practise properly once she got into the senior school and she much preferred to listen to Suzanne. Her favourite pieces were some of Mendelssohn's Songs Without Words.

When Mum was 9 or 10 she was taken to concerts at the old Queen's Hall and at the Albert Hall. She also sang in the choir at school.

She used to tell me that her most memorable experience was being taken at 12 or 13 to the Russian ballet where she saw Pavlova dancing in Swan Lake. Pavlova was reputed to be the most famous dancer of the 20th Century. Mum says that when she died they performed Swan Lake with a spotlight moving around the stage, following the positions where she would have danced. The English audiences worshipped her.

Mum was so enthusiastic about ballet that she was taken a number of times and remembered seeing what was then regarded as the highly avant garde Diaghilev productions of Stravinsky's Petruchka and the Rite of Spring.

Mum was obviously brought up to be bilingual. Sandy (her father) used to try his best when they spoke French at meal times or in France, but he always had difficulty with the accent and also with trying to remember which words were masculine and which were feminine.

Suzanne used to teach Mum French grammar and French reading and give her written exercises to do from the time she was 4, and as she grew up Mum acquired an extensive knowledge of French literature, as I did, i.e. she was given the sort of books that she would enjoy reading for pleasure, just as I was. Her French teacher would have liked to see her in the Modern Languages Sixth, but both her parents took the sensible view that languages are a useful skill in later life if you have shown yourself to be talented in another direction, but have little value on their own unless you want to spend your life as a French teacher, which Mum clearly didn't.

In the two or three years before 1914 Mum started a lifelong friendship with her cousIn Nicole (one of Thérèse's daughters). Although she was five years older than Mum and might have been expected to build up a closer relationship with Mum's older sister (and things may have started that way) it was always Tante Nicole with whom our family stayed when we went to Paris and Tante Nicole who used to come and stay with us in Tawchester. After the war she came to England in 1946 for Jean's wedding and then in 1948 for my wedding to John and she and Mum used to write to each other every week.

In those days children used to call most female adult relatives (other than grandparents) Auntie. We couldn't have called her 'cousin' and in those days children would not dream of calling an adult by his or her first name.

Nicole was one of a large family. She was intelligent but not given the educational opportunities of Mum. She liked being the expert made responsible for guiding her young English cousins around the sights of Paris (in fact they were usually accompanied by a responsible adult). She liked having a young girl that she could mother. She was even more appreciative of her visits to London where she was treated as somebody.

There was a great excitement during the Easter holiday in 1914 when Nicole married a handsome Cavalry officer and Mum was invited to be one of the Demoiselles d'Honneur. Stefan, her husband, was badly wounded in the Battle of the Marne in 1914. Much to his chagrin he had to resign his commission after he had realised that he would never be able to walk again without crutches. Tante Nicole used to speak of this as a blessing because she said that had he returned to the Front his chances of surviving the war alive were minimal. As it was, she had him until he died in 1928. They never had any children.

After Stefan's death Arrière provided considerable financial assistance to Nicole so that she could keep on her Paris flat. As an officer's widow she enjoyed a certain amount of priority when she applied for a job in the Public Service. She had not been able to work while Stefan was alive as she had had to spend all her time looking after him. She had no special qualifications and so she could only earn a low salary. Fortunately she accepted (soon after Arrière's death at the end of 1938) the invitation from Suzanne to go and live at La Tour du Pin as a friend, companion and helper, so she was able to escape the privations of living in occupied Paris. It would have been much more difficult for her to cross from the Occupied to the Unoccupied Zone after the 1940 Armistice with Germany. But she loved Paris and after the war she rented a small Paris flat as a pied-à-terre and we all crowded in with her in 1947 on our first post-war visit to France when foreign currency was restricted to £50 per person.

In the days before World War I Mum must have benefited enormously from having a close rapport with an attractive and older French girl over and above the joys such friendship can bring. She would have learnt all the colloquial expressions that teenagers use that wouldn't have been in the French vocabulary of her mother who had never lived in France except for holidays and a grandmother who had left France over 40 years before. She may well have started to pick up her impeccable dress sense at this period of her life, although it was Arrière who made it her business to teach her English granddaughters how they should dress.

Arrière was always highly critical of the way the English taught their daughters how to dress, although she was full of praise for the sort of education Mum was getting at St. Paul's Girls School. I found this surprising because I have always thought of London in the Edwardian era and the years of George V's reign before the start of the 1914-1918 war as a very elegant place where middle and upper class women spent far too much money on clothes that I certainly wouldn't have liked to wear. I hesitate to think what Arrière would have said had she revisited London in recent years and seen some of the dreadful scarecrows with rings in their noses, in their navels and wherever, as well as the horrendous clothes that would enable them to scare birds away better than Worzel Gummidge. She would probably have wondered how long the human race could be expected to go on propagating itself. What man would want to get into bed with creatures like these? But if you look at the scruffy men with rings in their ears and their noses attempting to communicate with each other in some incomprehensible series of grunts and noises, which is no doubt meant to be a form of English, you might ask the same question about the women.

Arrière did take Mum and her sister on shopping expeditions to buy party dresses, but as Mum was only a 13 year old when the war started and wore school uniform for most of her life in London, she was not quite ready for the education in clothes and dress sense that Arrière no doubt had in mind to give her as a 16/17 year old, but couldn't because of the war.

The 1914-18 war was not a period of austerity in matters such as clothes, but civilians didn't travel between England and France for holidays or pleasure. It was not only a matter of scarce shipping, but there was a risk of being torpedoed in the Channel. In any case it wouldn't have been seen as patriotic. Paris, of course, didn't suffer occupation. French and British Senior Officers who had the money went to Paris on leave and spent it freely on the women who would entertain them in the traditional manner and the ladies would spend a certain amount of this money on the clothes which they thought would attract more men to spend more money, and so on.

For Mum, however, the first serious education she received in the art of clothing herself was in the early Summer of 1920, at the end of her second year in Cambridge when she had already fallen in love and Arrière knew it and approved. Dad had loved her from the moment he first saw her but it wasn't for the clothes she was wearing but for what she was. I'm sure, however, that Mum's naturally good dress sense at that age didn't require a lot of tuition from Arrière.

Mum used to say that main lesson she learnt from Arrière at that time was that one of the secrets of keeping a man, or at any rate in retaining his amorous interest (and Arrière was clearly an expert in such matters) was in what a woman wore underneath her dresses and in what she wore in bed. I can only assume that Mum took this lesson to heart with enthusiasm. When it was my turn to become an amorous teenager, which was in the Second World War years when there was clothes rationing and everything was 'utility', I blessed Mum again and again for the lovely clothes she had bought and kept during the pre-war years and which I used to borrow freely.

Some of my women friends I know are very scathing about the way men go for this sort of thing, but I have never understood why they should be scathing. I suppose some women just want a husband as a social convenience, an odd job man around the house who can pay the rent and father her children and they find catering for men's appetites something of a bore. But if you want your husband to be an ardent lover and to remain an ardent lover it doesn't take much intelligence to find the things that turn him on. If he likes what you are wearing next to your skin then you do, because you instinctively like what you know he likes.

The subject of Mum's wish to attract and retain Dad as an ardent lover brings me naturally to his part in my family history or, more accurately, his early years.

His early life on the Fortingall Estate near Shrewsbury couldn't have been more different from Mum's. His mother died when he was 6. In the early years of his marriage James (Dad's father) and Jean (his mother) lived in the Dower House on the understanding that they would vacate it when grandfather Fortingall died, so that it could be used to house his widow. This was on the assumption that Uncle Henry, as the heir to the estates, would take up residence in the main house, which he didn't.

On their mother's death Dad and his two sisters moved in to the main house to live with their grandmother, who didn't move out to the Dower House because Uncle Henry said he didn't need the main house as long as he remained Headmaster where he had a magnificent house that went with the job. In the event, he didn't move there on retirement because he was offered the post of Dean of Tawchester, which gave him the right to live in the Deanery, another splendid house that went with the job.

Dad's father didn't want his son to suffer the miseries that he had endured as a boy, boarding first at a Dotheboys Hall type of Prep School and later at a Public School which was supposed to be good if you wanted an Army career. James didn't want his son to be pushed into the Regular Army. He wanted his son to choose his own career, although he hoped that he would be good enough to enter into one of the learned professions.

The children had a governess and later Dad had a private tutor who was in fact a retired Headmaster of a nearby Prep School, although he had started life as a History master.

From all accounts he was an excellent tutor and Dad learnt far more history, which was his favourite subject, than he would have learnt anywhere else. His tutor was an all-rounder who had got Dad up to a reasonable level in Latin and Maths. The governess, who looked after the education of Dad's younger sisters (Beatrice and Eleanor - whom I referred to Aunt Bea and Aunt Nell) claimed to be a good French teacher and therefore gave Dad his first French lessons, although he used to say it was very much the French of Stratford-Atte-Bowe.

Being at home meant that Dad was able to spend a lot of time with his Uncle William who used to spend his shore leaves in the family home. It also meant that after James had been posted back to England after the end of the Boer War, Dad was able to see something of his father. On one of his leaves when Dad was 9 James took him for his first visit to London to see Buckingham Palace, the Tower, Westminster Abbey and so on.

DAD AND MUM

When Dad was 10 it was felt that he would benefit from contact with other boys. In the days of motor travel he could easily have attended a good local Prep School as a day boy, but it was considered too far away to travel on a bicycle, so it was agreed that Dad would be a weekly boarder. Dad was solidly built and by then sufficiently sure of himself to hold his own with other boys. The school's academic standards were, however, far below what his father had expected and if Dad was to stand a chance of getting a scholarship to a leading Public School he would need a lot of private tuition during the school holidays.

It was already clear that Dad was academically gifted. Uncle Henry was keen to have him under his wing. He not only wanted to help Dad, but he wanted to help his brother James who had not had a good deal either from his parents or in the Army. Dad was successful in getting a scholarship. With the recall of James to the army when the war started in 1914 and his posting to what was to become the Mesopotamia front and then the death of Dad's grandmother (who had looked after James' children after the death of their mother), Uncle Henry and his wife Mavis took over most of the parental duties. Aunt Bea and Aunt Nell lived in the Headmaster's house with Henry and Mavis and were sent to a good local girls' day school. Dad was in a boarding house and spent his holidays with Henry and Mavis.

What I know about Dad's school days comes mainly from Aunt Bea, who was very fond of Dad. As children we used to stay in her house in Putney when we were travelling to and from France. In later life when she was a widow she quite often stayed with John and me and it was on these latter occasions that I learnt much of what I know about my Fortingall family history.

By the time he was 16 Dad was already a large, well-built amiable person who showed great enthusiasm for whatever he was currently doing. Although he was a loner in terms of his thinking he was popular with other boys. He had a dominating presence and was quick-witted in his replies. While he could pass muster on the rugger field and the cricket field, sport was not one of his main enthusiasms. On the work side he was an all-rounder but his strongest subject was History, where he won various prizes. He also dominated the school debating society and his first ambition was to follow in the footsteps of his Uncle Robert and enter Parliament in the hope of becoming a Minister. He was weaned away from this by Uncle Henry, who pointed out that he would need a lot of money to make a career in politics and with that nasty Welsh bounder (Lloyd George) at the helm public life had become pretty disreputable. Any old crook could buy himself an earldom or a knighthood by paying enough money into Lloyd George's private slush fund.

Dad's next ambition was to be a K.C. (as they were called when we had a king). This was partly the influence of his best friend Ian, whose father was a K.C. and who invited Dad on various occasions to stay with his family and go to the Public Gallery in the High Court to watch Ian's father performing in some high profile fraud trials. It was on one of these visits that Dad was introduced to Lord Curzon who became Foreign Minister and, in Dad's view, should have become Prime Minister when Bonar Law died suddenly in 1923. Dad often used to speak about Curzon in the 1930s as an intellectual and political giant for whom that 'nasty little impostor Baldwin' was not fit to act as a shoe-shine boy. Although it was only two years ago that I read David Gilmour's Biography of Lord Curzon, it presents a picture of him very similar to the one that Dad described, although David Gilmour doesn't share Dad's hatred of Baldwin.

Ian and Dad were both interested in politics and went together to the Visitors' Gallery in the House of Commons. Dad was mainly interested in the chance to see what leading Ministers and Opposition figures looked like in the flesh and I think he was singularly unimpressed. It was before the days of television and cinema news reels. When I read Max Beerbohm's wonderful essay "A Small Boy Seeing Giants" describing the way in which he used to spend his school holidays going to stand in Downing Street in order to draw sketches of Cabinet Ministers as they came out of No. 10, in the days when Gladstone was Prime Minister, it made me think of Dad's verbal portraits, although Dad did not have Max's genius as a caricaturist.

So in his Sixth Form years Dad had firmly made up his mind that he would like to go to Pembroke College, Cambridge (Uncle Henry's College) to read Law in the hope of becoming a Barrister. It was the sort of profession that if you earned enough you could afford to go into Parliament and if you lost your seat you could go back and practise at the Bar.

The death in early 1917 of his father (James Fortingall) in the Baghdad campaign put Dad's future in doubt. Would there be the money for him to go to university? There was also the shadow of the war. If it went on for another year and a half he would be 18 and have to join the army, although at that time his ambition was to join the Royal Flying Corps and be a pilot.

It was Uncle Henry who, at that critical period in Dad's life, provided the guidance and financial assistance that enabled Dad first to go to Cambridge and then to qualify as a solicitor. In those days it was necessary in most Law firms for anyone wanting to qualify, first to pay a substantial premium to the firm and then to be prepared to work for many years as an Articled Clerk without receiving any salary. This effectively restricted entry to the profession to boys whose parents were wealthy enough to pay such a premium and to provide their son with his living expenses for about 5 years.

We should at this point take a look at the world as Uncle Henry saw it. Following the death in 1906 of his father, Henry as the eldest surviving son had inherited the Shropshire Estate and, had he wished to do so, he could have retired from teaching and gone to live there. This was not his character. He was a man who needed to feel at the hub of things and he enjoyed the esteem in which he was held, both for building up the academic reputation of his school and for the way in which he had made a success of its financial development, so that in the pre-war days he had been able to embark on a substantial building programme.

But the war had taken a heavy toll. In 1915 he had lost his older son at Gallipoli. In 1916 he had lost his youngest brother William at Jutland and later that year his mother had died broken-hearted (it was said). If she had a favourite son it would have been William, her youngest. He was unmarried and spent his shore-leaves with her in the family home and so she had seen more of him than her other adult sons.

Early in 1917 had come the news of the death of Henry's only surviving brother James (my grandfather) and later that year he had lost his younger son.

In addition he had suffered the loss of hundreds of the boys he had educated, whom he used to describe as his 'other family'. As a Headmaster it had been his practice (a practice followed in many schools during both wars) to announce the deaths of old boys at the start of morning service in the school chapel and for the school to stand in silence for a minute before the first hymn. On many days he would have to read out a long list of names. Whenever I think of this period it calls to mind Wilfred Owen's Anthem for Doomed Youth -

> *What passing bells for these who die as cattle?*
> *Only the monstrous anger of the guns.*
> *Only the stuttering rifles' rapid rattle*
> *Can patter out their hasty orisons.*
> *No mockeries for them from prayers or bells,*
> *Nor any voice of mourning save the choirs -*
> *The shrill, demented choirs of wailing shells;*
> *And bugles calling for them from sad shires.*

Many of them were, in Uncle Henry's view, the boys he had expected to become the leading statesmen, thinkers and writers of the next generation.

Henry was also proud of his own family name and traditions. He was very conscious of the fact that Dad was the sole surviving male heir. He was determined that Dad should not volunteer for military service before he had to. He believed that the responsibility for the mass slaughter inflicted on our country was that of the ignorant politicians who had bungled their way into a war we couldn't win and which could bring no economic or military gain to the British Empire and that the responsibility for the series of military disasters was that of the same incompetent bunch of thick-heads that had prevented someone like his brother James from getting promotion to a top military job. "All these thick-heads can do" he used to say, "was to send men in their millions to be mown down by German machine guns in the hope that the Germans would eventually run out of bullets."

Henry knew that he would be expected to retire as Headmaster when he was 60 (i.e. in 1920) but he feared that if he were left to lead the life of a country gentleman in Shropshire, a life of contemplation would be unbearable, haunted as he would be by the memories of his lost family and friends who had died in what had been the holocaust for the British people.

In the Winter of 1917-18, the Deanery of Tawchester became vacant as a result of the early death of the previous incumbent. The Bishop who had been appointed only 18 months earlier, had been Chairman of the Governors of the school where Henry was Headmaster. The two had developed a successful working partnership and were close friends. The Bishop wanted as Dean someone who combined Henry's personal presence with his proven administrative ability. To achieve his ambitious scheme he would need to increase the revenues from the church properties which were under his overall jurisdiction. They were fortunate in owning some areas of land that had been developed for industrial use and where leases were due for re-negotiation.

There was also an educational dimension. The Dean and Chapter of Tawchester were responsible for two schools that had a long and respectable history, although they were not at that time academically in the big league. There was a boys' college which had started as a Grammar School and was also responsible for providing choristers. In the 19th Century it had as Tawchester College developed into a successful boys' boarding school, although it continued to take day boys. The Girls' High School had been founded in the 18th Century. It had been helped on its way by a number of enterprising members of the local clergy and college teachers and in particular by the wife (an enthusiastic education reformer) of the Dean who had held office between 1876 and 1896. It never developed into a boarding school although there were unofficial boarding arrangements where local families offered board and lodging to girls who lived too far away to travel. In due course I was to owe a great deal to the Tawchester Girls' High School, and its junior school, where I received all my education before I started university. I also received part of my education in the classrooms of Tawchester College because, as I shall explain, both schools coped with World War II shortages of specialist teaching staff by combining some of the College and High School classes.

Uncle Henry and Aunt Mavis visited Tawchester and liked what they saw. It was agreed that he would retire from his existing post as Headmaster at the end of the Summer Term in 1918 when he was 58 and take up his appointment as Dean of Tawchester.

As Dean he was provided with a spacious and pleasant house which meant that he would not be retiring to the Fortingall Estate which, on his death, would pass to Dad as the sole surviving male heir. He suggested, and Dad agreed, that the most intelligent arrangement would be to let the Estate on a long lease, if he could find the right tenant, and the income should be used for Dad's education and advancement and to provide some income for the four girls (Henry's two daughters and Dad's two sisters). Although Henry was entitled to all the income in his own lifetime he wanted to help Dad and he hoped, at the same time, to help his own two daughters whose income would otherwise cease on his death. The idea was that Dad, as a quid pro quo, would agree to continue paying what he could manage to pay out of the estate to his two cousins. Henry, however, was now treating Dad and his two sisters as part of his own family and so this was much more a gentleman's agreement than a legal contract.

Henry's view (and this later became Dad's) was that that 'nasty Welsh bounder' Lloyd George had it in for the traditional English landed families, clobbering them with high taxes and death duties whilst he (Lloyd George) lined his pockets selling knighthoods, baronies and earldoms to those with the cash to pay.

Henry, in fact, secured a very good deal with an American family (he had taught both father and son) who were nostalgic about returning to their ancestral English roots.

Henry not only exacted a substantial lease premium but secured the further advantage of an annual rental based on the 1918 value of the pound, which meant that in real terms the Fortingall family were getting far more in the mid 1920s when deflation pushed the pound back nearer to its 1914 value. Inflation in World War I had resulted in the 1918 £ being worth about half what it was in 1914.

While Henry had been negotiating this key career move and long-term financial planning exercise, he had nevertheless found time to make one or two visits to Pembroke College, Cambridge (his old College) where he now enjoyed considerable prestige (he was in due course to become an honourary Fellow). Arrangements were put in place for Dad to come into residence in October 1918. Henry's reckoning was that Dad would be able to complete his first academic year before being called up (if the war wasn't over by the Summer of 1919). Once the war was over Henry expected that there would be a rush of returning ex-Servicemen which would make university places much more difficult to obtain. The war wasn't over until November 1918 and so the big surge in returning ex-Servicemen didn't take place until October 1919. Conscription didn't continue after the end of World War I (as it did after World War II) so that Dad was able to complete the 3 year degree course without any interruption for military service.

Dad succeeded in obtaining an Exhibition which was a prestigious award even if it didn't have a very high annual value.

If Dad and Mum passed each other in the street during their first academic year they didn't notice. Like many undergraduates in their first year (just as I was in 1945) Dad and Mum probably spent most of their mental energies adapting to a totally new life, getting to grips with their work schedules, making new friends and finding their way around.

They met midway through their second year in February 1920 when they were sitting in adjacent seats at a concert conducted by Sir Henry J. Wood (of Proms fame - at that time Mr. Henry Wood). Mum told me that it was love at first sight and I believe her.

It is my belief that Dad and Mum's marriage, like both of mine, was made in heaven. By that I don't mean that I subscribe to a belief in predestination. I don't. I think we are guided by our guardian angels but it is up to us whether we follow that guidance or not. I believe the ancients understood this before the Christian era. Homer's description of the way Odysseus was guided by the goddess Athene in the final stages of his journey home and the recapture of his kingdom shows that Homer had an understanding of the process.

In later years Aunt Bea told me that Dad in fact had been trying for week and months to engineer a meeting with Mum. He had seen this unbelievably beautiful woman a number of times and didn't at first think she could possibly be an undergraduate. She had poise and was elegantly dressed. He must have been something of a 'stalker' but not in the unpleasant sense in which the word is now used. According to Aunt Bea, Dad as a boy had never shown any strong interest in music but of course he had not had the same opportunities to attend concerts as Mum. We didn't in those days have other ways of listening to music. According to Aunt Bea, Dad saw Mum and one of her friends going in to buy a ticket for a group of seats that were unreserved and followed her to the box office and then followed her until she found a seat in the stalls where he took the next seat.

Women students at Cambridge in 1920 were more restricted than in 1945 when I started at Oxford and certainly there is little comparison with student life today. Girls in the 1920s no doubt felt liberated as compared with pre-1914 days. Whatever the constraints, Dad and Mum were able to find opportunities to be together and they didn't waste time.

Families can help or hinder in such matters but Dad and Mum were fortunate in that both their families helped. Henry and Mavis made frequent visits to Cambridge during Dad's time there. Henry had a fond affection for his old College. He also liked finding out from Dad's tutor how Dad was getting on and it was an opportunity to meet some of the returning ex-Servicemen who had been his pupils.

In March 1920, when the daffodils on the backs were at their best, and Henry and Mavis invited Dad to join them for Saturday lunch, he asked whether he could introduce a young lady who was of course invited to make up the party and given the place of honour on Henry's right.

Henry, who was certainly no slouch in his appreciation of feminine talent, was immediately carried away. When he was told that Mum was a Mathematician he couldn't believe it and then when he learnt that she was the granddaughter of the famous Catherine Johnston who was due to receive her honourary degree the next term, he wondered what hidden talents his nephew must have to win his way into the affections of such a girl. No doubt if he had had his way he would have wanted Dad and Mum to get married immediately and start breeding young Fortingalls, but he was more circumspect. I think his main concern was that Mum might change her mind, but fortunately she didn't.

Before Mum left Henry had asked her whether she would like the opportunity to come and stay at the Deanery in Tawchester and whether she thought her parents might be persuaded to spend a long weekend. Henry was already in his mind planning how he would lay out the red carpet, something he loved doing for any of his visitors.

After they had said goodbye to Mum he accompanied Dad back to his rooms in Pembroke for a discussion, first with Dad's tutor and then with Dad on his own career path. The upshot was that Dad made up his mind to train as a solicitor rather than reading for the Bar. This may have been Henry's idea all along but his knowledge of young men had taught him that they have to be left to come to their own conclusions rather than be pushed.

Dad's tutor probably did most of the work, explaining that to succeed as a barrister one really needed a family law firm that would feed him cases, and Dad didn't have such a family law firm.

Dad was more motivated than he had ever been in his life. Marrying Mum was a far more important objective than succeeding at the Bar and by the time he returned to

Tawchester for the Easter vacation his first serious discussion with Henry was what firm of solicitors should he approach for his Articles, what would it cost and when would he qualify.

Henry had his eye on one particular firm where he knew and liked the senior partner who had acted professionally for him on a number of lease re-negotiations and land sales. Dad was introduced, terms were agreed and Dad was to start his Articles in the Summer vacation of 1920 and be given leave of absence during the three remaining terms until he took his degree in June 1921. Although this practice became standard in later years enabling graduate entrants to the profession to cut down the time between being articled and the date they were permitted to sit the Law Society exams, such arrangements were one-off at this early period when there were not many graduate entrants.

This didn't solve all the problems because Dad would get virtually no salary from the firm until he qualified and although he had a share of the rental income from the Estate sufficient to live on as an undergraduate, it wasn't likely to run to the cost of maintaining a wife and possibly bringing up children. Henry might have helped out of his own pocket, but the answer came from Mum's family.

Her parents were delighted to receive a formal invitation from the Dean of Tawchester. I would hope that they were both intelligent enough to understand the look in their daughter's eye, just as Mum in later years understood my feelings when I first came home with David. Unfortunately Catherine was in demand to speak at an Easter holiday education conference and hence unable to accept Henry's invitation. Mum then asked Dad whether she could bring her other grandmother, Madame la Baronne (also a widow). The idea was accepted with enthusiasm and Henry sent his own handwritten invitation to her. Dad knew already that Madame la Baronne was the wealthy fairy-godmother in the family and a lot more besides.

Arrière (as I later called Madame la Baronne) took Tawchester by storm. She loved red carpet treatment, particularly in an old English context. But much more important than this she took an instant liking to Dad. He was in her view 'serious' by which the French mean (in this context) a solid reliable person, unlike many typical young Frenchmen of that period who were good at playing court to ladies but not much else. Dad was much more cut in the mould of her 'companion' from Barings. She also liked Henry, whom she saw as a practical man of the world who had got where he had by his own efforts and who, at the same time, had great urbanity and charm.

Arrière didn't waste time or mince words. If these young people were to make a proper start in life they needed help and she would make her granddaughter an allowance which she thought a far more sensible way of doing things than the old-fashioned idea of providing a capital sum as a dowry. "What was it going to cost to live in Tawchester? What was Dad's allowance?..." All the questions followed in quick succession and Henry liked her way of doing things, even though her English was not conventional English. Her manner of speaking probably added considerably to her charm. I was often reminded of the way she spoke English when I listened to Françoise Rosay on the radio during and after the war. She had escaped from the

German occupation and participated in a lot of live radio discussions on such programmes as The Brains Trust.

Arrière and Henry shared many feelings about the world and the people they had seen swept away with the war. They also shared a deeply felt need, a sense of duty, to play their part in rebuilding. Just as Henry saw Dad as the symbol of the future for the Fortingall family, so Arrière saw her attractive and intelligent English granddaughter as a ray of hope for the next generation in her own family and as one of the key custodians of the 'patrimony' (a lovely French term for that part of a family's stock of worldly goods and money intended to be passed down from generation to generation and not squandered) that she, Arrière, had amassed painstakingly during her lifetime. In fact, as I shall show at the end of this book, Mum proved to be the only surviving custodian after World War II, of those financial assets that Arrière had prudently invested in Trust Funds in the U.S.A.

The upshot of this meeting of minds between Henry and Arrière was that Arrière was to pay Mum an allowance during her lifetime, reviewable at 5 yearly intervals, and the total paid in her lifetime would be deducted from Mum's share (expected to be 25%) of Arrière's capital as bequeathed in her will. Likewise, Dad would receive an allowance from the Fortingall Estate income during the life of Henry, and this likewise would be a loan made by Uncle Henry on the security of the capital (which Dad was due to inherit) so that on Henry's death his two daughters would be no worse off as a result of the arrangement.

Henry also undertook to use his influence to find a tenancy for Dad and Mum in one of the properties over which Henry, as Dean, had some influence as regards allocation. At that period very few people owned their own houses and the ecclesiastical establishment in Tawchester had within its gift a substantial number of good quality houses which were normally allocated to senior Church figures and administrators.

It was also agreed that Dad and Henry would put considerable pressure on the law firm to which Dad was articled to start paying a proper salary as soon as Dad could show that he was making a contribution to the business. Henry could put a substantial amount of commercial contracts to whichever law firm he thought best capable of handling them. Much of the work involved could be done by someone in the firm who was not qualified, but was clued up. Henry reckoned that Dad could do a large part of this as Dad was far abler than most of the partners in most of the law firms with which he had to deal and therefore could generate a lot of revenue for his employer who, as a quid pro quo, should be prepared to pay Dad a rate for the job and not the pittance (which might in some firms be nothing at all) that was traditionally paid to articled clerks.

Whilst both of them wanted to help the young couple, they happened to share the view that expensive and opulent wedding festivities were an indulgence designed to boost the social status of the parents and grandparents and totally unnecessary for the happiness of the bridal pair. This is also my view on which I shall comment further when I come to describe my marriage to John in 1948.

In France the custom is that the bride and groom's families plan the marriage as a combined operation and share the costs 50/50, in my view a more equitable arrangement than the English custom of leaving it all to the bride's family to foot the bill for the lot, which falls heavily on families with more daughters than sons. Arrière had married one of her daughters to a Frenchman and the other to a Scotsman. Of her two English granddaughters, Mum's elder sister, Aunt Simone, had had a 'shotgun' khaki wedding with Uncle Fred in 1915 when she was five months pregnant.

Uncle Fred was an officer in the Australian army medical corps whose father had been a visiting Research Fellow, or similar, in the hospital where Sandy (Mum's father) was doing his clinical and hence the red carpet had been rolled out to welcome young Fred into the Johnston household whenever he had any leave periods to spend in England, and what could be more natural than making love to his hosts' 18 year old daughter who Mum, in later life, described as a 'stunner'. In spite of his medical training Fred must on one occasion have failed to take the necessary precautions, but he may have been using a defective condom. In any case he did the honourable thing and married Aunt Simone and, from all accounts, they had a very happy life together. He survived the war and Simone returned with him to Melbourne in 1919 and their descendants still exchange Christmas cards with my children. In fact we have had a number of Simone's grandchildren and great-grandchildren to stay when they have been on education courses or getting work experience in England.

I am sure that Aunt Simone's courting experience was typical of many both in World War I as well as before and after. I have broken the thread of narrative to mention it because from the time that Mum first told me, I have always identified with Aunt Simone. Her lot could have been mine. I am afraid it has alienated me from the memory of my maternal grandfather Sandy (who died before I was born) because Mum described him as insufferable at that time. He got on his high puritanical, holier than thou, horse and apparently gave Simone a rough time, wrote unpleasant letters to Fred's father at the way young Fred had abused Sandy's hospitality. Fortunately Simone got warmth, comfort and understanding from her mother and from Arrière, which she needed because she continued to live in her parents' house until she left for Australia.

I have mentioned Sandy's 'puritanism'. This brings me to the religious question. Sandy's parents were Scottish Presbyterians. In fact Sandy's grandfather had been a member of the 'Free' church which was a break-away sect from the Church of Scotland. Scots in the Kensington area could worship at St. Colomba's (Church of Scotland) not far from Harrods, but Sandy had no ties to the Church of Scotland. His wife Suzanne was from a Catholic family, except for the fact that her mother Arrière had, soon after settling in England, decided that when in England one becomes a member of the Church of England. Given her lifelong liaison with an Englishman who was a communicating member of the Church of England, this was natural. She used to say that French children were incorrectly taught that England was a Protestant country, which was untrue, because when she came to live here she found a much greater similarity between Anglican Church services and those in the Catholic Church she had known as a girl than between services in the Church of England and

Protestant services in France, which she tended to typecast as 'Presbyterian'. In my view she was right, but she was probably a hundred years ahead of her time in terms of the ecumenical attempt to bring the Christian churches together.

The net result of Arrière's approach was that Sandy and Suzanne had been married in the Anglican church of St. Mary Abbots in Kensington, which was the Parish Church that Mum and her sister (who lived in Hornton Street) attended as girls. For some reason Mum didn't like St. Mary Abbots. Possibly she had taken a dislike to the vicar or rector who had been the incumbent of this church when she was a teenager or student. She once, later in life, described it as a 'rather formal specimen of decorated work which conveys no hint of inspiration'.

On her first visit to Tawchester she accompanied Dad and Uncle Henry on a visit to a little Saxon church in the village of Bishop Wantock where Henry had just succeeded in installing one of his former pupils, Gerald Wakehurst, as 'perpetual curate'. The Rev. Gerald Wakehurst (in later years we all called him Father Wakehurst) had been a padre in World War I who had gone too near the front line and had lost his left arm when a shell had exploded in a trench where he was ministering to his flock. His future had been uncertain, but Henry's successful effort to find him a congenial job had made him a lifelong friend of our family and he played a critical role in my own life, which I will describe when we get there.

The moment Mum took the step down into Bishop Wantock Church she felt God's presence and decided that this was where she wanted to be married and that was where she and Dad were married. This was the church where I married David and then John. It is the church where I too felt God's presence first as a child, in my two marriage ceremonies, and in the saddest moment of my life - after I had learnt of David's death.

As a result of Mum's decision, Dad and Mum were married at the end of June 1921 in Tawchester and not in London. The reception was held at the Deanery, which I am sure Arrière felt was far more prestigious than any London hotel. I am sure she was generous when she took out her chequebook. She also provided Dad and Mum with their honeymoon travel costs and let them have exclusive use of her villa at St. Jean-cap-Ferrat to which Dad and Mum returned every year until 1939 and I am sure each visit rekindled the memories of the wonderful three weeks they had enjoyed in July 1921.

In fact in 1920, a year before their honeymoon, Arrière had invited Dad to join Mum and other members of the family in Paris. It was his first trip abroad and (according to Mum) he enjoyed himself immensely. According to Mum he had not only done the usual sightseeing, but had been taken by some male relatives to such places as the Folies Bergères which I am sure suited Dad's tastes. As the provincial country boy he had very quickly adapted to life in both London (where he had also spent holiday periods with Mum's family) as well as Paris. Whether he made love to Mum before they married I know not. I suspect not. Mum must have had the fear of God put into her by the stink her father had kicked up when her older sister had confessed to being pregnant, but even if they had made love Mum is the sort of person that would have kept that secret with her to the grave. Her relationship with Dad was sacrosanct and I believe, as I have already said, that Dad and Mum's marriage was made in heaven.

The rest of their story will unfold in later chapters. Henry found them a wonderful house which was vacated when a Canon retired and went to live with his family in New Zealand. It was the home where Jean and I grew up. Dad did an even better job than Uncle Henry had expected. The law firm to which he had been articled prospered. Soon after he qualified Dad was made a partner and when the senior partner (who had built the firm) died in 1933 Dad became the senior partner.

Mum didn't work when we were young, but as the firm grew in the late 1930s Dad decided that they needed an administration manager to control the billing, chase up the outstanding accounts, etc. By then Dad had learnt that most of his partners were not really clued up as far as money was concerned. He was also looking ahead. I believe that from 1934 onwards he had a shrewd idea that we would be involved in another war (as a result of the incompetence of Stanley Baldwin and his colleagues) and he trusted Mum more than anyone else to keep a grip on the firm's finances and administration. He couldn't have been more right.

As I shall explain in a later chapter, the partnership and Dad's share in it would have been worthless had it not been for Mum's far-seeing perspicacity combined with her determination and diplomatic skill in finding the right people and persuading them that the firm was worth something and that with her continuing involvement it could be worth a lot more.

CHAPTER 4

MY EARLY CHILDHOOD

For many years I looked back on the pre-war days of my childhood as analogous to a Garden of Eden in my own life. I was the baby of the family (my sister Jean was three years older) and no doubt indulged and perhaps spoilt. I had a happy home. We lived in a grey stone house set back from the road with a pleasant garden, at the bottom of which was an old coach-house, part of which had been converted into a garage, attached to which there was a stable which was used to keep things like lawn mowers, a wheelbarrow and the garden shelter and deckchairs. We didn't have a horse. I can remember Mum and friends having afternoon tea in the shelter (no doubt designed to act as a windbreak as well as keep out too much sun) and I rode around on a toddler's version of a tricycle known then as a fairy car and it always seemed to be Summer.

I can remember walking proudly to school on my first day with Jean on one side holding my hand and Mum on the other. I can also remember those painful moments when I was 4 or 5 and I was squirming around over Dad's knee while he gripped both hands against my back and stopped me kicking by holding my legs between his while he smacked my bare behind with his large hands and I kept shouting "Don't do that, Daddy" but he didn't stop. It couldn't have been the first time because I clearly knew what to expect. When he eventually let me go I would sob plaintively "Why did you do that, Daddy?" and he would tell me that it was because I had been naughty.

I was a plump little girl and no doubt mischievous. I had no idea that what I was doing was naughty, but then children quickly forget.

Every child of my age probably had similar memories and so would children of every generation up to the present, when parents for some peculiar reason find themselves arrested and taken to Court for trying to teach their children to obey. In later life I often heard about parents who used to thrash their children in fits of anger or according to the mood they were in. This wasn't what happened with us. Dad would leave me to cry for a time and then both Dad and Mum would come in and Mum would say "Do you promise to be a good girl?" and I would say "Yes" and they would both kiss me goodnight.

When I was older, perhaps 7 or 8 and had been "broken in" like a young horse (I can't remember seeing either Dad or Mum riding a horse, but my parent's generation had inherited the riding metaphors that were current before most people had bicycles or cars) and had learned that struggling would do me no good, I used to go down to

Dad's study when I was in my pyjamas and ready for bed and obediently bend over a chair while he punished me with one of his slippers and, as I grew older, with the little swagger cane that he had as an officer in the Territorials. By then I had learnt that it would be far worse if I struggled or didn't do as I was told. He had large feet and his slippers had leather soles, not like the moccasin slippers that John wears. Whatever he used, each occasion was always worse than I expected and I used to yell and shout, but I knew better than to get up before he told me I could. When Mum came to kiss me goodnight she used to look at me reproachfully and say "You're a big girl now. Big girls don't cry."

Dad's principle was that an older child should not be demeaned in front of a younger sister. Jean was probably more obedient than I was and I discovered later that if she had to be severely punished he would do it on a Saturday morning when I was at Brownies, so that I wouldn't hear her if she yelled. I was expected to look up to my elder sister as a model of good behaviour. There were exceptions. Once when Dad and Mum were giving a dinner party and there was a lot of excitement in the house, which Jean and I probably sensed, we ran excitedly along the landing, fooling about while guests were arriving. We had been told to shut up and get back to bed or there would be trouble. Then came the stern warning from Dad "You have been warned to get back to bed. I'll deal with you both tomorrow" and Jean and I each slunk back to our rooms with heavy hearts. Neither Dad nor Mum said anything at breakfast or at teatime the next day and it was only after I had got down from Dad's knee when he had been telling me a bedtime story that he told me to be in his study in five minutes time when I was ready for bed. By God it did hurt and I did yell. "The next time" he said "I'll use a real cane". After that I heard Jean sobbing as she came upstairs and went into her room which was next to mine.

He never in fact used a "real cane" on me because by the time I was 13 he was away on active service. When he came home on leave in the first year of the war he was never home long enough to catch us doing anything bad enough to be punished and so I got off scot-free for the rest of my school years, apart from the little episode which I will recount in due course. If this sounds bad, I ought to say that I would far rather have had Dad at home and still have him, however much he might have punished me in my later school days, but that's history.

I did know what a real cane was because Louise, who was my closest friend, showed me.

I should say that Louise was the youngest of four children in a family that we saw a lot of. Louise and I were not only at school together from kindergarten through to High School, but her parents and mine were close friends. Her father was first a House Master at the College and then promoted to Second Master in 1938. Dad, at one stage, had hoped that he would be Headmaster, but the Dean, as Chairman of the Governors, had preferred a candidate with a strong academic record who could build the College's reputation for gaining Oxford and Cambridge scholarships.

Louise's father knew how to handle boys. He had a nose for sniffing out what they might be up to, maintaining good discipline and stamping on typical Public School bullying that was likely to blight the academic careers of potential scholarship winners. Walford Squires (Louise's father) was not in Dad's league or a person of much intellectual grip as to what was going on in the outside world, but Dad respected Walford because he did a good job and Walford respected Dad as his de facto boss (the Deputy Chairman of the Governors who chaired nearly all the Governors' meetings). Both men had married academically gifted wives who were Cambridge graduates. Millicent Squires (Milly) had played a large part in getting Walford his job as Deputy Head and (before that) turning him into a successful Housemaster.

In those days at the College, the role of being Housemaster was that of running a business. The House received the fees and passed on a tuition fee component to the school. The Housemaster's wife had to do the hard work of recruiting and managing the catering and domestic staff, buying the food and feeding nearly 100 boys during the term out of the fees the House was permitted to retain. She had to be available to speak to parents on the telephone when they were anxious and to do a good public relations exercise whenever parents came to visit and when they were invited to formal teas in the Houses at certain school sporting events. A Housemaster's wife was not officially recognised as an employed person in the school hierarchy and not paid a salary. Masters were promoted to the position of Housemaster on the basis of an informal assessment of a wife's potential by the Headmaster or by a perspicacious member of the Governing Body, such as Dad. A successful Housemaster's wife therefore had to be a good business manager, and from all accounts Milly was just this.

On the plus side a Housemaster's family enjoyed free accommodation in a spacious house - they lived at the front and the boys at the back. They had their meals prepared by the House domestic staff and if the Housemaster's wife could manage the money without too many complaints from the parents about the quality of the food, etc., her efforts could make a reasonable contribution to the family standard of living.

During her time as a Housemaster's wife Milly had borne four children - Richard (Dick) 9 years older than Louise, Helen 6 years older, Michael (Mike) 2 years older and Louise.

Walford and Dad were, in many respects, ahead of their time not only in having a high respect for their wives' abilities, but also in their firm belief that girls' education was as important as boys'. It is important to understand this in context. Even after the war when I was an Oxford undergraduate the number of girls in the university was only about a fifth of the number of boys. Even in later years when I was taking my turn as Chairman of the Parent's Association in a school that one of my daughters attended, I found myself dealing with one or two fathers who appeared to think that all a girl needed from school, apart from learning how to read and write, was the ability to sew and to knit and to look pretty enough to find a husband. I didn't believe that such people still existed in the 1960s, but they did.

So in the 1920s and 1930s some credit has to be given to people like Dad and Walford Squires who wanted their daughters to achieve the academic distinction that had been achieved by their respective wives.

Both Dad and Walford were also rigorously fair-minded. They understood the way children perceived things and how they might interpret relatively trivial matters as unfairness. Thus when Walford (who always had a suspicious nose for what boys or children might be up to) walked down his garden one Saturday afternoon in November 1938 and found his 14 year old son Michael and 12 year old daughter Louise puffing at a 5d packet of Red Label Woodbine cigarettes, he told them both to report to his study in 5 minutes time and told Louise to put on trousers. It would have gone against his spirit of fairness to cane Michael with the protection of trousers and underpants if Louise were not be caned in like manner. It would have gone against his principle of fairness to cane Michael and not Louise.

I remember the occasion because I had cycled over to the Squires to spend the afternoon with Louise on the Sunday afternoon when she was still feeling sore. We were in any case accustomed to commiserate with each other on mishaps and so I heard all about it. Her parents were out. There was only the maid and Michael in the house and so she took me furtively into her Dad's study and showed me the frightening array of canes that he had in a rack to the right of his desk. I think I was so scared about what might happen to me if Dad had decided that now I was 12 he would punish me with a real cane that I must have minded my Ps and Qs and been exceptionally well behaved for the year 1938-39. But it was a year that Dad was also preoccupied with world events and of course the consequences for his family, his firm and himself if war materialised.

But our home education didn't simply consist in being punished. My sister Jean and I learned a tremendous amount at home in addition to what we learned at school. Mum taught us French at a very early age. She had been brought up to be bilingual herself and wanted us to be. Apart from getting us to do exercises and read in French, she always insisted on speaking French to us on days when the three of us were together for afternoon tea and also during the school holidays. I knew all my tables before I went to school and I was usually top of the Maths class just as Jean had been in hers before me.

Dad taught us a tremendous amount of history in the form of bedtime stories. I knew all about Columbus, Nelson, Wellington, Clive of India and General Wolfe's capture of Quebec at a very early age. Dad used to speak about these people as if they were friends of his youth.

I remember being taken to see Hadrian's Wall and Fountains Abbey, walking round the walls of York and many other places. He used to explain the different types of architecture in the churches and cathedrals. He had an old Austin 16 which was a sit-up-and-beg type car that people don't seem to collect nowadays as vintage cars, but which got us around comfortably in the days when there were not many other cars on the road. We acquired all this information effortlessly and a lot of it influenced our thinking in our later lives. Jean, for example, was so inspired by her memory of the way Dad described Nelson's victory at Trafalgar and the way he described the Battle of Jutland where great-uncle William's ship went down, that she joined the Wrens when she was 17 because she wanted to be part of the British Navy.

An important part of our education was provided by the many interesting people who used to come to stay with us. In the 1930s when we still had an important world-wide Empire, a substantial part of the educated population of the UK was employed abroad either in Colonial administration or building bridges, railways and harbour installations in remote corners of the world. Dad had distant cousins, family friends, school friends and Cambridge friends who worked abroad. Before the days of air travel they used to be sent on three-year assignments and then come home for three months leave in the UK. A substantial number had Scots parentage (possibly distant) and many used to take up Dad's invitations to stay with us when they were on home leave. They might come by train or more often they would drive around, calling on many friends, and we were a convenient staging post on the route to Scotland.

Dad was not only interested in meeting these people as friends, but he wanted to know what was going on. He had an encyclopaedic knowledge of the economic conditions and political developments in many countries and he always felt that by talking to people whom he knew and liked, and whose judgment he respected, that he would get far more valuable first-hand information than by reading newspapers, although he also read such papers as the Times and The Economist as well as a lot of specialist magazines. The Times, in those days, used to contain far more precise information on political events than it does now when many of its pages are filled up with the type of lawcourt gossip that we used to associate with the News of the World.

Typically, Dad would announce that the Browns, or the Greens, or the Blacks or whoever, were on leave from Tanganyika or wherever, and would be coming, and we were immediately instructed to find in our atlases the country and the place where they lived, and read something about the country in the encyclopaedia, so that we could ask intelligent questions. Dad would, of course, tell us a lot more before they arrived.

What Jean and I always loved (apart from getting the usual presents that were given to the hosts' children) was the way our normal life was transformed. Mum used to recruit an assistant for our maid. The silver was all polished. We used to have wonderful social English breakfasts with the usual choice of porridge or cereals followed by a mixed breakfast grill of egg, bacon, sausage, tomato and mushrooms followed by toast and marmalade. Nobody seemed to slim in those days. Jean and I had to get on our bicycles and rush off to school at quarter to nine, leaving the grown-ups talking about the future of the world. Dad would go into his office late and come home early. Jean and I would usually have afternoon tea with Mum and our guests before Dad arrived home and we would have much more time to talk. We learned all about the problems of building railways in Patagonia. The Argentine was not a British colony, but before the war the English (including the Scots) dominated the country. We had invested so much money there that English firms got most of the contracts and English consulting engineers and contractors in the Argentine and other South American countries were major contributors to our invisible exports.

Another of Dad's friend was working on the construction of the naval base at Singapore, which was lost so disastrously to the Japanese in 1942 because our military strategy was geared to defence against an attack from sea and no-one had thought about Japanese hordes swarming down the Malay Peninsula and attacking Singapore from the rear, which is what happened. Another friend had been to Russia, working on a Hydro-electric plant. There were friends from New Zealand, India and Hong Kong.

Not only did they tell us about the countries where they were working, but many had been in other overseas postings before their present jobs and quite a number had used their home leave periods to travel in Europe. These were not people who went to lie on Mediterranean beaches. They went to places like Berlin, Vienna, Budapest, Warsaw. They explained how poverty in many of these countries was worse than in England and how this made it easier for Communist parties and the Nazi party in Germany to recruit members to their private armies. This was long before the popular press became interested.

I shall talk about Dad's strongly held views of the German threat and its linkage to Britain's return to the gold standard in 1925 in a later chapter. My point here is that whilst we didn't have television news every night of the week, as children in a modern household, we acquired a considerable knowledge of world events at an early age in an effortless way from all these family friends. Jean and I were expected to be on our best behaviour (and woe betide us if we were not) but we were highly motivated because all these interesting people talked to us as if we were adults and I think we responded by trying to behave as adults.

In later life John and I never seemed to have the opportunity to entertain on this scale. We didn't of course have a live-in maid and the ability to recruit a reliable short-term daily in the way my parents did. We lived in a modern house, whereas my parents lived in a large old house with a splendid guest-room, a large dining room with a big table as well as a drawing room and a study.

An important part of these 'Garden of Eden' years before the war was the time we spent each Summer in France. I can remember, even as a four year old, playing with our French cousins and second cousins in the rambling old house and nearby farm of our great-grandmother's country home near La Tour du Pin, which is about 35 miles east of Lyon and 30 miles west of Chambery and Lac du Bourget.

We didn't have air travel. There was great excitement as we boarded the train to London, where we stayed with Aunt Beatrice (Dad's sister) and her family in Putney. We would then get a taxi to Victoria and take the train, the boat and the train to Paris, where we would stay with one of Mum's cousins whom we called Tante Nicole, who lived near the Bois du Boulogne. We would then get a train down to Lyon, which probably took four or five hours in those days before the TGV. We would be met by my great-grandmother's chauffeur, Georges, who used to drive the type of big Citroen car that you saw in the Maigret films. Over the years they probably had a number of cars, but this was the one I remember.

It was a lovely part of the country. It was an old house which was called the Chateau. I always called my great-grandmother Arrière and so did Mum and Dad. In French arrière-grand-maman means great-grandmother. I had learned the word arrière at an early age, and simply called her Arrière because I couldn't remember the rest of her name and she liked it. There were hosts of cousins and different children of about our age with whom we used to play and we quickly adapted to speaking French all the time.

Mum and Dad used to leave us. Georges would take them back to Lyon where they would catch a train to Nice and then be driven to a lovely house with a garden going down to the sea on St. Jean-cap-Ferrat. This was where Arrière, Grand-maman and their companions spent the Winter. In Summer it was not the fashionable place it now is, but Mum and Dad wanted warm sun and sea to bathe in, saying that they needed it because they lived in a cold climate. This gave them a chance to be together and go out in the evenings without having to worry about us children, knowing that we were in good hands, which we were.

Rural France in the 1930s was a totally different country from what we know today. In many ways it was more primitive than England at the time. Very few people had telephones in their houses. Even in the towns there were no flushing loos and even where there was running water there were no proper drains. When you took out the plug to let the dirty washing-up water run away, the pipe merely carried it to the gutter in the street outside. The roads and streets were highly cambered, so the gutters could be quite deep. In the country people had to rely on oil lamps and candles because there was no electricity. You hardly ever saw a tractor on the farms and milking was done by hand. Few middle class people wanted to live in the country, and even round the towns there was relatively little of the suburban growth of houses and gardens such as we knew in England.

About 40% of the population still lived "on the land". Farming was often inefficient because farms were too small. Since Napoleon (perhaps longer) French law has prevented parents from willing their property on death as they may choose, so that instead of being able to leave the farm to their eldest son, they have been compelled to divide their property equally between their children, and so their farms got smaller with every generation. There was little incentive to introduce labour-saving devices when many farms were teeming with people who had to be fed, who were presumably under-employed in real terms, but no doubt believed that they were working to capacity. There were of course labour shortages following the mass slaughter of World War I, but if French farmers had never been exposed to any alternative modes of farming, there was little chance of their understanding that there might be better ways of doing things. In England a lot of middle class and upper class people had bought farms as a hobby and were putting money into their farms as well as new ideas. These sort of people, if they existed in France, were so few and far between that they made little impact. Even in the 18th Century when English upper class landowners were spending a lot of time and money developing their own estates, the French equivalent had a greater tendency to pocket their agricultural rents for what they were worth and spend their time hobnobbing with the people that they thought of as good and great in Paris or whatever.

Of course I knew nothing of this historical background in my childhood visits to a house in the country in France, but this knowledge helps to explain what I saw and why it was different. My first-hand knowledge was, however, helpful to me in later years when I was studying European History and having to write essays on such subjects as the causes of the French Revolution.

We didn't in fact live in primitive conditions in the country house that was called a Chateau (like most French country houses) but there were reasons for this. Arrière had lived for a large part of her life in London following the death of her first husband during the war and troubles of 1870-71 and her lifelong liaison with a director of Barings. She had also made a number of visits to the United States, on one of which she had been invited to the White House to meet 'Tayodor' (Theodore Roosevelt who was President in the early years of the 20th Century). She not only had access to good investment advice but was a shrewd investor in her own right. She had a better understanding of the political fortunes of countries and the likely effect of investments in those countries than most of the men advising her. Starting with the considerable wealth left to her by the two men in her life, she had built a very considerable family fortune. Most of her investments, however, were held in the US and UK, including some gold bullion held for her by a bank in New York. Her wealth in France consisted mainly in real estate, her house in Paris, her villa in St. Jean-Cap-Ferrat and of course her country house and surrounding farmland near La Tour du Pin.

Like many people of her kind she was averse to wasting money. In 1925 when her son-in-law (Grand-maman's husband) died, Arrière decided that she and her daughter would move back to France. It was the year that Winston Churchill, as Chancellor of the Exchequer, had put Britain back on the gold standard (something for which Dad would never forgive him, but more of this anon) and there is no doubt it gave her a further reason for moving back to the land of her birth. The income which she and her daughter earned from their interest on UK and US Government bonds (like Lady Bracknell, she believed in having her money in 'the funds', although she also had substantial shareholdings) would buy much more in France. Apart from that, London was no longer quite such a wonderful place to be as in the days of 'le bon roi Edouard'. In any case, she was now much older and had a certain nostalgia for the part of France where she was born and had spent her early days.

In 1914 there were 25 French francs to the pound and one French franc was worth the same as one Swiss franc. These old French francs are now centimes. At the time of writing you can get 10 new French francs for the pound, which is the equivalent of 1000 old francs, and only 2½ Swiss francs.

By the early 1930s the exchange rate had already moved to the point where she could buy as much in French francs for the equivalent of £1 as she had been able to buy for £7 in 1914. By the late 1930s the equivalent was £10.

Whether she had inherited this rambling old building and some farmland from her husband, or whether she bought it in the 1920s, I do not know and neither did Mum. After the war when John and I visited La Tour du Pin, Grand-maman was no longer in the land of the living and none of her granddaughters or great-grandchildren knew any more than Mum and I.

What was important was what she achieved. Regardless of what made up her mind to live near the village or farm where she had first seen the light of day, she devoted a tremendous amount of time, energy and money into making her enterprise a success. Even by the time of the first visit I can remember (when I must have been about 4) she had renovated enough of the semi-ruined stately home to provide very comfortable living quarters for herself, her daughter, her business manager and various people in her entourage. There was electricity (they had their own generator), running water (their own supply and water tank) and there were at least three telephones. She was said to have her own short-wave radio transmitter, but this may have been one of the apocryphal stories told about her. What in England we call the 'Home Farm' had been renovated and she had found an American farmer who had married a French wife during his spell in France in 1918 in the US army and wanted a job in France.

She managed to buy a number of neighbouring farms as they came on the market or, more usually, when the owner thought he might be able to do a good deal with Madame la Baronne.

Madame la Baronne had a number of other ambitions apart from rebuilding her chateau and running the neighbouring farm in the way she believed that an English gentleman would look after his landed estates. She wanted to be the personage to whom all the local notables would defer and she set about building this position with all the shrewdness and peasant cunning that she could muster. Whilst on one side she maintained the mystique of being the elegant and autocratic 'grande dame' she was at the same time much more 'modern' than the sort of person the French rural population would expect to find as a Baronne living in a castle. She didn't have a patronising, distant demeanour. She didn't need to play-act. She knew she had the power and money and she could therefore relax, which is what she did. What's more, she was genuinely interested in the day to day concerns of the people with whom she conversed. She quickly understood a problem that might be bugging a particular individual at a particular time and she had the type of mind which she had trained to deal with all problems as problems to be solved.

Her relations with the local Curé were a good example. Although Arrière had no doubt been baptised as a Catholic, she had to all intents and purposes been a Communicant of the Church of England from the time she had established her lifelong liaison with an English banker. Back in rural France, however, she was happy to revert to the religion of her childhood, and presented her card to the Curé and invited him for tea. She discovered that he had been having battles with the priest of a neighbouring parish. Her Curé's Church was in urgent need of repair, the local mayor was a communist and anti-clerical and her Curé got no support from his Bishop.

Arrière didn't believe in throwing money at problems, but rather in drip-feeding in a way that would keep the recipient hopeful. Her big coup with the Curé came when, after she had restored her magnificent dining room and salon, she invited the Bishop and various members of his entourage to lunch (the main meal of the day for most French people at that time). What's more, the Bishop accepted and was charmed to hear her talking about how she had been presented at Court to Queen Victoria and later to the Bon Roi Edouard. She had of course also invited M. le Curé, prefacing her introduction as the champagne was passed round with some such remark as "it would have been lacking in courtesy on my part not to include in our party M. le Curé who represents you so well in our Parish", and so on.

She could likewise handle the left-wing Mayor, the local Deputé (MP), the local schoolmistress, the doctor, the dentist, or whoever. She had them all on side. They respected her as a hard-headed business woman. She got them to accept her as one of them and yet somehow different. She was not involved in politics or intrigue. However friendly she might be, none of them wanted to make an enemy of such a formidable lady as Madame la Baronne. In fact none of them would have wanted to be ill-thought of by a grande dame whose elegance and charm still worked wonders in spite of her age.

This background goes some way to explaining the dynamic of the world in which I lived during these nine Summers from 1930 to 1938. We had only a short holiday in 1939 because Dad was worried that there might be a war and so Jean and I accompanied Dad and Mum on a Wagon Lit Sleeper-Express from Paris to the villa in St. Jean-cap-Ferrat for the warm sea bathing and a different idyllic type of Summer holiday before returning to England after only a 3 week absence.

During our Summers at the chateau we were, as the great-grandchildren of Madame la Baronne, put in the charge of a matronly lady, Marianne. In some years there might be a dozen of us at one time. All the others were French and so Jean and I were fluent in child French. I was at any rate from the age of 4, although I tended to get rusty during the rest of the year. I needed a few days for adaptation when I first arrived each Summer. There was considerable age spread and so we tended to break up into separate groups. I was the youngest and as "La petite Anglaise" I probably got more attention from my great-grandmother. Although she particularly liked Mum, as she liked all her grandchildren, she also had a high regard for Dad as 'un bon travailleur', 'un homme sérieux'. I think the respect was mutual. Apart from her personal liking for Dad, I think her general view of the Englishman was that he took his work more seriously and didn't strut around like a turkey-cock pretending to be God's gift to women (my view of a lot of Frenchmen, a prejudice which I shall explain in a later chapter). In contrast, Arrière was highly critical of the way English mothers brought up their daughters, failing to teach them how to dress properly, and failing to teach them how to be a good 'maitresse de maison'.

She had taken to Dad at their first meeting and was delighted in later years to learn how successful he had been. Although Dad had strong political opinions he was also diplomatic. He would certainly not have argued about Churchill and the Gold Standard if the subject had ever cropped up when he was at La Tour du Pin (and it may not have done) and I am sure he would not have made denigrating remarks in her presence about 'young Stanley' (Stanley Baldwin, English Prime Minister 1924-29 and 1935-37). Mr. Baldwin used to spend his Summers nearby at Aix les Bains. When I was old enough to be interested in politics I used to hear Dad describing him as the worst political disaster Britain had ever had, with the possible exception of Balfour, Lord Aberdeen and Lord North. Baldwin was no good at anything except intrigue and he went around masquerading as a cross between Farmer Giles and John Bull. Dad would have understood perfectly well that Arrière's sole interest in young Stanley was the fact that she was able to say that she had had afternoon tea with him on one of his sojourns to Aix. She didn't need to hire a PR consultant to know that her casual reference to such events along with her invitation to the White House and presentations at Court did wonders for her image.

Whether it was because she had a soft spot for Dad and Mum, whose marriage she had helped to facilitate, or for whatever other reason, I appeared to bask in her favour. Looking back over some 65-70 years I now like to think that there was an intuitive rapport between us as creatures of a common kind. At any rate she is the ancestor that I have always wished to emulate, even if I have been only a poor copy.

I was, even as a child of 4 (so Mum tells me) respectful in Arrière's presence. Dad of course warned us before each holiday that should he hear bad reports of our behaviour, we would be severely punished when we got home, and we knew what that meant. Although I may have got into a number of scrapes on various occasions that would have resulted in painful moments over Dad's knee or over a chair, had he been there, Mum and Dad were always greeted with glowing reports of our model behaviour when they returned to collect us.

Arrière may have liked me for the efforts I made to speak good French, even when I was only 4, and the clear way I answered her questions. I think I was a more coquettish child than Jean. I liked wearing a pretty dress and I showed it in a way which she approved.

The children had a playroom, a reading room and a dining room. I quickly got used to drinking a bowl of very milky coffee or chocolate for breakfast and dunking French bread in it. We drank a little wine topped up with a large amount of water (which had been boiled or sterilised) with lunch and we thought we were very grown-up. If we were good in the afternoon we were given a chocolatine, a piece of French bread with a bit of chocolate in the middle.

After lunch on a warm day Georges would drive Marianne and a number of the smaller children to a little stream nearby which had been dammed up to form a bathing place and which was sandy. He would leave us with Marianne and go back to collect the older children. We were not far from the Valley of the Rhône, which curves south on its route from Geneva to Lyon and then north again not far from La Tour du Pin, but this was only a small tributary and not dangerous. Although Jean and I wore bathing costumes (and in those days they were full bathing costumes and not just trunks) most of the local children who played about in the pool were naked. As I didn't have any brothers this was the first time I had seen little boys naked.

Marianne used to say that if I was good she would allow me to sit in the front seat beside Georges. I liked this because it was the seat where Daddy, the driver, sat in an English car and I could pretend to be driving.

The French roads were highly cambered, sloping fairly steeply from the middle towards the sides, and the only comfortable way to drive was in the middle. Roads were made like this because it was cheaper to construct roads with a thin layer of tarmac and the high camber allowed the water to run off to the sides. The frost and the sun used to make the roads very crinkly, which was bumpy for the passengers unless your car had very good springs and shock absorbers, which the big Citroen had.

In later years I always had a soft spot for these Maigret cars and I remember a young second or third cousin taking John and me for a ride in one when we visited La Tour du Pin in the early 1950s. I sat in the front and John in the back but I failed to close the door properly. It was hinged from the pivot in the middle and not from the front and therefore flew back dangerously. John was very contemptuous. Fortunately our host and driver didn't understand English while John inveighed against the incompetent designers of such a car who had failed to think of the obvious. However, when he came and opened the door for me to get out he changed his view. "I can see why only a Frenchman could have designed a car like this" he grinned. The angle at which he could stand with a rear opening door offered a much better view of both my 'undercut' and pants as I lifted my right knee to step out.

We were driven on a number of occasions to Aix les Bains, although we never had tea with Mr. Baldwin. On one occasion we travelled in style with Arrière herself and Marianne to Geneva and stayed overnight at the Hotel Les Bergues, which has a marvellous view over the Rhône where it comes out of the Lake of Geneva. Jean and I shared a room and had dinner with Marianne and Georges in a nearby restaurant. Arrière had gone to have dinner with either an English MP or Lord who was involved in League of Nations affairs. Geneva, as the headquarters of the League of Nations, was a very important city at that time, particularly for the English who played a dominant role in the League.

The Hotel Les Bergues was the hotel where all the influential Ministers in the various countries stayed and had varying informal meetings when there was a threat of a crisis. Arrière proudly told us how it was in this hotel that she had met and shaken hands with the former French Prime Minister, Pierre Laval, two years ago when he had prevented a war between Yugoslavia and Hungary by his skilful use of diplomacy. Although Laval is now remembered as Prime Minister under Pétain in the Vichy government after the defeat of France in 1940, he was greatly admired in the late 1930s as the Prime Minister who had restored stability and confidence until he was thrown out of office in 1936 by the man Arrière described as that "nasty little socialist Blum, who had let in the communists and undone all the good work of the previous five years."

In 1934 when King Alexander of Yugoslavia had been assassinated in Marseilles by a Croat gunman (who had also killed the French Foreign Minister Barthou), the Yugoslav government threatened to attack a demilitarised, weak Hungary for aiding and abetting the Croat gunman, whilst Mussolini threatened to send in the Italian army in support of Hungary. Laval succeeded in persuading Mussolini to back off in his support for the Hungarians by promising that he would not interfere with Mussolini's proposed colonising expedition in Abyssinia (as we then called Ethiopia) and that he would use his best endeavours to persuade the British to do the same. This resulted in the famous Hoare-Laval pact, when Sir Samuel Hoare was the British Foreign Minister. Unfortunately it backfired in the House of Commons and Hoare was forced to resign. Laval (in my view and Dad's) was right. Hitler had come to power in Germany, and Laval wanted to retain solidarity among the European countries such as Italy and Yugoslavia that he saw as allies against Germany (as they had been in World War I) and not to have them quarrelling amongst themselves.

Laval used his influence with Mussolini to persuade him to back off, persuaded the Yugoslavs to hold their horses for 48 hours and persuaded Anthony Eden (who was then British Minister Resident at the League) to lean on the Yugoslavs (which he did) and to extract an apology from the Hungarians. All this was happening at the Hotel Les Bergues during a weekend when Arrière had chosen to stay there. In those days leading politicians were less cocooned on such "social" occasions (all the key negotiations took place informally) so her chances of meeting the key players and talking to some of them were much greater than they would be today.

I knew nothing of these top people events at the time, but I intuitively sensed that Arrière was in her element.

In 1944, however, when I was writing an essay on the strengths and weaknesses of the League of Nations in answer to an exam question in the History paper for my Higher School Certificate, I had read up the incident and felt very bucked about squeezing in a reference to my stay at the Hotel where these events took place. I was arguing the case that the League had done one or two useful things and stopped some minor wars, even if it had not stopped major ones.

The Hotel staff clearly knew her well and were accustomed to according her the status of a great lady. Marianne said that Madame la Baronne wanted us to have breakfast with her the next morning. We were given the traditional English breakfast. A number of apparently important people came up and presented their compliments. We were introduced as two of her English great-grandchildren and duly got up and curtsied. We felt as if we were part of the Royal Family and were anxious not to make mistakes.

After breakfast Marianne walked with us to the landing stage where we got on the boat that took us to Montreux at the other end of the lake. We stopped at a lot of places to pick up and put down passengers. We had lunch on the boat. We thought Switzerland was a wonderful place.

Arrière in the meantime went to her bank, was entertained to lunch at the Lion D'Or by one of the partners in Barings and was clearly on top form in the afternoon when Marianne brought us back for Georges to drive us home.

Whenever I go to Geneva it brings back these wonderful childhood memories. It is a beautiful city. It has all the advantages of an important business centre without masses of sprawl and has no slums. Whenever I drive across the bridge from south to north and see the Hotel Les Bergues (and I have stayed there many times in recent years) or across the bridge in a southerly direction and see the imposing Lloyds Bank building (I suppose it is now Lloyds TSB - it used to be Lloyds Bank International) I remember my first visit. It also makes me think about that same period of history when so many of my parents' generation believed fervently in the League of Nations and when England was clearly the dominant country in Europe and when people like Arrière (who had quickly turned back into an Englishwoman when she crossed the Swiss frontier) enjoyed red carpet treatment everywhere.

Geneva was the city which Arrière had adopted when she moved from London. Today it is less than two hours from La Tour du Pin on the motorway. It probably took 3 hours or more for Georges to drive there in the 1930s. The road he took twisted around a lot, but there wasn't very much traffic and people like Georges made a habit of sounding their horns very loudly whenever they got to a bend or crossroads.

One of the endearing things (or so I thought and still think) about Arrière, who died a few days before Christmas 1938, was her simplicity and directness. On the one hand I was in awe of her as a regal figure, particularly after she had invited us to accompany her on her visit to Geneva, and yet she would come into the children's room when we were about to have lunch or afternoon tea and converse with us about what we were doing just as if she were another child, as excited as we were about what we were going to do that afternoon. Until the last year of her life (when Jean and I spent the Summer of 1938 as her guests at La Tour du Pin) she was as vigorous, elegant and as quick on the uptake as she had ever been. When in due course my time comes to go it would be wonderful to leave the earthly dwellings of men and women in like manner, but we have no control over such events. She was spared World War II. Although she lived in a part of France that was not occupied by the Germans until the British and Americans landed in North Africa in December 1942, she would have suffered a great deal. Her substantial income from the US and UK would have stopped and she would, above all, have been saddened by the third invasion of France by the Germans in her lifetime. Somehow, I feel, she would have got out in time and taken ship to the US, but even there she would have been unhappy with the knowledge of what was happening in Europe. When she died a lot of the old world died with her.

Arrière had another characteristic that I found surprising and perhaps amusing. She didn't use euphemisms. As an English child I had been brought up to use the normal euphemisms for bodily activities and still do. It is part of a civilised way of living. If someone asked me where Mum was or Auntie was, I would say "she's in the bathroom" or possibly "she's in the lavatory" (which would be less polite), whereas if someone asked such a question in Arrière's presence she would typically reply "Elle est en train de pisser" or "Elle crotte" and she would probably be right because she had an uncanny knack of knowing what everyone in the house was doing.

Marianne was the person to whom I became attached over the years. She looked after me like a Mum and was very attentive. She had a lovely round face and never seemed to get into a bad temper. She used to talk occasionally about her big boy and big girl who were working in Paris and her grandchildren. Her husband was the postman

MY EARLY CHILDHOOD

who used to say hello to me when he cycled up to bring the letters. I always think of him as the postman in the Jacques Tati film Jour de Fête, although I don't think I can ever accuse Marcel (Marianne's husband) of being drunk when he delivered the letters, but even at that age there was something slightly absurd (to my mind at any rate) in the funny hats that the French postmen used to wear on duty, just as the funny hats that a lot of French army officers wore.

But Marianne had another side to her life, which I discovered when I was 9 or 10. The children divided up more or less naturally into groups. After lunch the people we might have called the seniors used to do serious things like playing chess or snakes and ladders or read books. It was generally considered too hot to go out. The 'gosses' were left to their own devices. Most of the adults, including Marianne, used to disappear for a siesta. I found myself with a bossy girl, Monique, and her younger brother, Alphonse. Monique clearly liked being in charge of the gosses and keeping them out of mischief. She also liked demonstrating her superior knowledge in all sorts of areas. She is the sort of girl that Beano readers would have described as Keyhole Kate or Meddlesome Matty.

I remember her taking us to stand by the gate of the farmyard while a bull was serving a cow. She explained that this was how they got veaux. I thought that this simply meant veal, which I rather liked when we had it for lunch and I therefore didn't immediately cotton onto the fact that what she meant was that it enabled a cow to beget calves.

Much more importantly she announced to us on one occasion that she would show us how a baby was made. Even In those days children in families like ours were not fed the stork nonsense, or the cabbage patch nonsense that some people imagined. We knew that babies grew in a mother's womb and were delivered either at home or in hospital, and often rather painfully for the mother, so we were not ignorant.

Monique must have followed Marianne one day, or at any rate watched her walking towards one of the wings of the chateau that had not yet been restored, and then found some way of getting into this building by a different door. Alphonse and I were strictly instructed not to say anything to anybody, but keep quiet and to follow her as she led us to a loft that overlooked a large room, that might even have been an assembly hall, full of old couches, cupboards, bedsteads, washstands and other furniture that had been dumped there while the rest of the house was being renovated.

We saw Marianne come through the door. She didn't see us. I don't think she even looked up, although we had quickly ducked down. A few minutes later Georges came in and locked the door from the inside. We saw them kiss and then they moved out of sight under the gallery where we were standing. They must both have partly undressed, because the next thing I remember seeing was Georges without his uniform on top of Marianne on the couch below us and her large bare knees on either side of him.

Georges seemed to be working very hard for a long time but saying nothing, while Marianne, who now had her hands on his behind, kept saying "Encore Georges, encore". I started to say to Monique that it appeared to be taking an awful long time and there was no sign of any baby, but she immediately said "shush", so I obeyed.

Apparently Georges and Marianne spent all their siesta period this way every day, except on the days when Georges was expected to drive Madame la Baronne to some rendezvous.

When they had gone and we came back downstairs Monique said that it took 9 months to make a baby. When I came back next year (when I was 10 and knew a bit more) and there was still no baby, Monique was also wiser and told us that grown-ups did this sort of thing for fun, just as we enjoyed eating ice-creams or chocolatine.

Although Monique had enjoined us not to tell anyone where we had been, I was sufficiently curious when we got home after the second Summer, during which I had had a grandstand view of this lovemaking pair, to ask Mum whether making babies was such fun that Mums did it every day after lunch, even if they didn't want any, and as a result I was given a more comprehensive explanation.

Mum could have been annoyed, but she had the good sense to know that this was probably one of the best ways in which a child can acquire its early sex education. There was nothing naughty or smutty about it. It was just a natural thing to do during the siesta hour. In the class-room or from a book, or even from an explanation by Mum, I could never have acquired an insight into the wonderful experience of being loved by a man in the way that I somehow sensed it as I watched Marianne and Georges. It wasn't so much anything that they said or did. It was just something in the atmosphere. It was also probably in the warmth and happiness that Marianne radiated with us.

I have often thought that this type of experience would be the ideal way to teach most children the facts of life, but somehow I don't think it would be the same thing if the people concerned knew they were doing it for an audience and not just for each other. Nowadays they probably make videos like this. A child might believe them. An adult with my cynical frame of mind would automatically assume the participants were play-acting, which they would be. I still believe that there was some invisible form of communication between Marianne and anyone like me who wanted to understand and who understood and I shall always be grateful to her, not only for her wonderful kindness to us children but for teaching me something important in my own life in the pleasantest possible way.

Sadly my Garden of Eden days in La Tour du Pin ended when we returned to England in 1938. It was the time of the Munich crisis. We were issued with gasmasks at school and everyone was digging great pits in their gardens to put in air-raid shelters.

Arrière died in December 1938. Dad and Mum went to the funeral but Jean and I stayed with the Squires. In 1939 we had three wonderful weeks holiday at St. Jean-cap-Ferrat. Jean and I were both well developed and being goggled at by saucy Frenchmen, although we had the luxury of a private beach at the villa. Dad listened to the news every day and told us we had to be ready to pack up bags at a moment's notice if war started. He said it was typical of the Germans to want to start a war while everyone was on holiday. We nevertheless travelled home on our original return tickets, feeling very grown-up as we ate dinner in the Wagon-Lit restaurant car before trying to sleep in the Sleeper on the way back to Paris.

The real shock was the defeat of France in 1940. Everyone believed that the French had a bigger army than the Germans (which they probably had). Everyone we knew talked of giving the Germans a 'whopping', but in June 1940 France signed an armistice.

La Tour du Pin was not in the zone occupied by the Germans and people living in the country area didn't suffer the privations of those living in large towns where food distribution was appalling. We had no means of communicating with any of our French relatives until late Autumn 1944. We then learned that grand-maman had died in the Spring of 1944, before the Normandy landings. La Tour du Pin was liberated when British troops landed on the Mediterranean coast in August 1944 and advanced very quickly up the Rhône valley. The Germans had of course occupied the whole of the previously unoccupied part of France in December 1942, when the Allies landed in North Africa. Most of our family survived except poor little Alphonse (who was about my age) who had been deported to Germany in 1943 as a factory worker and never returned.

All Arrière's long-term plans for restoring the chateau to its one-time glory ended when she died and the flow of money from her British and American investments stopped. Mum, in due course, benefited from a substantial share in Arrière's investments, but neither she nor any of her cousins and second cousins felt that they had the knowledge or capability to continue with the restoration work. It was only in the late 1950s, when the great French economic expansion got under way that the chateau was eventually sold to be turned into a country house hotel. John and I stayed there once in the 1970s. My memories of the chateau and all the countryside round about which I saw as something of my family heritage made me too sad to enjoy myself. With the money which I eventually had from Mum I would have enjoyed (or think I would have enjoyed) finishing the rebuilding and running of the hotel, but each to his own. It was better that I did the job that was suited to my capabilities than trying my hand at something for which I may have had no flair.

What no-one has taken from me is the wonderful memory of a pre-war rural world that has gone, a knowledge of the French language that I acquired effortlessly, an extensive knowledge of French literature, thanks to one of Mum's cousins who spent a lot of time with me and ensured that I read good books every evening (I am talking about the years 1936, 1937 and 1938) which was what we all did between our early evening meal and bed, and the warmth and affection of the many people like Marianne and Georges, who were so good to us and who always seemed to breathe goodwill to all the men and women and children who surrounded them. If this sounds unreal, so be it. At this remove in time, it is the memory that is important rather than the original events.

CHAPTER 5

POLITICS AND WAR

Neither Dad nor Mum played any part in conventional politics in the sense that they were not personally involved in local Party organisations. I can only assume that Dad and Mum voted Conservative in the only pre-war election I can remember (it took place in 1935), but international politics was one of the main topics of adult conversation in our house during the period 1934-39 when I was growing up and taking an increasing interest in the adult world. In the previous chapter I mentioned the breakfast discussions with our many guests who were enjoying home leave in England from their overseas postings and that Dad was always keen to get their first-hand assessments of local conditions either in the countries where they worked or on their travels in countries such as Germany, Austria, Hungary and Italy. People with three months leave had time to travel out of season in places that a family such as ours (before the days of air travel) would not think of going to in our relatively short Summer holidays, particularly when Dad and Mum were able to go to Arrière's wonderful villa at St. Jean-cap-Ferrat and leave Jean and me where we would be well looked after by Marianne and learn a lot of French in the process.

My first memory of the impact on my life of the events that were to lead to World War II was when we were sitting round the tea table when I was about 8 (probably Autumn 1934) listening to the 6 o'clock news and of Dad suddenly becoming angry and saying "Those tomfool idiots. They have no idea of what is important."

I was quick to observe that Dad was not in the least angry with Jean and me. A normal worry was that the first thing Dad would do when he came home from work (usually just before 6) and sat down with us to drink a cup of tea was to ask Mum whether the children had been good, because woe betide us if we hadn't. We used to look anxiously at Mum and unless we had done something that had really annoyed her she would usually give us the benefit of the doubt and Dad's leather-soled slippers would hopefully stay on his feet that evening. But here was Dad getting very angry about something the man was saying on the wireless.

Our family routine in those days was that Jean and I would come home from school and have high tea between 5 pm and 6, typically scrambled egg on toast or baked beans followed by bread and jam and a piece of cake, and we would listen to Children's Hour.

In those early days of broadcasting children were (in my view) introduced to a much more loving and friendly outside world than they are given in present day television programmes and children's videos. We used to begin with stories read by Auntie Doris (Doris Gambell, later to become famous for her music programme "These You Have Loved") or by Auntie Muriel (Muriel Levy). There used to be historical plays about William the Conqueror or Charles I and Cromwell in which Richard Goulden (later to become famous as Moley in Toad of Toad Hall) played "The Man in the Street". There was an exciting adventure story that ran for weeks called "The Island in the Mist" and one of my favourites was Toy Town with its distinctive signature tune, Larry the Lamb (played by Uncle Mac, Derek McCullogh), Denis the Dachshund, Ernest the Policeman and Mr. Grouser ("This is disgraceful") which most people in my age-group still remember.

The wireless (as we then called it) was still something of a novelty in most British households and was treated with respect and a certain amount of mystique. I can remember the man from the wireless shop who used to bring a heavy glass leclanché battery every week and take the other one away to charge. It was believed that the bigger the aerial you had the better the reception and so our aerial wire went up the side of the house and then from the roof right across to the garage roof. The first loudspeaker I can remember was separate from the wireless and looked like the old advertisements for His Master's Voice. Because wireless sets in those days were not cheap or portable we had an extension speaker in the kitchen which could be left on when our dining room speaker was switched off. Mum used to ask our maid what she wanted to listen to (there were only two programmes that we knew of - North Regional and National) and our maid usually used to ask for dance music - the bands of Jack Payne and Henry Hall were favourites at the time.

In 1935 or thereabouts we had a new Art Deco Philips wireless with a built-in speaker that worked off the mains and which could pick up German, French and other foreign stations. It was called a Jubilee model, so it must have been brought out to coincide with the 1935 Silver Jubilee of George V. In fact I remember listening to the King's radio broadcast on the afternoon of May 6th (Jubilee day which was a public holiday). In 1939 we acquired a state of the art radiogram which would start playing a record when you pressed the button and stop automatically when the record had finished. The playing time on one side of a 12 inch 78 rpm record was about 5 minutes, so if you wanted to play a Mozart piano concerto you needed to load the radiogram with a pile of records. The radiogram would automatically play the top sides in sequence and then you would turn the pile over. This invention played an important part in my musical education. The quality of the sound was very much better than that on the old clockwork portable gramophone that Dad and Mum must have bought before I was born.

News bulletins in the early days of radio were much more detailed and informative than anything you hear now or see on television. It was no doubt assumed that the sort of people who had wireless sets and who would listen to the news would, like typical Times and Telegraph readers in those days, have a good working knowledge of international affairs. Dad would normally get home from the office towards the end of Children's Hour and sit down with us to drink a cup of tea as he listened to the

6 o'clock news. If Jean or I talked or made any noise he would frown and say "Sh!" His brows used to furrow and I could see he was annoyed.

The first time I remember him getting annoyed was over the prospect of a war between Italy and Ethiopia which was then called Abyssinia. Dad's annoyance was not with Italy but with the incompetence of the British Government and, in particular, with Stanley Baldwin, who was Leader of the Conservative Party and was then Prime Minister in what was called a National Government. Dad used to describe Baldwin as a pretentious nobody who was good at nothing but backstairs intrigue. Having got himself appointed Prime Minister in 1923 in place of Bonar Law's very able and natural successor (Curzon), Baldwin's sole objective, in Dad's view, was to keep potential rivals out of his Cabinet and put mediocrities into all the key jobs.

Dad, in fact, had a much more favourable view of Neville Chamberlain, who in 1934 was Chancellor of the Exchequer, and of Sir Samuel Hoare, who had a short spell as Foreign Secretary, than either of them has been given by the general run of historians. In Dad's view Neville Chamberlain was essentially a Civil Servant, a competent administrator but without the vision and charisma to be a political leader. We owe the existence of an independent Royal Air Force to a policy decision Sir Samuel Hoare persuaded the Cabinet to accept during his period as Minister for Air in the early 1920s, and without the RAF one shudders to speculate on our ability to prevent the Germans gaining mastery in the air in 1940. And yet Hoare was ditched by Baldwin for adopting a sensible policy on Abyssinia when this policy became unpopular with some noisy back-benchers.

The yardstick against which Dad measured the achievements or failures of British Governments and individual Ministers during the inter-war period was comparable to the yardstick we use as shareholders to measure the achievements of a Board of Directors in a Company in which we choose to invest. The Board's primary role is to make money for the shareholders, to foresee risks and to take whatever pre-emptive action may be necessary to minimise the potential capital losses to shareholders should some of these risks materialise. It is an unfortunate fact of public company life today that hordes of lunatic fringe fanatics buy one or two shares in order to attend AGMs of many well-known companies and to get reported in the national press and on television. Most of us can remember the nutcases that used to heckle at Barclays and Shell AGMs attacking the Board for doing business in South Africa at a time when South Africa was probably the only country in Africa where an intelligent company would want to do business. Now another shower of nutters (in all probability the same people who have learnt a different tune) tackle oil companies for drilling in the North Atlantic or Alaska.

A good chairman does what he can to humour these yahoos in the knowledge that the only thing that matters to the solid body of shareholders is whether the share price goes up or down and whether the dividend can be regularly increased. It is, however, unfortunate for the cause of "shareholder democracy" that big company AGMs can so easily be prevented from carrying out their proper role as a forum for serious discussion and that the antics of the lunatic fringe element are all that apparently interest the press and television.

Dad's view of Parliament in the inter-war period had much in common with the view I have just expressed about Company AGMs. But while it is a simple matter to sell your shares in a Company whose board starts catering for the whims of its lunatic fringe constituents instead of sticking to its guns, you have in practice little choice but to live with the follies of a Government which allows itself to be swept along by the whims of its unintelligent back-benchers and the fashionable emotions that the press are able to whip up. I fear to think what Dad would have said about Parliament in the age of televised debates. He used to blame our ills on the silly competition of Disraeli and Gladstone to extend the franchise and on the growth of the popular press. His annoyance over the Abyssinian crisis was that the tomfool British Government and tomfool popular press were making an unnecessary fuss and creating diplomatic problems over an attempt by the Italians to turn a God-forsaken bit of Africa into a colony after Britain and France had grabbed all the best bits.

To people who spoke of Mussolini as a wicked fascist dictator his answer was that Musso was a typical Italian gangster and if somebody shot him he would be replaced by another Italian gangster who might be worse. If only Italy had succeeded in colonising Abyssinia in the 1880s when they had first tried, they might have exported a lot more of their surplus population to a part of the world where they could do little real damage instead of which the Italians were left to emigrate en masse to the United States where they had done untold damage. All the American gangsters like Al Capone were goddam Wops and if the US Government had any sense it would forcibly repatriate all its Italians to Italy or send them direct to Abyssinia and give the Italian Government whatever subsidy it needed to develop that God-forsaken country.

Dad's irritation over the public preoccupation during 1934-5 with Abyssinia and with all the righteous indignation of people calling for sanctions against Italy was that Britain and France had a much more serious problem - the Germans. Hitler had come to power in 1933. Dad wasn't too fussed about the beliefs of Hitler's National Socialist Party. In Dad's view, any strong man who appeared, whatever his views, who could promise to reverse the defeat inflicted in 1918 had a reasonable chance of success and if France and Britain were to avoid another war they would have to act promptly before the Germans had time to re-arm and re-organise their armed forces.

Dad used to describe the situation as no more than two boys in the playground. One gets the other down and agrees to let him get up when he says "Pax you win" and as soon as he's on his feet he will return to the attack. Dad's view of the situation was that Britain had stupidly destroyed its own economic power by Churchill's ill-considered return to the gold standard in 1925, forcing us to cut our defence expenditure to absurdly dangerous levels, and that even if the French had a big army of conscripts sitting underground in the Maginot Line we would be no match for the restored might of a proud German nation hell-bent on removing the recent stain on its honourable military record. This time we couldn't count on the Russians who had tied down a lot of German troops in the East in World War I before they caved in and we certainly couldn't expect to be rescued by the US. It was essential, therefore, that Britain and France should have a secret military agreement to pick on the first suitable pretext (which might be only a minor breach of the Treaty of Versailles conditions) to march in and knock out whatever token army the Germans could muster. This would quickly destroy the credibility of Hitler amongst the military, which might reasonably be expected to leave us a few more years before some other strong man got into power.

Instead of this we seemed to be wasting our substance in getting hot under the collar with the Italians. It was not that the Italians were likely to be much use as allies, but there was no point in handing Italy to the Germans on a plate so that the Germans could establish air bases in Sicily and Libya to create havoc with our Mediterranean shipping. Even more damaging in the short term was the way in which we allowed the German public at large to see what a bunch of confused and toothless clowns their World War I enemies had turned into, capable of nothing but empty posturing at meetings of the League of Nations.

Dad had a major educational advantage over most of his contemporaries and certainly over children educated since World War II. He had received a firm grounding in international politics from a private tutor who must have been born in the 1840s and who had been first a Public School History master and then Headmaster of a Prep School - coaching Dad had been one of his retirement jobs. An intelligent History master growing up in the 1840s and 50s would have learnt to see international affairs entirely in terms of real politik. Lord Palmerston, who had been Foreign Minister for a substantial part of the early 19th Century before finishing as Prime Minister, would have been seen as a heroic figure of his era. At any rate, Palmerston was one of Dad's heroes along with the two Pitts, Lord Salisbury and later Lord Curzon.

Dad thought Britain's involvement in World War I was a disastrous mistake. The Austrians should have been left to deal with the evil Serb terrorists who had assassinated the heir to the Austrian throne in any way they might choose. He saw Serb terrorists as pathological criminals in the way we now regard the IRA and the Austrians had just as much reason to be angry with foreign interference as we are angered by those foreigners who are so ignorant as to treat the IRA as if they had anything to do with being Irish or being Catholic. If the Russians were so pig-headed as to try to interfere with the way the Austrians treated terrorists, then they deserved what they got, because the Russians had more terrorists and revolutionaries than any other country. If the French wanted to aid and abet the Russians in the hope of getting back Alsace-Lorraine, that was none of Britain's business. You should only get into a war if there is something in it for you or if you are defending your own territory against attack. The British Empire had nothing to gain and everything to lose by becoming involved in World War I. We lost 'a myriad and of the best among them' - the men who, in Dad's view, should have been running the Empire in the inter-war period instead of the dunderheads that we were left with, and the war had lost us our economic supremacy.

This view was certainly Uncle Henry's view of international affairs and he, like Dad, was very embittered by the fact that we had got into one disastrous war on the worst possible terms and by the late 1930s seemed hell-bent on getting into an even worse war in which we would probably lose our Empire and possibly our independence.

From the war years onwards it has been fashionable to make Neville Chamberlain the scapegoat for what is referred to as 'appeasement', though he didn't become Prime Minister until the Summer of 1937. In Dad's view Chamberlain had little option but to buy time with the Munich Agreement in 1938. The real fault was the failure of the Baldwin Government and the French to make a pre-emptive strike against the Germans when they re-occupied the Rhineland in 1936. The Germans had two divisions and the French twenty. The German generals were shaking in their shoes because they were thinking in military terms and had no understanding of politician's minds. Hitler had such an understanding and his hunch proved right. The French and British in his view would do nothing except bleat in their newspapers and bang the table at meetings of the League of Nations, which is what happened. Until this episode the senior military figures in the Germany army had regarded Hitler as a low-level political spiv. Our failure to act quickly and decisively meant that we had handed him moral authority amongst the military and many others in his own country, and for the next 2½ years he was able to consolidate his position and break as many of the clauses in the Treaty of Versailles regarding re-armament and limits on the size of the German army as he cared to break.

Although Dad frequently attacked Baldwin for his failure to act promptly on this occasion and for failing to understand foreign politics or having the good sense to appoint a Foreign Minister who knew what he was doing and to give him proper backing, the guilt for this disastrous failure was shared with the French Prime Minister of the day, Leon Blum, who had just taken over from Laval as Prime Minister of France with a communist/socialist 'Popular Front' government. Blum was a man detested with equal venom by Arrière. In retrospect popular historians have failed to allocate a part of the blame for World War II and the defeat of France in 1940 to this trade union happy, hyper-inflating Popular Front government in France which abandoned attempts to contain German expansion and no doubt drove most of the Conservative middle classes to take a defeatist view and make what terms they could with the German victors. History has treated Laval unkindly. He was the Prime Minister and Foreign Minister who had been the architect of a strong pan-European set of alliances against Germany and a sound monetary policy against which the Popular Front rebelled. Laval was only brought back into Government in France after the armistice in 1940 in the hope that he could secure the best day-to-day modus vivendi on an ongoing basis and for his pains was put in front of a firing squad and shot after a trial by a kangaroo court after the French (with the help of the British, Canadians and the US) had regained their independence at the end of the war. He was made a scapegoat for the defeat of France, for which Blum and his Popular Front cronies deserved a much worse punishment - and yet Blum was given a further spell as Prime Minister after the war.

In the late 1930s when the popular press had started treating Hitler as an ogre, Dad used to complain that people were attacking Hitler for being a madman or a National Socialist (NAZI). It didn't matter what Hitler's political beliefs might be, the danger to the British Empire was that he had succeeded in gaining control of one of the most powerful military machines backed up by an advanced industrial economy. Dad had a copy of Hitler's 'Mein Kampf' (in an English translation) prominently displayed in his library alongside Karl Marx's 'Das Kapital'. He used to enjoy teasing people who asked whether he was a Nazi or a Communist by pointing out that it was vital in any war to understand the mind of your enemy and that even if your enemy were either a Nazi or Communist he was no less dangerous because he might be mad or appear to be mad. There had been plenty of dangerous madmen in history.

National Socialism (and Dad never made the mistake of using the Italian term fascist to describe the Nazis) and Communism were similar in that they advocated an all-powerful State which would leave very little choice to the individual in the way he ran his life, and hence both political ideologies would inevitably attract power-hungry zealots who saw opportunities for their own advancement, including people who had the skills to hypnotise millions of gadarene swine to follow their leadership and destroy themselves in the process. Communism was a more dangerous doctrine because it had no frontiers and it could in due course be as dangerous to the world as the rise of Islam. Although National Socialism had a limited German appeal it was more immediately dangerous because it was better organised in military terms.

The only practical course of action for the survival of the British Empire was the traditional British policy of balance of power. We should do what we could to get the Germans to attack the Russians before they attacked us, which is why Dad was so angry with the British guarantee to Poland in 1939 when we couldn't do anything to assist them. It was inviting the Poles to commit suicide. The Poles were a headstrong impractical nation and it was obvious to all concerned that their army would be defeated within a few months (in fact it was five weeks). We should have leant on them to give up the Polish Corridor, Danzig, etc. as the sole means of keeping the rest of their country intact. The Western Allies' strategy should have been to encourage the Germans in their anti-Communist crusade. Britain and France could then have attacked Germany in the rear once the Germans were fully stretched in the East, enduring the rigours of the Russian Winter.

With this strategy we could have started our attack on the Rhine instead of having to land on the Normandy beaches. Furthermore, when the Germans attacked Russia they would not have had the backing of French, Belgian and Dutch industrial output. With the fall of France in 1940 the Armistice with the French virtually doubled their industrial output including the output of military supplies - a fact that is often overlooked by 'popular' historians.

The practical obstacle to Dad's strategy was the vociferous body of public opinion for whom Communist Russia had become more important than their own country. They may have been a small minority but they made a great deal of noise. The second obstacle was the UK political set-up which seemed congenitally incapable of adopting a tough real politik approach to international affairs. It could only take the country into a war in a spirit of frenzied righteous indignation, which probably meant going in at the worst time. With a small well-educated electorate a charismatic Prime Minister might have been able to adopt a strategy where you only get into a war when you have a reasonable chance of winning and you pick your moment.

I have summarised Dad's views on the basis of Mum's recollections in later life. But in conversations with Jean and myself at the time Dad was much more interested in getting us to understand who was who in the various European countries, the political systems that operated, the population sizes, military strength and industrial capabilities. Many of his discussions of military strategy used to take place during dinner parties when fellow Territorial officers and their wives came to our house or Mum and Dad were invited to their respective homes.

The Territorials played an important part in Dad's life. He joined in the 1920s when (in our part of the world) they were partly an 'old comrades' association and partly a gentleman's club. Dad, like most Public School boys at the time, had been a member of his school OTC (Officers' Training Corps) during the 1914-18 war years. This school military training was pretty thorough. It meant that most school-leavers would be commissioned as soon as they joined the army and could be sent on active service with very little further training. Even in the 1920s when there was no obvious threat of war there was a strong tradition amongst those who were active in the Territorials that it was only by keeping a strong army and navy that we could avoid another war. But this was not the view of many politicians. A number of Ministers in the two inter-war Labour Governments had been conscientious objectors in World War I.

In those days the men of military age (and some long past it) in most county families in our part of the country held commissions in the Territorial Army, which was very much a regional affair. Dad, as a personable young man with a Cambridge degree, quickly built up a good rapport with many of the Territorial officers who in future years would turn to him whenever they were buying or selling land or renewing leases. He was always being asked for legal advice and Mum used to say that he would have made a lot of money if he had been able to charge for it, but as Dad pointed out, this was the best way to establish his reputation amongst people who wouldn't normally deal with lawyers. What is more, Dad's blunt homespun way of putting things went down well with these sort of people who were ill at ease with the type of lawyer who tried to establish his mystique by talking in what was perceived as mumbo-jumbo.

Mum used to say that some of the people she met in Dad's early Territorial days were not simply veterans of World War I, or even of the Boer War, but talked as if they were still fighting the Zulu War or fighting their way up the Khyber Pass.

By the mid-30s things had changed. There was a major attempt to recruit younger men in which Dad played an active part and he was promoted to Captain. He used to go away for a fortnight in May or early June each year. Dressed in his smart uniform complete with Sam Browne, he used to hold up his swagger cane menacingly as he kissed Jean and me goodbye, saying "And you girls had better be good, or else..." and we knew what that meant. Fortunately Mum was usually kind and gave us good reports when Dad returned. Even if we had blotted our copybooks she gave us the chance to retrieve the position if we were 'extra-specially good' for the rest of Dad's absence.

In post-war years there has been a tendency to denigrate the effectiveness of these 1930s training camps. One heard snide comments that the only strategy discussed was over the bar and the only manoeuvres taken seriously by many of the officers were those needed to get their lady-friends into bed and once in bed the manoeuvres best suited to bring mutual delight to the said officers and their ladies. I am sure most enlightened people shared Mum's view that such small and harmless perks were a minimal reward for the many men who were giving up their free time and the opportunities to earn money, so that they would be ready to defend their country when the call came, as it did in 1939. One should also spare a thought for the millions of women who had either been widowed in the slaughter of World War I, lost all hope of finding a husband, or who had suffered the fate of Lady Chatterley but without the consolation of a game-keeper ready and willing to oblige. No-one but a flint-hearted bigot would have begrudged any of them who were able to take advantage of the all too rare opportunities, such as those offered by territorial camp fortnights, to participate in the sort of amorous dalliance that most women of nubile age, in the post-pill era, have been able to take for granted (should they so wish) as an almost nightly occurrence.

The Territorials were (like Dad) immediately ready for service when the war started in 1939 and many were in the Front Line in the fighting in France and Belgium in May and June 1940. A number of my Oxford friends had been in the Territorials in their first year 1938-39 and had immediately been called to their units in August 1939, only returning to complete their studies in October 1946, like my friend Clifford Dobb (of whom more in Chapter 23). One has to remember that the country also contained a lot of vociferous pacifists and communists who were prepared to fight for the Republicans in Spain or for Russia but not for their own country. When the Russians signed a peace treaty with Germany in 1939 these communist sympathisers attacked Britain's entry into the war as a wicked capitalist plot and only changed their tune in 1941 when Germany attacked Russia. The most entertaining description I have read was written by the poet Roy Campbell, who was very scathing about the constant changes of tune of the communist and 'fellow traveller' writers of the 1930s who either escaped to the US in 1939 (as Auden and Isherwood) or got themselves safe jobs out of the firing line (as Stephen Spender) in the NFS (National Fire Service).

In 1950 Clifford Dobb sent me an anthology 'First Words', published by his college (St. Edmund Hall), which included some of the poems he had written and discussed with me over afternoon tea at the Kemp. Roy Campbell had been invited to write the introduction and I still recall his punchy phrases in which he refers to the 1930s as "an age of hypocrisy, of peacetime belligerency and bogus egalitarianism on the part of those guzzling and steatopygous poltroons, the fire-eating profiteers of the left-wing Parnassus... Nothing was more striking than the collective simultaneousness of their changes of ideas and opinions to suit their personal safety and financial welfare... And we saw how the fire-eating belligerents of the pre-war years all volunteered simultaneously as chair-borne parasite troopers in the Knife and Fork Brigade (Crosse & Blackwell's regiment)... None of these fat-bottomed chair-bashers found his way into any but the most safe and lucrative positions. They held the Fort to a man, by digging into cushions with the most prominent and hindmost part of their anatomy - which they had once tried to pass off as a 'Popular Front'."

Although the people Roy Campbell was describing were the vociferous element in the 1930s political scene, one has to remember that the 1930s was a period in which the educated middle class in many provincial towns like ours took part in a great deal of serious political discussion, much of it outside the realm of the conventional political Parties. Because the Conservatives had a vast majority of MPs in what was referred to as a 'National Government' and because they were led much of the time by the man Dad used to describe as an uninspired 'impostor' (Baldwin) and because the Government had demonstrated itself to be particularly incompetent in two key areas - foreign affairs and the management of the British economy (areas which concerned most serious middle class people) - there was a widely felt need for relevant information.

The late Sir Allen Lane launched Penguin books in the late 1930s with a series of highly successful 'Penguin Specials' which included Europe and the Czechs, Mussolini's Roman Empire, Searchlight on Spain and Germany Puts the Clocks Back. The immediate success of these books consolidated the success of Penguin as a publishing house, which at that time aimed to cater for thinking people who took a serious interest in international affairs. This success was indicative of the widespread concern at the time that Britain could soon face a re-run of World War I.

Later historians have tended to treat this period in a simplistic way as if it amounted to no more than disapproval of Neville Chamberlain's 'Appeasement' policy at the time of the Munich crisis in 1938. Dad considered Chamberlain as a fall-guy left at the tail-end to carry the can for the 15 years of incompetent government of Baldwin (with a two year break from 1929-31 under Ramsay MacDonald). And Dad didn't have much time for Anthony Eden, who resigned as Foreign Minister in 1938, ostensibly because he disagreed with appeasement. He always talked of Eden as a matinée idol totally lacking in the substance that a Foreign Minister needed to play whatever cards he might hold at any given time when he was up against a bunch of card-sharpers as all British Foreign Ministers inevitably are. As I have already said, Dad used to measure people like Eden by the standards of Lord Salisbury, Lord Curzon and Lord Palmerston.

Had Dad survived the war I think he would have respected Ernest Bevin, the Labour Foreign Minister, who had to deal with the wiles and treachery of Soviet post-war diplomacy. Dad would always respect a man for what he was and held the view that whilst political parties had a right to differ in the way they handled domestic affairs, there should be little scope for differences when it came to the task of fighting for the best deal for England and for the British Empire against all the slimy foreign toads who were jealous of our position and would use every trick in the book to do us down. In that context I am sure he would have said that Ernest Bevin was a man of substance.

It would have been surprising if someone of Dad's temperament, whose first ambition had been to enter Parliament as an MP and who had demonstrated his powerful debating skills in the Cambridge Union - it would have been surprising if Dad had been content to limit his political activity during the 1930s to dinner parties or bar room chats with his Territorial friends.

POLITICS AND WAR

Dad was a person who formed instant judgments about people once he had met them (I like to think that I have inherited some of his skill in this domain). By the same token he was highly sceptical of second-hand judgments of people. He believed strongly that a person should be given the benefit of the doubt until he had been proved guilty. However much a politician or military figure might be attacked in the press or in conversation, Dad would wherever possible reserve his judgment until he had met the person concerned. Meeting people in order to get 'horses' stuff from horses' mouths' was therefore a major driving force in much of Dad's political activity.

With an introduction from Uncle Henry, Dad quickly became an active participant in a local Rotary Club where he used his influence to invite a lot of speakers of note. In those days the Rotary was taken very seriously indeed as a means whereby professional men could keep abreast of affairs outside their own professional circles. Perhaps it still is. I suppose that Uncle Henry, and later Dad, contributed significantly to our own Rotary in their ability to persuade leading public figures to travel north and speak at the monthly lunches or dinners, and also in their abilities to guarantee a good attendance and a high quality of debate.

But a lot of political figures and topics were not suited for Rotary meetings and most of the controversial people I remember meeting used to come to the other Society which Dad effectively ran - 'The Scientific and Constitutional Association' which dated back to the 19th Century and possibly to the time of the 1832 Reform Bill and which was transformed into a flourishing debating society when Uncle Henry arrived on the scene as Dean and was soon elected Chairman, which he remained until he retired in 1935. Uncle Henry had a vast network of friends in high places. All those who had been boys at the school where he had been Headmaster continued to hold him in very high regard and were no doubt flattered that he followed their careers with such interest, as he did. Dad used to say that most of them became schoolboys again in his presence.

The result was that this society was able to pull in a succession of top line political speakers and the audience from miles around used to pack the old town hall to capacity. Radio was in its infancy and there was no television, so there was a much greater demand then for tickets.

Dad had started off as secretary to the Society and done most of the work for Uncle Henry, so that he was the natural successor to step into Uncle Henry's shoes in 1935. It was between 1935 and 1939 that I met some of these speakers if they came to have dinner at our house or stayed the night. Jean used to be allowed to attend certain meetings and when I was 12 or thereabouts I was occasionally allowed in if I promised to be well-behaved, as I am sure I was.

It was said that Churchill had spoken in the early 1930s, but that was before I was old enough to know who such people were. The names I remembered best were J.M. Keynes, the economist, for whom Dad had considerable respect. Dad, like many of his friends in the north, felt particularly strongly about the disastrous economic policy that had been pursued between the wars which resulted in mass misery and unemployment in many northern towns at a time when our productive capacity and our resources could have enabled us to achieve a high standard of living. One of his bêtes noire was the 1925 return to the gold standard for which he blamed Churchill as Chancellor of the Exchequer. I have already mentioned this in the last chapter.

The speaker who caused the biggest flap in our household was the Marquis of Tavistock (later Duke of Bedford) who had established a substantial following which constituted something like a mini political party. He liked to meet people and to stay with them and learn something about them, so he was delighted to accept Dad's invitation to dinner and to spend the night with us, but can you imagine poor Mum's consternation. Was our dinner service going to be good enough to entertain a Marquis, and so on. She needn't have worried. Dad used to say that one of the advantages of going to Cambridge was that you could be equally relaxed and at ease with a Duke as with a dustman. Life in a women's college in the early 1920s was no doubt more sheltered. Nevertheless, when our guest arrived Mum turned up trumps and I am sure produced a far better dinner than the future owner of Woburn was accustomed to eating when he travelled around the country. What was more important to me was that Dad had decided that his daughters' education would be well served by meeting a member of an historic family that had drained the Fens and been responsible for the building of that part of London which we still know by names such as Russell Square, Tavistock Place, Bedford Square, etc. We were told to do our homework before the great day and read all about our guest's illustrious ancestors. For a girl of 11 it was a wonderful experience and I still remember with gratitude Dad's thoughtfulness in allowing me to stay up late and sit at dinner with the adults.

One of Dad's speakers was highly controversial - the late Sir Oswald Mosley who had started his own political party, the British Union of Fascists. After distinguished service in World War I he had become a Conservative MP and married one of Lord Curzon's daughters (when Lord Curzon was Foreign Minister and expected to be Prime Minister) and was expected to progress rapidly to a ministerial career. He left the Conservative Party and, after a period as an Independent, joined the Labour Party and became the youngest Minister in the 1929 Labour Government. He resigned and allied himself with John Strachey (who later became a communist) to form a 'Keep Left' group and when that didn't work he presumably thought that calling his party the Fascist Party would be the most fashionable thing he could do to catch the political tide that seemed to be flowing in much of Europe, and this would enable him in due course to become Prime Minister. I'm speculating with the benefit of hindsight, but this was I think Dad's view of him at the time.

About 1934 the communists started to make systematic attempts to break up all his meetings and this resulted in a lot of honest middle class English people sympathising with Mosley because they saw the disruptive communists as the main threat to law and order at the time, and certainly the photos that I have seen of the 'rent a mob' crowds look very like the pictures in more recent times of the yobs demonstrating against the City or desecrating the statues of Churchill and the Cenotaph War Memorial.

Dad had decided that Sir Oswald Mosley was entitled to an opportunity to put his case, but for security reasons the issue of tickets to attend was tightly controlled and members of the Society were given strict instructions not to publicise the event. The meeting gave Dad the opportunity to make quite a long opening speech on the importance which the British public attached to the rights of the individual to say what he thought and that the British sense of fair play was outraged by the way in which the British perceived the communist and fascist governments were in the habit of treating their political opponents.

I was not at the meeting. After the meeting Dad made the comment that Mosley was an extremely good speaker and an extremely good debater and that he could put a good case when he was given the opportunity. He was in fact arguing for massive public expenditure on a road building programme and re-armament on the grounds that we had vast unused resources in terms of unemployed people and that we needed strong defence forces to maintain our position in the world and a modern transport infrastructure. He also made the point that Great Britain should not dissipate its resources getting involved in European quarrels where there was nothing for us to gain but a lot to put at risk. In Dad's view, the people who went to break up Mosley's meetings did so purely because they saw him as a very capable rival in the power stakes. They didn't believe in democratic government but wanted a dictatorship. He was perceived as one of their own kind who had a lot of advantages that they lacked.

Dad's considered view of Mosley, however, was that any man who changed his shirt as often and as quickly as Mosley had done (in those days the colour of one's shirt was a form of political uniform, as with Hitler's Brown Shirts, Mussolini's Black Shirts and the communists' Red Shirts) posed a big question. It suggested to Dad that Mosley was power hungry and would climb on any bandwagon that he believed would enable him to become a home-bred Napoleon or Adolf Hitler. That didn't mean that Dad thought he would become a traitor in the event of a war with Germany (Dad gave him the credit for being a genuine patriot) but rather that Dad considered Mosley's record made him unsuitable for high office. Joseph Chamberlain's high profile chopping and changing was a bad precedent. The British people needed someone much more solid and reliable and with much greater patience when the going was tough. We needed a Pitt, a Palmerston or a Salisbury.

By far the most interesting person that I met (I think in 1938) in the course of a dinner party at our home was Clifford Hugh Douglas who was invited to speak on the economic causes of the forthcoming war. He was not a politician or an economist in the conventional sense of either of these terms, but a professional engineer. He did, however, have quite a large political following at that time when political parties were elected in British Colombia and Alberta, Canada (known as Social Credit Parties) pledged to put some of his economic ideas into practice.

Like Dad and Uncle Henry, Douglas was a Pembroke College man, born in 1879, who after working for Westinghouse in India had been responsible for much of the design and construction of the London tube system. The early Underground trains had simply been steam trains which ran near the surface, such as the Circle and

Metropolitan lines, whereas the Tubes were dependent upon what was then state of the art technology of electric motors combined with the development of deep tunnelling apparatus. In recent times we have all read of the problems and delays caused in the building of the Jubilee line extension running through to the Dome. Not many of us stop to think about the tremendous achievement involved in building London's vast network of Tubes in a relatively short time in the early years of the 20th Century.

In World War I it was realised somewhat belatedly by the UK government that aircraft had a potentially important part to play. The first cross-channel flight had taken place in 1909, only 5 years before the war started. A lot of young men like Dad wanted to train as pilots, but the planes available were still rudimentary and liable to conk out and crash without any enemy intervention. Large scale production had to be started almost from scratch and Major Douglas was drafted in to mastermind the exercise. In fact, in the 1930s people tended to call him Major Douglas because he had been given the honourary rank for his role in turning Farnborough into a major aircraft manufacturing establishment, and the name Farnborough has been associated with the aircraft industry ever since, or until relatively recently.

While he was running the production side of Farnborough, Major Douglas pioneered the development of the punch-card and tabulating system (the forerunner of computerised accounting) to enable him to keep personal control over accounting and budgeting. Surprisingly this state of the art accounting technology received little attention in either political or business circles between the wars, but his mention of it fascinated Mum, who for once dominated the conversation for much of dinner - in contrast with most such dinners for political guests when she left it to Dad to play the lead role and did her best to make suitably diplomatic comments.

After Major Douglas' visit I remembered Mum pulling Dad's leg that the Society was supposed to be a scientific and political society and they ought to invite more speakers like Major Douglas. In fact he was invited to speak on a political subject and he was very pessimistic as were many other people at that time, including Dad.

Instead of simply blaming Adolf Hitler for the coming war, Douglas' theme was that Hitler would never have attained power in Germany if we had managed our monetary system intelligently, a view repeated by Churchill in 'The Gathering Storm'. Would-be Hitlers have existed at all periods of history but well-fed and prosperous middle class people don't usually treat them seriously. The traumatic defeat of Germany in 1918 followed by the disastrous inflation when many of the middle classes lost all their monetary assets and then a slump with over 6 million unemployed was what enabled Hitler to seize power.

Even I, as a 12 year old, was able to follow the logic of this argument, and a good deal of what Douglas said. Jean and I were allowed to attend the meeting as well as the dinner party. Although Uncle Henry had retired, he came back to stay as a guest at the Deanery and attended. It was the last time that we saw Uncle Henry who died that Autumn at the age of 78. Dad became the owner of the Shropshire estate, but we never lived there.

I did, however, have the chance to learn a lot more about Douglas' ideas later in life. Mum had continued to correspond with him and he wrote to Mum when he read the news in the Times of Dad's death in 1945 and invited her to visit him in Scotland (where he had retired) if she had the opportunity to do so. In 1950 when William was one and we were worried about travelling with a baby to France, we decided to go to Scotland. John and I both wanted to see Fortingall and we stayed in a small family hotel at Fearnan on the north shore of Loch Tay, only a mile from Fortingall.

As Mum came with us (to help us with the baby and because we wanted her to have a holiday) she decided to take up the long-standing invitation to visit Major Douglas, who would have then been 71 and who lived in a beautiful house on a hill near Fearnan which had a superb view of the Loch and the mountains beyond.

Major Douglas limped very badly because I think he had had a fall from a horse some years ago. John volunteered to remain at the hotel with baby William, so that I could accompany Mum. What I remember most is the large painting of Douglas by Augustus John and comparing it with the subject of the portrait himself who was walking around and eventually sat down where one could compare the sitter with the portrait. I found it fascinating. Augustus John had got the high-domed forehead right and something about the look in the eyes, but it wasn't quite right and I believe the Douglas family wasn't entirely happy with it, but that remark was made by a third party many years later and may or may not have been true.

Mum's creative mind was at that time exercised by the need to introduce some system of management accounting for the various law firms that she was trying to integrate. Nowadays all professional firms operate computerised time-sheet systems, but believe it or not in the post-war years a lot of firms were still operating book-keeping systems that didn't seem to have changed since the days of Bob Cratchit and Scrooge. Large financial institutions were using Hollerith cards, but the idea of a professional firm investing money in accounting machines was alien to the culture of most law firms and Mum was determined to change this. She succeeded in her own enlarged firm, but it was a long up-hill task. My recollection was that she was hoping to get some ideas and help from Major Douglas and I remember him frequently reminding her of the difficulties of any consultant trying to get any organisation to introduce changes which it didn't properly understand and hadn't thought of itself. This, he said, had been his life story and he was essentially a consultant - a role which I have filled for much of my later life, which is perhaps one of the reasons why I have come more and more to see things in the way he did.

I had two reasons for taking an interest in Douglas during the 1980s. The initial trigger came from my inner feeling following my marriage to David. British Colombia in Canada had become my second homeland. It was not until the 1970s that cheap long-haul flights and the fact of being freed from a growing family meant that I could make the pilgrimage (accompanied by John) to David's home city, Victoria. We were enchanted with British Colombia and had a number of holidays in the 1980s. I met a number of the MPs and Ministers of the Social Credit Party who had a Parliamentary majority and were, therefore, in government in the Province for much of the time.

The same people who had voted for Social Credit in the Province were voting Conservative in the Federal elections. The Social Credit Party seemed to me at the time to have a considerable amount in common with the aspirations of the British Thatcher government.

The second factor that stimulated my interest was the much greater understanding of financial matters that I had built up running a business. Like Douglas, I was much more concerned on a day to day basis with money management at the practical end and in guiding many small companies, as opposed to pontificating from on high as a politician or an academic. This makes one more aware of the gaps between the way financial matters are perceived by someone who merely has to stand up and answer awkward questions in Parliament or on television and the perceptions of a person who has to find money to pay the rent and the salaries and yet combine this day to day practical sense with a vision of where you are going to take your company in the years ahead.

I had initially perceived Douglas as a reformer similar to Keynes, who had advocated deficit Government spending in periods of recession and mass unemployment as a means of generating purchasing power in the way that the Hitler Government in Germany from 1933 onwards had built a network of motorways, making use of the vast pool of low-cost labour that was recruited from people who would otherwise have been unemployed.

I later learned that Douglas was a much more radical thinker than Keynes, which is no doubt why a much smaller number of people understood what he said. At a time when the conventional wisdom of people in the Bank of England, the Treasury, and most University Economics Departments maintained that the money supply in a country was limited to the volume of gold held in the vaults of the Bank of England, Douglas argued that the only real relevant measure for a nation's money supply was its ability to produce needed goods and services. A country could base its money supply on that country's industrial and commercial capacity and this principle has been understood and applied for war purposes at a number of key periods in our history. William Pitt the Younger, as Prime Minister during the Napoleonic wars, had abandoned the gold standard in 1797 'because there was no alternative'. He had enabled the UK to develop its resources at a rate at which no-one had believed possible, not only to wage total war against the strongest army in Europe but in addition to finance all our feeble and sometimes useless Continental Allies to put armies into the field. We had finished the Napoleonic wars as the most powerful industrial nation in the world, but then we had thrown this advantage away by going back on to the gold standard in 1819 (on the bad advice of Ricardo).

Likewise, in 1914 we had abandoned gold and expanded our productive capacity to fight another total war. We had increased living standards even though we were using a vast part of our human resource asset not to produce goods and services for consumption, but to fight in the trenches or to produce shells, guns and warships that were not available to supply consumer demand. But then the Bank of England and the Treasury had twisted the arm of Winston Churchill (as Chancellor) to go back on the gold standard in 1925, so that large parts of our productive capacity would lie idle and vast reserves of trained manpower would remain unemployed.

Douglas demonstrated that Governments had power to create credit and should do so in a way that companies created shares on the basis of shareholder confidence in the company's ability to deliver. It was widely believed that the only way Governments could create credit was by creating debt, i.e. to borrow from people who had savings to lend. He showed that the expansion of the money supply at critical periods in our history was far beyond the stock of savings whether in this or any other country and that if borrowing had been restricted to available savings then the money supply would have been static over the years instead of increasing exponentially during periods such as the Napoleonic wars and the 1914-18 war.

He argued that the credit-worthiness of a nation belongs to its people and that this credit-worthiness should be recognised by treating all citizens of the UK as shareholders and issuing them with periodic dividends based on realistic estimates of the value of these shareholdings. He referred to this form of wealth distribution as the "National Dividend" and the term he coined to give recognition to this ownership by a country's citizens of their country's credit was 'Social Credit' and the first article he published using these terms appeared in the National Review in 1918 before the end of World War I during the period when he was running Farnborough and had become closely involved in the accounting as well as the production side of the business.

By the early 1920s Douglas had spelt out in a number of books and articles many of the answers to questions that had been raised about the way his proposals would work in practice. He had recognised that if you increase the money supply you could suck in imports and offer scope for suppliers to increase their prices to 'what the traffic would bear'. He had therefore included provision for a compensated price mechanism. Instead of distributing all the available credit in the form of National Dividends, a proportion would be distributed to UK providers of goods and services if they guaranteed to hold their prices at an agreed level. In other words, suppliers could increase their profits by increasing volume (but not their prices) in response to increased consumer demand. This would keep the prices of UK produced goods and services competitive. It would not be an export subsidy because goods sold in the export market would not be eligible for the compensated price.

There was also a lot of work done to demonstrate that the money distributed in a given time period as wages, salaries, dividends, etc. was not sufficient to generate the purchasing power needed to buy the products and services manufactured or provided during the same time period.

To get off the ground in the UK the Douglas proposals needed a powerful political backer. We saw in more recent times how difficult it was for someone like Sir Alan Walters as economic adviser to Margaret Thatcher to get his ideas implemented. The best example I can think of is the way in which Pitt the Younger understood the writings of Adam Smith in the late 18th Century and decided that they should be the basis of UK Government economic policy. In the 1920s we didn't have anybody of Pitt's calibre at the head of Government. After the Welsh bounder Lloyd

George we had Baldwin who was a major disaster in virtually every area of policy, two short interludes of Ramsay MacDonald and the sad few months in 1922 when Andrew Bonar Law was 'the unknown Prime Minister' (the title of Robert Blake's excellent biography of him). He sadly died of cancer of the throat a few months after taking office.

Inevitably the radical thinking of someone like Douglas would generate a lot of opposition. Professional economists, like professional anything else, don't like an outsider coming up with an idea they haven't thought of. They can in fact be pretty acrimonious about a lot of their own profession. Alan Walters and Patrick Minford (both opponents of ERM and a common currency) have had to put up with plenty of flak in recent years.

The Lefties of course had a further reason for strong opposition to Douglas. They wanted power and they wanted to destroy the existing social system and for this they needed a strong State and the tide they hoped to harness was the tide of mass hunger and deprivation which would disappear in a relatively short time horizon if all citizens were to start receiving National Dividends. In fact, if the boost to the economy worked the Dividend could be gradually increased to a level where it could be enough to live on and it would not therefore be necessary to employ vast numbers of people collecting social security contributions and paying the same money out in benefits. Unemployment benefit, sickness benefit, means tested supplements to state pensions etc. would not be necessary. We would not need to pay in taxation the sums needed to pay the salaries and wages of all the people employed in Central and Local Government and their various agencies to collect people's money and pay it back to them. Furthermore, these people would be available in the labour market to do useful productive work.

The original rationale for much of our tax-based spending on State funded education and State funded health services was that the State had to provide such benefits for people who couldn't afford to pay for them. Experience has shown that the State and other Government agencies are totally unsuited for organising the provision of such services as health and education. There is a reasonable chance that if Douglas' ideas had been implemented in the 1920s when Britain was potentially much wealthier in terms of our claims on world resources and we still had our Empire, that a much higher proportion of the population would have had the money to pay for private education and health care, possibly using health insurance as a large proportion of salaried staff do today, and we would not now be suffering the problems of a badly educated and illiterate population (caused by a rotten and politically sick education bureaucracy) and an NHS bureaucracy that can never hope to deliver the healthcare our people can now afford.

I believe that if we had been able to harness our economic resources in the inter-war period in the way Douglas showed was possible that we could easily have afforded to maintain a strong peace-time army, navy and air force and that this might have been an effective deterrent, discouraging the Germans from risking another war. Furthermore, as a wealthy country instead of a poor country at the time of the 1929-34 slump, we might well have provided the economic dynamo which Europe needed to achieve prosperity. Other countries may well have been tempted to follow the UK example, as they did when Margaret Thatcher pioneered the concept of privatisation.

This could well have enabled Germany to avoid the appalling conditions in which over 6 million of their people were unemployed, so that the Nazis would not have found it so easy to recruit large numbers of desperate men to their private armies and to tempt so many voters desperately clutching at straws.

I therefore believe that the failure of Baldwin and his ministerial team to take serious note of the new economic technology demonstrated to be feasible by Douglas, just as he had demonstrated the feasibility of the London Tube system and of the mass production at Farnborough of aircraft for military use, makes them bear a heavy responsibility for the death and destruction suffered by so many of our people in the Second World War which that Government could have prevented and that this must weigh even more heavily in the scales than the failure of the Baldwin Government to take prompt pre-emptive action when a minuscule German army re-occupied the Rhineland in 1936.

But politics, like charity, begin at home. The politics that took up a great deal of Dad's spare time and energy between 1935 when Uncle Henry retired as Dean, and August 1939 when Dad joined his Territorial Unit, were mainly ecclesiastical and school politics and the critical role he played proved to be all-important for my own educational future.

Uncle Henry had remained as a very powerful figure in public life, not only as Dean but as Chairman of the Governing Bodies of both College and High School, as a contributor both to the Times letter columns and as the writer of occasional feature articles. He had, however, made it known for some time that he would retire at about age 75 when a suitable successor could be found. Fortunately Dad had already become senior partner in his firm in 1933, but there was predictable speculation both by Dad and many local worthies and unworthies as to the extent of his continuing influence once Uncle Henry's successor had taken up office.

Fortunately Dr. Wilding, who was appointed Dean in 1935, liked Dad and immediately appreciated the role he could play. Dr. Wilding was a distinguished historian who had been the Principal of an Oxford College and who, when approached, had decided that the role of Dean suited his temperament, providing an agreeable halfway house in a gradual progression to retirement. He had expected to stay for five years, but in fact stayed for 12, the six war years proving far more demanding than he had envisaged.

When it came to the chairmanship of the Governing Bodies of College and High School, he was much less 'hands on' than Uncle Henry, who had tended to be something of an overlord Headmaster because headmastering was the job he had done for much of his professional life.

But after the appointment of Dr. Wilding as Dean, Dad soon found himself as Deputy Chairman (he had previously been Secretary) of the Governing Bodies of both College and High School. At the time nobody seemed keen to 'volunteer' for the job of Secretary, so Dad volunteered Mum for the job. Dr. Wilding left it to Dad to chair most meetings. Although Dr. Wilding (who was much in demand as a speaker at various historical gatherings) took leave of absence on two occasions to give lecture tours in the US and Canada, he had a firm grip on essentials, decided what decisions he wanted to make and Dad proved to be the type of No. 2 who was quick to perceive what his boss wanted and ensure that it was done, no doubt one of the reasons why Dad was later to be promoted to Brigadier during his period of service at Mountbatten's Headquarters in SEAC.

In 1937, the Rev. Arthur Wilkinson told Dr. Wilding that he would like to retire early as College Headmaster at the end of the current school year. His health was not good and his wife had died 18 months previously. One of his daughters who had emigrated with her husband and two children to Wellington, New Zealand, wanted her father to come and live near them and this option appealed to him. His timing was absolutely right. He was able to sail in the Autumn of 1938. If he had waited another year before retiring he would have probably found it difficult if not impossible to get a passage and he would have had to sail through U-boat infested waters.

This meant that the Winter of 1937-38 was one of much politicking and speculation about who would take over from 'Uncle Arthur' as he was known by most of the College boys as well as the masters. One of his nephews had once attended the College and his mode of referring to his uncle had quickly become part of College folklore.

Walford Squires looked the natural candidate. He was the Senior House Master. He was personable and had a distinguished sporting record. He appeared to be the person who, in large measure, ran the school for Uncle Arthur and had a good rapport with Dad as he had had with Uncle Henry. Dad backed him on those matters where Walford needed decisions made quickly and, furthermore, we were close family friends. Walford no doubt assumed that the job was his if he played his cards right.

Dr. Wilding, however, was of a different view. With the benefit of hindsight I think he was quick to assess Walford and recognise that it was Milly (Millicent) Squires, the able and efficient housemaster's wife, who was the power behind the school and not Walford.

Dr. Wilding had a very clear understanding of the change in priorities in middle class parents' perceptions of what they wanted from a Public School. In the 1920s many middle class parents had no doubt felt that the mere fact of Public School education would be sufficient to guarantee their sons good jobs. The 1929-34 slump had changed this. The College had been very dependent on the use of church funds in the form of scholarships in order to avoid a catastrophic fall in College revenues. Good academic results and the ability to gain university scholarships had become much more important for a school's success than the ability to beat a few other well-known local schools on the cricket and rugger fields more times than they lost.

The candidate favoured by Dr. Wilding was an Oxford double-first who had taught first in a well-known boys Grammar School (a Day School) before being appointed a

Housemaster at a Public School. He had taken his doctorate in Divinity and edited biblical texts. Like many Headmasters at that time he had taken Holy Orders. He was an extremely good teacher. When I became a Sixth Former at a time when many College and High School classes were shared, I was in his divinity class and also in his Confirmation class and at that time I had a high respect for him as an excellent teacher. Dr. Hanscombe proved, in my view, to be a very good choice indeed, which Dad supported, but in the short term it left him with a diplomatic problem and also a school organisational problem. What to do about Walford if he was to be motivated to support the new regime.

Dad hit on the idea of creating an official post of Second Master, which was further enhanced by allocating to him the very imposing 18th Century house that had used to be the home of Uncle Arthur (known by the boys as 'Arthur's Seat'). A new house was being built for Dr. Hanscombe. Finally, Dad suggested in his discussions with Dr. Wilding that it would be sensible to recognise Milly's major role in running the school by inviting her to be a member in her own right of the High School Policy and Administration Committee which would provide a direct line of communication with Dad and Dr. Wilding on policy matters concerned with the running of the College.

Walford, however, remained resentful vis-à-vis Dad for 'letting him (Walford) down' and failing to land him the Headmastership. This was Mum's view and I'm sure she was right. I certainly felt that some of this resentment was still seething in 1942 when I found myself at the receiving end of his cane (but more of this in Chapter 9). Milly, however, was (in Mum's view) relieved. Milly knew Walford's weaknesses as well as anyone. She knew she could hold the fort for him in his job as Second Master, organising his time-tables, handling relations with parents, etc., but she knew that the job of being Headmaster would require a lot more than in the past and that if Walford had got the job he would have been a classic sad case of over-promotion and disaster could have resulted not only for Walford but for Milly herself and the whole of the family. In later chapters I shall have a number of occasions to comment on Milly's capabilities, strength of character and wonderful loyalty not only to Walford and her children but also to Mum and me at the time we learnt of Dad's death when we desperately needed help.

In the event it was this appointment that provided a bed-rock for a successful wartime regime when Dad was away. Mum and Milly proved to be the key players during the difficult period when College and High School had to work much more closely together as a single unit during the war years. It would have been hard to find two volunteers of this calibre who were able to work so harmoniously together. Dr. Wilding was a delegator but he knew how to assess the people to whom he was delegating and I am sure he knew in his bones how well he had chosen his team. And so did I, or rather so I came to understand, particularly in the critical years of my life in the Sixth Form which I will describe in later chapters.

CHAPTER 6

THE FOUR MUSKETEERS

In the Autumn of 1940 I entered a new phase in my life. There were a number of contributory factors. Firstly I was now alone in the house with Mum. She was working long hours and she gave me as much responsibility as I was willing to take for running the house. Our only help was an old lady who was known as 'the treasure' who would come in for two hours on a Saturday morning and possibly one or two other mornings a week. I did the shopping either after school or on Saturday morning, hoovered the house and did most of the cooking. I had lunch at school. We used gas and electric fires as much as possible. We didn't have central heating, but we had an Ideal boiler in the kitchen which heated the water and heated the kitchen, which we used as a breakfast room and on most nights for our evening meal. I used to get in the coke as soon as I got home from school and take out the ash if it was cold before I went to school in the morning. We used it to spread on the paths in the garden. We had a gas poker to light the boiler, which was lit by whoever got up first in the morning.

One of the biggest chores was shopping for food. You had to be registered with a grocer and with a butcher and they were all as bad as each other in terms of efficiency. They knew they were in a seller's market and could laugh up their sleeves at the way they kept their customers standing in queues. People who talk or write nostalgically about old-fashioned family grocers are talking through the seats of their trousers. They obviously never suffered the misery of having to shop at one. I had to stand waiting impatiently while some dim-witted moron took a long time to find the right piece of bacon to put on the bacon slicer which he had to move whenever he then needed to use his steps to reach the biscuits on the top shelf. Even the simplest of simpletons could have told him how to re-organise and put things so that he could work his way through this exasperating routine in a twentieth of the time for each customer. Presumably he was paid a fixed wage and couldn't give a damn how long he kept busy people waiting in a queue. Give me my out of town ASDA supermarket any day, where I can drive in once a month on a day when I've got someone to help me, fill two trolleys in 20 minutes and that's it. Mind you, the people who block the gangways looking as if they don't know what they want and where to find it still exasperate me. It only takes one or two visits to a store to know where everything is and you write your shopping list out in that order.

Food offices were another irritation. They were set up from scratch to issue ration books, emergency ration cards for people travelling, special tickets for expectant mothers and children under six, and so on. The rationing system under Lord Woolton (who wasn't a politician but a business man brought in by Churchill and most of us think he was a very good choice) compared very favourably indeed with the systems used in European countries, because it was in the main respected and fair, so that far less disappeared onto the black market. At operational level, however, it had to be run by the left-overs in the labour market. The women who were any good (at any rate in a City like ours) could walk into worthwhile jobs replacing men on active service, so places like food offices tended to get the left-overs.

The food office, where I used to have to queue for the renewal of ration books, was an experience that persuaded me from an early age that I hated the idea of socialism. I saw it as making one more dependent on Government and hence dependent upon the behaviour of low-level trogs who any Government would have to employ to implement their systems. One queued impatiently for a hell of a long time at a counter that said 'Ration Book Renewals'. There were much shorter queues at the other counters. You eventually got to the front and you said to the lady, "Why don't they have more people dealing with ration book renewals?" She would reply, "We are far too busy to work to a system. Everybody's doing everything" which meant that I could have renewed our ration books in a quarter of the time had I queued somewhere else.

The fault may not have lain with the individuals working in the food office, but with the person in charge. You must remember, however, that labour shortages in the war years reduced the effective power of bosses in any organisation to say "Do as you're bloody well told or you're fired".

In retrospect the golden age for an employer, particularly a small employer, was the 1930s when you could do just that. It was hoped that when Margaret Thatcher came to power in a period when there was considerable unemployment, that we could get back to this happy situation, but we were wrong. Her Governments failed to repeal the unfair dismissal and redundancy legislation brought in by previous Socialist Governments.   Furthermore, she failed to disband such busybody Quango organisations as the Equal Opportunities Commission and the Commission for Racial Equality, so that if an employer dismisses a woman because she is incompetent she will predictably waste his time and money at an Industrial Tribunal defending himself against some fatuous claim for harassment or sexual discrimination, and if he dismisses a black, a Pakistani, an Indian, or whatever, he will likewise have to divert precious time from the task of running his business to arguing the toss against ridiculous claims that the employee is being dismissed for racial reasons and not because he is incompetent or no longer wanted.

Although I was only a 14 year old, I was already forming judgments on the incompetence of people much older than myself. Fourteen was at that time the school leaving age for the majority of the UK population. I was hardly likely to turn into an adolescent rebelling against authority when there was no authority to rebel against. Mum would think of me as an adult and as her companion I did my best to live up to her expectations. Before Jean left home I had no doubt had a complex about being 'the kid'. Many younger children have this. I don't think either Jean or Mum treated me as a kid. It was probably all in my mind. In the period of 1938-40 Mum seemed to spend a lot of time with Jean, which in retrospect was perfectly natural. Jean was doing the equivalent of what we called (when my children were at school) Double Maths plus Physics and Chemistry in Higher School Cert. and Maths was Mum's subject. Mum wanted Jean to get the highest possible marks and Jean did. Mum was disappointed that Jean joined the Wrens rather than taking up the place which she could have had at Newnham, but she understood and respected Jean's patriotism.

The Autumn of 1940 was the period when Britain stood alone. We had listened in recent months to all Churchill's broadcasts on the wireless about 'fighting on the beaches'. We were encouraged by the success of our fighter pilots against overwhelming odds in what is now called 'The Battle of Britain' and, in spite of the tremendous damage caused by the blitz on London, the message was going out 'Britain can take it'.

We had heard that Dad had arrived safely in Egypt without being torpedoed and that he was now an Acting Colonel in Staff Headquarters and then we had our first victories against the Italians just before Christmas. In Libya we first took Bardia and then Tobruk. Mum and I used to tell our friends that Dad was at long last having a chance to give these greasy little wops a kick in the pants, something we knew he would enjoy doing.

On the school front life was beginning in earnest. I was in the Lower Fifth, which meant that we would be taking our School Certificate (the equivalent of 'O' Levels) in July 1942. At the beginning of term the Headmistress gave a pep talk to all the sets (streams in present-day language) of the Lower Fifth, making it plain that our results would depend upon the work we did this year. By the time we were in the Upper Fifth our ability to 'sprint to the winning post' would depend on our efforts in the school year 1940-41.

Not only did we sense that we were being closely watched in our day-to-day schoolwork, but we also felt we were being treated seriously. What we did mattered. Not only this, but the work was much more interesting. Whilst I had enjoyed writing essays about Henry VIII, Charles I and Cromwell, I became much more involved when we were doing the 19th Century and covered the period right up to 1918. I got the highest marks and was first in History in the class exams in December 1940. One of the questions was on President Wilson's 14 Points. From one of Dad's books on the Treaty of Versailles I got and remembered all of them. Our school text book just talked about the 14 Points without saying what they were.

Likewise Lloyd George's 1909 Budget and the 1911 Parliament Act were things that Dad used to talk about and I felt on home ground.

Whereas Mum and Jean were much more circumspect and kept themselves to themselves, I was probably more of an extrovert like Dad and I enjoyed opportunities to express myself. Our set play that year was Julius Caesar and I was given the part of Mark Anthony for our dramatic class readings. I read the play right through at home and rehearsed the famous 'Friends, Romans and countrymen' speech in front of the mirror in the bathroom umpteen times and I think I impressed everyone including Mrs. Rainham (our English teacher, of whom more anon) who didn't need impressing. She knew I loved the subject, otherwise she wouldn't have given me the part. If we had been in a mixed class I couldn't have read this part because it would have been given to a boy. In fact this would have happened if I had been one year younger, by which time Lower Fifth English at the High School had been 'integrated' with Lower Fifth English at the College.

I was obviously good in French, so French, English and History were clearly my best subjects, but as I managed to get credits in both Maths and Additional Maths as well as Physics and Chemistry, Latin, Geography, etc., I had achieved a reasonable position as an all-rounder.

Personal friendships were also important. Louise and I had been friends from our kindergarten days and, in fact, earlier as our families were already close friends before I was born. By the time I was in the Lower Fifth I was also developing a close friendship with Elizabeth Gundry (Liz). Liz and I were what would now be called 'pace-makers' to each other in a number of subjects. She had a first-class mind, worked hard and was totally unconventional in her attitudes.

Liz had spent much of her early life in India where her father had been working to build up the Church of South India. When his time of service had ended he had obtained a position as a Canon in the Cathedral hierarchy. I am not exactly sure of what his responsibilities were during this pre-war period, but at the time I am writing about he was back in the Far East as an Army Padre. Although I never met him, I can only assume that he must have been born into a family that could afford to send him to Eton and Christchurch Oxford, where he had taken an Honours Degree in English Language and Literature before studying for Holy Orders. He had accumulated one of the most interesting libraries of English Literature that I have ever seen. I am sure I would have enjoyed meeting him.

Maureen O'Hagan was a close friend of Liz, probably because their families were close friends. Maureen had also spent most of early life in India. Her father had served throughout his life in the English Army and had retired as a Major in 1938 and found an administrative job in the Cathedral hierarchy. With the coming of war he was back in uniform and back in the Far East. In spite of his Irish name the family was as English as ours (which after all had a Scots name). At that time there were probably twice as many people of Irish origins living in England as there were in Ireland. As far as I knew, Maureen's family didn't treat the people running the 'Irish Free State' Government in Dublin seriously. In History discussions Maureen used to refer to de Valera as 'that Spaniard'. The O'Hagans, like the Fortingalls, were proud of their pedigree and no doubt this was one of the reasons why Maureen was given a traditional Irish Christian name.

Maureen was fairly large (in terms of bulk), a bit awkward, particularly during exercises in the gym, not particularly gifted academically but managed to keep up, and was a pleasant girl. I think Maureen's mother was glad that she had schoolfriends who worked hard, because it meant that Maureen would also work harder than if she got in with a clique of layabouts. I don't think that Maureen's mother was particularly bright. She had conventional second-hand opinions on most things and seemed to spend any spare time she had reading psychology articles in women's magazines. Whenever I met her she spent her time talking nostalgically about life in India where she was, presumably, a lady of leisure with servants to do everything for her. She was now, to her credit, doing an admin. job in the Town Hall, so it would be unkind on my part to belittle her ability.

Liz had a brother, Malcolm, nearly 3 years older, who was at Eton (his father's school) and only appeared during the school holidays. Maureen had an older sister, Meg, who was in the ATS, so although they were both like myself younger children, they tended to be treated more as adult companions by their respective mothers than might have been the case had there been no war. Because Maureen, Liz and I were on our own at home when our respective mothers were at work, we tended to spend more time with each other than might have been the case had there been no war. We used to have discussions about all sorts of subjects and I'm sure we gained a lot from each other - at any rate I did.

Because we used to interact with each other a lot in discussions in class, and used to sit together at lunch, etc. one of our teachers (I think it was Mrs. Rainham) gave us the nickname 'The Four Musketeers' pointing out that if we took the trouble to read the Dumas novel we would know that in reality there were four and not three. This didn't mean that we were always getting into scrapes or creating havoc. The only scrape that involved us all in getting sore bottoms on the same occasion (of which more anon) was not a scrape at all but something totally ridiculous when Maureen had the ill-luck to light a cigarette to celebrate her 16th birthday when we were having tea and toasted tea-cake in the Copper Kettle café in March 1942.

The only Musketeer that showed any propensity to disobey authority was Louise, no doubt because she was the only one of us living in a normal household. She was the youngest of four children and, although the two oldest were away in the forces, she seemed to feel the need to rebel against parental authority and it cost her dear.

For some reason she had an addiction to smoking and she was always being caught by her father and getting her behind caned. Mum let me smoke whenever I wanted to at home, although she made it clear that this was conditional upon my not smoking in public because "Girls who smoke in public look common". I used to invite Louise to our house after school and on Saturday mornings so that we would do our homework together in Dad's study and I used to let her keep her supply of cigarettes in our house because her father would no doubt have punished her had cigarettes been found in her bedroom.

One Saturday she turned up with three bottles of sherry. The Squires were presumably running low and Milly had 'phoned the wine merchant to say that she was sending Louise to collect two bottles, or whatever. This gave Louise an excuse to pay for an extra bottle out of her own money (the shop mightn't have served her if she hadn't been sent as a message-girl for her parents) which she wanted me to keep. We had a glass each, but at that time I was neither an enthusiastic smoker nor had I developed a taste for sherry. Louise in her 70s is still a smoker and drinks a lot of sweet sherry and red Martini, although I probably down much more wine and Scotch than she does.

We were at the age when we were obviously interested in boys and boys were interested in us. Theories are propounded from time to time about girls developing earlier now than in earlier time. I am sceptical. I think that the pace of development in any child depends more on the individual. Some small children walk and talk much earlier than others, just as the aging process affects some people sooner than others. Climate and race may have some effect. We used to read at school in notes to Romeo and Juliet that Juliet as an Italian girl in medieval Verona would have developed at a much earlier age than an English girl. I have no opinion on such matters because I have never had the curiosity to study any relevant data. Apart from my first-hand knowledge of the ages at which my two daughters had their first periods, my only first-hand knowledge of the subject in based on my memory of how I thought and felt when I was a 14 year old.

My recollection is that pretty well all the girls in our class (although there were a number of notable exceptions) had become interested in boys. Some were no doubt giggly and others would laugh furtively at smutty jokes. Liz and I tended to think that we were the avant garde and modern and we pretended to be very blasé about the whole subject and the other two followed suit. We no doubt thought we were superior to previous generations. Liz had lent me a copy of one of her father's books, Christopher Isherwood's 'Mr. Norris Changes Trains' or 'Goodbye to Berlin' (I can't remember which) in which there was this woman Sally Bowles talking openly in a loud voice about how she had slept with this man or that man the night before, and we convinced ourselves that this was the way 'intellectuals' lived and we had decided that we were going to be 'intellectuals'.

Sally Bowles, of course, became famous after the war in a musical called 'Cabaret', but at the time the Christopher Isherwood books were known only to a minority of readers and 'intellectual' would be a most inappropriate description of her. The word 'intellectual' was, however, very much in vogue at the time and in fact remained so for some years after the war. It tended to become discredited and associated with pimply-faced lefties, but it served our purpose at the time.

Both Liz and I probably had stronger libidos than the average for our class, but this may or may not have been true. Where we differed was that we were both more articulate and didn't have inhibitions in talking about our desires and aspirations. Maureen appeared to go along with this, often bringing us copies of various magazines that her mother apparently took seriously, which had articles talking about inhibitions being a bad thing and all the old clap-trap about people dreaming of narrow passage ways which was supposed to indicate that they were repressed and desperately needed sex.

We all used to day-dream about film stars like Errol Flynn, or Leslie Howard or Clark Gable or whoever coming into our bedrooms, where we would be doing our best to look glamourous so that we could enjoy the romantic love-making that would follow. In practice all we could aspire to was being fondled in the dark by spotty-faced College boys.

We did, however, use our initiative in one or two areas. In one of our animated lunch-time conversations I said it was a stupid convention that girls would have to stand or sit around the dance floor waiting until some boy would pluck up the courage to come and ask us to dance and it probably wouldn't be the boy we wanted to dance with anyway. There was no law to prevent girls from asking boys to dance. It was merely a custom and we could easily change the custom. Maureen dared me to do this at the next dance and I asked her if she would give me half-a-crown if I did. She said "yes" but then we agreed that she wouldn't have to give me half-a-crown if she did the same.

So I walked confidently up to a boy that I liked the look of and said to him "I'd love to dance with you and I'm sure you are not the sort of person who will refuse when a lady asks you" and he couldn't and didn't, although he might have done. Of course it took a bit of nerve and I thought of all sorts of opening gambits before I hit on this one. Nevertheless, I might have chickened out if I hadn't known that the other three Musketeers were watching me closely and unless they did the same I stood to gain 7s/6d, which was a lot of money in a period when many people earned less than £5 a week and the pay of an Army Private was 3s/0d a day.

Of course the other three had to do the same, or each would have to pay me half-a-crown, so they all went up to boys and got them on the dance floor. Whilst most of the boys were no doubt too timid to ask a girl to dance, they were likewise too timid to say no if a girl asked.

I enjoyed my dance. My partner kept apologising that he couldn't dance, so I told him that all he had to do was to hold me tight and remember that dancing was the vertical accomplishment of the horizontal ideal. I probably embarrassed the poor chap more by saying things like this than by asking him to dance. Once we got going I had a lot of dances with him until we had a Paul Jones. Anyway, the four of us succeeded in dancing most of the evening while a lot of our classmates remained sitting or standing patiently waiting to be asked by boys who were too timid.

After this experience the Four Musketeers agreed that we were going to choose our own husbands and not wait passively until some would-be suitor (who might not be the right man at all) went down on his knee to press his suit. I don't suppose that even then we took all this stereotype nonsense seriously about the way gentlemen were supposed to propose to ladies and that ladies could do it only in leap years, but there were few mothers then (and I don't suppose there are many more now) who were likely to tell their daughters that if they really wanted a man for a husband they had to be prepared to use every trick in the book to get him rather than sitting back and waiting for Mr. Right to come along like Father Christmas.

I'm not in fact being accurate. With Mum and Dad it was love at first sight for both of them and so it was to be in my own life, both with David and John, but generally speaking a stereotype of a woman knowing what she wants and getting it is more true to life than a stereotype of a girl passively waiting for Mr. Right to go down on his knees, at any rate amongst the circle of people whom I have known and who have talked about such things.

One area in which our education was unusual for the times was in our knowledge of what is popularly called 'porn', which I think is a singularly inappropriate term. Nowadays magazine racks in most newsagents usually stock a wide collection of publications full of pictures of naked women facing the camera, or of naked men (depending on the market) and anyone can buy copies of books like Lady Chatterley in paperback. So-called adult films are shown on television and can be bought on video. We had no television or video, and censorship of films under the Hays Code (because most films were American) wouldn't permit a husband and wife to be seen in bed together on the grounds that the actor and actress who played the parts (and who in real life were not married to each other) would have to get into bed to make the film. As a result married couples were always shown in single beds, even though the film might be an historic one portraying a 19th Century or 18th Century scene. The only magazines that used to be furtively passed around were Men Only and Lilliput, plus a naturist magazine 'Health & Efficiency'. Lilliput used to have occasional photos of naked women from the side which were of little interest to girls.

Liz, however, had by chance or for some other reason found some very interesting books in her father's library. It was no doubt assumed that as a clergyman he would have a lot of dull collections of old sermons in dingy leather bindings which would fill the top shelves where no-one would even look at the titles. When her father was at home no-one would even go into his study except to dust and Hoover it, but when he was away Liz used to go there to do her homework and she read a lot of his books just as I used to borrow from Dad's books for history.

One day when Liz was on the steps looking at some of the books in the top two shelves, either to dust them or just out of curiosity, she picked out John Cleland's 'Memoirs of Fanny Hill'. She started reading it and couldn't put it down. She had never read any book like it and neither had I when she lent it to me. Nowadays it is a cheap paper-back, but in those days such books used to be retailed at high prices by specialist booksellers and often bound to the specification of the purchaser in a dull cover with a misleading name on the spine.

Although the book is no doubt classified as 'porn', the Memoirs of Fanny Hill are highly readable. Some 250 years after it was first published it remains a robust piece of 18th Century writing and for me, when I first read it, was a far more useful piece of education than any Freudian nonsense that was being pushed around. It enabled me at an early age to feel that my thoughts and desires were perfectly normal and nothing to feel guilty about and that human beings hadn't changed very much over the centuries.

I don't think I ever met Canon Gundry, but I've always respected him as an enlightened and intelligent member of the Church of England hierarchy and I don't think he was by any means unique. Liz's researches enabled her to turn up a number of interesting books that were nearly all on the same shelf. She often found that when she took a book in her hands it would open at the pages that were most frequently read. Right at the back of the last volume of the Complete Works of Thomas Nashe (one of Shakespeare's contemporaries) there is a beautiful poem called The Choice of Valentines which I still enjoy reading. There was also a limited edition of Marlowe's translation of Ovid's Amores, a number of beautiful love 'elegies' translated into wonderful Elizabethan English.

I always think it is unfortunate that so many teenagers are left to pick up an important part of their sex education from the most uncouth, sordid and sometimes cruel bits of latter-day porn because their parents and teachers are too inhibited to introduce them to classical pieces like these which respond to a permanent need for an imaginative and realistic description of what it is like to make love and at the same time can provide a romantic and enriching experience which we all hope to achieve in real life.

I know it's difficult for parents because most of us pretend to go on treating our 13 and 14 year olds as if they were much younger and because it's very difficult to track the phases of mental development, particularly in matters where any teenager is likely to feel secretive and possibly guilty. Of course the problem has no doubt changed. I would expect many sensitive and intelligent 13 and 14 year olds to become quickly bored and irritated by the repetitive banality of so much of the sex they see on television and video screens. This is an area where I am probably too old to adapt to the perception of children born in the late 1980s.

Apart from helping to educate each other and boosting each other's provocative class discussions, the fact that we thought of ourselves and were proud to think of ourselves as the Four Musketeers had various other spin-offs. Three of us have in fact maintained links for most of our lives, so this says something of the strength of the team spirit forged in our school days.

Whilst Louise (who is still my closest friend) might not have been in the front line in some of our escapades, she was a much more determined rebel in others. She may not have been as voracious in her bodily appetites as Liz and I, but she wanted her share of the fun. College boys were a little bit cautious about being too forward with her because they were scared stiff she would tell her father and that he would beat the living daylights out of them. They needn't have feared. Louise was not that sort. She used to come up with 'dares' which neither Liz nor I would have dreamed of, but we were sports and if Louise wanted us to play ball we would.

I remember on one occasion - I think this was when we were in the Upper Fifth - when Louise said "Let's all go to the College dance wearing no knickers. Then we can tease the boys to our heart's delight."

None of the boys who Liz and I danced with needed any encouragement, but if Louise had an idea we would go along for the ride. It was just as well there weren't any boys who were good at jitterbugging, which was an acrobatic dance at that time where the girl was picked up and virtually turned upside down. Anyway, we all agreed to her 'dare'. I don't know how she fared with the boys that she told, but she seemed reasonably happy with her evening.

Soon after the war Maureen married an Australian and we never saw her or heard from her again. Louise and I are as close as ever. Liz has not had a happy life. She made one bad marriage and then at last she appeared to meet Mr. Right. He turned out to be Mr. Wrong. She had a particularly nasty time because he was not only Mr. Wrong but he turned out to be brutal about it and ill-treated her in a unforgivable way, even breaking one of her front teeth in a drunken explosion of wrath.

She is now somewhat embittered, poor girl, but I love her as much as when we were Musketeers together and try, whenever I can, to help her, but it's not easy. We are not talking about money or friendship, but what you can do to help a real friend who has had a series of on-going raw deals. I may have suffered the most tragic loss early on in my life, but I subsequently married a wonderful second husband and I have had the joys of bringing up a family that I love and the stimulus of running a successful business. Liz has not had any of these joys, yet deep down she is a wonderful woman whom I respect and love and I would do anything in my power to help her, but in blunt terms nothing I can do will make a ha'p'orth of difference at this late stage in her life.

CHAPTER 7

ENTERING A NEW WORLD

Soon after I was 14 I entered a new world of the spirit and began to form a view of life which has stood me in good stead ever since. For this I owe an eternal debt of gratitude to Sylvia Rainham who joined the High School staff in September 1940 and became my English teacher.

Had it not been for the war Mrs. Rainham would not have been teaching at all and certainly not in a small provincial city. Although she had obtained a degree in English in the 1920s after studying at Birkbeck College in the University of London, she had, soon after qualifying, married Jonathan Rainham (not his real name), a poet and literary critic who had become something of an impresario in the world of letters, starting magazines to launch the careers of various poets and novelists, so that Sylvia, apart from bringing up two young boys, found herself doing a number of unpaid jobs as editor, treasurer, hostess at literary gatherings and so on. Her husband Jonathan must have had enough money and been prepared to use it to back a number of his ventures, because I can't believe that his literary earnings would have brought him enough to enable them to live as they did during the 1930s.

Sylvia herself wrote a lot for these various magazines, mainly book reviews. The articles that she showed me are well structured, clear and to the point, not like a lot of the literary criticism one reads by critics who are merely anxious to show off their own versatility.

As we were much more formal in those days we always called her Mrs. Rainham, and this is how I shall refer to her. Some teachers were always referred to by their Christian names or nicknames. We always referred, for example, to our gym mistress by her first name Mildred. She wanted to be treated as one of us and was popular with some girls because she gave them practical advice on contraception instead of pretending that this sort of knowledge would only be useful in the distant future when we were married. There was, however, something ludicrous about the way in which Mildred chased after a succession of men. Many of us disliked her other hobby-horse which was her vigorous campaign for the High School to introduce caning as a punishment for girls as it was used in the College for boys. We all assumed (probably rightly) that this was because she wanted to do the job herself. Anyway, we all thought Mildred was a slightly comic name and well suited to her, so we all called her Mildred.

We would address most of the other women teachers as 'Miss' or 'Miss Brown', etc., just as in later years we addressed the College masters as 'sir'. We would always address Mrs. Rainham as Mrs. Rainham because it was considered very ill-mannered to address a married lady as 'Mrs.' on its own and we certainly wouldn't have addressed her as 'madam', a term normally used by shop-assistants to women customers.

Jonathan Rainham was a patriot, unlike many of the avant-garde writers of the 1930s and had joined the RAF Volunteer Reserve. He would have been one of the 'weekend pilots' who played such an important role in the Battle of Britain but for the fact that his eyesight wasn't good enough. Nevertheless, like Dad, he was recalled to his Unit shortly before the war. He survived the war and finished, like John, with the rank of Squadron-Leader.

His absence on war service meant that all his pre-war activities as an editor, impresario, etc., were at an end, although he did continue to write both war poems and articles. Nevertheless Mrs. Rainham found herself alone without work and two boys to bring up on her own. They were at a day school which had been evacuated to Taunton and she went with them in the hope of getting a part-time or perhaps a full-time job as a teacher. It was the classic situation of two schools that didn't match being put together. She wasn't happy with the job opportunity and didn't think that the school where they had finished up had much to offer for her sons. When a vacancy occurred at the High School (the previous teacher had found a much better paid job in a boys' school replacing a man on active service) she applied and must have made a good impression at the interview. Part of the deal was that she would be eligible for greatly reduced fees for her two boys at the College, where they would be day boys. The Governors felt that her family situation would anchor her to the school and there was less risk of her being poached by a boys' school than with many of the other applicants.

Even if she had done nothing for me personally, she was a great success as a teacher. She could motivate the girls and get them enthused so that they worked hard. What's more she got them to enjoy what they were doing. There were years when she succeeded in getting 39 out of the 40 entrants Credits in English Literature. It was not simply a question of enabling the brightest and best to do better. She was able to get the average and below average up to scratch and was respected for this by both parents and school.

Inevitably, however, she aroused professional jealousies and there were always teachers prepared to put down the poison. Mum told me how Mrs. Rainham had put her appointment in jeopardy by talking enthusiastically to some of her Sixth Formers about James Joyce's 'Ulysses' which, even if it was not banned at the time, was regarded by many people as a book they wouldn't have in the house and certainly not the thing to mention in a girls' school. I know that Mum and Milly came to her defence and she kept her job, but that was the work situation with which she had to cope. In 1940 I was merely a member of the most junior class for which she was responsible.

I remember her explaining in her first lesson that although we would have to study a number of set books for School Cert. we needed to read much more widely in order to have a basis of comparison. How could we possibly argue in an essay that Julius Caesar, Macbeth or Hamlet was one of the greatest of Shakespeare's tragedies unless we knew a number of the others. We mustn't think of great authors of the past as if they were monuments in a museum. They were only great because they had something worthwhile to tell us. We had to learn to read what they said as if they were friends talking to us in our own homes, and this is where she produced her lovely quotation: 'It is dawn at Jerusalem while midnight hovers over the pillars of Hercules. All ages are contemporaneous. It is BC let us say in Morocco. The Middle Ages are in Russia. The future stirs already in the minds of the few. This is especially true of literature, where real time is independent of the apparent, and where many dead men are our grandchildren's contemporaries, while many of our contemporaries have been already gathered into Abraham's bosom.'

The author was one of her favourite poets (and in due course became one of mine) Ezra Pound, whom she had met when she had visited Rapallo, where he lived before the war. In 1942 or 1943 he became, like P.G. Wodehouse, persona non grata in the popular US and UK press because he had given some talks on Rome radio when Italy was at war with Britain and America. He was not a Lord Haw-haw. All his income had come from royalties from books published in Britain and America. He was an American citizen and when America entered the war in December 1941 he was refused permission to travel on a diplomatic train out of Italy. How the hell could he live? Even the talks he gave on James Joyce, Eliot, Cummings and other writers made the Italians suspicious that he might be a spy speaking in code, but that is by the bye.

What was fascinating to me was that Mrs. Rainham seemed to have met all these famous people. She had been closely associated with Geoffrey Grigson, editor of New Verse and she talked about Auden, Isherwood, Louis McNeice, Roy Campbell, Frederic Prokosch, etc. as friends. She had been to Paris and met Cocteau and Hemingway, plus a host of other famous literary names in the 1930s. She had even met the great T.S. Eliot and written an article for one of his magazines 'The Criterion'. She knew F.R. Leavis and his wife Queenie Leavis who ran a Cambridge literary magazine called 'Scrutiny'. It was an electrifying experience to have a teacher who had lived in the real world of famous authors and so I enthusiastically started reading a number of the Faber modern poetry books in the library, buying some myself and borrowing books that Mrs. Rainham was kind enough to lend me.

To put her in context, it is worth noting that she succeeded in keeping her distance from the highly charged political views of many writers of the day. She may have done this for diplomatic reasons to prevent her enemies finding a pretext to get her the sack, but I think she was genuine. Her husband had been a patriot, whereas a number of the writers whom she knew were fairly militant lefties, always praising Russia as the workers' paradise, attacking the wicked warmongers in England who served in the territorials and favoured a strong national defence force.

Mrs. Rainham was my English teacher for the five remaining years of my school life. It was thanks to her that I made English Language and Literature the subject that I wanted to read at Oxford, and thanks to her that I decided that I wanted to go to Oxford rather than following Mum to Cambridge. She had a high opinion of a number of Oxford professors at the time, notably Tolkien, Wrenn and F.P. Wilson, although she also spoke very highly of Professor James Sutherland who was then at her old College, Birkbeck. I don't think she thought much of the Leavis's whom she knew. If I hadn't gone to Oxford I wouldn't have met John.

Mrs. Rainham was someone to whom I could turn for help and advice in all sorts of school situations. She did a lot more than teach me English, introduce me to authors outside the syllabus and show me how to get the best out of what I read. I absorbed from her something of her philosophy of life, which was the antithesis of puritanism, but it was not materialistic. She believed firmly that the good things of life are gifts from God (and so do I) to be savoured to the full, although she rarely expressed herself in religious terms.

We have to remember that for many centuries large numbers of people were led (and no doubt this is still the case in many parts of the world) to believe that such activities as making love, wanting to make love, enjoying a good meal, and so on, are temptations of the Devil and that is why Adam and Eve were thrown out of the Garden of Eden (which is factually incorrect) and so being holy or devout meant going around looking as miserable as sin and criticising everybody who looked as if he might be enjoying himself. Mrs. Rainham's words (and I have never succeeded in finding them in any of the authors that she regularly used to quote) were "Live the best moments in life to the full. God gives them to you to enjoy so that you can re-live them in testing times of sadness and endurance."

In my case losing David could have destroyed me as losing Dad virtually destroyed Mum. But I have a good visual memory and whenever I wanted to I could recall some of my wonderful moments with David and I could say to myself, "God brought him to you. This was for a purpose. You will have to do your best on your own for the time being, but if you don't blot your copy-book you'll be reunited with David in eternity."

I have tried not to make too many big blots on my copy-book. However much I may have suffered by losing David I am eternally grateful to the Almighty for bringing him into my life. But if I hadn't had Mrs. Rainham for a teacher, I might never have been capable of interpreting these same events in the way I did. I fervently hope I shall meet her again among the blessed.

On more down to earth matters, there were a lot of things about traditional English education which she disliked. She was glad to have a congenial job (at least I hope she thought it congenial) in a pleasant school away from the London bombing. Her boys were getting a good education at the College for which she was paying substantially reduced fees, but she nevertheless thought traditional English education was 'barbaric'. It was not the teaching standards of which she complained. Her two sons were day-boys. One of her bêtes noire was compulsory games. She regarded it as a tremendous waste of time for intelligent boys to be forced to spend five or six afternoons a week on the rugger field, risking serious injury, if it was a sport in which they were not the least bit interested. There were plenty of other ways of keeping healthy. I would agree with her.

Her other bête noire was corporal punishment. Her oldest son Benjamin (Benjy) had taken a short-cut on a compulsory cross-country run during his second term (Spring Term 1941) no doubt following most of the other boys who were doing the same thing on a day when two prefects had been positioned to tick the names of the boys who ran round the most distant point. All the short-cutters (including Benjy) had been duly summoned to Senior Study the next day and had their bottoms caned by the prefects in the customary manner. It had been a painful experience for Benjy, as it had been for all the other boys in the same boat, but poor Mrs. Rainham was outraged when she saw the stripes on his behind. No doubt he had a lot more and likewise his brother Tim before the two of them ended their schooldays, but she never ceased to cite this particular episode when she was arguing the case against corporal punishment in the High School Policy & Administration Committee of which she was a member. As this subject is covered in a later chapter I will not dwell on it now. I have merely mentioned it at this point in order to set her in context.

Although Mrs. Rainham was the person who had by far the greatest influence on my intellectual and cultural development during my school days, this didn't mean that I agreed with everything she said. I don't think she would have thought much of me if I had. In my school reports she praised me for having an enquiring mind, for not being afraid to be in a minority of one in a class discussion and that when I wanted to argue a case I was conscientious in my search for correct factual information which I was able to marshal and put together effectively.

Many of the ideas that I absorbed in the course of her lessons and discussions out of the class were not her ideas but ideas that she had absorbed in the course of her own education. She was a channel through which I was able to make my initial contacts with many of the great thinkers of the past, and this is what a good teacher should be. She did not stand in the way and try to impose her own personality or impose a dogmatic view. If it hadn't been for Mrs. Rainham it would have taken me decades to discover many of the sources of her ideas and some I would never have discovered. To this day I have never found the source of her wonderful advice about living life's best moments to the full. It was more than advice. It was a philosophy of life which I took to heart and made my own. In my prayers I have thanked her and blessed her memory hundreds, possibly thousands of times for these words of good counsel. If they originated in her own mind in a moment of divine inspiration, as they may well have done, humanity owes her a tremendous debt of gratitude, for she dispensed her counsels freely to many generations of High School girls in the course of a long life as a teacher, which she made her permanent career after the war.

Surprisingly I often bump into people who had done literature courses and all it seems to have meant to them has been mugging up on a few texts and getting to know the sort of model answers that examiners are supposed to like. They seem to have spent most of their time reading chat books by critics turned academics or academics turned critics rather than try to understand the texts for themselves. My principal tutor at St. Hilda's once told me that I had a knack for seeking out the most imbecile remarks made by any literary critic and quoting them in my essays in the hope of making her laugh. My favourite was Rymer who (in the 18th Century) wrote that the moral of Othello was that "a young lady should look to her linen and not run away with blackamoors".

Many people are brought up to think of literature as icing on the cake, a fancy use of words to impress less educated people, and no more. What Mrs. Rainham impressed on us was that we were looking back over centuries, over thousands of years and getting at first hand the insights and precise observations of gifted and enlightened men and women (some possessing genius) on the lot of human kind. If we were studying Macbeth it was to enable us to share Shakespeare's understanding of the minds of a man and a woman who had succeeded in getting to the top and who were struggling to stay there and how they faced practical problems as well as the struggles of their own minds. We have seen many Heads of State (not all of them dictators of the Hitler/Stalin type) who in their own way have been as unscrupulous as Macbeth and Lady Macbeth in getting there, and in due course have been driven out.

There are of course large numbers of pretentious nonentities in the literary field who will string together the clichés and fashionable phrases of the previous generation of writers but who have nothing of substance to offer.

Another of Mrs. Rainham's favourite themes was that poets are the guardians of language. Words are devalued every day, just as money can easily be devalued. Precise terms are picked up in conversation and used in an imprecise way by people anxious to impress their listeners (we can't blame everything on tabloid journalists). Look at the way people in recent years have talked about 'a quantum leap' when all they mean is a big step in one direction or another. Poetry, Mrs. Rainham taught us, is concerned with gists and piths when the precise meaning of each word is important. A lot of so-called poets merely trot out lines that sound like imitations of 'the boy stood on the burning deck', but a great poet is constantly re-working the language in order to provide us with a means of precise communication on matters that are important to us.

One of the most important insights into the proper understanding of great literature, that I absorbed in Mrs. Rainham's classes, was that contact with the past enables us to detach ourselves from present day thought habits and to see them in perspective. Each age tends to wrap itself up in its own form of parochialism and to imagine that it has a monopoly of wisdom in the understanding of human affairs. You read Chaucer's prologue to The Canterbury Tales and you find yourself looking at the world in the way he sees it. In one sense a lot of what he sees is no different from what we see, but there are a lot of points of difference. We may have the motor car, the aeroplane, computers, television, etc., in our own age, but apart from the small number of people who succeed in developing these inventions the vast majority of us don't have to be more intelligent than our medieval counterparts to use these gadgets. Chaucer's monk wouldn't take any longer to learn to drive than anyone who nowadays attends a driving school and he might well have taken less time.

I was fortunate not only with Mrs. Rainham but also in my time at Oxford to have teachers who saw it as their job to help their students to understand the texts of the past. Beowulf for example was a very difficult text to interpret, but someone like Professor Wrenn, who had devoted a large part of his life to the study of the text, played a major part in helping us to understand, and yet he was a very humble man and so was Professor Tolkien. I loved Tolkien's British Academy lecture on 'Beowulf - the Monsters and the Critics', in which he pokes fun at most of the critics. I have read horrifying stories of English lecturers in some universities who have merely used classical texts as a footstool to promote their own egos, subjecting their students to pernicious rubbish with fancy names like 'structuralism'.

An unfortunate tendency in recent decades has been for universities to offer mish-mash courses with fancy names such as 'Literary studies', 'English studies', etc., many of which do no more than to familiarise students with a hierarchy of names of authors that they can trot out in exam papers. It is no substitute for the real benefit of study which is to learn to understand important texts from the past where the student can feel he is conversing with an author with a first-class mind and who will help the student to view the contemporary world with a certain amount of detachment.

Some of my grandchildren have been fed the idea that, if they are going into business, they should read something useful, practical and 'immediately relevant'. There seems to be a belief that if one reads a subject such as Business Studies or Marketing and Finance it will be much more useful in the job market than a degree in English or Greats (which I suppose they now call Classics). The trouble is that most of these apparently fashionable subjects tend to contain little of practical use and much of the information on the course will be obsolete by the time the students are on the job market. One boy, I think a friend of Ruth's, was said to have obtained a university place to study Brewing and Industrial Fermentation. In a declining beer market and an expanding wine market this may not be a subject with a future.

In the late 1960s my Company paid for me to spend three months attending one of the first Executive Development Programmes at the London Business School. Women were very much loners at that time on such courses. Sheila Cross was the only girl on the first two year M.Sc. course. Most of the people attending my type of course had risen to positions of responsibility in their companies and it was interesting to note that those with degrees who had been successful had obtained them in classical subjects. A number had left school at 14 and also been very successful, so that it isn't education that makes people. It is something that can help or hinder them. Fortunately in England we still attach more importance to a person's native ability than to a piece of paper that a person carries round called a Diploma and in this respect we are more intelligent than the Americans or the French.

As a postscript on English as a discipline, I believe that if you study it the way Mrs. Rainham taught me to study it then it helps you to see round corners and to use your imagination to solve problems. Milton Grundy, who developed the concept of the Cayman Islands as a tax haven, bringing untold wealth to a small population that might otherwise have been living near the breadline, was an English scholar. Oliver

Stanley, who became an Inspector of Taxes and who for many years was the Times and Sunday Times guru on taxation, was an Oxford English scholar, and so is my present editor. Other examples abound:

The final and most useful nugget from my days in Mrs. Rainham's class-room was the phrase that 'education is about getting wise in the most hard-boiled and basic sense in which that word is used' in the context of which she cited Odysseus as the perfect example of an educated man. He was never at a loss and he managed not only to help the Greeks win the Trojan war but to get home and re-conquer his kingdom because he knew how to use his loaf. He could apply every bit of technology and information that he had learnt whether it be in the cave of Polyphemus or in knowing how to placate the supernatural. In later years I found this same piece of advice in a book by Ezra Pound, but if it hadn't been for Mrs. Rainham I wouldn't have discovered it until long after I had finished at university.

Because she frequently referred to the Odyssey as one of the greatest books ever written and to Odysseus as the man who had learnt to use his loaf in all sorts of tricky situations, I made a serious attempt to read it once I no longer had to concentrate on the set books first for School Cert. and then Higher Cert. I was fortunate in getting the W.H.D. Rouse translation (I was never a Greek scholar) but I read a number of others including Rieu and T.E. Lawrence. It is a book I have re-read more than any other. Of course I knew bits of the story when I was a child, but as I have got older I have seen my own life more and more as an odyssey and I don't think I am unusual.

It is a book that tells you more about the nature of the world in which we live and the sort of people who live in it than almost any other book I can think of and yet it was written 3,000 years ago or thereabouts. We don't know when it was written down. We know nothing about its author except that he was a genius, although people have pretended from time to time that he didn't exist, just as they have pretended that Shakespeare didn't exist. One of the witty lecturers (mainly on Chaucer) of my Oxford days was Neville Coghill. He used to quote the clerihew:

> *Homer*
> *is a misnomer*
> *All the evidence goes to indicate*
> *That he was a syndicate.*

The other book, or as I prefer to call it, compendium, which tells us more than we can learn anywhere else about human nature at the level of those human beings who concern themselves with their ultimate destiny, is the Old Testament. I am deliberately separating it from the New Testament in which we are addressed directly by Our Lord. In my childhood we all grew up knowing the stories of Abraham and Isaac, Jacob and Esau, David and Goliath, Samson and Delilah and many others. They give us the most wonderful insights into what jargon-psychologists would now describe as human behavioural patterns. Some of these superb writings date back over a period of between 3,000 and 4,000 years, whereas most of the jargon comments of present-day psychologists will be forgotten before the psychologists in question are themselves buried.

Kids probably get puzzled and confused by some of the stories. How can they possibly be expected to treat a story which describes the way in which Jacob, a younger brother, cheats his poor blind father Isaac (Jacob being aided and abetted by his mother Rebecca) as a moral story, when it is highly immoral. Jacob was a cheat and had no justification for cheating. If the story is uncoupled from the attempt to teach moral behaviour and is instead regarded as a vivid and realistic portrait of the way human beings behave, then you learn a lot more. This is what you understand when you read the Old Testament as an adult, because it is good literature in the sense that it is a remarkably vivid and accurate way of presenting the way people behave in the situations in which they find themselves.

One of my hobby-horses over the years has been the importance of stressing the Old Testament as a common heritage shared between Christians and Jews. I am not saying this simply because I have a Jewish son-in-law, and have therefore spent more time than I might otherwise have spent trying to get to grips with current Jewish religious practice (and there are as many, if not more, variations between different branches of Judaism as there are between different branches of Christianity), but much more because I feel that as a nation we are losing an insight and familiarity with the Bible that we once had.

I can remember once in Market Square hearing an urchin shout out when a College boy appeared wearing his House Colours blazer (when a boy had distinguished himself in rugger or cricket matches against other Houses he might be awarded what were known as House Colours, which conferred the right to wear a blazer displaying the colours of the heraldic emblem of his House - a great status symbol): "Look, like Joseph, a coat of many colours!".

In those days a working knowledge of the main Bible stories was almost universal. It was imparted at an early age in schools of virtually all denominations and in Sunday Schools to which most working class parents as well as middle class parents were keen to send their children. Attendance at Sunday School was often seen by parents as something that might help the children to get on as well as making them more Godly.

It would also keep them out of mischief as well as giving the parents some time to themselves on Sunday afternoons. A vast army of unpaid volunteers, many of them professional people as well as small shop-keepers and teachers, gave their time freely, and I am sure the children benefited from these contacts with adults other than their own immediate teachers in many ways apart from the biblical knowledge which they gained.

This knowledge provided a universal sphere of reference. It didn't matter to whom you were talking, you could trot out an analogy from a well-known biblical story and take it for granted that the other person or people would immediately understand. The fact that you can no longer do so is a sad reflection on the way we as a Nation have been steadily jettisoning an important strand in our cultural tradition. We have not only become a more ungodly society where churches have to be locked because of the risk of sacrilege (virtually unknown when I was young) but a more philistine society in the way that Oscar Wilde used the word.

One of the saving graces in this decline has been the fact that traditional animosities between different Christian sects have disappeared (there are of course exceptions such as Ian Paisley) and there is a much greater readiness of denominations to focus on the things they agree about rather than the matters which were the subject of discord in times past. I know this at first hand because two of my sons became Catholics when they married Catholic wives and I always attend mass in their respective churches when I visit their families.

My daughter Suzanne (the barrister) married a Jewish husband, Simon. He does not in fact practise his religion and, although I think he alienated some members of his family by 'marrying out', I think John and I have succeeded over the years in establishing a good rapport with many members of his family.

In our case, close family ties have played an important part in building up a good rapport between denominations, but it doesn't always work. It has to be accompanied by mutual respect and not be one-sided. You have also to recognise the tremendous amount of common ground (e.g. the Ten Commandments) between Christianity and Judaism. Man needs a religious framework in order to get some bearings on where he comes from and where he fits in to the universe and if you take away a genuine religious framework you leave most of the population a prey to the first impostor that knows how to exploit the gullibility of the mass of human kind, knowing as they do that man is essentially a religious animal.

I've entitled this chapter 'Entering a New World' and in it I have tried to explain my particular good fortune in having an English teacher during the important years of my spiritual development and who introduced me to the concept of world literature, explaining how truly great creative writers and artists used their God-given talents to try to understand and explain the ways of God to man, to enable us to achieve a better understanding of the world in which we live and the people with whom we have to live.

If I've strayed from my narrative by taking time to describe some of the ideas with which I was starting to grapple at this period of my life, it is because what went on inside (what still goes on inside) my head is as important in my life story as many of the events in the outside world to which I had to react. The way I responded to many challenges at critical moments in my life resulted in part from the way I perceived them, although instinct and intuition have, as with everyone else, accounted and account for much of what I have done and do.

In my next chapter I move from the domain of my spiritual and cultural awakening to another type of awakening, what in clinical terms would now be called my 'sex life'. Here again, girls can be fortunate or unfortunate in the ideas that are put into their heads at this period in their lives. I was fortunate in being left to grow up with the view that my bodily desires were normal and natural, so I suffered no inner conflict or feelings of guilt. I was also fortunate in growing up in a social context where no-one forced me to have sex before I wanted it or was ready for it. In fact I probably had to wait for about two years from the time of my first strong yearnings until the most wonderful first time that any girl can dream of. This was no doubt because I lived in a sheltered world where my only male contacts were schoolboys who were not particularly enterprising in such matters. I suspect that in the more 'liberated' world in which my grandchildren have grown up I would have been subjected (voluntarily I am sure) to an 'early learning' experience which would no doubt have been satisfying in physical terms but I fear would have left me blasé and, who knows, unable to muster the intensity of the spiritual and emotional ecstasy of my first time with David. I am not preaching, because I had absolutely no merit in the matter and I have always been eternally grateful to God for his kindness in this wonderful period of my life which I shall describe fully in Chapters 16 and 17.

CHAPTER 8

A DIFFERENT KIND OF EDUCATION

The war years brought a number of permanent changes to daily life in the High School and the College, although very little notice was taken of them at the time. Pre-war most of the High School teachers had been spinsters, many of the generation that had lost the chance of marrying as the result of the carnage of World War I. The professional and middle classes probably suffered the greatest proportionate loss. Their family ethos tended to make them produce the first volunteers and the same ethos required them as junior officers to lead their men "over the top".

Most of these women were not embittered when we knew them. Teaching for them had become a calling rather than a job. They would do anything for their pupils and we owe them a debt that many of us would only comprehend when we became involved in the education of our children and grandchildren. In the debunking 60s it became fashionable to mock such stereotypes as Jean Brody because the writers were only concerned with making a story out of private personalities rather than focusing on what was important in their lives - their very real contribution to the education and quality of life of the next generation - just as some current biographers tend to devote large chunks of their Lives of the Great to unimportant trivia and minor peccadilloes - many of them invented.

As soon as war was declared virtually all the College teachers who had been active in the territorials left to join their units. With the College's strong patriotic tradition, territorial recruitment had been encouraged both by the Governing Body and the Headmaster, particularly since Hitler came to power. As the same Governing Body ran both schools it knew the capabilities of the senior High School staff and could offer them jobs in the College without worrying about the risk of employing people who were unknown quantities. Traditionally the College had been able to pick and choose its young recruits and groom them in junior positions before entrusting them with senior posts. This meant that there were soon many gaps to be filled in the High School. There were, however, substantial reserves of unused talent. Many masters' wives had good academic qualifications and many mothers with children at the College, the High School, or both, were qualified to teach at senior level - many with Oxford and Cambridge degrees. The jobs had not existed pre-war. Although teachers' salaries were low (many were earning salaries of £200 - £300 a year) the jobs were congenial and could offer worthwhile inducements - what we might nowadays call 'perks' - such as specially reduced fees. Boarding fees at the College were around £120 a year. For families surviving on the low Service pay of the absent fathers, these fee reductions were a godsend.

The result was that a substantial proportion of our teachers were much more involved in the family lives of the girls and boys at both High School and College. The staff shortages also meant that the Governing Body started combining the teaching of a number of subjects in both schools. At the start many girls attended Chemistry and Physics classes at the College and this probably led to more girls opting for these subjects - for whatever reasons. Teaching in Latin, Modern Languages, Chaucer and History gradually went the same way.

Pre-war the College had been much more monastic and there had been very little contact with the High School except when a brother in one had a sister in the other, or for furtive rendezvous between the more enterprising older boys and High School girls. Most of the senior boys at that time were pretty gauche in such matters and didn't have much to say when they met a girl, whatever desires might be popping up inside them. In any case, the awareness of such desires probably made them feel guilty and hence even more sheepish.

Mildred, our gym mistress who was unmarried, but reputed to have a string of boyfriends who came to see her when they were on leave from the various Services, was said to favour closer links with the College as a means of providing a better social (and probably sexual) education. On top of this she was the teacher most trusted by the senior girls as someone who would never pass on anything said in confidence and who appeared to give sound practical advice. Instead of preaching about restraint and remaining pure before marriage, she gave practical advice on contraception and avoiding VD (venereal diseases - a subject of much Government publicity at the time). It may have seemed good Girl Guide - be prepared - stuff at the time, with repeated warnings of "Don't leave it to the boys or even to the men - they are surprisingly inept in such matters". This may seem run of the mill stuff today, but in the early 1940s it was probably light years ahead of most current practice. She was a teacher to whom many of us owed a debt of gratitude, even if we didn't realise it until later in life. She did have a not so pleasant side to her character, but more of that anon.

The appointment of a young, good-looking Music master at the College, who for some reason was classified as medically unfit and hence exempt from military service, provided a stimulus to Mildred's enthusiasm for social contact between the two schools. She obviously had a crush on Alec Horsman and so did many of the senior girls who met him. He was not a fuddy-duddy Music master, but one of those people who enjoyed entertaining the boys playing jazz tunes on the piano and Mildred soon got him interested in starting a ballroom dancing class (it could have been his idea) and the start of a tradition of College dances each term in Big School.

At that time some of the girls attended dancing classes, most of which tended to be run on an amateurish basis in upstairs rooms above a small cake shop - a café where middle class women (who had no jobs) met to gossip over morning coffee or afternoon tea. An instructor, who might be the proprietor, attempted to explain steps to a background of Victor Silvester records played on 78 gramophones. For partners the girls had to dance with each other. Dancing was considered a useful accomplishment, like playing the piano, if the girls were to stand a reasonable chance of finding a suitable husband when the time came.

The chances of a boy being able to dance reasonably by the time he was 18 were pretty remote. The idea of boys dancing with each other was absurd and probably immoral and it wouldn't have worked. In the schools where there was a dancing class one would typically see 20, 30 or more boys advancing across the floor trying to practise the steps that were being taught by the instructor. And those who attended the classes ran the risk of being ridiculed by their classmates for being sissies. As a result they tended, in later life, to stand around talking to each other and looking gormless when they attended formal dances, while their expectant dancing partners sat around the wall feeling bored and frustrated, noticing the way they were eyed up from a distance and describing the experience as being in a cattle market.

Both Mildred and Alec had lived this experience and felt that they could do something to bring about a change. They had considerable success in the two schools for which they worked.

To start with they needed enthusiasm and the powers of persuasion, which they had. The Headmaster gave his consent (necessary because the dances and classes were to take place on College premises) and the Headmistress (although her consent was not needed as all the events were taking place on College premises) expressed her approval and said she would come to the first dance. In fact she came to every dance, making it known that she expected to dance. Thus the number one priority for the organisers was to prepare a rota with a sufficient number of compulsory volunteers who would invite Miss Blantyre to dance. Presented as a challenge, the dance committee got its 'volunteers'. She was a voluminous, determined person who knew where she was going. One College Sixth Former afterwards remarked that when his turn came to ask her to dance the polka (which he claimed he had never tried to dance in his life) he had to hold on for dear life as she bounced around the floor and he kept thinking of himself as Sisyphus holding on to the rock that would at any moment come tumbling down the hill.

For the rest of us it was the dancing classes in the evenings at the College that had the most to offer. We were the keenest. When we saw Alec we all wanted to dance with him and he did his best to oblige. He used to do demonstrations with Mildred, so that we were all convinced that they were lovers and so we all dreamed of being able to dance the tango, but we were all told that we had to start at the beginning. The practical problem was that although there were a lot more boys in the College (being a boarding school which took a certain number of day boys) there were a lot more girls at the classes, so some of us had to dance with each other.

In the course of these lessons I was asked to dance by Jacko (in those days the name given to everyone called Jackson). I liked his attentions but I didn't particularly like Jacko. He had a lewd grin permanently on his face and no doubt thought he might get somewhere with me. I was only 15 and he may have been 17. I subsequently came to know a lot more about him when I was 20 and an undergraduate and we had a number of one-night stands together (it didn't merit the term "affair") but more of that anon.

Jacko was a day boy at the College. His parents were agricultural auctioneers. He was different from the run of the mill sons of Service officers, clergymen, teachers, civil servants and solicitors who appeared to constitute the bulk of the College population. He probably had local female contacts in the village where he lived and I later learned that he had a girl cousin, two years older, who taught him quite a bit.

Whatever the explanation, he was more enterprising than most of the other boys who turned up at the dancing classes and who (as I saw them) stood sheepishly around even though I desperately wanted to dance with a number of them. As I have explained at Chapter 6, we Four Musketeers used to dare each other to ask boys to dance, but that didn't mean we had the self-assurance to take the initiative on our own whenever we wanted to dance with a boy at every dancing class.

Jacko, however, danced close. At the slightest pretext his cheek came against mine whenever the opportunity occurred and it was obviously clear to him that I didn't recoil. At the slightest pretext his right hand moved down to my bot or took a firm grip of my left thigh and no opposition clearly sent the signal that I wanted it as much as he did, although he may not have been intelligent enough to comprehend the full extent of my desires.

Because I had to cycle home and he, as a day boy, had to cycle back to his village three miles away, he made a detour to see that his "young lady" was safely home. At 15 it was flattering to my self-esteem. When we got to our drive we put our bicycles against the gate and in the shadow of the yew hedge I had my first kiss. What's more, when I had my arms round his neck his right hand shot like lightning under my dress and gripped the left side of my bottom firmly through my knicks, the ends of his fingers exerting on and off pressures that helped to make me feel increasingly randy, although at that time I didn't know what the word meant. Then his hand drifted down and wedged its way between my thighs, just about the stocking tops and below the knicker elastic. I relaxed and then squeezed.

In later years I have always felt that this initial contact is the key. You know straight away whether a warm, firm clasp of a handshake gives you confidence or whether a wet, cold, clammy hand like scales of a dead trout on a fishmonger's counter would give you confidence in an insurance salesman's intentions. Likewise, it was what made a man decide whether the touch of the skin on your inside leg would make it worth venturing his fingers inside your knicker elastic - or so he would have done when faced with the clothes that we wore in the 1940s. One French doctor, whose right hand was equally determined, told me that sex attraction was all a question of 'épiderme'.

There is a lot to be said for his view. I think girls who wear tights miss out on this important initial step, except in the Summer months if they are intelligent enough to go bare-legged. And the men miss out a lot more, which is why when women who wear stockings and ostentatiously cross their legs to show they are wearing stockings have a much better chance of getting the man they want into bed than those that wear tights, except for work or workaday activities.

If one believes what one reads in the newspapers, girls can now get any man they want into bed without all the amorous preliminaries that were so important to us in the 1940s. If I had my time again I think I would still prefer all the conventions I grew up with as a better filtering system. By the time you have made love with a man, or let him make love to you for the first time, you had a high level of confidence that he was someone you really wanted and were less likely to be disappointed, even though you sometimes were.

Jacko's right hand moved slowly and imperceptibly up between my legs until it began to massage ever so gently my most sensitive area. The intensity of my desire and its concentration in one part of the body may have come as a surprise to him, but that was what he was hoping for. At that stage of my development many girls that I knew, or so they said, had their sensuality spread more evenly in other parts of their bodies and it took a period of successful love-making to focus their sensual expectations where it mattered.

Although I am very sure (judging by his later ineptitudes) that Jacko had never made love to a girl before this first encounter on a cold night in our front garden, his hands must have acquired some useful experience groping their way into the sensitive areas of other girls or women. Either that or he was much more intuitively intelligent than I believe. 'Groping' tends nowadays to be used as a disparaging term, but at that time many women had to make do with it (as did many men) as their sole sensual relief until their marriage. And for middle class girls planning professional careers and who ended up marrying men who, having spent a number of years in the forces, wanted to take a degree, acquire professional qualifications and settle into a proper job, their first proper love-making was in their late 20s. In fact, I had a close friend, an art teacher, who didn't marry until she was 30 and often spoke to me about the strain of the 15 years love-making she had lost. She was attractive, very flirtatious, had a large number of boyfriends (the word was used differently in those days - it often meant no more than an occasional social escort), many at the same time, whom she no doubt encouraged to grope to their heart's content, although I would be surprised if most of the men she went out with needed much encouragement. I think she was genuine and remained a virgin until her wedding night. Most of us were genuinely afraid of becoming pregnant and some of us (but not me) still believed the old wives' tale that it would be difficult for a girl to find a decent husband unless she remained a virgin until her wedding night.

'Groping' (the word was not in current use at that time) and the 'everything but' formula provided the best consolation prize that we could get. If you were unattached and didn't get into quasi-marital situations at an early age, as happens today, most warm-blooded girls could enjoy being kissed and groped by a reasonable selection of boys and men. In some ways this border experience of the opposite sex had educational advantages. Its main drawback was that it caused many of us to build up excessive expectations about the physical side of marriage. Given that I was only 17 when I married David, I was an exception to this general rule.

I may not have been the first girl to be groped by Jacko. I was 15. I may not have thought very much of him as a boy in other respects, but he had the nerve to try his luck where no other College boy had shown any enterprise and no way could I have hidden from him the heat of the fire he was stoking. Once he had found a way, he was a frequent visitor. If I mention Jacko in a number of later chapters, it is no doubt because this first encounter did establish some sort of a bond between us, although in many respects I could never treat him seriously. The Jackos of this world have their uses, and one could even say that every girl should have one.

Watching Georges and Marianne and reading books like Fanny Hill had played a useful part on this side of my education, but I was still 'on the outside looking in'. I knew far less about the clinical niceties and so-called techniques that nowadays fill modern manuals and generate cash for their promoters, but I knew what mattered and I realised that I had reached the stage when I desperately wanted to start the practical side of this important part of my education - if I could do it safely.

Finally I have to remind you that the habits and sexual behaviour I have just described were those of a particular social circle in a sheltered school world. It is the only world I knew at that age. I am not making any claim to knowledge about the way girls grew up in other circles such as industrial towns, where they left school and went to work at 14, which was then the school leaving age.

CHAPTER 9

"THREE OF THE BEST FOR BOADIE"

One element of school life in the 1940s merits comment - at any rate as an introduction to one of my escapades. Public schoolboys were caned for a vast number of offences, some of them trivial. Schoolgirls were not (at any rate not in my school) but if their fathers were brought up in the 'spare the rod and spoil the child' tradition like Dad and Mr. Squires, we didn't escape, as I have explained in the chapter on my childhood.

Those of us in the Lower Fifth up to the Sixth forms who attended a number of classes in the College were inevitably made aware at close range of this aspect of school life. A system for the administration of justice existed, which was largely run by prefects. In the boarding houses the prefects would meet once or twice a week to review the list of defaulters that each had prepared, decide who they were going to punish, and the 'defaulters' would be sent for from their various dormitories, usually during the half-hour before lights-out. The defaulters were called in one at a time, or in groups, and given a chance to mount whatever defence they could muster and then sent to wait outside. Those who were to be punished were called in and given two, three or four stripes according to the gravity of the offence. Part of the punishment was waiting outside listening to the very audible noise of the cane doing its work on whoever was inside, knowing that it would soon be one's own turn. The boys were all in pyjamas and woe betide them if they tried to wear anything underneath, or stood up before they had been given their full count.

Both of our sons were at the College in the 60s. They were boarders and the same regime was still in operation at that time.

For School, as opposed to House offences, the school prefects would forgather on certain afternoons between lunch and afternoon school and dispense discipline in like manner in a room called Senior Study, which was never used as a study and where the sole piece of furniture was said to be a low armchair with wooden arms which provided the anchorage for defaulters to grip.

Boys could find themselves caned for all sorts of trivial things such as taking a short-cut on one of the standard school runs (games were compulsory at that time) on a day when a prefect was ticking off names at the furthest point, being a few seconds late for a game, and so on.

The big blitzes, as they were called, used to be for smoking and being seen in pubs. The girls coming back to school in the afternoon might see long queues of anxious boys outside Senior Study and see some of their classmates shifting their weight uneasily from hip to hip during afternoon school and we breathed a sigh of relief at the fact that we were girls. Some girls used to take a malicious delight in giving a not so playful smack to a boy when she knew he was feeling tender, possibly when he was trying to kiss her and she wasn't so keen.

Anyway, this was the folklore and it probably didn't differ very much from that of most boys' boarding schools at the time. Different schools used different euphemisms, but they all meant the same thing. Some schools talked of tanning, others of being beaten. In the College they talked about 'going for the whacks', and Walford Squires, who as Second Master dealt with the most serious cases, was known as 'Old Whackers' and had the most fearsome reputation.

Whilst I have never had strong views on the pros and cons of caning boys (or girls for that matter) in schools, I do think this is a matter that should be decided by the schools and the parents as customers of the schools and not by some governmental body or some kangaroo European Court of Human Rights in Strasbourg or wherever.

A good example of a situation where a cane had its uses was when a High School girl was caught shoplifting in W.H. Smith, who reported it to the Headmistress, who in turn referred the matter to the Governors with a suggestion that the girl might be expelled. The girl in question was intelligent and had a good school record. This happened about a year before the war and Dad thought it was a bit unfair to ruin a girl's school career by expelling her when a College boy would probably have been given 'six of the best' by Walford Squires or whoever, and that would be the end of it. As there was no provision for corporal punishment in the High School, Dad suggested that as he knew the girl's father who was a sensible sort of chap, he would speak to him and suggest the obvious solution. From all accounts the father treated her as severely as if she had been sent to someone like Walford, and that was the end of the matter. Neither he nor the girl, nor anybody at the school wanted to broadcast the fact that a girl had been caught shoplifting, but the Governors knew they had a practical solution should such problems occur again.

If there were any similar problems I never got to hear of them, but by the Summer of 1941 different concerns were being voiced both by teachers and a number of others. With so many absent fathers and most of the mothers doing full-time jobs (quite a number of the jobs were voluntary) a lot of girls were said to be unruly and difficult to control.

I remember Mum coming home late one evening because a school committee meeting had gone on for hours and hours and saying, "If only Dad had been in the chair he would have sorted the whole thing out in no time."

The committee was in fact the High School Policy and Administration Committee which included a number of High School staff as well as representatives from the governing Council. Mum was the Committee secretary.

Mildred Pierce, the somewhat masculine gym mistress (who was in fact very feminine in other parts of her life) had repeated for the hundredth time her long-standing suggestion that troublesome girls should be sent to the gym and she should be authorised to give them 'a bit of stick'. Mrs. Rainham would always rise to this particular bait. She had been militantly anti all forms of corporal punishment from the time she had seen the stripes on her eldest son's (Benjy) behind for doing no more than taking a short-cut on a run. She went into a tirade against the scope for abuse by bullying teachers and prefects. Everyone seemed to be letting off steam. According to Mum, the Headmistress and Milly just sat back with their arms folded. They had heard all the arguments on both sides so many times before. It was known that these two teachers would be at daggers drawn on almost every conceivable subject.

Eventually the Headmistress intervened and said, "We are not here to debate the pros and cons of giving girls the cane. We are here to address a problem. Has anyone got a constructive solution?"

That shut them up, at any rate for a time, but it didn't solve the problem. After the meeting, Milly in her usual pragmatic way suggested a solution: "Why don't we deal with this matter entirely outside the school. If parents are having problems with their girls, I'll get Walford to deal with them in the way he has dealt with my two girls. The College pays him for caning troublesome boys, so he can do a bit of voluntary work with any girls that are sent to me on Saturday mornings, or at least on the Saturdays that he is not away with the First Fifteen."

I breathed a sigh of relief. I couldn't imagine Mum getting so angry with me that she would send me to Walford for punishment. She treated me as an adult, let me smoke when I liked and didn't mind what I did with Jacko when we shut ourselves away in Dad's study for a kiss and cuddle.

But there was a sting in the tail to this proposal, which proved to be a very painful sting in my tail nearly a year later, but more of this anon. Teachers were to be authorised on an individual basis to write to the parents of a girl who was being unruly or difficult, with the recommendation that the said girl should be suitably dealt with. In those days virtually all parents were very respectful of school instructions and requests, and would automatically send their daughters to be caned by Walford Squires if this were politely suggested to them.

The idea didn't get off the ground straight away. Even in those days schools were concerned about the risks of legal actions for assault and battery, or whatever. The normal terms on which boys were accepted for admission to the College, for example, put the College in loco parentis, although this point was considered to be established in Common Law at the time. In other words a school could exercise the powers of correction and discipline that a parent would be expected to exercise and a parent had (or was assumed to have) the right to chastise his or her child in any manner that he or she might think appropriate.

College boys were given the right of appeal to their House Master when they were told they were going to be caned by a prefect and they were even expected to say "I want to be caned/beaten/whacked or whatever by you" to whoever was going to administer the punishment, and believe it or not they all did.

Walford was an old hand at the game (he had been caning boys since he had been appointed a prefect in his own school at the age of 17) but he wasn't going to play this new game unless somebody would organise the paper trail (he would have used other words because this jargon phrase did not come into use until relatively recently). This was done. In appropriate cases the teacher would write a letter (countersigned by the Headmistress) to the parents suggesting that they might care to take appropriate disciplinary action and this enclosed a draft letter for the parents to send to Mrs. Squires, and so on.

When these arrangements were announced at Speech Day in the Summer Term 1941, a day or two before letters went to all parents, there was consternation among the girls, particularly among those who spent a lot of time at the College and knew how severely some boys were caned. They assumed they were now to be brought fully under College discipline and they knew that Mr. Squires had the most fearsome reputation when boys were sent to him to be caned.

As the Headmistress had hoped, the mere threat was enough to achieve a significant improvement in school discipline without any girls having to be caned. And so it was until the end of the Summer Term and almost to the end of the Autumn Term.

The catalyst for change came with a combined College and High School production of The Gondoliers. In those days amateur productions of Gilbert and Sullivan operas could be crowd pullers. You didn't need to have the star performers necessary to attempt, say, The Marriage of Figaro or some serious opera.

The performance was to be in the old Town Hall as one of the high spots for a 'Wings for Victory' week. These were attempts to boost National Savings, which were in turn an important part of Government policy aimed at mopping up money that might otherwise be chasing the very limited goods available in the shops and causing inflation.

Alec Horsman, the senior Music master at the College, was in charge. He was a handsome young man who, for some medical reason, had not been called up, and it was an open secret that Mildred Pierce had a crush on him. So did a lot of the girls.

Mildred had volunteered her services as stage and properties manager, and in her typical sergeant major-ish style had dragooned a number of High School 'compulsory volunteers' that she could order about. It seemed a fun thing to be in on, so many of us were involved as assistant this, that, or the other.

Where the girls went the boys would follow. The boarding houses were normally shut up like fortresses in the evenings but boys found it easy to get leave to go out through the House Master's front door if they claimed to be singing in or otherwise involved in this mammoth production. As a result a considerable number of boys and girls who had no useful role to fulfil spent the time in the traditional manner. The old Town Hall, apart from having a stage and an auditorium, was something of a rabbit warren of corridors and little rooms in which the boys who had found willing accomplices (and vice versa) could kiss and fondle in the dark. If the light was turned out it didn't matter that there were two, three or more couples doing the same thing. The only stupid thing some of them did was to smoke at the same time. Quite how any boy managed to hold a cigarette when both his hands had more interesting things to do, beats me, but I can't believe the only people who were smoking were girls.

Fortunately I had decided that doing odd jobs for The Gondoliers was a waste of time. There was nothing useful for me to do. If I wanted to smoke I could do so at home. Mum had no objections. If I wanted to canoodle with Jacko, he came round to our house and I went into Dad's study and I knew that Mum would never disturb us. I was thus spared the troubles that followed.

It was said that Mildred was becoming irritable because jobs were not being done. She was complaining that vast numbers of girls appeared to be wandering around the old Town Hall doing nothing in particular and so the day before the dress rehearsal she did a walkabout, smelt smoke in the corridors, quickly sensed what was going on and told the head prefect he ought to do something.

On the night of the dress rehearsal a number of school prefects were instructed to post themselves in front of every door, and at the agreed signal open every door and switch on the lights and prevent anyone from escaping. The embarrassed girls were usually much more concerned with pulling their skirts down than worrying whether or not they were holding cigarettes, and I don't suppose many of them were.

The boys' names were all taken and Mildred, bless her cotton socks, went from room to room taking all the girls' names.

The next day the girls in question had the doubtful pleasure of learning that their canoodling partners of the night before had all be given 'four of the best' (more if they failed to stay down) and some of them no doubt felt guilty about getting off scot-free. But they didn't.

Mildred had at last scented victory. The High School, she explained to the Headmistress, would lose all credibility if it failed to act. The boys had all been punished and it would be grossly inequitable to do nothing about the girls.

So in due course 20 or so apprehensive girls reported to the Squires' house on Saturday morning dressed as per the instructions which specified trousers, only one pair of pants and no padding. They reported in groups of three or four at half-hourly intervals from 9 o'clock onwards as the guinea-pigs of the new system.

From all accounts they 'didn't let the side down'. In those days we hadn't dreamed up propagandist terms like Women's Lib, but we had our pride. We could hold our own with the boys on the work front and we believed that we could take it on the punishment front as well as the boys, even if we were shuddering in our pants at the thought of the ordeal to come (I speak from a later experience). The boys were no different. If a girl stood up, clutched her backside and yelled like fury after a particularly painful shot, so did lots of boys, but she would grit her teeth and get back down again until she had had her quota and was allowed to go.

I don't think Walford let them off more lightly than the boys, although he may have been more indulgent on certain points of etiquette. Boys would have had an extra stripe for every time they got up to a maximum of six, whereas none of our lot had more than four, but that was more than enough for a first-timer. If a girl had masterly self-control she would have got away with three, but Walford made sure that none of them did.

They all must have been pretty sorry for themselves for the rest of Saturday, and were no doubt sitting down rather gingerly on the Sunday, but by Monday most of them were acting like heroines showing off their 'campaign stripes' in the changing room when they were getting ready for gym lessons or games.

Obviously my turn was going to come, otherwise I would not have spent time writing the initial part of this chapter, but before we get to that point I need to slot in some other bits of background.

The post Gondoliers 'blitz' sent shock-waves around the school. This was no doubt what was intended. Whilst the heroines could boast (whilst hoping to God they would never have to make a second visit to Walford's study) the rest of the senior school who were familiar with College discipline were worried stiff. If only one girl had been punished for doing something obviously wicked it wouldn't have been so bad, but it was obvious to all but the stupidest that most of the girls who had been whacked by Walford had not done anything wrong. They had just been unlucky in the way that most of the College boys who were whacked were unlucky.

Some of the girls stupidly thought that they could protect their backsides by wearing their grandmothers' flannel drawers and sewing in two or three extra layers of flannel, believing that this wouldn't be the first thing that Milly would spot as they came through her front door. All they achieved by their enterprise was the immediate order to go up to Louise's room and change into a spare pair of Louise's pyjama trousers with nothing to be worn underneath. And if a girl was wearing pyjama trousers when she went into Walford he knew damn-well that it was because she had been a cheat, and this would certainly earn her an extra stripe. But the message never seemed to get around, so there were always girls who thought they would try. No doubt some of them were so desperate that their brains weren't working properly at such times.

The other noticeable factor was the high proportion of girls who were done for smoking related offences. After The Gondoliers episode Mildred had persuaded a number of her colleagues to take a tough line on smoking, which was forbidden not only in the school but anywhere in public (it was considered 'common'). However, even if Walford had two or three girls to deal with on many Saturday mornings in the Spring Term of 1942, this was nothing as compared with the large numbers of College boys who were typically caned each week, so the fears of many girls that we would all be subjected to College style discipline did not materialise. I had no fear of being caught smoking as Mum allowed me to smoke at home, but asked me not to smoke in public which I didn't. I gave up altogether when I married David.

I have always considered that punishment is a totally unsuitable way of dealing with addictions such as smoking and drinking. Nowadays I suppose this would have to

THREE OF THE BEST FOR BOADIE

include drug taking. If you want an example, take Louise. She was always an addictive smoker. She was unfortunate in choosing to have a father who was a non-smoker, who could smell smoke anywhere and who had an uncanny knack of knowing all the places and times where boys would smoke. As a House Master he had the reputation of wandering along the corridors in his dressing-gown at 2 am or whenever he woke up, and catching boys smoking in their studies. Likewise he was always catching Louise, who must have been caned for smoking more often than the most unfortunate College boys were ever caned in the whole of their school careers, and yet Louise is one of the few people I know who still smokes like a chimney.

I suppose I should also explain this chapter heading - Boadie, as you have no doubt guessed, is me. I acquired this nickname in the course of my Latin lessons during the Winter of 1941-42 and it has remained with me ever since. It is the abbreviation for Boadicea. We were doing Caesar's Gallic War, books IV and V, as one of the set texts for School Cert. Latin. The other set text was Virgil's Georgics IV, all about how to keep bees.

Latin was a more difficult subject. It was not my best, but I was in the top set. You had to do far more work than in any other subject, but you could get a Credit for about 45%. You were advised to spend part of the Summer and Christmas holidays preparing word lists and trying to construe the texts with the aid of a crib. I never learned to read the language in the way I could read French, because the Latin words always seemed to me to be arranged in a totally illogical and higgledy-piggledy order. I accept, nevertheless, that Latin was an extremely good way of learning to think in English and to understand English grammar.

Caesar's Gallic War was interesting to me because it was all about the invasion of Britain by Julius Caesar in 55 BC. As Dad had been an enthusiastic military historian I was able to read up the background both of the 55 BC invasion and the 43 AD invasion by Claudius Caesar, and Queen Boadicea became one of my heroines.

The Winter of 1941-42 was one where the war was going very badly for us. The Germans looked as if they were about to capture Moscow. The Japanese had captured all our Far Eastern colonies, including Singapore, and sunk the battleships the Prince of Wales and Repulse. The only victory we had been able to claim was against the Italians in Libya, where even Wavell's victories in early 1941 had been reversed when Rommel had arrived on the scene with a few Germans.

I came out with a theory that Julius Caesar was nothing more than a pretentious wop like Mussolini, a bully and a thug, and that the books we were now studying had been written by him as propaganda for the ignorant wops back home in Rome, similar to the propaganda Mussolini had been pushing out about his retreat in Greece, when the Greeks had been giving him a good hiding.

I had enjoyed telling the class that just as Boadicea had given Claudius' troops a good hiding in 43 AD it was probably a determined woman who had sent Julius Caesar packing (who knows it might have been Boadicea's great-grandmother) but he didn't like to admit it. But if he wasn't sent packing by someone, why on earth did he come here only to leave?

The rest of the class liked my theory, but the Latin master, who was clearly a traditionalist, brought up to think of Julius Caesar as a godlike figure, was irritated, although I think he forgave me when I got higher marks in School Cert. Latin than anyone else in his class that year.

I was quickly nicknamed Boadicea (a name which I liked) although it was soon reduced to Boadie. When I told John he loved it. Boadie is the name he has always called me when he doesn't call me darling.

To come back to the painful aspect... one bit of College folklore was the incentive used to make boys stay down. It was sensible to tell them that they would get an extra stripe every time they got up, but this tradition was abused by Walford and many masters and prefects. They would deliberately plan their shots with uneven pauses in between each shot so as to catch a victim at a moment when he wasn't gripping the chair arms like fury and provoke him into standing up. Walford had succeeded in doing this with all the girls. This normally happened to most of the boys the first time they got caned and many boys never acquired the skill and determination to stay down.

The unpleasantest part of this provocation game was that the extra shot was always landed at the top of the thighs, i.e. just below the crease. This was known as the coward's shot. In other words, a boy could have any number of stripes above the crease and he wasn't branded as a coward. It simply meant that whatever he had done had merited four, five, six (the maximum at that time) instead of the basic three.

The coward's shot was usually administered with venomous force and precision, which made it far more difficult to find a comfortable way to sit down. Most of the College desks were double desks with a plank to sit on and a plank as a back-rest. I think the wood in fact was polished hardwood that had been carved upon by many generations of boys. A boy could slide his bottom so far back, but no further. If he hadn't suffered the coward's shot he might be able to slide sufficiently far back to sit comfortably during afternoon school on his thighs. If he had suffered the coward's shot there was no way he could find a sitting position on his return from Senior Study that wasn't as painful as hell.

The girls had a different problem. In those days our school knickers used to have tight elastic that would bite into the tops of our legs and usually leave a mark. The elastic would certainly have shown as a ridge when the girls were bent over tight and Walford would probably aim just above it, although in some cases he might go below. It didn't matter where he hit, the elastic would have an unpleasant knack of working its way into the painful spot, and the only solution was to remove the elastic altogether or to remove the offending garment.

After The Gondoliers episode, news of this particular refinement in Walford's technique quickly spread around. The boys laughed like drains and looked forward to a bit of fondling without any elastic to get in the way.

The girls decided to defend their honour by renaming this stripe below the crease as the 'knicker elastic shot' and refusing to accept the term 'coward's shot'. Amusingly the term was still in use some 20 years later when my sons were at the College, and had by then become lost in College folklore.

The 6th March, 1942 was Maureen's 16th birthday. She was the first of the Four Musketeers to reach the age of adultery, as we called it. A girl in one of Mrs. Rainham's classes had written an essay on 'growing up' which began "Sweet are the pleasures of childhood, but they are nothing as compared with the pleasures of adultery" and this little tag had quickly become part of High School folklore.

Maureen invited Louise, Liz and myself to come and have tea and toasted tea-cake at the Copper Kettle immediately after school, and we did.

We were all in a punch-drunk Friday afternoon mood. We lifted our tea-cups as if they were champagne glasses to toast Maureen on being able to enjoy some of the pleasures that had previously been denied us. She was legally entitled to smoke. With the Bishop's permission she could marry. She already had a front door key, so she wouldn't have to wait until 21. If she put on high heels and enough make-up she might even pass for 18 and have a drink in a pub.

She was holding forth on the ideal presents a Fairy Godmother might give her, including the right to spend the night with the man of her choice (I think it was Leslie Howard) and we teased her that he might be drunk and disinterested. She was going on about what it would be like to lie back in bed sipping a glass of whisky, smoking a Passing Cloud (an up-market cigarette at that time) whilst waiting for Mr. Right to mount her. We were probably making a lot of noise and attracting attention. She then took a cigarette out of her handbag, lit it with a match (after a few unsuccessful attempts with a lighter) and flourished it in the air saying "Adultery here I come".

Whether we were seen by a teacher or by a friend of a teacher, or by someone serving behind the counter, the news got back to the school that a bunch of rowdy High School girls had come in on Friday afternoon, made a lot of noise as if they had been drinking and were all smoking like chimneys.

By Tuesday our respective parents had all received what we referred to as the 'dreaded letter' and we immediately knew what was in store for us on Saturday the 14th. We had three days and four nights unpleasant anticipation. This was part of our punishment. Liz, Louise and I had been chastised by our respective fathers in the traditional manner and were accustomed to 'grinning and bearing it' whatever punishment came our way. Louise had been caned by Walford her father on so many occasions that she might have had reason to be relaxed, but she was in trepidation like the rest of us. One's hide doesn't acquire insensitivity.

For some reason Maureen was in a blue funk, hoping her Mum would get her off by failing to co-operate with the system. We were disappointed with her. Our opinion of her dropped even more when we heard that she had turned up on the day with loads of padding, which we knew would do her no good and merely earn her an extra stripe. As far as we were concerned she deserved it.

Of course the news that we had to report to Walford's study quickly got around and I had to put up with a lot of teasing. A girl who had been play-acting as Boadicea, the champion defender of Britain against Caesar couldn't suddenly pretend to be a damsel in distress, so I had to bluff it out. I was repeatedly told that this time it was Walford Caesar who was going to whack Boadicea and not the reverse and the boys in the Latin class were forever moving their index fingers in the manner of a cane heading towards its target, so I had to pretend to be not the least perturbed, although I was shaking in my pants whenever I thought of what lay in store. But I never knew a boy who didn't do likewise however much he pretended to play the tough guy.

There would be little point in elaborating on what followed. I was caned and it hurt. So were the other three. Most men over 40 who were educated at boarding schools will remember what it felt like to be caned. I suspect that only a small minority of women had any comparable experience. Even our High School temporary war-time practice disappeared after the war when the Dads had returned and were deemed capable of keeping their daughters under control. Mildred had found herself a rich husband and left, and even Walford Squires had become a shadow of his former self in the years up to his retirement - after Dick was killed at Arnhem. Nowadays it seems that since we have banned caning in schools it has become a sexual fetish. I would never have allowed any man who wanted to get into bed with me to treat me in such a barbaric way, but my view on such matters is obviously influenced by the experience of knowing it for real. Nowadays one reads a lot about deviant practices that sound even more unlikely.

To return to this particular episode in my life story, its significance for me was not the simple fact of being 'punished' but rather that my painful session with Walford Squires was the first major confrontation of my life. I was three months short of 16 and he was a senior and very powerful person, but in my view I won, although the result could equally have been regarded as a draw.

This didn't mean that I behaved like a stroppy teenager and refused to take my punishment. In my view I took far more than I merited, particularly as I hadn't been smoking in the first place, but that was not the point.

We were both playing the game by the rules and I believe I was observing the spirit as well as the letter. Like many of his kind he was merely observing the letter and keen to exploit any unfair advantage he could possibly take.

To understand what was really going on you have first to understand something of his character. He had a tremendous respect for Dad as someone who had given him a helping hand to get his present job as Second Master, but deep down there was an underlying resentment of Dad's intellectual superiority, Dad's power in the hierarchy and Dad's personal wealth, and the fact that Dad hadn't got him the job of Headmaster. Mum knew this as well as anyone. She had a tremendous insight into people and their motives. I didn't, but my antennae told me as much in terms that I couldn't put into words at that time. Now he had one of Dad's daughters in his power he didn't intend to let the opportunity slip. I sensed this by the way he looked at me when we sat face to face in his study before he gave me the treatment.

The second factor is sex. Nowadays people use sex to explain almost anything, but without in the least being clever, it is easy to understand that the streak of lechery to be found in most men wielding a little power had a part to play. I may have been under 16 but I was reasonably well developed for my age and everyone with the courage to do so used to tell me what a sexy behind I had. Some of them still do so. I was wearing the sexiest pair of trousers that Mum had worn on the French Riviera before the war and no-one is going to convince me that he was insensitive to what he saw when I was 'bent over tight' over a very low armchair with arms which I was grasping like fury.

On my side I had built up a reserve of Dutch courage by thinking about the brave women who were being parachuted into occupied France to liaise with the Resistance Forces (in which French women played a major role) and the French girls of my own age, who were actively involved in sabotaging the German military machine. One frequently read newspaper stories of the way they were captured and tortured in attempts to make them reveal the whereabouts of their comrades. I used to wonder how much it would take to make me crack under such treatment. If I was going to let myself worry about an old man hitting my backside with a cane, it didn't say much for my courage, and so I managed to maintain my tough Boadicea mood when I marched into Walford's study on Saturday 14th March, 1942.

Fortunately I had built up a good enough flow of adrenalin to make light of all the demoralising irritations that had beset me that morning.

First, Mum had annoyed me by insisting that I should wear a smart pair of beige slacks that she had last worn before the war on the Riviera. I told her I wasn't going on a picnic where I could hook a lot of College boys and it would be much better if I were to wear some ordinary cords that would give me more protection. But she had heard Milly complaining about the cowardly girls who tried to cheat by turning up in padding and she was determined, for the good of our family's reputation, that her daughter should be clearly seen to be the opposite of a cheat. The sentiment was no doubt sound, but I was nonetheless irritated by the way Mum was treating family pride as more important than the protection of her daughter's backside. In the event, what I wore would probably have made little or no difference. The only consolation was that the pants she had lent me to go with the trousers were intended to be nearly invisible and therefore didn't have any elastic round the legs. Thus Boadicea, the good girl-guide, was prepared for the worst.

The next bit of demoralisation came when I arrived last of the Four Musketeers to sit and wait my turn in the Squires' morning room (next to Walford's study) while the other three Musketeers went in one by one for Walford's kind attention. The party wall was solid brick and you couldn't hear what was being said, but by God! You could hear each whack as it landed and all the Ows and Ohs and yells that followed.

When I arrived Louise had warned me that her Dad was not in a good mood. She also said that she been done so often for smoking that she was unlikely to get away with less than four as a repeat offender, although the rest of us shouldn't get more than three, except Maureen, who had been caught cheating and made to change into Louise's pyjama trousers and was now moaning continuously about being treated worse than the rest of us. Nevertheless, I heard Liz, who went in second, get four and give a loud yell after each, and she was a pretty tough creature. She had obviously stood up. When it came to Maureen I thought she was going to get hysterics. I kept hearing shouts of "no more", "I can't", "I won't", but after a few minutes I would hear another whack, so Walford had succeeded in getting her to bend over again, and then there would be a repetition of the same charade. Overall I reckoned he had succeeded in giving her five painful whacks before I heard her running into the corridor and up the stairs and yelling all the way. Talk about morale boosting.

The third attack on my morale was deliberate and part of Walford's standard game plan. When he called me into his study and invited me to sit down opposite him as he sat at his desk (while I could still sit down) my eyes had the pleasure of studying his collection of canes that were stored neatly on a rack on the wall to my left and his right. Over the years this must have unnerved a lot of boys.

I have never been a particularly subtle person and I don't think I have ever had a particular gift for playing clever psychological games. A talent I do think I possessed in reasonable measure is to size people up as soon as I see them and to make a quick judgment of where they are coming from and what they are trying to do. In my business life this has been a tremendous asset. Sitting in front of Walford on a one-to-one basis (no longer as a family friend) I saw him as something of an impostor. His pretentious benevolent air combined with his would-be dandy appearance (speckled bow tie and camel-haired waistcoat with top button undone) didn't disguise the fact that he didn't have much in the coco (as the French say), nor did his benevolently brushed back white hair, but in conventional terms he was highly personable.

I had to listen to him reciting his usual spiel to the effect that he was acting as a friend of my parents and that what was to follow had nothing to do with the College and nothing to do with the High School, etc., etc. and if my father had not been absent on active service he would no doubt have dealt with me far more severely than he (Mr. Squires) could be expected to deal with me.

This annoyed me. If I have been unkind to poor Dad's memory by making him sound like a tyrannical father, then I apologise to him and to you. He was not. He didn't punish me often, but when he did I remembered and still remember. He may have made me feel sore, but he also made me feel sad that I had upset him. "I didn't expect to have to tell a daughter of mine…" were words of his that used to make me feel contrite and miserable. But Dad didn't mess about playing silly games of cat and mouse with me. It was over "over that chair" bang, bang, bang, and that was it.

Walford made it plain that he was intent on inflicting as much mental anguish as he could in addition to physical pain. After he had finished his introductory speech he handed me a piece of paper to sign which merely repeated what he had just said, but then finished with my acceptance of the fact that I had been a wicked girl (or words to that effect) and humbly requested him to give me _____ strokes of the cane. It may sound silly, but once you were in his study there was no way you could chicken out.

All this time I looked him straight in the eye. I sensed that this annoyed him. Maybe he saw something of my father in me. If so, I was glad. One of the proverbs current at the time was that 'Slaves look down. Free men look their masters in the eye'. In those days women didn't have hang-ups about English grammar. We knew that the word 'man' was a neutral particle as in 'man cannot live by bread alone' and we weren't so stupid as to imagine that you ought to say 'man and woman cannot live by bread alone'. Most of us remembered the corny joke of our Latin master about the shop-keeper who had put up the Latin motto 'mens sana in corpore sano' to impress his customers being upstaged by the shop-keeper across the road who had affixed above his shop the slogan 'mens and womens sana in corpore sano'.

When I had read and was about to sign his bloody form I looked up and asked him "How many strokes am I supposed to be asking you to give me sir? It doesn't say here." "I'll fill that in later", he said. "It will depend on you".

"But I want to know, sir. Can I get up and leave the room after you have given me three, or are you going to give me four?"

Clearly he wasn't used to this kind of self assurance at such moments. He was accustomed to his victims being so tongue-tied and scared that they couldn't think or speak clearly.

He handed me the next piece of paper which simply set out the standard rules about not standing up before I was told to and standing at attention when I was allowed to stand up. It was a tatty piece of paper which he must have had on his desk for years. I knew what his game was before I came in. He was determined to give me such a nasty one at some stage that I would stand up and give him the pretext for delivering the 'coward's shot' and I was determined not to let him.

As to the modus operandi of our hero Walford it was this. After I had reluctantly signed the piece of paper which was too much of a blank cheque for my liking, I was 'invited' to go and bend over the low armchair at the far end of his study. There was a great deal of open space for him to manoeuvre between his desk and this little armchair. I have never seen this type of chair in anybody's house. It had wooden arms for you to grip and it meant you had to bend right down, but if you had been using it as an armchair it would have been a bind each time you wanted to get up, because it was so near the ground. For the purpose for which Walford was using it there were obvious advantages. Apart from making you bend right down, it had decent anchorage so that you weren't toppled over by the momentum with which his cane hit you. He had eventually conceded that if I didn't get up he would give me three whacks and would allow me to enter the number on the form and that he wouldn't require me to sit down to do so. Big hearted of him!

So I bent over in the traditional manner and took a firm grip of the wooden arms of the chair. Instead of giving me three of the best and letting me get it over, he seemed to take an interminable amount of time moving around. From where I was I couldn't see what he was doing. Eventually I sensed him behind me with whatever cane he had chosen and he started tapping my behind provocatively with it as he took aim - at first a little bit more on the left and then a little bit more on the right, and then a little lower down. I suspected that it was more of a teasing operation for my benefit (or rather mental discomfiture) than anything he needed to do to take aim.

Then I sensed that he was stepping back and I gripped like fury. I was right. He seemed to be running at me as if he was bowling in a game of cricket. I felt the impact at the same time as I heard the noise and the whistle, or that's what it seemed.

I was told afterwards by one of the boys that Walford's technique was that of the 'low swing', which would suggest more of golfing than a cricketing parallel. This presumably meant that the trajectory was down towards the ground and then up to hit the underside of the victim's bottom at an angle of 90° and hence to achieve maximum impact, which it certainly did, although how anyone could possibly have observed his technique from the position I was in, heaven knows. With that sort of impact, the texture of the trousers one was wearing could not have made much difference.

But as he hadn't provoked me into jumping up I sensed that he was annoyed. Instead of following number one with number two, he started his silly tapping game again, only this time he tapped a little harder until he had found the tender spot of the first stripe. I must have made some sort of involuntary movement when he had found it, because he immediately started identifying the place for his second shot, so I began to brace myself and grip as I sensed him moving back again for his next run at me. If it could have been worse than the first, it was, but with that sort of impact you lose all sense of relative hurt. To me both shots were ruddy painful and that was all there was to it.

I sensed that he was now really annoyed but I had no means of knowing. It sounded as if he had walked back to his rack and picked another cane. In my opinion that was cheating, but in my book Walford was the sort of person who would cheat in any game if he could get away with it. But it didn't enable him to make me stand up.

When he had done his worst with number three, he still left me in suspense for a few minutes before he said gruffly "You can get up" and I did. I walked to his desk and picked up the scratch pen.

"May I put the number in now sir?" I asked and he nodded assent. In a moment of defiance I even thought of sitting down, just to show him, but I'm glad I didn't. I stood to attention with my hands by my side and when he said nothing I asked "May I go sir?" and again he nodded assent, so I went.

The adrenalin was beginning to run out. I wanted to burst into tears and cup my hands around my hips but I wasn't going to give in until I got out of the house and out of sight.

Milly came out of her office which was near the front door. She had presumably heard me come out of Walford's study and I would be surprised if she hadn't heard a lot more, but in her bland amiable way she took my raincoat off the peg to hand it to me. It swung against my behind and I realised how sensitive I was. I said I would carry it. I commented on Maureen being in a pretty bad way, but Milly shook her head.

"She'll be all right. They always are. We are used to her type. They make a song and dance in the hope of getting off, but they don't." She was right. By Monday Maureen was proudly showing off her stripes, holding herself out to be the ringleader who had got it worse than the others.

I was edging towards the door, because I didn't know how long I could continue my bravado act. "See you tomorrow." Milly smiled as she opened the door. God, I had forgotten, Mum and I were due to have Sunday lunch with the Squires and the thought of them all gloating as I gingerly tried to sit down was horrendous. Still, tomorrow was another day and I was now free to go.

And so I closed the door on an unpleasant episode of my life which, fortunately, was not to be repeated. I don't regret it. In later life I was the one (not John) who had to do the smacking and, later, caning of our children and, in fact, some of our grandchildren. I don't think anyone should do this unless he or she knows what it's like to be on the receiving end. I don't think the College got it right and I don't think Walford was a suitable man for the job. He was too absorbed in his own ego. But bad examples do not form the basis for good law.

I had nevertheless learnt a number of useful lessons from Walford, lessons in how not to do it. I believe the cane can be useful at certain times and for certain things, otherwise I wouldn't have used it.

I have already said it is totally useless for addictions such as smoking and drinking. It is totally unnecessary to go through the fatuous charade of taking aim and of keeping a child in suspense with a build-up of mental anguish. It is totally unnecessary to apply a cane with the ferocity and force that Walford used so that the stripes would last for weeks and weeks. I managed perfectly well to put the fear of God into my family with a fairly thin swishy cane, which is not much different from the sort of bamboo stick you use in the garden to tie up chrysanthemums. The punishment should follow the offence as soon as possible and the offence should be of a kind that is clearly understood by the person being punished.

A good example is my granddaughter Ruth. She was staying with John and me when she was nearly 15. She was beginning to have expensive tastes, whether in clothes or CDs or whatever else I know not. I am one of those people who normally knows how much money she has in her purse (at any rate in terms of notes) and I was short on two occasions, so I put pale pink crayon marks on the corners of all the notes before leaving my handbag unattended in the lounge. Next time I checked I noted that a £10 note was missing, so I challenged her and asked to see the money in her purse/wallet. She knew she had been found out and burst into tears. Her mother (Catherine) had always been careless with money from her childhood days, so Ruth could have been helping herself to £5 and £10 notes from her mother's purse for weeks or months without being detected.

I told Ruth that I wasn't going to keep a thief in my house and that if her parents hadn't been on holiday I would have sent her home straight away. I warned her that if she carried on stealing like that when she grew up she would finish in Holloway Jail.

Nowadays people talk about kleptomania and all sorts of silly excuses for stealing. All this is nonsense. People will help themselves to anything they want if they think they can get away with it. A minority are basically honest, but if more parents kept an eagle eye and punished their kids at an early age and more schools attached importance to detecting and punishing petty thefts we wouldn't now be living in a country where even churches have to be kept locked up for fear of thieves and vandals.

Ruth could see how angry I was and she was no doubt worried stiff at what her parents would say, so I told her that if she was a brave girl and took her punishment from me that would be the end of the matter, and I kept my word.

I marched her straight up to my bedroom, made her bend over the back of my armchair. It was a comfortable velour chair which had velour arms and not wooden ones. Luckily for her she was still wearing schoolgirl knickers which fully covered her bottom and once I had tucked her dress into the waistband that was the only protection she had. I took my little swishy cane from the top of my wardrobe and I gave her the option of staying down and getting three, or getting up and having more, and to her credit she stayed down until I had finished, but with me there was no playing around. It was three whacks in quick succession and then "Good girl. Go and wash your face and don't let me ever have to do this to you again."

It was a short, sharp lesson, but it was all that was needed. I am not an athlete or a sporting person. Any man or woman can do the job effectively, so bang goes the myth that you have to be someone with Walford Squires' physique to do the job. If you don't believe me, just try getting your wife, husband, best friend or whoever to hit your backside with any old garden cane. I am sure they will be delighted to do so and you won't enjoy it in the least.

By supper time (John was away so Ruth and I were alone together) I could see that Ruth was still sitting uncomfortably, so I suggested sitting sideways as I had done.

"You have no idea how much it hurts, Gran", she said wryly, so I told her that I knew perfectly well and how I once suffered the attentions of Walford Squires.

Some two years later when John and I were staying with Catherine (my younger daughter, the barrister) and her husband Simon, the subject came up at dinner time of the unruly kids next door and the poor mother who couldn't cope. Catherine turned to me and said:

"Gran, you should have brought your cane. That's what they need" and turning to Ruth and her younger brother Michael, she went on:

"You two never knew how lucky you were. When we were kids Gran used to put the fear of God into us whenever she got her cane out."

I looked at Ruth and our eyes met. She gave me a conspiratorial smile. She obviously hadn't resented what I had done. After dinner she came to me. "I'm eternally grateful you didn't tell Dad and Mum. I would have been accused every time Mum was short of money". She was right. Catherine was and still is one of the most careless and feckless girls when it comes to money. She can earn large sums, but her housekeeping's chaotic.

One final point - if caning comes back into vogue, as it certainly will, it will have to be applied equally to boys and girls. Historically it was boys that were caned and not girls, except in households like ours and the Squires. Because our two sons were away at boarding school it was, as Catherine remembered, our two girls who were at day schools who were much more often at the receiving end of my cane. On balance I think a cane can be used much more effectively in the home than at school, but this of course depends upon the home. Dad's idea of ringing up the father of the girl caught shoplifting in Smiths was the best solution, but it depended upon the co-operation of a sensible father.

Like all problems, there is no perfect solution, but this is no excuse for pretending the problem doesn't exist, which is what most homes and schools are doing at the present time. Kids have to be taught to obey, which means punishing them if they disobey. We are slowly rediscovering the fact that we have to teach kids the three Rs in school, so I hope we don't take too long as a nation to rediscover the fact that the quality of civilised life depends upon kids being brought up who have learnt to obey and have a healthy respect for authority.

Coming back to my own life story, I apologise if I have taken up so much of your reading time with such a trivial event, but for me it wasn't trivial. I had stood up to Walford. I had proved to myself that I wasn't a coward. Whether or not I would have cracked sooner or later if I had been subjected to real torture by the Gestapo is a different matter. I had also proved to myself that in addition to competing successfully with the boys in terms of academic ability, I also had the stamina to take the same punishment. I had undergone my trial by ordeal, as they called it in the Middle Ages, and I had not been found wanting.

CHAPTER 10

JACKO - THE IMPERFECT ENJOYMENT

When I left the Squires' house after getting my behind whacked, that wasn't the end of the matter. For one thing it was hurting like hell. Almost as soon as I got into the road I met Jacko, who had obviously been hanging around for the last half hour or longer. So I couldn't stop acting my amateur heroics.

"So you've come here to gloat, Jacko", I said.

"I've been worried about you for the last three days", he said. "Old Whackers is merciless."

"I know, Jacko. He's just knocked the stuffing out of me and it's hurting like hell. I thought you were supposed to be working in the Chemi labs. There is no point in your getting a sore behind for playing truant just to say hello to me".

"I'm OK. I have an official excuse", he said.

We walked together for a short distance and then he stopped and said:

"Boadie, I have never seen you look so beautiful. There is something noble and courageous about you."

"There's a time and a place, Jacko", I replied. "At present I am not capable of either giving or receiving compliments. You just think I look a bit more fetching in these slacks of Mum's."

"Kiss me, Boadie", he said.

"Not here, Jacko", I answered, and so he guided me into the driveway of one of the houses where the garden was something of an overgrown shrubbery. I think it was a College house let to one of the masters where the driveway curved around so that we were quickly out of sight of both the road and the house. As we kissed, his hand, as I knew it would, ever so gently cupped my behind.

"Gosh, he's really given it to you, Boadie", he said. I nodded.

"With the amount of heat he generates with his cane he could heat the school and save central heating costs."

"Jacko! This is no time for corny jokes!"

"Sorry, Boadie", he apologised sheepishly, and then "Are you going to show me?"

"Not here, Jacko. In my present mood I'd be quite happy to do it on the stage in Big School and let the whole College walk by in single file just to kill the wicked slander that girls are let off with a few light taps." Jacko was horrified.

"They'd be all wanting to mount you", he said.

"What a wonderful time I would have, Jacko. If you'd studied the interesting bits in classical mythology you'd have known that a woman's pleasure in such moments is greater than a man's." He looked puzzled, so I went on.

"Tiresias, you remember." He obviously didn't. "He started life as a woman and then became a man, and so he knew at first hand but Juno punished him by making him blind for giving away a woman's best kept secret, but Jupiter tried to make amends by giving him the gift of prophesy."

"How is it that you have the knack of finding the spicy bits, even in the dullest of subjects?" he asked.

"Because I'm not asleep, Jacko. In any case, the subject isn't dull. You should try reading the spicy bits of Ovid. Some of the best are in English in the last few pages of Marlowe's plays. It looks such a dull book so nobody reads that far."

Talking about a subject dear to my heart was the best thing I could do to take my mind away from the horrible pain in the butt, although it had no effect on the pain.

"I'd love to mount you, Boadie", he said, "but I've never had the courage to ask. Not to ask straight out like that, anyway."

"No courage, Jacko?", I went on "you disappoint me. Here am I prepared to face down Old Whackers and you say you haven't even the courage to ask me to do something you know I want to do anyway."

I made it plain that I wouldn't do anything unless he were properly equipped and I assumed he knew what that meant. We agreed to meet about 6 o'clock on Sunday evening in the West Ground cricket pavilion to which he claimed to have a key. This was some considerable distance from the College buildings and no-one was likely to go there outside the cricket season. I promised to let him have a sight of my striped behind and, if I was not too sore, he might have the honour of pleasuring me. In retrospect I'd probably unnerved the poor boy.

As soon as I got home I told Mum that I was going to have a look at myself in her full-length wardrobe mirror. She was still treating the whole episode as a joke, although I think she relented a bit when she saw the severity of the stripes that old Walford had laid on. She brought another mirror from the bathroom so that by juggling it around I could get a better view. Even then, all she could say was:

"If I needed to spank you this would be the ideal time."

"But I've done nothing wrong, Mum. How could you be so cruel?"

"I know", she said, "but it seems too good an opportunity to miss."

Fortunately she was joking and let the opportunity pass by. She was nevertheless impressed by the accuracy of Walford's aim - three parallel lines with not much more than an inch between the top and bottom one.

For lunch I put a cushion on a dining room chair and sat sideways so that the painful bit projected over the back. It wouldn't have been so easy if he'd given me a fourth one below the crease. I pitied the boys who had to go straight into afternoon school and sit on hard benches after a visit to Senior Study.

I managed to spend most of the afternoon and evening finishing off the preparation of Gallic War Book V, which I had planned to do that weekend, but it wouldn't have been so easy if I hadn't found a comfortable way of sitting down. I tried a bath. After that, sleeping on my side or on my tum wasn't so easy. I kept waking up with a twinge when, in my sleep, I rolled onto my behind.

I tried to sit normally at breakfast and managed church without too much aggro as long as I sat down gingerly. Mum remarked that this was an excellent way of training teenage girls to sit down in a ladylike manner as opposed to merely plonking themselves down. She was always telling me that I would have been the despair of Arrière (had she still been alive) whose constant complaint about the English was that they didn't know how to bring up girls, which was why she had insisted on Mum and her sister (when they were teenagers) spending their Summer holidays with her.

So far so good. I was more apprehensive about lunch with the Squires. During term time Walford and Milly would invite most of the masters and their wives by rote plus members of the Governing Body. Their dining table comfortably held ten without anybody sitting at either end. Walford normally sat in the middle. This was official College hospitality in the sense that College servants cooked and served the lunch. It was plain English fare, where the only drink was water. Food rationing limited the menu, although the College sponsored its own pig club and most of the boarding houses had chicken runs. Scraps of food from the boarding houses were thus recycled. The Second Master would naturally enjoy favoured treatment in the supply of pork, bacon, chicken and eggs.

Mum and I were fairly regular guests. I was invited only as a matter of courtesy to Mum and Dad and whenever I was invited Louise joined us, so that the two of us could sit at the end of the table and have our own conversation, provided that we were on our best behaviour.

Guests were offered sherry in the morning room. Louise and I normally joined the adults when the gong went to announce lunch. Given the fact that Louise and I had both enjoyed Walford's kind attention the previous day, we naturally took the opportunity of showing each other our respective campaign stripes. Even she was horrified by mine.

"Dad must have really had it in for you", she said. "I can't see why. This was your first time."

I would never have dreamed of criticising her father to Louise, so there was no point in talking about possible reasons.

When the gong went we found, to our irritation, that the grown-ups were all talking about us. I think it was Mum's fault and she apologised to me afterwards. She couldn't resist complimenting Walford on his skilful marksmanship and his ego naturally enjoyed being massaged. The other guests consisted of two masters who had joined the school the previous term, Mr. Harris a Physics master and his wife, and Mr. Hanahan, a History master plus his wife. Mr. Harris may have been medically unfit and hence exempt from military service and Mr. Hanahan was an Irish national, who was likewise exempt. As relatively junior in the College hierarchy they were clearly on their best behaviour. Walford and Milly sat opposite each other at the middle of the table and at our end Mum sat between Walford and Louise and a dreadful woman called Phyllis sat on my left.

Phyllis was an inquisitive gossip whom nobody seemed to like. She was, nevertheless, on the visiting list because she was married to Canon Henderson, a flamboyant Billy Graham hotgospeller who preached sermons in the Albert Hall and on the wireless, but who was at that time in Egypt on active service as an army Chaplain. The Hendersons had no children.

Phyllis, who at that time was probably in her early fifties, dressed coquettishly. She may have had a crush on Walford, but I don't think it was reciprocated. It was said that but for his wife Canon Henderson would have been a Bishop, but Mum thought differently. His gifts as a rabble-rouser hardly fitted him for the role of a position of responsibility in the Anglican hierarchy.

Phyllis was introduced to us just as we all moved to stand behind our chairs for Walford to say grace. I could see her slyly watching the way I sat down before she burst out:

"So I'm to sit with the naughty girls, am I, Walford. I'll keep an eye on them and see they don't get out of hand."

Milly politely pointed out that College tradition required punishment to be the end of the matter and she would not, therefore, tolerate other guests referring to Mavis or her own daughter as "naughty girls".

So the conversation lurched along with desultory comments on yesterday's match. But it took more than a tactful reproof from Milly to stem the tide of Phyllis' curiosity. She was, as I have said, one of nature's busybodies, Meddlesome Matty and Keyhole Kate rolled into one, so she turned to Walford:

"I suppose you now have to pay for your job when it gives you such marvellous opportunities to feast your eyes on all these lovely young ladies while Milly stands obediently holding their skirts up so that you can get at them with your cane. You wicked old man."

I seemed to be the only person who was amused because, in my book, she wasn't far wrong, but even the unflappable Milly was annoyed. Walford stopped his conversation with the lady on his right and turned angrily to Phyllis:

"Canon Henderson will not be amused when I tell him the wicked thoughts you have been harbouring in his absence. He will have you over his knee and you will know about it when he returns." This gave Mum her opening:

"But Walford, surely you're the man for the job. If you are replacing absent fathers you can surely find time to replace absent husbands. Phyllis is dying to know what it is like to get six of the best". And turning to Phyllis: "The girls have to wear trousers."

"That doesn't matter in the least", Milly chipped in. "Walford can do it here and now before they bring us our chicken. I'll hold up your dress with pleasure while Walford feasts his eyes, as long as he gives you six of the best good and proper. If he has given these poor girls three for doing no more than taking a furtive puff at a cigarette, you deserve a lot more than six."

However much Phyllis would have enjoyed the prospect of Walford having a chance to feast his eyes (and I am sure she was even more coquettish underneath than she was on top) even she had the sense to realise the banter was going too far in the wrong direction. Who knows Walford and Milly might mean it. So she sat comfortably, and not uncomfortably, on her chair for the rest of lunch. Louise and I were the only ones who were still shifting a little uneasily and so were glad when lunch was over, although we would no doubt have taken impish delight at the thought of one of Walford's canes having a field-day on what was no doubt the decorative underside of Phyllis.

My morale for most of that Sunday was boosted by the thought that I might at long last have the chance of doing it for real with Jacko. I felt reasonably safe with him because I reckoned he would do what I said if I decided to stop. For some reason I was much more excited at the prospect than I had ever been, but I was still a bit nervous.

I even managed to ride my bicycle, not too uncomfortably, to this relatively isolated wooden hut that served in Summer as a cricket pavilion in one of the more remote College sports fields. Jacko was there before me and it was still light enough to see. There was a little public footpath that ran along the edge of the field and as there were no dog walkers around when I tapped on the door I knew I hadn't been seen. Apart from the usual cricket clobber there was the padded matting for the batting side to sit on the grass and two or three of these could serve as a mattress on the floor.

Jacko was aroused all right when we were both stripped from the waist downwards. He had made the expected 'gosh' and 'golly' noises when he saw my stripes, but he was far more interested in the object of his desire and, likewise, I had a firm grip on mine, but the incompetent fool had funked going into a chemist or barbers to buy the necessary, and I point blank refused to go any further. At the time I was angry with him, but in retrospect I was grateful that he had served as the agent of providence and that my first experience should be with the man whom I loved more than I believed it was possible to love anyone and to whose memory this book is dedicated.

The Monday gym lesson, as I expected, brought the predictable slap on the rump from Mildred, who always made sure she knew the names of the previous Saturday's 'defaulters', but because I expected it I was braced to playact my air of indifference. Of course I was still tender and of course it stung, but I wasn't going to give her the satisfaction of showing it. I was not one of her favourites. In fact very much the opposite.

Much more fun was the weekly coaching session after school on Monday with Steve, the House Tutor of Blenheim (one of the boarding houses). House Tutor was the title given to a young master (usually a bachelor) who, in addition in his normal teaching duties, assisted a House Master. For this he received residential accommodation in the boarding house where he had a study and was paid a salary supplement. He was one of our Latin masters and I was one of ten 'high flyers' who were expected to get a Credit or even a Distinction, in Latin. Our late Monday afternoon tutorials were held in his study in Blenheim House.

Normally boys' boarding houses were out of bounds to girls unless they were on official business, which I was. I was in fact the only girl in this group of ten.

On the way out a group of them persuaded me to drop in to the study that Chris Wilson shared with two other boys. Chris Wilson was a Sixth Former whom I knew well, or rather I knew him because he had often kissed and fondled me at dances. They all wanted to have a look at my stripes, or rather that is what they said. I knew perfectly well what they really wanted to have a look at and I had no reason to be reticent about showing them both. The stripes still looked pretty fierce and provoked a few 'goshes'. All I wanted them to know and spread around was the fact that Boadie could take it and that girls weren't let off lightly. If I also achieved the reputation of being a good sport, so much the better.

Being a vain woman (almost as vain as the boys) I did look at my back view in the mirror every few days and as it was nearly five weeks before the marks completely disappeared I reckoned that I had got as good as any of the boys, probably worse than most.

If you think this wish to prove myself means that I felt insecure, then I was insecure. So what. In those days it hadn't yet become fashionable to waste time trying to psycho-analyse oneself à la Woody Allen and I would still regard it as a waste of time. In recent decades large numbers of girls have found themselves in small minorities in the Sixth Forms of boys' Public Schools and I am sure many of them will understand the way I felt.

In those days single sex boys' boarding schools were much more like the closed world of monastic institutions than they are now. They had their own closed world set of values. These were often unhelpful to a boy when he came in later life to build (or try to build) a lifelong working relationship with the woman he would choose as a wife.

For girls to be respected and make the running as anything more than desirable bits of crumpet (and many boys had been induced by their upbringing to feel guilty about their desires for crumpet rather than treating them as normal and natural) it was bound to be a challenge. For someone of my temperament this challenge was not to be ducked even if it meant getting a sore behind. Anyway I didn't have any choice, but having taken my punishment in a way I knew the boys would respect, it seemed perfectly normal to me to want as much of that respect as I could get. Whilst I was perfectly happy to go on being regarded as a desirable bit of crumpet, I wanted to be regarded as a lot more besides. Having earned the nickname of Boadicea as the result of jocular comments in a Latin lesson and decided I liked it, I was keen to keep it, although I didn't want any more Saturday morning visits to Walford Squires. Fortunately I was spared further ordeals of that kind

CHAPTER 11

JEAN'S LIFE IN THE WRENS

The weekend after my bottom had been tattooed by Old Whackers, Jean came home on leave with the wonderful news that she had been promoted and was now on an Officer's Training Course. We drank to her good health and promotion prospects before our traditional Saturday evening meal, and as I was knocking on 16 I was allowed to have my glass of Dry Sack, which I enjoyed. When Jean filled all the glasses up for a second I enjoyed it even more. It was certainly better than the sherry that Louise had produced when she had brought a bottle to our house for us to drink in secret. I suppose my enjoyment was much more related to the fact that I sensed that both Mum and Jean were now treating me as an adult and this mattered more to me than sherry or anything else that I might have drunk on such an occasion.

In retrospect, it was clear to me that Jean had an agenda on this occasion as on all other occasions. She was a highly organised person and also very close. In this respect she resembled Mum. I suspect that she may well have spent quite a bit of her leave entitlement in the company of various naval officers at quiet Scottish country hotels, because we didn't see much of her. Now she needed more money. She had her Wrens pay, but this was peanuts. Mum made her an allowance and she had obviously been over-spending it. Now she had to point out that as an officer she would have to pay for her uniform and would have to pay Mess bills and although her service pay would increase she would have difficulty in making ends meet.

At first I wondered what on earth a Wren would need money for when she had no living expenses in the sense that she had her board and lodging and clothes provided (until she became an officer that is) but I had overlooked the fact that if she wanted something to eat in the evening (after high tea at 6) morning coffee and a cake, she would have to pay for it herself. It was assumed that Wrens would sleep in their shirts unless they bought their own pyjamas and if they wanted to look more glamourous out of uniform, or underneath their uniforms, or in a hotel bedroom, clothes had to be bought and clothing coupons would probably have to be acquired on the black market. In addition it was clear that Jean had acquired a taste for booze.

Whilst she was with us Jean must have trawled around the booze shops to buy bottles of gin and red Martini which she offered to Mum as presents, but which she poured liberally into her own glass whenever she felt so inclined. Gin and It (i.e. Gin and Italian, which meant red Martini) was a popular cocktail at the time, although Mum preferred sherry and I did at that time, although I later became a gin and tonic person.

After having got through the congratulatory phase, and Mum had said on a number of occasions how Dad would be overjoyed at Jean's success, the subject inevitably turned to my recent little misadventure in Walford Squires' study. Fortunately this triggered off some general remarks about my getting off scot-free because Dad was away and hence to a recollection of occasions when Jean 'had been given the hiding of her life' by Dad and this gave me the cue to intervene: "Mum, we're here to celebrate Jean's promotion. This is hardly the time to remind her of when you used to change her nappies. We have all had to endure unpleasant moments, so let's look on the bright side."

Jean gave me a lovely smile, which did more for me than anything else that weekend. It gave me a warm feeling as if she were now accepting me as an adult, almost as an equal, and no longer did I have to feel that I was merely the kid sister.

Late that evening, as I was getting into bed, I heard a light tap on the door and I said "Come in" and it was Jean. Our rooms were next to each other at the front of the house. She was already in her pyjamas and came in and sat on my bed.

"Thank you for having the presence of mind to get Mum off of one of her favourite topics", she said.

"I thought I was the one who was going to be made the butt of everyone's humour, and I can tell you it was bloody painful and certainly no joke. See for yourself."

And I showed her. She whistled.

"Jean", I asked, "I need your help and advice on an important question" and I explained the fact that as I was nearly sixteen and that there were one or two boys (I was exaggerating) that might soon want to bed me, I wanted, in the best Girl Guide tradition, to be prepared.

"Good God, girl. It's illegal if you are under sixteen."

"But that doesn't stop me getting pregnant if it happens, does it Jean!"

I knew Jean too well to ask her what she did. Good sisters know not to ask intimate questions. If information is volunteered, that is totally different. I wanted to move from the particular to the general, so that she could give me some help without talking about herself. So I said:

"With all those attractive Wrens at Rosyth and all those sailors coming back from spells at sea, there must be a lot of occasions when they get into bed together. So how do the Wrens not get pregnant?"

"Good God, girl, you're living in the dark ages. In any case most of them never get into bed. They have to do it on the floor, or in all sorts of unlikely places. The Service takes care of such matters very efficiently. As any girl who gets pregnant is lost to the Service, proper precautions are taken to ensure they don't."

I could sense that Jean was already talking as an officer with a sense of responsibility for the girls under her command and that if I managed to pursue my enquiries from this angle I might get the answer I wanted.

JEAN'S LIFE IN THE WRENS

"I suppose this means that men are all given orders that they must use French Letters."

"Good God, girl", Jean interrupted. "The first thing they teach the Wrens is never to rely on the men. If a man's on heat, and not sure whether he'll be able to get his end in, the last thing he'll do is to stop in his tracks and fumble around for a French Letter, because he knows the pause at that particular moment might well cause the girl to reflect and change her mind. No, the Wrens are all trained on the day they join the Service to carry at least six French Letters in their handbags, and if they mean business at least two dozen. And they are usually given training in how to put them on. A number of male medical orderlies volunteer for the job in the hope that some of the girls will be sufficiently on heat to recompense them."

I gathered from Jean that quite a lot of the girls had considerable experience in such matters before they entered the Service, where they clearly had a whale of a time. "Don't get the wrong idea", she went on. "We are only talking about 20% or 30%. The vast majority are either virginal or don't do anything except with their husbands or fiancés. Discipline is very strict, so none of the girls is pressurised or molested, and in any case the men usually have the sense to queue up for the girls they know will play ball."

"You make it sound as if some of the Wrens must have little time for anything else, if they have dozens of men queuing up. Where do they go if they can't do it in bed?" "It's just about that at times" Jean went on. "Sometimes there are ten times or twenty times as many men as girls in our Unit and you'd be amazed at their ingenuity in finding places to do it. The women's billets are out of bounds to the men and the men's out of bounds to the women, but mother nature has her way. When I first joined up I was astonished at the amount of shagging that went on in our Unit, but I would now be surprised if things were different when I'm posted to any other Unit."

I was clearly on heat and trying to refrain from asking whether I would have to wait until I was 17 before I could join, but somehow I managed to keep the conversation on a detached enquiring mind level so that Jean could maintain her stance as a wise, knowledgeable elder sister, although I suspected that she enjoyed talking about such things as much as I enjoyed listening - as long as I could steer clear of asking any questions about what she might or might not do herself.

From what I could gather the Wrens could get unlimited free supplies of Durex from Sick Quarters and no questions asked. They were also advised to stuff little tablets (called pessaries) into themselves before going into action, but that didn't tell a person like me where I could buy such items if I didn't want to feel conspicuous in a chemist shop. Eventually Jean gave me an address of a London Mail Order shop called Georges in Irving Street which posted such things to you in plain envelopes. I think this was the address given to all the Wrens and no doubt plenty of other girls, so that if they were posted where there was no free issue, or back in civvy street, or wherever, they wouldn't be caught short.

Jean and I had plenty of long chats during the next few evenings. We covered all sorts of topics. For me it was wonderful to be treated almost as an equal by a big sister who had been used to regarding me as a kid. Like many younger sisters and possibly many younger brothers, I suspect that this was an idea that mainly existed in my mind. Whatever the reasons, I now felt more relaxed with Jean and I loved being treated as an equal by someone who was just that little bit older and more experienced and to whom I felt I could turn for advice and help.

CHAPTER 12

'GIVE THE BOYS A TREAT'

The topic covered by this chapter involves leaping ahead in many parts of my narrative, but it follows logically from Jean's description of one aspect of Service life. It certainly impinged on my life and attitudes and also on the way many of us thought and behaved until the early 1950s. The term 'permissive society' became fashionable in the late 1960s and some may equate it with the kind of permissiveness that Jean described amongst some of her Wren colleagues and which also existed in the other women's Services and amongst many civilians during the war and early post-war years.

I believe that people generally were more loving and emotionally involved in their short-term affaires than in the more callous era of the 1960s. Although I wasn't myself in any of the Women's Services, I was closely involved in many ways. Apart from what I learned from Jean, I became closely involved in the demands of Service life when I met and married David in 1943 and then when I met John in 1946.

There was a close esprit de corps amongst RAF pilots who were very much a band of brothers and they remained so for many years after the war. In John's case the bonds were even stronger with those of his RAF colleagues who had shared life with him as prisoners of war. We had many reunions in which the wives considered themselves as honourary members of this very exclusive Club. A number of John's friends married WAAFs whom they had met when they had been stationed together. Whenever a few of us met for a meal, reminiscences would be the order of the day, particularly when the wine, beer, whisky or whatever had begun to flow.

In my Oxford days I was mainly mixing with men who had been on active service. Many of the women with whom I became friendly had also been on active service.

The women who had enjoyed the uninhibited lives of some of the Wrens described by Jean married and settled down as respectable wives and mothers and the last thing they could be expected to do was to tell their daughters 17 or 18 years later how they had spent some of their free time. As a result, the next generation no doubt grew up believing it was breaking new ground by imagining that it was sexually liberated, and no doubt this is an inevitable inter-generational communications gap. I nevertheless think the war years were special in many ways, which is why I have paused to describe this part of our lives more fully in this chapter.

The prevailing ethos can be summed up in the phrase "Give the Boys a Treat", which engendered greater tolerance.

Just as the authorities responsible for Jean's Unit were concerned not to lose trained woman-power and were therefore prepared to spend money on providing free contraceptives both for men and women, so the public at large (at any rate those in positions of authority and influence) recognised that successful prosecution of the war effort could best be achieved by recognising the needs of mother nature.

There were other considerations. The Service authorities didn't want to lose manpower or womanpower as a result of the scourge of VD. We hadn't reached the stage of anti-biotic treatment. There were great poster campaigns and education campaigns. The most horrifying films were shown to young recruits, who were also warned that if they went into dock (hospital) for VD treatment their Service pay stopped immediately. Bromide was mixed with the tea (which was served in large urns) in the cook-houses in the hope that this would reduce natural desires, but the Service authorities knew as well as everybody else that nature would have its way.

Unless they were actually fighting or on fighter or bombing operations a great deal of evening time was spent in idleness. There was no television and apart from a communal radio in the NAAFI or other canteen, there was not much to do or think about except booze and sex. For home-based troops trucks might be sent in to neighbouring towns to pick up women for dances that might be run once or twice a week in the NAAFI. The women were probably leading dull lives while their men were away. Opportunities would not be lost for quick sex wherever a place could be found out of the cold and wet, but the majority of service personnel contented themselves with sentimental cuddling and fondling when the lights were turned out, as they usually were on a number of occasions.

Where the Service authorities had established mixed Units the situation was different. Jean had been at Rosyth which for many decades had been one of the most important naval bases in the UK. Having Wrens to do a lot of the administrative work made good sense. It also meant that naval officers and sailors had a fair selection of 'wholesome women', the term used for female naval personnel, to consort with. They were assumed to be less infected than the prostitutes in any nearby town. This may not be a heroic way of presenting the role played by Service women in the war effort, but there is reason to believe that they did play their role in keeping active Service personnel disease free and, if Jean's comments at the time were valid, those that played this role enjoyed it to the full.

Whilst I would not wish to elevate one of the women's Services more than another (because my sister was in the Wrens) I think that the Wrens did succeed in attracting many more good-looking girls than the other Services. The Duchess of Kent (Princess Marina, the present Duke's mother) has been credited with designing the Wren uniform as it was in 1939. It was certainly the most chic and I know that many of my schoolmates were determined to join the Wrens for that reason, although they may have had others. I do not know whether she designed what went on underneath, but you don't have to be all that knowledgeable in erotic matters to know that a combination of black pants, black stockings and a bit of white thigh in between will send most men over the edge even if the girl who is wearing this ensemble doesn't have much above the neckline to commend herself to masculine attention. If Princess Marina of Greece (as she was before she was married) was responsible she deserves a mention in our history books for her contribution to the morale of the British Navy and to a lot more besides.

The WAAFs and ATSs were not so well served. John was naturally reticent. I believe he was abstemious until he returned from PoW camp. He was desperately in love with the girl who let him down. When he was liberated in 1945 and learned that his fiancée had married someone else, I think he plunged into the first WAAF who was willing to give him solace. I think he had felt ashamed of himself ever since, but if I ever meet the girl I would like to shake her by the hand and thank her.

The WAAFs and the ATSs didn't have the sexy underwear of the Wrens. They were issued with uncomfortable droopy drawers which the ATSs referred to as 'passion killers' and the WAAFs as Service Issue. John and most of the ex-RAF personnel that I have met said that very few WAAFs wore Service Issue, but the word was a great joke. The standard ploy was to say:

"I'll spank you on your Service Issue" to produce the response "You'll have a job - I don't wear any" and this got the conversation going.

The live and let live spirit of Service life was an important feature of the world in which I grew up and had a strong influence on many of my attitudes, even though I didn't participate until I met John in 1946. The boys in uniform who were fighting to defend our lives deserved our support and if 'giving the boys a treat' was making a contribution to the war effort, few people frowned on it. The girls who participated enthusiastically were away from the constraints of parental control and censorious eyes and made maximum use of the opportunities. Those who wanted to retain their virgin purity or wished to remain faithful to the men to whom they had pledged their troth could do so without any let or hindrance, but they were encouraged to take a tolerant view of their frailer sisters and be grateful for the way in which the latter were diverting the attentions of the men who might otherwise be pestering them.

The less attractive women were often the first targets, on the male theory that they would be less likely to say no on the grounds that they wouldn't normally have the same opportunities, but with ten men to one woman (and in many cases more) many attractive as well as unattractive girls made the most of their opportunities and few of them got pregnant.

When the war was over and everyone was yearning for homes and husbands, this part of Service life was quickly forgotten.

In fact I learned much more in later years about the ways of men and women in uniform than I learned from Jean or from John. John was naturally reticent on detail because in a successful marriage husband and wife must each learn to leave each other some private space. I knew that if I tried to encourage him to talk about the fun and games many of his randy air crew friends had with the WAAFs on the various RAF Stations to which he had been posted at different times, he might have told me some things which he would live to regret on a day when he knew he was in the dog-house.

To put some other slants on the overall picture, the comments and attitudes of two men whom I didn't meet until some 30 years after the war are worth noting. Firstly, there was Joe, who worked for a large client company and whom I wined and dined on a number of occasions, but no more. If you fed him a few leads when he had drunk deep and well, he gushed like a burst pipe and his fantasy no doubt took over from reality in a lot of what he said, but a certain amount rings true. He joined the RAF late in the war when they no longer needed air crew, so he never did much more than work in the Orderly Room as a clerk general duties, with the rank of AC2, which is the most junior rank in the Service. When I teased him of the fun he must have had with the WAAFs he described how when he lay on his bed in the billet, he and the other occupants would be woken late at night as the enterprising womaniser of their group would try to find his bed in the dark and then lie down, too exhausted to undress.

"Did she let you shag her?" said one voice.

"Who?" said another.

"The tall blond girl in Equipment Accounts", he replied nonchalantly.

"Ooh, I'd love to shag her. What's she like?" said another voice.

"Lovely. Shags like a rattlesnake. Wouldn't let me go."

"Was she wearing Service Issue?" said another voice.

"Not when I shagged her, she wasn't" said the exhausted shagger of the evening who wanted to get to sleep.

The rest of the billet were all now wide awake and picturing themselves shagging, or almost shagging a woman they knew well and saw every day in the Mess and the NAAFI and didn't know how to approach.

This was probably a fair sample of the intelligent and articulate conversation that would take place in men's billets. Not that I would be able to put into words anything much more meaningful if another woman asked me to describe what it was like being shagged.

When a new WAAF was posted into the Station the two questions that provided food for speculation in most of the men's billets were "Does she shag?" and "Is she wearing Service Issue?"

In general, air crew stood a much better chance with the WAAFs than ground staff. What started as a casual relationship often blossomed into a close attachment which lasted until one or other was posted away and in a number of cases led to engagements.

My friend Joe, as an 'AC Plonk' ground staff, stood little chance of getting his end in and only managed to do so on one occasion (or so he said) because a girl with a voracious appetite was posted in and happened to work with him in the Orderly room which she used as a base for some of her encounters on the dark Winter evenings. By

The Village of Fortingall, Perthshire (Chapter 2)

Although I have found no Church records I like to believe that the Founder of the Fortingall family first saw the light of day in this beautiful village, just north of Loch Tay, before he set off in the late 18th century, like many more Scots, to seek his fortune in England. Some of the cottages and certainly the Fortingall Hotel (an old Coaching Inn) date back to the 18th century (or earlier) and would therefore have been known by my great great great grandfather in his early life.

Hornton Street, Kensington - Mum's home as a girl (Chapter 3)

"Only a Frenchman could have designed this car" (Chapter 4)

My great grandmother's big Citroen (to me the Maigret car) was the king of the road in pre-war rural France, giving a comfortable ride on the badly surfaced bumpy roads. The weakness of its design was that the front doors hinged on the central pillars and if not properly shut the car's momentum would swing them wide open. Its big plus was the unobstructed view that was offered to the 'gentleman' who gallantly opened the door for his lady front-seat passenger. In an era when there were very few cars on the roads and only the wealthy could aspire to ownership of a large Citroen, every vamp in the business who could manage to get into that front passenger seat would be sure to use all the time-honoured tricks to hook her companion - whether as a fare paying customer for the evening or for life. Even if chauffeurs didn't pay for their jobs, a perk like this would suffice to retain and motivate them.

Quai de Bergues (Chapter 4)

In the early years of the 20th century with the Hotel in the background.

Hotel Les Bergues as it is today (Chapter 4)

Whenever I drive or walk across the bridge over the Rhone and see the Hotel Les Bergues where I was taken to stay by my great grandmother in 1936 (and I have stayed there many times since then) it brings back nostalgic memories of the period in history when so many of my parents' generation believed fervently in the League of Nations and when England was the dominant country in the League and in Europe.

Although the cane was excluded from the curriculum in most girls' schools (including mine), during my school era many of us got our fair share at home from parents who had been taught to believe that sparing the rod would spoil the child. Sod's law ensured that I would cop it when a zealous College master volunteered for the extra-curricular task of replacing fathers absent on war service - hence Chapter 9. Once was more than enough for me, but if I had been a boy a well-striped behind could have been my lot a dozen or more times in the course of my school days. The compulsory trousers were to protect our supposed schoolgirl modesty and not our behinds.

As a convinced believer in the merits of the cane as a deterrent and punishment for both boys and girls, my own experience has helped me to argue my case on many occasions - although I would have done anything to chicken-out at the time.

Taking Aim - This girl (not me) knew she wasn't going to enjoy the next few minutes of her life.

If you tried to hold your dress down you would have been jeered as a spoil-sport. We preferred our boys to ogle at us rather than spend their money to ogle at the girls in our local equivalent of the 'Windmill'.

'Give the Boys a Treat' (Chapter 12)

Victoria, British Columbia, David's home town (Chapter 15)

Victoria is generally regarded as the most English part of Canada, even having its own red double-decker buses.

Canadian troops landing on the Eastern Sector of Juno Beach on 6th June 1944 (Chapter 19)

The photograph was taken by one of the Canadians taking part in the landing and is reproduced by the kind permission of the Imperial War Museum.

St. Hilda's College, Oxford, my College 1945-8 (Chapter 21)

For me it was a haven of peace after the turbulent years of World War II when I was still trying to come to terms with my loss of David.

The Cherwell, a view from St. Hilda's

Two pen and ink drawings by Lt. Lawrence Gilling-Smith, 1899-1963 (Dryden's father) of the Royal Flying Corps (before it became the RAF) who had rooms in BNC while attending a short course prior to gaining his pilot's licence in 1917.

BNC (John's College) and the Radcliffe Camera (Chapter 23)

BNC and St. Mary's, the University Church (Chapter 23)

getting a copy key and (after she and her companion had let themselves in) leaving it on the inside with the door locked, she had a reasonable chance of remaining undetected by any Service policeman who might be patrolling the corridor, as long as no lights were switched on and no voices were heard.

As Joe was the most likely person to guess what had been going on, it was presumably worth getting him on side with a few minutes that he would remember for the rest of his life as he sat in the dark on a Tansad chair as she mounted him in the astride facing position and gripped him in a way he claims he has never been gripped since. Although I have never been a Kamasutra enthusiast, I suspect that I might well have adopted a similar posture in preference to being on my back on a concrete floor.

If some of these women had been articulate enough to write about their adventures in and out of uniform (from most accounts they remained fully clothed), we might have learnt more. Skirts were simply rucked up and WAAFs were skilled at getting them back down in double quick time if they were disturbed. If they were naked underneath when they started the evening there was little risk of leaving incriminating evidence if they had to move quickly.

Another man on whom such a chance encounter left a lasting memory was Douglas, whom I have known and loved for many years. He had (or so I gather) his first amorous encounter with a Wren who was, from his account, a stunner. The memory of those black stockings, white thighs and black ETBs (as they were called) still seemed capable of giving him an erection. Admittedly the black stockings and black pants I put on for him to remove when I felt like indulging his favourite fantasy, were more fetching than anything the Wrens would have had to wear during the war years, but I would expect his reaction to be typical and that the 20% or 30% of the girls in Jean's unit who gave the men what they craved for, were in fact making a major contribution to the morale of the troops.

I have mentioned booze as well as sex as one of the activities that compensated the troops for the anxieties, the boredom and the lack of home comforts and affection that were inevitable in service life in war years and are no doubt inevitable in much of peace time service life.

As a Nation we no doubt consume infinitely more wine and spirits than were consumed during the war years. Many more families now drink wine with their meals and with friends than in the past. During the war many households like ours consumed virtually no alcohol while the men were away, but servicemen consumed vast quantities of beer, although most of them were continually complaining about it being watery, which it was probably was.

Gin was cheap for naval personnel and most of them drank it with water. Jean's habit of drinking it with red Martini made her a more expensive woman to entertain, but 'she presumably had what it took' in the language of the day and there were therefore enough naval officers with the financial means who were prepared to indulge her 'pretensions'. I have already noted how surprised I was at the quantity of gin she consumed when she was home on leave and she was no doubt typical of many others.

Although most drinking was convivial, a certain amount was lonely and nostalgic and I can best encapsulate the mood of these nostalgic drinkers in the parody that one of my ex-Service friends had written of 'Begin the Beguine'.

> *When they come in with the gin*
> *It brings back a night I'll always remember*
> *It brings back the cries of barmaids so tender*
> *It brings back the state I was in*
> *I'm with you once more close to the bar*
> *And I cannot recall a word you were saying*
> *It seemed as if all the room started swaying*
> *When they came in with the gin*
> *To drink it again is past all endeavour*
> *Except when that booze goes to my head*
> *And then next day I'm swearing TT forever*
> *And wishing that I were dead.*
> *What oceans of wine*
> *What raptures obscene*
> *'Til fate came along to destroy the joys we had tasted*
> *And now when I hear people curse cognac methylated*
> *I know but too well what they mean*
> *O don't let them come in with the gin*
> *Let it stay on a shelf in the bar from January to December*
> *Let the bottles contain the fire I only remember*
> *Let them come here just with beer*
> *O yes let them insist that we're pissed*
> *Let them say we're approaching half seas over*
> *While the vermouth lasts*
> *We know we'll be in clover*
> *We suddenly know what heaven we're in*
> *When they come in with the gin*
> *When they come in with the gin*

Dancing, at that time, was also immensely popular. We used to talk about it as the vertical accomplishment of the horizontal ideal. People were always being posted around the country, so most of one's dancing partners were strangers. No-one would dream of running a NAAFI dance or a Town Hall dance and leave the girls sitting around for unknown men to pluck up courage to come and ask them to dance, so the girls all took to the floor in Paul Jones circles and danced with the man opposite when the music stopped. When the lights went out a girl would respond to the passionate kisses of her partner even if she didn't know who he was and had never seen him before.

I met John at this sort of dance, albeit at a French Club social, when we were both at Oxford. Within ten seconds of our bodies touching I knew. John later admitted that although he had the rapid reflexes needed to make him a successful fighter pilot, it took him 20 seconds. This was 55 years ago, so the dance floor didn't do badly as a dating agency in those days. What's more, John and I paid only 2s/6d each for our tickets.

It's easy to forget how lonely most men were in Service units, particularly for a man who wanted a woman. John is an emotionally warm person who cuddles snugly against me every night as we go to sleep and every morning when we are both at home together, just as I need to cuddle against him. For John and men like him dancing to soft nostalgic music, holding a girl who lets her head rest against his or on his shoulder, provided the emotional therapy that he needed, even if he had never seen the girl before and might never see her again. And the girls were caught up in the same atmosphere. We wanted to be accepted by the boys who were fighting the war for us. We looked up to our men in a way that it may be difficult for many young women today to comprehend, and we were happy to indulge all their boyish pranks.

Boys of 19, 20, 21 had tremendous responsibilities thrust on them at an early age. A 21 year old Squadron Leader organising the tactics of a team he was leading in a fighter attack had the lives of his colleagues in his hands. He knew it and so did many men of that age or less who had gained promotion for their ability to do their jobs, but they were still boys when they were off duty and needed to be kept sane. They needed girls to cuddle and also to provide entertainment. They loved leading us to places where they knew our skirts would blow up (in those days wind machines designed for this purpose were an important part of any fairground or amusement arcade where girls could be trapped). A girl who tried to hold her skirt or dress down was jeered as a spoil-sport by other girls as well as the men, but most of us didn't. Some of us enjoyed it. We would rather the men looked at us than queued up to look at the girls at the Windmill.

And if the men weren't looking at us in our knickers they were talking about them. Elimination dances where the girl who remained on the floor at the end would win a prize such as a pair of nylon stockings (like gold dust in those days) were a regular favourite. Couples were eliminated at different stages according to the colour or design of the woman's knickers. "Will all ladies wearing ETBs (elastic top and bottoms) please leave the floor" and if this resulted in all the ladies having to leave it was "as you were", so we were all back dancing and then they would try something like "Any lady wearing pink (or some other colour) undies please leave the floor' and this would give your dancing partner a good excuse to start asking you whether you wore camis (a great favourite with men at that time) or to suggest that you take off whatever you were wearing next time the lights went out and he would keep them safely in his pocket, and so on. In fact this was often the best bet for the girl who really wanted to win those nylon stockings (and didn't we all). And if that was the way she won her nylons, the boys would not only give her a big round of applause but start singing "For she's a jolly good fellow" and she would become the most popular dancing partner of the evening. Such were the simple pleasures of life that kept many of our boys happy.

If you are of a later vintage, you may be amused at our wild passion for nylons which lasted until the early 1950s. Manufacture of nylon was started only in the war years and it was initially used to make the vast number of parachutes needed for the RAF.

Even in 1943 farmers in Scotland were being subsidised to grow flax, as the linen was desperately needed for parachutes. The early nylon stockings were made in America and the US troops who succeeded in obtaining them were said to find them an excellent item of barter when they wanted to get an English woman into bed, although I think that most of those who succeeded (and there were many) relied on the more traditional means of persuasion and many of the girls didn't need persuading.

This whole era, together with many of its thought habits, conventional attitudes and values went out like a lamp about 1950, although I saw it briefly rekindled in the eyes of some veterans whom I met on our pilgrimage to the Normandy War Cemeteries in 1994 to mark the 50th anniversary of the D day landings.

For John and me the swan song of the era was the weekend, or rather an evening, which we spent with John's fellow pilot and PoW Jim and his wife Ann, whom he had met when she was a sergeant in the WAAF, a chance wartime romance that ended only when Jim died two years ago.

Like most recently demobbed couples, Jim and Ann were living with parents/in-laws (in this case Jim's parents). He had a low salary as a new boy in a house-building firm and Ann was earning what she could typing. Ann was an excellent tennis player and with the goodwill of her local Tennis Club had been able to have the use of the club house, a wooden hut that was large enough for a dance floor and separated from the nearest houses by grass tennis courts and a hockey pitch.

One of Jim's friends, a demobbed radar mechanic, got hold of or built one of the early style tape recorders, which was a very long piece of tape on two large spools, and spent weeks recording all our favourite wartime tunes from the various gramophone records he was able to borrow. This was probably illegal and so was the fact that we didn't have a music licence or a bar licence, but Jim and Ann had succeeded in gathering together enough of Jim and John's old RAF friends and her WAAF friends and Ann gathered up enough sporting girls from the club to balance the numbers.

Ann took an impish delight as mistress of ceremonies to have us play all the old games on the dance floor, including a prize for the first man to reach her with his partner's panties (and I wasn't dancing with John for that one). There were shrieks of delight everywhere, but we were already past it. John and I had been married for just over five months. This was December 1948. I was still at Oxford doing a Dip.Ed. and so was John starting to work on his B.Litt. thesis and I was casting an anxious eye at the dancing partner he was holding when the lights went out and he was no doubt looking as anxiously in my direction in the knowledge that experienced wandering hands would everywhere be exploring unfamiliar and yet very familiar territory.

Everyone was still demob happy, thanking heaven for being among the survivors, so the evening inevitably made us all think a great deal about those we knew who had not survived and above all those whom we loved and still love in a way no words can describe. I knew that John would be worried about me. Would I break into tears under the emotional strain, but we all had tears in our eyes (and I was now dancing in John's arms) as we all joined in with such lines as we knew from the song that epitomised so much of what we longed for.

> *Someone so good and true...*
> *And there beneath the starry skies...*
> *Just you and I...*
> *We'll find a home*
> *To call our own...*
> *A sweet little nest*
> *Some way out in the west...*
> *And let the rest of the world go by.*

Within a month I knew I was pregnant with William. He is now over 50 and may well become a grandfather in the not too distant future.

All the hopes of those who survived 'To build a sweet little nest' were about to be achieved. We didn't yet have a home to call our own, but the warmth and love of the nest into which William, his brother and two sisters were in turn received were all that counted for John and I for many years to come, and all that counted for Jim and Ann when their first born arrived a few months after William. All our friends were likewise preoccupied and we did let 'the rest of the world go by'. Many of us disliked the things the Labour Government was doing at the time, but we had no wish to argue with our friends who might think differently. Our friendships at that time were more important than our opinions.

I don't think we were politically irresponsible because I don't think we could have done much to change the course of history had we been politically active. The simple fact was that we had no spare capacity. In some respects we were emotionally exhausted and needed to recharge our batteries. In any case, most of the Conservative party activists that we met seemed to be pansified wets who talked as if socialism would be more acceptable if it were run by pansified Conservative wets rather than by Socialists. It wasn't until Margaret Thatcher came on the scene that I could muster any enthusiasm, but that was nearly 30 years later.

Looking back, I believe that while we may have succeeded in winning the war we somehow succeeded in losing a number of national qualities that are difficult to define but which people who were around at the time find easy to recognise, and this is sad. My only excuse for writing this somewhat disjoined chapter is the hope that not only those who were there will understand but, much more importantly, those of you who were not will also understand. Our heritage is much more important than old buildings. It is also the thoughts and aspirations of the people who lived not only in old buildings (many spent most of the time in Nissen huts) but who played an important part in our history, even if many of their roles were minor roles.

CHAPTER 13

SIXTH FORM

1942-43 Academic Success - but an uninhibited 'lecture' lands me in trouble

In this chapter I get back to my life as a sixteen year old schoolgirl in the Summer of 1942 after (in the last chapter) breaking the narrative to take a look at the wider context of the customs and attitudes that were prevalent at the time and would, in due course, have a bearing on the way I would think and would act in my relations with men.

My standing with adults and the confidence with which I was able to handle tricky situations by the time I was seventeen owed more than a little to the school and its education traditions, as well as to my good fortune in having a number of remarkable teachers. It is customary to praise a child for being intelligent if it does well and to blame its teachers if it does badly. This is a custom I deplore. Furthermore, it is counter-productive. Teachers, like the rest of us, are bound to be better motivated if parents and pupils give them the credit properly due when they do a good job.

I will start with School Cert. where I took nine subjects, many of which involved a number of three-hour papers, which meant that the latter part of June and most of July were spent in exam conditions. In those days Summer Term lasted until the end of July and we didn't get our School Cert. results until we started the Autumn Term in mid September. I got distinctions in English, History and French and six credits in other subjects. Latin wasn't my favourite subject, but there was no brilliant Latin scholar in my year and so I got the top marks for the year, both in the High School and in the College. I didn't have Mum's or Jean's gift in Maths, but as I had already reached the required level for elementary Maths by the time I started the Lower Fifth, I was put in the set that did differential, calculus and trigonometry and in due course entered for the paper in Additional Maths, which counted as a subject. I could, of course, get help from Mum where I had difficulty in understanding. Again, because there was nobody brilliant in Maths in my year, I got higher marks than anyone else, but I had worked steadily at all my subjects throughout the two school years 1940-42.

There were not many distractions and I had peace and quiet to work at home. I did, of course, enjoy my sensual moments with Jacko and one or two other boys and the occasional high-jinks with the other three Musketeers, but they, as well as the boys, were all living within a regime where work had to come first. Of course, if I was in the midst of reading a randy passage in a French novel or a book such as Fanny Hill, I might be tempted to finish it rather than getting on with my Latin word list, or whatever, but these were nothing like the distractions with which my grandchildren have had to contend in terms of television programmes and boys wanting to take them out to discos.

The advantage of the old style Sixth Form system (as opposed to sending children to separate Sixth Form Colleges) is that, as a Sixth Former in a Grammar type school, you were somebody and became a role model. You were treated as an adult and you tended to identify with authority rather than becoming a rebel.

In the College the boys stood a chance of becoming prefects, which gave them early experience in holding positions of authority and exercising judgment in the maintenance of discipline. We didn't have quite the same system in a girls' day school, but we were given a lot of responsibility in such matters as organising school assembly, doing the roll-call in junior classes and supervising prep. periods and, in some cases, supervising a class when a teacher was absent sick and there was no replacement.

In some schools there was a tradition of the Lower Sixth being a laid-back year after the hard work for School Cert. In the High School and the College, the practice was to stretch us to the full during the Lower Sixth year. We had the same sort of pep talk from the Headmistress in September 1942 as she had given us two years earlier when we went into the Lower Fifth - this time it was that we were starting a two year course for Higher Cert. and those who would get good results would be those who worked hard in the Lower Sixth.

Prestige can be an important motivating factor and I make no secret of the fact that I basked in the respect I now enjoyed from the staff who knew me in both College and High School. I was seen as a solid all-rounder who could have specialised in any set of subjects, but I chose English, History and French as my main subjects with Latin and German as subsidiary subjects for Higher Cert. In those days, the practice in the College and High School was to do two main subjects and two subsidiary subjects, but it was reckoned that with my existing knowledge of French literature (mainly novels) and the ability to speak the language since my childhood days, I should be able to cope with French as a third main subject.

Mrs. Rainham was delighted to have me in her English Sixth and Captain Ferrers (of whom more anon) likewise welcomed me into his History Sixth because they both thought I was Oxbridge scholarship material. Mrs. Rainham was said to have remarked in the staff room that I was a good example of 'slow and steady wins the race'. She also said my essays were my best work because they showed that I could think for myself and not simply trot out bits of information that I might have learnt parrot-fashion.

The encouragement that I was getting from my teachers (notably these two) did result in my becoming over-confident and as a result nearly getting expelled - not from the High School, but in being refused permission to attend further classes at the College.

When one talks about the threat of being expelled from school people may think I must have been guilty of some heinous crime such as being found in bed with a boy in a College dormitory, or having too much to drink, and so on, when all I did was to talk knowledgeably in class about some French books I had read and to express some opinions on these books. One of the sad lessons I, therefore, had to learn during my first year in the Sixth was that our much vaunted freedom of speech didn't apply if you said things (however innocently) that conflicted with the prevailing orthodoxy of someone in power. I had to learn that if I wanted to get on and stand a chance of getting an Oxbridge place, I must learn to be circumspect and avoid expressing opinions that might irritate. It was well that I learnt this lesson sooner rather than later.

In retirement, now that I don't have to worry about upsetting prospective clients, I have, of course, become much more relaxed in what I say. Normal politeness will prevent me from making insulting remarks about say vegetarian cuisine if I have been invited to dinner by a vegetarian, but, you will have noticed from this book, I don't nowadays pull punches in my comments on people who hold views that I regard as totally pernicious.

People who want to interfere with the traditional rights of Englishmen to ride to hounds, of English women to wear fur coats, the right of people to eat meat on the grounds that they are eating their brothers and sisters, or people who want to prevent the correct use of English grammar (trying to force the use of plural pronouns such as 'their' instead of 'his' relating to a single subject, as in the sentence 'everyone waved his good wishes') can count on getting the raw edge of my tongue. Sadly, however, I would have to advise a Sixth Former of today's generation against speaking as I do because he might be in the class of a teacher for whom such views have become holy writ.

Before we get to the events which could have got me banned from College premises, there are one or two items I want to include because they played an important part in the development of my view of life. I have spoken in an earlier chapter on the way Mrs. Rainham helped me to develop the concept of literature as a way of understanding why we are in this world and what we should be trying to do in our time here.

Learning to understand and interpret historical events and to make allowances for the slanted ways in which they are often presented was something I owed to my History master, Captain Ferrers.

He had fought at Gallipoli in World War I, going straight from school to the army and then to Oxford after he had been demobilised. The College boys nicknamed him "Old Ferret" presumably because he had the reputation of ferretting out interesting snippets of information and how little work they had done in order to write their History essays. But he was liked and respected. Apart from being a History master, he was a house master and he was also the officer in charge of the College corps (called the Officers' Training Corps [OTC]) at the beginning of the war and later the Junior Training Corps (JTC).

Not only was Old Ferret a goldmine of information, but he taught me how to exercise critical judgment, the most important thing I learnt in the Sixth Form.

Again and again he would repeat his dictum "You are now specialists. It's no good quoting the 'Bible' (his name for our Upper Fifth History text book) and saying 'the book says'. You needed the Bible to get through School Cert. where what you had to show was your knowledge of facts." He would set us an essay subject to write on an event of historical importance. He would give out a Roneo-ed sheet of paper with six or seven quotations from different leading historians, each of which put a different interpretation on the same facts. He used to tell us that all these were people with big names, that they all had opinions and had an interest in persuading us to believe their particular interpretations.

"Your task is to assess the various motives of these protagonists. Never believe anyone who says he is impartial. In the Sixth Form you've got to learn to think for yourself and form your own judgments."

For many years I assumed that everyone who studied History at Sixth Form level was taught in the same way. I didn't realise at the time, or for many years later, how fortunate I was to have such a wonderful teacher. Whether I was trying to reconcile the different views of different members of my family, or of clients and their antagonists in the days when I ran a management consultancy company, or simply in reading newspapers, I have had occasion to be grateful to and bless Old Ferret for what I learnt in his classes, which was infinitely more valuable than what I needed to get my Higher Cert. He is one of those people whom I hope I shall one day meet again if St. Peter lets me through the gate. The conscientious devotion which he gave to generations of schoolboys and later to girls as well as boys, as well as the devoted service to his country must surely have earned him a place in Paradise. He died in 1965.

The subject of specialisation in the Sixth Form is one on which I feel strongly. The chorus of attacks on the English 'A' Level system always makes me angry. If you were to replace it with something like a baccalaureat, Sixth Formers would get no more than a superficial knowledge of a large number of subjects, making it into no more than a super 'O' Level. With declining standards the knowledge required to pass is likely to be substantially less than we needed to take the old School Cert. Such an approach demonstrates total ignorance of the most important component of Sixth Form work - to learn how to learn, how to look for information that is relevant, how to weigh evidence and form a balanced judgment. With that experience one has the skill to master any new subject as and when you need to, just as in later years I had to master subject areas such as business finance, company law, taxation, marketing, personnel management and the multiplicity of skills needed to run a company.

I can still remember the essays I had to write on topics such as "The Church of England under Henry VIII was Catholic without a Pope"; "The Congress of Berlin - Peace with Honour or a Major Cause of the 1914-18 War? - Discuss."; "The American Civil War - Does it Prove that Federal Systems of Government Inevitably Result in the Extinction of Individual States' Rights?"

This last essay comes to mind whenever I read of the constitutional battles in the EU or the break up of the former Yugoslavia.

I knew that many of the opinions that I expressed and judgments that I made in my essays were the opposite of those held by Mr. Ferrers. At that time I was more of an idealist, believing for example that a federal system of government for Europe might have saved us from two world wars. Subsequent events have proved him right again and again, but at the time his sole concern was to correct us where we had got our facts wrong and to ensure that we learnt to marshal our arguments and present whatever case we wanted to present in the best possible light.

Our subject areas in History were vast - England 1485 to 1919 and US History from the founding of the thirteen colonies to President Wilson's fourteen points. Mr. Ferrers had chosen the US rather than Europe. This was pioneering on his part. Most History Sixth Formers in those days knew a lot about the wars of Frederick the Great and the battles of the Thirty Years War. We were, at that time, joined in alliance with the USA as the two democracies that were trying to save the world and he thought it more important for our generation to have an in-depth understanding of the totally different ways in which democratic institutions can evolve in different countries. His favourite quote was a remark made by Bismarck in the 1880s - "The most important, single fact of modern history is that the people of North America speak English."

In addition to the syllabus we were given every encouragement and assistance to extend our interests. We went to concerts. In those days very few people had gramophone records of complete concertos or symphonies. You would have to afford three twelve inch 78 records in order to play a single Mozart piano concerto. In those days the BBC saw itself as responsible for raising educational and cultural standards. People from all backgrounds seemed keen to improve themselves. A string quartet playing in the town hall would attract a large audience, including many men and women in uniform. Orchestral works such as Tchaikovsky's first piano concerto, Rachmaninov's second piano concerto and Beethoven's fifth symphony attracted large enthusiastic audiences. I remember going to see Benno Moisevitch play Rachmaninov's second on a Sunday afternoon in a local cinema as part of a "Wings for Victory" week aimed at beating the national savings target. National savings were a means of mopping up the excess money supply. If people could be persuaded to refrain from spending money on things (there was not much to buy in any case) it would be easier to prevent inflation getting out of hand and in the main the effort was successful. As this was not an easy concept to sell it was presented as if a school, or a village, or a town was actually subscribing for the purchase of a Spitfire, or a Hurricane.

Beethoven's fifth symphony had acquired a major symbolic importance. The opening bars corresponded to the Morse code for the letter V (...-). These opening bars were used to introduce most of the BBC broadcasts to occupied Europe, be they in French, Dutch, Danish, Norwegian, Polish. They were intended to provide hope and encouragement where the occupied peoples knew that they risked imprisonment, or worse, if they were caught listening to the BBC. In those days not everybody had radios. In later years I met many French people who are still emotionally stirred when they hear this magnificent Beethoven opening and remember the days when a large number might be huddled around a primitive wireless set in a cellar, wondering whether one amongst them might turn out to be a Judas who would denounce them to the occupying police.

In spite of the war, it was a wonderful year to be alive. I enjoyed my work. Up to then it had been work. Up to then playing the piano had largely been a matter of practising the piece I was set to learn for the next music lesson. There were many pieces that I loved, but it was in the Lower Sixth that I came to know and to love many of the famous pieces of music that I still find deeply moving whenever I hear them to this day, the slow movement from the Mozart D Minor piano concerto (number 20), Handel's Largo, Gounod's Ave Marie and above all "I Know that My Redeemer Liveth" from Handel's Messiah. As you can see, my tastes are quite ordinary in music as in so many other things.

I came to love the Messiah when I sang in the Hallelujah Chorus in a performance of selections in the Cathedral in December 1942. This was the most ambitious production that Alec had achieved with the College choir and College orchestra, certain guest singers and the Cathedral organist. The tremendous power of the resonant organ notes as they filled the high vaulted nave and the transepts symbolised for many of us the triumph of good over evil. It was at a time in the war we had heard of the victory of General Montgomery over Rommel at the battle of El Alamein, the news of the successful capture by the British and Americans of Morocco and Algeria and the turn of the tide on the eastern front, although victory against the Japs still seemed far away and we would not see Dad until the Japs had been defeated.

The Hallelujah Chorus enables ordinary people to feel part of something greater than themselves. I am reminded of this every time I see or hear a performance in the Albert Hall which gives the opportunities for school choirs, village choirs, women's institute choirs the chance to participate. In a century when the only opportunity that has been given to so many people to participate in something bigger than themselves had been political movements, whether the Hitler Youth or other, which had betrayed them, I think how much we owe to Handel, a German immigrant who was down on his luck because his operas on classical themes had gone out of fashion and who wrote his greatest work for its first performance in a Dublin church on 13th April 1742. There can be few musical works that have brought so much spiritual joy to so many for over 250 years.

I mention these events in my spiritual and cultural odyssey because they were important in shaping my future way of thinking, more important than anything I actually did during that year, and I did quite a lot.

I participated, for example, in debates in big school at the College and at the Sixth Form conference, which the College hosted for representatives of a number of schools within reasonable travelling distance. It was a period of widespread interest in rebuilding the world after the war. The Beveridge Report on the reform of British social security had been published a few months earlier. Everyone who had remembered, or knew about the conditions of deprivation and poverty during the 1930s recession believed fervently that such conditions should not be tolerated. We had demonstrated as a country our capability to wage war on an unprecedented scale and yet we were able to maintain much higher standards of living in conditions of U-boat blockade and with only a small part of the population available to provide food, clothing, heating and shelter for the whole population. Without an enemy to fight we could all enjoy a much higher standard of living.

Many of us, however, were annoyed by what we saw as the subversive political campaigns of the socialists and the communists to hijack this desire for reform and turn it into an attack on the middle classes and on our democratic institutions. We had enough potential manufacturing capacity to create plenty for all without pillaging everyone who didn't fall into the political definition of "workers" whether by confiscatory taxation or other means.

Although this was the view of many older people, I was sometimes in a minority of one amongst those of my own age group. I remember Mr. Ferrers, who was arbitrating and calling the speakers to order, winding up a debate by paying tribute to my resolute defence of my beleaguered position and reminding the debaters that we were fighting a war to defend the rights of individuals to hold their own opinions and to speak freely. I sensed there were a number of would-be little Hitlers in the audience who thought differently.

After the debate he said it would be wonderful for the country if I were to make a career in politics, but not wonderful for me and he didn't advise it. His advice was good and I am glad I took it, although I don't think I would have gone for a career in politics even if he had recommended it. I am too much of a believer to have the tactical skills needed for a political life and I couldn't imagine a more boring job than having to pass my days and nights sitting through the type of debates they have in the House of Commons, where the voting result is always a foregone conclusion.

The year was also one of spiritual experience. It was the year I was confirmed. Most College boys and High School girls were confirmed much younger, but by waiting until the Lower Sixth I had the advantage of being in the Headmaster's preparation class. He was a theologian, a Doctor of Divinity, who had written a number of books. The same rigour was expected of us in our discussions as we had come to expect in the analysis of a Shakespeare text. This is important. In many schools religious instruction is in the hands of well-meaning amateurs, but this can mean that many children grow up with a perception of the Christian religion, which remains relatively childish as compared with the perception of the subjects that they were studying for Higher Cert., or even for Matric.

Divinity was also a school subject which took up two periods a week. In the Lower Sixth we joined the College boys and were taught by the Headmaster himself. In the Lower Sixth we studied the Gospel of Saint Luke, in an edition which considered the motives of the various translators during different periods of history. The Headmaster, who had been a classical scholar, used to try and explain what the original Greek text might mean. In the Upper Sixth when the school knew we were all working flat out for Higher Cert. we had an easier divinity option, a comparative study of the religions of the world.

And the earthy side of me? My bodily desires were as powerful as ever but after the disappointing encounter with Jacko the previous year, I could no longer find any enthusiasm for him, or in fact for any of the other College boys. I was kissed and fondled on a number of occasions after such events as College dances and my immediate bodily response must have been enough to convince any man who knew what he was about that I wouldn't say no. Fortunately, none of them knew what they were about although I would not have said 'fortunately' at the time.

From May or June 1942 when I received my plain brown paper parcel from Georges (fortunately it looked like a book) containing a dozen French Letters, a tube of spermicidal cream and packets of the famous pessaries, I was always prepared, in the best Girl Guide tradition, so if Mr. Right had come along I could have responded without fear of getting pregnant. But no Mr. Right presented himself.

By now I was yearning for something more. One of my main questions was how to fit this earthy side into the same me that was at an important stage in her spiritual and intellectual awakening. The best clue as to the way these bits of the human jigsaw fitted together was in Chaucer, where the most moving lines I had read on the death of Troilus came from the same pen as the description of the two northern students making love in the dark to the miller's wife and daughter while the miller snored. Yet even this tale was not simply bucolic. The fact that Chaucer described the miller's daughter as someone in tears as her lover left her, made me identify with her.

My third main subject, French, catered for my enjoyment of what is now called 'soft porn' (a totally ill-fitting term which suggests that it is inferior to 'hard porn', but more of that anon).

Although the war had put an end to my annual Summer holidays in La Tour du Pin with my French grandmother and her family where I had spoken nothing but French, Mum was determined that I should not lose the advantage of being bilingual. She had always spoken to her mother in French, but as she always spoke to Dad in English, English had become our intimate and child language which she felt enabled Dad to be part of our closely-knit family. When we were alone together she made a point of speaking French with me so many days a week, in order to keep it up, but more importantly she got me interested in reading. When grandmaman had gone back to live in France in 1925, she had let Mum keep most of her books. Apart from the obvious classics, there were lots of paperback novels which are no longer read, but which even at 14 and 15 I had raced through with enthusiasm. To me they were light reading, whereas my classmates would have had to struggle through, looking up most of the words.

In those days English books (or at least those printed in England) were meant to be 'respectable'. The A. W. Verity edition of Hamlet for schools for example had been bowdlerised to the extent of cutting out all references to adultery in spite of the fact that this altered the plot and left no sound reason for Hamlet to be annoyed with his mother. In contrast, there were many more French books that wrote about life 'as it is'. That was the way I saw it and the bits of life that a teenager with a lecherous mind like mine wanted to know about were better catered for in my French reading than in English.

Fortunately, Mum never attempted to restrict the books I read. In fact I could guess by the way in which some books seemed to open at the erotic pages which had been folded back more than the others, or by little slips of old, faded newspaper that had been inserted as bookmarks a generation ago, that Mum, her sister, and grandmaman had been as lecherous in their choice of teenage reading as I was. And if they were like me, as they probably were, they would never have grown out of this innocent form of enjoyment.

Unfortunately, Mr. Porteus, the French master at the College who took most of the French literature classes, was an old style boarding school bachelor who knew the texts and the sort of answers that were needed to get good marks in Higher Cert. where the papers were, no doubt, going to be marked by other people like him. Apart from having little or no sparkle, he appeared to treat the French language as a dead language, like Latin, although I have always regarded Latin as much more alive than most of the people who learn it, but this is a quote from one of my Latin teachers and not something I have made up on the hoof.

With Mr. Porteus I must have appeared insufferably arrogant and self-opinionated because I had an unfair advantage. Most of the boys in his class had struggled to get a credit in School Cert. French. They would be examined on nine set texts, which included Tartuffe, Le Pere Goriot, Tartarin de Tarascon, Merimee's Chronique du Regne du Charles IX and he knew he would have the devil's own job to get them to read even half of these books in French (most of the class would get hold of translations), let alone read anything outside the syllabus. But he wanted to encourage them to read what they could and circulated suggestions for further reading. It didn't matter if these books were read in English translations. He was doing his best to get his class familiar with French literature.

Early in the Autumn Term he announced, no doubt in accordance with his normal practice, that he wanted boys (he wasn't yet used to having girls in his class) to volunteer to talk to the class at the next lesson about their favourite French books. I was the first (and I think only) member of the class to put a hand up. His first reaction was presumably to think that with a few girls in the class he stood a chance of producing better results next year.

It was the first opportunity I had in my life to stand behind the master's desk and see whether I had any capability for public speaking. I worked hard to prepare a set of legible notes and as all first timers I produced far too many and the ideas came bubbling forth a little bit higgledy-piggledy. The poor man must have been in danger of a heart attack, but the boys sat spellbound. I doubt if he had ever in his life been able to arouse so much interest and enthusiasm in a class of boys for French literature.

I started with Madame Bovary, which I still think is the greatest novel ever written in French, although I hated much of what it says. I must have read it six or seven times over my life span, learning something new each time. I hated it, no doubt as Flaubert hated Emma Bovary.

My next book was Maupassant's Une Vie. I said that although both of these books had been written by men, they were both books which interested me because they attempted to understand and explain what it was like to be a woman in 19th Century France.

Although I was in the main repeating things that my mother and grandmother had told me some years earlier as reasons why I should read these books when I was old enough, I had really worked hard in the week that I had to prepare my notes, reading Une Vie for the first time. I was now at an age when I became emotionally involved. I'm sure I had tears in my eyes when I described how this woman with substantial money of her own had felt it necessary to marry a syphilitic boor with aristocratic pretensions, who spent her money on gambling and other women, got her maid pregnant and was killed by the husband of the woman whom he had made his mistress.

My theme was justice. I knew nothing about things like the Married Women's Property Act in Britain and the fact that there had been no such Act in France. It just seemed to me a contravention of natural justice that a man should get his hands on a woman's money just because he married her. I now think it equally unjust that some gold-digging female should acquire a right to half a man's property.

And so I gradually built up to my intended shock piece, Maupassant's Maison Tellier. This was a short story that had fascinated me when I first read it when I was sixteen, so I had immediately understood what it was about. It was pornography in the literal sense, which means writing about brothels and Madame Tellier's house was a brothel for the upper middle classes, although the term brothel is as inappropriate for her type of establishment as the term "boozer" would be for an English country pub where men and their families sit out in the gardens. Boozer was the term appropriate to places where hard drinkers stood over a bar (and no women dare be seen) in Scotland when I was a girl.

In my Fifth Form days I had got used to posing as the strong woman Boadicea (hence the nickname Boadie, by which I was still known). Now that I could show the boys that I had been able to beat virtually all of them in every subject in School Cert, I was tending to posture as the knowledgeable and sophisticated woman of the world who could talk in a relaxed, casual way about what went on in places like brothels, even though the slim knowledge that I might have gained at that age was all derived from books.

There were a number of historical facts that I knew, of which I assumed most of the boys in the class were ignorant, so I did my best to impress them by explaining that such establishments as the Maison Tellier were legal in France (they were until 1946) and an eminently civilised way of satisfying basic human needs or bringing buyers and sellers together, rather than leaving the women who practised the oldest profession to ply their trade standing out on cold street corners. I explained that Maupassant had grown up in what was the golden age for modern France, the era of Napoleon III when all the Parisian boulevards had been built. I explained that France in 1850 had been twenty years behind England in constructing railways, but had caught up during the Napoleon III era and this meant that new opportunities were opened up for women from all over France to travel to Paris and find jobs in Paris that were much better paid and congenial than the wretched conditions in which most of them had to slave as servants and peasants.

I pointed out that in a period of prosperity there were lots more men with money to spend and I was sure that many of the women who had found jobs as can-can dancers or entertaining wealthy men in brothels enjoyed their jobs and this might be a way of finding a wealthy lover, or even a husband. I said that one of my own family's legends was that my French great-grandmother had started that way and finished up marrying a wealthy French Baron and inheriting his fortune.

I went on to say that Maupassant had learned from Flaubert the art of 'le mot juste' which is to describe life as it was and not to wrap everything up in a romantic haze.

Although Maupassant set many of his stories in Paris, some of his best stories are set in his native Normandy. The Maison Tellier is set at the small port (now a seaside town) of Fécamp. Madame Tellier and her late husband had originally been proprietors of an inn, but in another small Normandy town. They inherited the brothel, which was a much more profitable business, from an uncle and, as Maupassant explains, the Normans didn't have any hang-ups about working in this sort of business, neither did their regular customers have any hang-ups in patronising the place. They included a banker, a tax collector, an insurance agent and a wood merchant who had done his turn as mayor. They used to sip Chartreuse or Champagne (at ten old francs a bottle) in the drawing room, talking and laughing with the three girls who constituted the establishment and each, when he felt so inclined, would discreetly disappear with his favourite girl through the door to the stairway leading to the bedrooms. The establishment is presented as a homely and friendly place where the three girls appear to enjoy their life, or at any rate regard it as a better option than many of the alternatives.

On the floor below two other girls (assisted by a barman, who was no doubt also available as a chucker-out) served cider and catered for a rougher type of customer, including the English and French sailors who came in by a different entrance.

One of the merits of the story (and this is still my view) is that it enables Maupassant to present these people as human beings, as opposed to being treated as type-cast automatons. He describes their adventures on a railway journey (when the establishment was closed for the day, to the consternation of its regular customers) to attend the first communion of Madame Tellier's niece and the moving scene in the village church service, where the girls are no doubt seen by the villagers as sophisticated city ladies.

I finished by saying that one of the most important things I had learned from Maupassant's books was that it taught you to look behind the job to the person who did it and to try and understand that person. I wished that one of the girls in the Maison Tellier, or a similar establishment, had written her life story and it had been published.

I sat down to an enthusiastic clapping of hands. But poor old Mr. Porteus, who had been used to translating any expletive that he found in a French text by "dash my buttons" quickly ended the lesson with a curt comment "For obvious reasons none of the books that Miss Fortingall has chosen to talk about is in the syllabus, nor are any of them likely to be." We filed out to go to our next lesson.

The repercussions of my lecture on French literature were much more serious than I could have anticipated. Although feminists in recent years may have banged the drum at a time when they were old enough to hold their own in the national press, I doubt if many of them would have stood up at the age of sixteen in an all male establishment such as the College (although there were four or five other High School girls in the class they tended to be reticent and passive in a mixed class) and put the case, as positively as I think I did, for a sympathetic understanding of what life must have meant as a woman in 19th Century France. I was not asserting any rights, or making any claims. All I was saying was "think", which is what I had been trying to do. My reactions were genuinely spontaneous reactions to the books I had read and was talking about. I was not trotting out other people's ideas. If I had done a rotten job I don't think I would have been in such deep trouble.

Later that week my name was read out as one of those required to report to Mr. Squires before lunch. The school prefect of the week brought the list round with the notices in the third period each day, after the 10.45 - 11.00 break. Boys knew that this would inevitably mean the whacks and they were teased by their class mates who silently made indicative finger movements.

I knew it was serious by the expression on Mr. Squires' face when he eventually called me in. This time there was no question of being told to sit down in the morning room. I stood in the hall behind three boys, each of whom went in and was given six. Only serious offences were referred to him and no boy got less than six. The poor blighters were yelling pitifully after the first three (one after the first two) and staggered out sobbing, with their hands clutching their agonised backsides.

I knew that College and High School rules would not permit him to cane me or any other girl, regardless of what I had done and I also knew that he wouldn't have subjected me to the painful ordeal of listening to those three boys having the living daylight knocked out of them unless I had done something dreadful. I gathered that all they had done was to skip their ATC field-day manoeuvres so that they could spend the afternoon with their girlfriends, who worked in various shops in town (it was early closing day) and who would be suitably impressed at the sight of these boys in their uniforms.

I also knew that if Walford wanted to get me he could, whatever the rules. If I had committed a heinous crime it merely had to be suggested to Mum that she should write him a letter requesting him, as a friend of the family, to do her a favour and punish her little girl in the way her Dad would have done if he had been at home. In this way neither the College nor the High School would be officially involved in the matter and, of course, neither Mum nor any other parent in those days would have failed to do what someone in authority in a College or School suggested. It would, therefore, have been no relief for me, or anyone else, to walk out of Walford's study at lunchtime on a Tuesday with my behind unscathed, in the certain knowledge that I would be back again on Saturday as 'a friend of the family' clad in suitable punishment trousers for Walford to do his worst, as he had just done to these three 'truants'. And the four waiting days would have been added punishment. I had managed to keep a stiff upper lip when he had done me for smoking, six months earlier, but I reckoned that three was as much as I could take and I reckoned I would crack if I got any more, just as these tough, sturdily built, seventeen year old 'truants' had cracked.

I was not, therefore, in a happy frame of mind when Walford called me in. I also felt a bit like the hero in Kafka's novel 'The Trial' because I had no idea of what heinous crime I was supposed to have committed. I didn't know I had any enemies who would want to put down the poison.

This time when I went in he didn't tell me to sit down, so I stood awkwardly in front of his desk as he sat and looked at me. He noticed me glancing apprehensively at his rack of canes and shook his head.

"Your offence is much too serious for that. It's touch and go whether you will be able to attend any classes in the College in future, but you can take it from me that if I had been able to deal with you in the conventional way you would now be in a much sorrier state than any of the boys who came in before you."

"But what have I done, Sir?" I said. I was really surprised. I thought I was going to be incorrectly accused of smoking or drinking, or some similar 'crime' of which I knew I was innocent.

"Good God, girl, don't try that on me! Everyone knows you are intelligent, so don't you dare come in here pretending to be stupid or I will change my mind. But that won't help you."

"But what school rule have I broken, Sir?"

I had never seen a man so angry. He threw his pencil down on his blotting pad in a gesture of rage.

"Don't tell me you haven't the intelligence and common sense to understand that when you are allowed to attend classes in the College, you are benefiting from a special war time dispensation. The College is where Christian parents send their sons for a good, moral education. Not just to pass exams. If Mr. Porteus asked to be excused from teaching you in future, as he has, it would simply be a matter of telling you to abandon French in Higher Cert., or learn it some other way. But what are we to say to the parents who have sent their sons to a boys' Public School when we allow a girl to stand up in class and tell them that women are much better off working in brothels than getting married, and that Frenchmen go to brothels every night of the week just as Englishmen go to pubs and, oh yes, that your grandmother was a prostitute and you are proud of her. You have become the scarlet woman and no parent would want his son to be contaminated by you."

Even in that frightful moment I couldn't help but smile inwardly at the memory of all those lecherous College boys who had never missed an opportunity to get their fingers inside my knickers, but I kept a straight face. When he had finished I said:

"But that's not what I said, Sir. What I said was..."

"I don't give a damn what you said, or thought you said, that's what boys are repeating. It's not within our jurisdiction to expel you from the High School, but if a boy had said what you said, we would seriously be considering his expulsion. And for a woman to say it, and you are a woman..." He left the rest of the sentence unfinished.

I was about to ask why a woman should be more guilty than a man for saying the same thing and to go on and say "I thought this war was about the defence of freedom of speech", but I thought better of it. I was already thinking about how I could get Higher Cert. and could I get to Oxford if I was to be expelled.

"You're not to attend any lessons or extra curricular activities at the College for the rest of this week, so you had better collect your things and go home straight away. I'll have to speak to your mother. I'm sorry for her and as for your father, by God he'd have thrashed you to within an inch of your life if he'd been here. All right, you can go."

So I walked to the door and let myself out. It would have been tempting providence to go into the College dining room for lunch as I normally would on days when our French and History lessons kept us in the College until lunchtime. Hungry as I was I didn't go home to make something to eat. I didn't want to disturb Mum at the office. I decided to go to the High School library while the girls were in the dining hall. I hadn't booked in for High School lunch so there wouldn't have been a place for me. On the way I saw Mrs. Rainham go into her study so I followed her and knocked on her door. She often spent the lunch hour marking while she ate a sandwich.

Before I had said a word she had interpreted my facial expression to indicate that something serious was up. I'm one of those people who has always looked hale and hearty, with plenty of colour in my cheeks, even when I have had a temperature of 102 and felt at death's door. I wasn't pale and wan, but she knew me well enough to know that I didn't get worked up on minor matters.

"They're threatening to expel me", I said as she sat down and waved me to a chair. I imagined a whole series of possible misdeeds wafting through her mind, but she merely stood up, picked up her handbag and keys and said:

"Come and have a Welsh Rarebit, I'm hungry and I bet you are."

So we walked to the Al Hambra, the pretentious name for a scruffy little caff (the only word for it) where you paid for your food and tea at the counter and took it to a series of tables separated by plywood partitions, which ran along the side of a corridor.

"I've brought you here so you can talk to me as a friend and not as a teacher. I'm something of a misfit, both in the College and High School. You must understand that no teacher must be seen, or suspected of criticising another member of staff to a pupil. I would be more in danger of losing my job than anyone else. I can listen to what you say and sympathise but no more."

I nodded agreement. I then told her what had happened. She was silent for a moment as she ate and then she turned to me.

"You know I want to keep you and I'm sure Mr. Ferrers does. You're our best hope for an Oxford or Cambridge scholarship in 1944-5, whether you decide to read English or History. We can find someone to coach you in French if Mr. Porteus refuses to teach you. The Headmistress doesn't have power to expel you without the agreement of the governors and I don't think she would want to, so our task is to negotiate a compromise. We want the College to agree to your continuing to attend History classes with Mr. Ferrers, but I won't say a word to him until I've talked to your mother.

"If Mr. Squires was as angry and ill-tempered as you say that may be a good sign. Nothing ever ruffles him so something else must have got him into that state. Let's hope he regrets his wild outburst. In the meantime you've got to be tactful. You produce some powerful arguments in your English essays, which some teachers would find outrageous. People generally tend to get more annoyed with someone like you who can marshal your arguments and make a strong case than with someone who dabbles and who is easy to destroy."

I agreed that the only thing that mattered was my future, but I couldn't help referring to freedom of speech. She shook her head.

"Most people only pay lip service to freedom of speech. Look at the way the Americans are threatening to shoot Ezra Pound as a traitor because he broadcast a few talks on James Joyce, Eliot and Cummings on the Rome radio. You can thank your lucky stars Squires didn't use his cane on you. Mind, he has no right to because you are not a College pupil, but if he was in the rage you say he was there would be no holding him."

"In a way I wish he had", I said. "The whole thing would have been over then and there."

"You don't know what you're saying, girl." This time she was annoyed with me. "If you'd seen Benjy's (her eldest son) bottom after he had been caned for nothing more than taking a short-cut on a run when the poor little mite was barely fourteen, you wouldn't say things like that. You could see the marks nearly five weeks later and Mr. Squires is feared in the school far more than any prefect."

I told her about the three boys who had been in front of me that morning. She suspected they were the three that Benjy had mentioned who had played truant the previous Thursday when the ATC and JTC were away from the school on field day and I said they were. They were day boys who had left home in their ATC uniform and worked out there wouldn't be a roll call on a field day and there wasn't, but they'd been seen in the town by the local bank manager, who was a voluntary ATC instructor (who knew they should have been on field day manoeuvres) and who telephoned the Head. The school had obviously feared the worst.

"So I was the scarlet woman who led these morally upright boys astray. I have, in fact, been at the receiving end of his cane when I was supposed to be smoking and wasn't."

When I saw the frown on her face I immediately wished I could unsay those last words.

"No-one can be expected to help you, Mavis, if you go on saying things that are bound to get you into trouble. I know you have an impish sense of humour, but your situation is serious and you've got to keep your tongue in check. Remember the famous Latin tag 'tempus loquendi… tempus tacendi' - there is a time to speak up and a time to shut your trap. And as for getting the cane, everyone knows he only plays with his cane when he taps the girls in the hope that he can frighten them out of further mischief."

I disagreed, but I wasn't going to argue.

"On reflection I don't think those truants could have got him into that sort of rage. He dishes out that sort of punishment every day of the week, often for things that are far worse. I'll keep my ear to the ground. Ask your mother to do the same. In the meantime it's back to school. You're with me for most of the afternoon and you're in Mrs. Brown's German class, so act normally and don't say anything to anybody. If they ask what Mr. Squires wanted to see you about you can say it's because your timetable was giving problems because you are taking more subjects than anyone else. And if they ask if you got caned you can tell them truthfully that you didn't."

I waited until Mum and I had started our evening meal before I told her. Even at that age I found it easier to think and talk while I was sitting at a table eating. Perhaps that's one of the reasons I have always eaten slowly.

Mum, didn't seem the least excited, but that's her character and one of the reasons she has always been the diplomat in the family.

"You've got Arrière and Grandma both coming out in you", she mused. Arrière would do the most scandalous things, but she always acted the part of the noble lady to the chateau born. She wasn't attending a Church of England boys' Public School. She would never have dreamed of using polemic or argument to justify what she did.

"Grandma (Catherine, her father's mother) could beat anyone in an argument on any subject. She was whiter than white and shrewd enough to restrict her crusading to one or two issues that could command widespread moral support, such as university education for girls, and using the rest of her talent to make herself financially independent by writing best selling popular novels. I am sure she'd have liked your crusading spirit, but would have taken you on one side and told you not to waste your time trying to persuade men to do something about the injustices suffered by women. She'd have told you to save your breath to cool your porridge. Get yourself a good education and make yourself financially independent and then you can teach other girls to do the same.

"Dad would say the same. No-one could be more of a crusader than Dad, but by the time I knew him he rarely got into a fight unless he knew he could win and he quickly pulled out whenever he discovered his ground was weaker than he first thought. I remember his enthusiasm to get Walford appointed Headmaster until he realised that

Walford would never be more than a good number two, or as he put it 'an amiable overgrown schoolboy, who's perfect as a factory overseer but incapable of running the school as a business, and not capable of holding much else in his head."

Mum had restored my confidence. Instead of being a dirty little schoolgirl I was upholding the best family traditions. I needed confidence to help me think straight. She went on:

"You've got a far better chance than most girls of your age of getting into Newnham, but if you want to get the best out of the High School and College teachers, you've got to learn tact."

I knew that she wanted me to follow in her footsteps to Newnham more than anything else, but this wasn't the moment to argue. She went on:

"I could probably shame old Walford into letting you back to the College tomorrow by telling him you came home in tears, because everyone would think he'd whacked you so hard that you couldn't take it."

"No, Mum" I said. "I did not come home in tears." I probably would have done if he'd caned me the way he caned those three boys, but he didn't. I was extremely angry when I left Walford's study and by the time I got to school I had calmed down and the only thought in my mind was the problem of getting through Higher Cert. if the school threw me out. Could I do it on my own? I mentioned Mrs. Rainham's comments.

"Poor girl, she's been in a number of scrapes herself. Some parents were outraged that she mentioned James Joyce's Ulysses in a lesson on modern literature because the book is banned. I'll speak to her."

Thanks to Mum I was allowed back. It appeared that Mr. Rogers, one of the College Latin masters, a misogynist who had waged a continuing war in the staff room against the admission of girls to any College classes, had heard about my French lecture, either from Mr. Porteus or from some other source, had pounded the staff room table to complain that the terms of his contract were to teach boys and not girls. He had repeated this tub-thumping performance in the Headmaster's study and the Headmaster had told Walford to 'deal with that troublesome girl'. Hence Walford's explosion when I saw him.

Mum picked this up from Milly, spoke to the Dean who, as a retired Principal of an Oxford College, had a relaxed view about student expression of unorthodox opinions. He was said to have maintained a friendship from student days with Bertrand Russell whose opinions on sex and marriage were well known. The financial advantages of co-ordinating the resources of High School and College had been self-evident to him from the start and he was gratified by the improved academic results, particularly amongst the girls who had benefited from the improved teaching resources of the combined schools. On top of this he recognised how much support he had received over the years from Dad, probably more so now that he no longer had Dad on hand to sort out the Dean and Chapter's financial and administrative problems. But it was

Mum who had the skill to remind him of all these things in a way that made him believe that he had thought about them himself, and I knew this.

The Headmaster was persuaded that it would be extremely bad policy for the College if a person like Mr. Rogers was seen to gain tactical victory on this particular point. He was a known trouble maker and if he was seen by the staff as winning this battle, there would be no holding him. Unlike most of the other masters who had failed to be appointed housemasters, but who had accepted their lot, Mr. Rogers' jaundiced attitudes to teachers, boys and the world in general made him a problem that had to be contained. The Dean saw him and told him in so many words that if he wanted to keep his job he had better pipe down.

So I was called to the Headmaster's study where I apologised profusely, both to the Headmaster and to Mr. Porteus, who was then asked if he would agree to take me back, which he did.

After that I kept my head down and made no comments in or out of school when I heard Mr. Porteus translate 'par les boyaux du Pape' as dash my buttons in Merimee's Charles IX. I felt free to say what I thought in English literature and in History, but I was more circumspect than I might otherwise have been, not only in French classes, but in school life generally.

This episode marked an important watershed in my life. Up till then I had been a bright schoolgirl who had won approval for her hard work and scholastic achievements. I had tended to treat adults like Mr. Squires and most of my other teachers as omniscient and more knowledgeable in every conceivable area of human understanding than I could hope to be. With a jolt I had been pitched into a world of adult politics (albeit school politics, but no matter) where a conviction of being right and the ability to present a good case had proved to be woefully inadequate. I knew I couldn't have won on my own. We all go through this experience. My memory of it is as vivid now as it was in the Autumn Term of 1942. I knew then, as I know now, that I got through it without mishap thanks to luck and not to me. My luck was to have a wonderful Mum who was bringing me up single-handed.

As children grow up many of them begin to see through the shortcomings of their parents and are quick to spot their parents' limitations. Dad's public position had given him a mystique, but Mum's unassuming way of seeing what had to be done and doing it could easily have passed unnoticed. It was only in later life that I understood the critical role she had played during the war in Dad's office, as well as on the governing bodies of both schools. My respect and admiration for her continued to grow in later life and I know that I can never hope to live up to the standards she set.

In later life it has often cheered me to look back and note the number of judgments I formed as a sixteen year old schoolgirl, which seemed to me sensible and obvious at the time and which I still regard as sensible and obvious and yet this is not the way other people, in the main, have tended to view things.

The Maison Tellier theme which nearly got me expelled is a case in point. Men and women need sex at different times, in different ways and to different degrees at various stages in their lives. They may not want to get into long-term entanglements. Even if they get good sex at home they may occasionally want to try something else, as people who eat well at home enjoy going out to good restaurants, so there is a continuing demand in the marketplace and there have always been plenty of people willing to cater for that demand.

What I find so incomprehensible is the vicious and often barbaric ways in which people who cater for this demand have been vilified and ill-treated throughout the ages. Even in our own time poor Cynthia Payne faced a prison sentence for organising a quiet, unobtrusive service for elderly clergymen, solicitors, etc. This pathological persecution of women prepared to do a useful job has always puzzled me. I don't think you can pin it down to any particular religion because it seems to have operated in all civilisations, in all times. The only result is that organisations like the Mafia in Russia and the US earn vast sums of money at the expense of the girls who ought to be keeping it themselves.

My favourite analogies are running a restaurant and accountancy. There are good and bad restaurants. It is much more enjoyable to have a meal out in pleasant surroundings, with friendly service, so it is with sex - hence the rationale for places like the Maison Tellier. My analogy with accountancy is based on the fact that, during my business career, I helped four women to set up their own accountancy practice. They were all able and hard-working accountants who felt they were doing most of the work as underpaid assistants in their respective firms and would never be made partners because the male senior partners in these firms thought they would leave and have children and never come back. In the present day and age this would not be regarded as unusual, but at the time I helped them to get started (in fact I lent the firm some money because the bank would not give them an overdraft) it was pioneering.

I have often thought that if the stupid law about 'living on immoral earnings' were changed in England, groups of women could set up in partnership to market their 'intimate personal services'. Fortunately for me I never got involved in such activities, otherwise I might have finished up in jail myself for living on 'immoral earnings'. As a postscript, I have often wondered why groups of men haven't got together to offer a similar service to women like me who no longer attract in the way they once did. Perhaps they do and I've merely been someone who has led too sheltered a life to be aware of their existence.

Wars, of course, change embedded attitudes overnight. Women who are one day treated as social lepers are transformed into patriotic heroines and immortalised in songs such as Lili Marlene. Something similar happened in my home town where a local hotel was effectively turned into an English Maison Tellier and a blind eye was turned by all the authorities. From what I can gather, similar transformations took place in hotels in garrison towns in many parts of the UK.

During the period 1942-44 we saw the gradual build-up in England of one of the biggest armadas ever known in preparation for the 'second front', the Normandy landings in June 1944. US troops, Canadians, Australians, Free-French, Free-Poles, Free-Czechs, Free-Norwegians and a host more nationalities were being organised and trained for the landing.

For me, the most important decision by the military authorities was to hand over an army camp ten miles from our city to the Canadians.

The Canadians were better paid than the British (although not as well paid as the Americans) and were known to be fond of ice-skating and Tawchester had the nearest ice rink. Women of all ages hired skating boots, put on white socks and wore short skirts, hoping to look like Sonia Henie, an ice-skating film star of the period.

Truckloads of Canadian soldiers would arrive on various evenings and for the weekend. A large number of the women never went onto the ice or had to fall over to show an expanse of knicker. They didn't even need to hang around watching. Many were picked up in the streets and whisked to the Rose and Crown, which had become the Canadian headquarters. Those Canadians who had got sleeping out passes and invested in a room for a night defrayed their cost by letting their rooms out to their mates for half an hour at a time in the evenings, Saturday afternoons and Sunday mornings. So a lot of Canadians were able to get what they desperately craved for at the cost of a half-hour slot, plus the money they paid to the girl, if she was doing it for money, and a lot were not. The operation was organised with military efficiency so that bells rang in the main corridors used for this purpose every half hour and the staircase at one end was used for entry and the other for exit.

Various other buildings in this seedy part of the town catered for the soldiers whose pay (or what was left of it) didn't run to a half hour slot in a hotel. Some were doing it three or four at a time on the floor of a room, with little or no upholstery except the odd blanket, but this didn't appear to detract from their enjoyment. If the woman was willing, that was all that mattered.

The Canadian authorities seemed to be much more concerned than their British counterparts to avoid their troops leaving a trail of women 'in the family way'. French Letters were dished out free in vast quantities and the troops were even told to give the girls a supply, in the hope that it would encourage them to take precautions if they were doing it with other men, so the Canadians wouldn't be blamed.

If was then that a number of High School girls, some of them as young as fourteen, were dressing up in the hope that they wouldn't be recognised and having the time of their lives. Maybe, if I hadn't got myself into such serious trouble over my French lecture, I might have been tempted, but getting to Oxford had now become more important to me than anything else and I wasn't going to take any chances. But even if it hadn't been necessary to keep out of trouble, I might have desisted. I was already yearning for something more than the proverbial randy poke, the apt term used by a not very attractive Fifth Former to describe the all too brief experience that she somehow believed had transformed her from a schoolgirl into a woman.

As I shall explain in a later chapter, the Rose and Crown did, a year later, play an important role in my life, which is why I still remember it with fond affection. I did not go there for a clandestine rendezvous, but as a married woman spending an all too brief hour with a husband who was about to be posted away. I sensed something of the atmosphere which I found far more sympathetic than I had expected and it is possible that this experience has left me with a deeper awareness and understanding of the role of places such as the Maison Tellier in many people's lives.

CHAPTER 14

SCHOOL FARM CAMP 1943

When I had finished my exams at the end of my first year in the Sixth Form I knew my results were good. I, therefore, started to focus more sharply on my chances of getting a place at an Oxford women's College. (There were no mixed Colleges until the late 1970s.) I began to feel more confident that I had a reasonable chance, but I had one major problem - Mum.

Because Mum had blazed the trail by getting a place to study Mathematics at Newnham College Cambridge, I knew she had set her heart on one of her daughters following her. With Jean in the Wrens, this was the role I was expected to fulfil.

Desire to go to Oxford had been stimulated originally by Mrs. Rainham, but I suppose at some stage along the road I must have decided that I wanted to blaze my own trail and not simply be a poor imitation following in Mum's footsteps. In any case, her main subject was Maths and mine was English and Mrs. Rainham frequently told us that Cambridge was the university for Maths and Science, whereas Oxford had far more famous people teaching English than Cambridge. This could have been no more than a matter of opinion, but I firmly believe it was true at the time I became an undergraduate at St. Hilda's. We had Professor Tolkien, Professor Wrenn, Professor Wilson, C.S. Lewis, Neville Coghill, Helen Gardner (my tutor) and many other great names.

Mum thought it would be a good idea to ask the advice of Alice Draper, one of her Newham friends with whom she still exchanged Christmas cards, who had read English and was now head of the English department in a girls' Grammar School in south east London. Alice had never married. She still lived with her parents. They had had a rough time in the blitz and their house had been so badly bombed that they had been forced to rent two rooms with shared bathroom and kitchen in the house of some nearby friends.

Mum thought it would be a nice idea to invite her for a week's holiday with us, which she did. For much of the war, access to coastal areas and beaches was severely restricted. The Lake District, the Pennines, the Welsh Hills and Scotland were the main places where our friends took walking holidays. There was no basic petrol ration for private mileage so one couldn't go on holiday by car. Accommodation in country areas was limited because people from towns had been evacuated. Servicemen with homes in the London area tried (if they could afford to do so) to rent accommodation in country areas for their wives and children, who were enrolled in local village schools.

Alice's father walked with a stick and so a restful holiday for the three of them with us was something I think they enjoyed. Living alone with Mum I had learnt to share all the household jobs and very often prepared the dinner, particularly on evenings when Mum was late home. Although food was rationed and limited in variety I was still able to learn a lot about how to present meals and make them look attractive and I was grateful in later life for this important part of my education.

When Alice and her parents came Mum asked me to be 'maitresse de maison'. It was school holiday for me. I was seventeen and it was an opportunity to learn how to plan the meals for a week for five people, as well as organising visits to the historic sights.

Fortunately, Mr. Draper was the sort of person who felt the ideal way to spend a holiday was to sit on the lawn in a deckchair, with his Panama hat shading his eyes, reading various books of Dad's - Liddell Hart's History of World War I, Churchill's two volume biography of his illustrious ancestor the Duke of Marlborough, T.E. Lawrence's Seven Pillars of Wisdom. Mrs. Draper wanted to do all sorts of things about the house that Mum never had time to do, such as cleaning the silver, so Alice Draper used to take Mum's bicycle and go for cycle rides with me to some of the country villages and churches that I wanted to show her. We talked a lot. She told me of her surprise at finding how busy Mum was.

"I somehow used to think of your mother as a lady of leisure. She never wrote about what she was doing."

I told her about the way Mum had the gift of getting things done without talking about them and about the way she solved my own problem when I was threatened with expulsion.

But in these rides (and we would stop for a cup of tea and a teacake, cake or whatever) I had the chance to talk about what I was doing and what I wanted to do and my wish to go to Oxford, if Mum would agree.

I understood from our conversations that she had, for some years, been sending the best girls in her English Sixth to St. Hilda's, Oxford and was a friend of the Principal. She understood my predicament and said to me one day:

"I don't think it is a good idea to rest your case on the argument that Oxford is better than Cambridge for English at the present time. I happen to agree that it is because the most important thing you can learn is how to interpret such texts as Beowulf, Sir Gawain and the Grene Kniht or the Layamon rather than listen to some pretentious nonentity such as F.R. Leavis pontificating on what he thinks about Jane Austen. If you have been reading authors such as James Joyce, Ezra Pound, Percy Wyndham Lewis and T.S. Eliot you're not likely to take kindly to other people's clotted opinions. But your mother is the sort of person who is likely to dig her heels in (as I think I would) if you started preaching the superiority of Oxford to her own university.

"If I were you I would take the line that your mother was a pioneer and trail-blazer. She was the first girl in her family to go to university and she achieved a first in Maths at Cambridge. I think you're like her in many ways. You want to be a trail-blazer. You want to be the first member of your family to go to Oxford. If you put it that way I think she'll support you. After all, if you are together, you can celebrate no matter which crew wins the boat race."

What's more she found a way of saying this to Mum herself. She was even more complimentary about me behind my back. She promised to write to the Principal of St. Hilda's suggesting I should travel to Oxford and meet both the Principal and Helen Gardner, the senior English tutor (of whom more anon). She also said that if my English teacher thought I might be scholarship material I should stay on at school for the extra year.

"You learn a tremendous amount in that final year after Higher Cert., whether or not you get a scholarship and this will enable you to make much better use of your time at Oxford and your chances of getting a better degree at the end."

Mum took the idea to her heart and gave me all the support that I could possibly need during the next two years, not only in my ambition to go to Oxford, but in the critical period of my personal life, which I shall describe in the following chapters. I can never thank Mum or Alice enough for this. If I hadn't gone to Oxford I would never have met John.

After Alice and her family had returned home I had another interesting experience. I was one of fifteen girls who had volunteered to go to a school farm camp. During the war years the harvest season posed major problems for farmers. We didn't have combine harvesters. We had old-fashioned binders which cut the wheat, the oats or the barley and bound them into sheaves. It was left to farm workers to pick up the sheaves and put them into neat stooks so that the grain could dry out. When the grain had dried out, these stooks had to be loaded onto carts in the process known as "leading". There was a chronic shortage of labour because all able-bodied men were in the forces. An organisation known as the Women's Land Army had been formed at the beginning of the war, to provide assistance on farms, but they obviously couldn't cope in peak work seasons such as harvest time.

For some years College boys had volunteered to do two or three weeks at a school farm camp about 50 miles away and it was suggested to the Headmistress that High School girls ought to be given the opportunity to volunteer. Fifteen of us did volunteer, whether out of devotion to duty or because it sounded an interesting adventure, no matter.

The driving force behind this experiment was an old High School girl called Peggy Johnson. She had joined the ATS at the beginning of the war and had been invalided out. I don't know why because she always seemed as strong as a horse, but I believe this apparent strength was due to her indomitable spirit. She became a Land Girl. She was a true patriot and a worker. She was also something of a card, but it was thanks to people like her that we were able to maintain the food supply back home (when German U-boats were sinking our supply ships at a rate that was frightening to the people who understood the implications). I have a tremendous respect for her memory.

But she was a no-nonsense woman who didn't mince words and when she gave orders they had to be carried out, or else.

Most of the farms on which it was intended that we should work were owned by the Church of England, although they were let to individual farmers. We were all to wear corduroy trousers (presumably to avoid getting our legs pricked on the stubble and jeans had not yet established themselves as workwear). We referred to them as cords and most of us wore them for doing odd jobs around the house. We were told to bring sleeping bags and what to pack as essentials and we were also told that we would have to rough it. Land Army girls drove us in two trucks the fifty-odd miles to the camp site to which we were to report. We were allocated one tent which had camp beds. We didn't have to sleep on the ground.

Peggy gave us our marching orders on the afternoon we arrived. She told us there were strict camp rules and that she was determined to demonstrate that fifteen High School girls could do at least as much work, if not more, as fifteen College boys. We heartily agreed.

"The first thing you've got to understand is that this is not a Butlin's holiday camp. I won't tolerate any larking about or indiscipline. I have two assistants. The first is Wilfred who can be trusted to keep any unwanted marauders out of our tent." So Wilfred, a large shaggy dog with a fringe over his eyes, came forward and was patted behind his head by his mistress. I didn't know at the time, but he was in fact a Briard, reputed to be a very aristocratic dog who could frighten the life out of an Alsation (which is what we used to call German shepherds) and any human being to whom he might take a dislike. Wilfred was invited to go round and sniff each of us, so that he would know that we were friends of his mistress.

"If you have to go out in the night to the shit-house and anyone tries to attack you just call Wilfred and all he'll leave will be a few bones for the canteen soup next week", she said.

"My other assistant is Fred. Come here, Fred", reaching for a half inch thick bamboo stick that was about three and a half feet long. She then whacked it down on her bed.

"Fred's pleasure in life is making painful ruts on the rumps of girls who don't do as they are told, so now yer know."

None of us was keen to make Fred's acquaintance. Peggy went on:

"That little square tent on the left as you came in is our very own shit-house. I wasn't going to have my girls walking a 100 yards over the field to queue up with the College boys, so you ought to be grateful that I sweated blood to get it. If you need a piss-pot in the night there are two over there, but don't you dare tip one over. The last girl to get out of bed when I blow my whistle for reveille at 6.30 each morning has to empty both of them. Understood?!"

"The ablutions are in that corrugated iron Nissen hut before you get to the barn. This end is supposed to be reserved for the girls. I didn't want to have all the boys goggling

SCHOOL FARM CAMP 1943

at you while you wash your tits and your fannies. The old dust sheet they've hung up as a divider won't stop the boys ogling round the side, so you'll just have to lump it."

"That old barn building is the canteen or cook-house where you go for breakfast and high tea. You will be given packs of sandwiches to eat during the day in the field where you work. Any questions?"

There were no questions.

"Next topic, discipline, you are to be in bed by 10 o'clock. If you're not, Fred will ensure that you sleep on your face. Drink. Fred won't touch you if you're drunk but when you sober up you'll wish you'd never been born. Men will tempt you with beer and cider. You know perfectly well why. My advice is never take more than half a pint of either, and never more than two halves."

"Topic number three - men. Out here you've got men as well as College boys. They are not the sort of men you dream about. Most of them are horrible, ugly, toothless, hairless and incapable of walking. God knows what they do in the daytime, but they come out of the hedges, ditches, ruined cottages and they've only got one interest in life. You'd think they'd be incapable, but they're not. Most of them are capable of sniffing fuckable cunt from five miles away and that's all you are, so don't get ideas above your station. The buzz will have gone all round the district that fifteen fuckable cunts have just been delivered to this camp site. Keep your cords on at all times."

"I'd rather you stayed together when you walk across to the cookhouse, but I don't want any girl walking round on her own. I want you to walk in pairs so that one can raise the alarm if any of these Frankenstein monsters attempts to give you trouble. So now yer know."

We were beginning to feel like rookies who had landed in France in World War I believing we were heroes fighting for our country, but being introduced to the realities of our new life by a sergeant reading a list of our comrades who had just been shot for cowardice. We suddenly felt very small and insignificant.

"Next item on the agenda", Peggy went on. "I don't want any of you getting a bun in your oven. By the time you find out it will be too late for Fred to deal with you. I'm the person who'll get the sack, and what's more I'll have my name expunged in ignominy from the old girls' lists and my name removed from all the boards in the school hall. Your fate will be worse. You will not only be condemning a poor, innocent child to a life of misery, but your life won't be worth living. No-one will want to employ you. Your parents will throw you out. So my advice is, don't take risks.

"Which of you can recite the golden rules that your mothers taught you on how not to get pregnant? You either pass or fail on each rule. If you fail on any one question, you've failed on the lot because that's what happens in real life. You only need to make one mistake and you could be pregnant and spend the rest of your life regretting it."

"First question, anybody. What should you always carry with you?"

I answered "Six French Letters" and noticed admiring glances from some of my subdued colleagues.

"Pass, on the first question you're obviously experienced enough in such matters to know that once you get going, you'll have used up six before you can say Jack Robinson."

"Next question, where do you keep them?"

"In your handbag", I said.

"Fail" came the put-down response. "You won't be able to find your handbag and even if you could, your French Letters would be lost in all the junk." Obviously no experience of the speed at which these things happen. Anyone else?"

Hilda, who had been paying close attention, came up with what we thought was the intelligent suggestion that the girls should put them in pockets that they should sew onto the insides of their knickers.

"Fail!" she said, adding emphasis by hitting her bed sharply with Fred. "The first thing a man does is get yer drawers off and God knows where he puts them, so what chance have you of finding what's in the pocket? If this is all you remember of what your mothers teach you, I shudder to think about your abilities to learn anything in life."

So where were we to keep those all important protective items? Eleanor tactfully suggested that there were large gaps in our education and that we were keen to learn.

"The first thing you have to learn is to keep your shirt on, even if it's up round your neck. Let him take everything off. It can even pay to take your bra off yourself and let him play around with your titties. It can help you to buy a little time while you decide what to do next. And you sew your pocket inside your shirt and if you change your shirt, you change what's in your pocket."

So now we knew.

"What do you recommend we should do while we are buying time?" said Eleanor, who was as keen to learn as the rest of us, "Particularly if he's one of these ugly men we don't want."

"Intelligent question" said Peggy. "It may not work, but the advice we were given in the ATS was not to panic, but to give the impression that we weren't going to resist and when he thinks it's going to be easy to stuff his prick into you, you take a gentle hold of it as if you're trying to help him and then give an almighty twist, but you've got to twist a long way round with all the force you can muster. The bastard will still be able to hurt you, but his erection will be gone and he'll have a job getting another one during the time you try to get away."

So now we knew.

In recent decades we've been used to reading a lot about the enlightened sex education that is given in schools, as compared with what was given in the olden days when people like me were at school. I reckon it's declined, just as the teaching of English grammar and things like tables have declined, and I often think that if we had people like Peggy instructing our teenage daughters, there would be a lot fewer unwanted teenage pregnancies. She didn't mince words and some of us may not like the coarseness of her language, but she said it like it was and the fifteen of us learnt a lot more at the farm camp than how to pick up and stook sheaves of corn.

For the first week most of us were so exhausted with the heavy open-air work that we just flopped onto our beds and slept long before the 10 o'clock curfew time. I had made up my mind that, in spite of all the idyllic pastoral propaganda being put out during the war years about the wholesomeness of farming life, I never wanted to work on a farm again. I have a tremendous admiration for farmers' wives and for people who work on farms, but I am eternally grateful that I was not born in an age where the bulk of the population had to slave all day as agricultural labourers.

Peggy, to her credit, got a lot of work out of us. She counted the stooks in each of the fields to which we were sent on the various farms where we were driven in trucks each day and, I think, succeeded in convincing her lords and masters that a 16 girl power (including herself) output team had achieved more per unit (one girl/day) of labour than the College boys and she may well have been right. Even if she didn't win on that point, the message got through that the High School team had shown its mettle and done a good job on the home front and she would be given the opportunity to bring another group of volunteers next Summer.

By the second week we had become accustomed to working long hours in the open air without falling asleep over high tea and this gave us the opportunity to have the odd glass of cider or beer in the local pub with some of the College boys we knew. In fact I narrowly escaped the attentions of Fred when I finished up lying on the grass behind a hedge with next year's head of school on top of me going through the motions of lovemaking. Nowadays we might call it simulating. It was his idea and I felt reasonably safe, as long as I had my cords on. He got a terrific thrill out of being gripped between my legs as I crossed my ankles in the air, as I imagined they did it in real life. Suddenly I said:

"God, what's the time?"

It was about two minutes to ten, so I unceremoniously had to roll him over, jump up and run. Peggy was already toying with Fred in anticipation.

"Saved by the bell!" she said. "Fred was looking forward to the fun he was going to have when he got those cords off you."

I shuddered with relief. I hadn't realised we would be made to take our cords off, but even with cords on it would have been bad enough.

"I am not going to ask where you have been", Peggy added. "With all that grass in your hair."

"I kept my cords on all the time", I grinned.

"Good girl", she said and with that a hearty slap on the rump, but I didn't mind as long as it wasn't Fred.

When I returned I used the rest of the Summer holiday to work on the English and French set books prescribed by the Oxford and Cambridge Joint Examination Board for the Higher School Certificate in 1944. It was fortunate that I did, given the time I would spend on things other than schoolwork during the following term.

CHAPTER 15

ANNUS MIRABILIS

At 3pm on Saturday 16th October 1943 my life changed. The time and the place remain pictured in my memory more vividly than anything that had happened before, or has happened since. We were nearly a month into the Autumn Term. It was a crisp, sunny day. Mum was at work. I had done most of the week's household shopping in the morning and I was in Market Square trying to find a silk scarf to buy Mum for her birthday on the 21st. I never remember seeing a market in Market Square. Part of it was cobbled. There were some 18th Century buildings and an equestrian statue of a member of a local titled family who had won renown in the Crimean War.

As I came out of the shop with my small parcel I almost walked into a young Canadian soldier who was looking up intently at the roof of the old Town Hall building. He had a small notepad in his hand. He was half facing the weak afternoon sun. The words 'noble countenance' went through my mind. You may consider these to be the words of a schoolgirl steeped in the literary language of the plays of Shakespeare, when English literature was playing an important part in her life, which it was, but I still use these words when I think of David and they still describe the essence. I loved him from that miraculous first moment. His true nobility, mind and soul, was manifest in everything he was, everything he did and everything he said.

I asked whether I could show him some of the old buildings in our city. I told him that my great-uncle had been the Dean and that my father, who was serving in the army in the Far East, had often spoken about the loyalty of the Canadians to the Mother Country in both wars. They had no other reason to be involved and I knew Dad would want me to do anything I could to help a Canadian soldier who was visiting our city.

We started walking up the narrow, cobbled street to Cathedral Close. He told me that his name was David McBain, that his home was in Victoria, British Colombia, that he had studied architecture for a year in Vancouver University before volunteering and that his father had emigrated to Canada from Aberdeen in Scotland in 1912 and had later served in the Canadian forces in France in the 1914-18 war. His father had wanted to be a doctor and had studied medicine for a year at Aberdeen University until David's grandfather became ill and died, so there was no money for David's father to continue at university. He had been recruited in

Scotland by the Canadian Bank of Commerce which had paid his fare to Canada and provided him with a job in Vancouver.

David had just turned 20. After posting to England he had been selected for promotion and sent to the Officers' Training Unit attached to the large Canadian camp about ten miles from our city. This was his first free day after being posted in.

Dad had attached importance to our knowledge and understanding of one of the most famous cathedrals in Europe. Even as an 11 year old I knew the different styles of architecture of the columns and buttresses that had been added at different periods and the particular themes in the more famous stained glass windows. I could therefore acquit myself reasonably as a guide to someone like David and we spent some time walking around and I then suggested that we should sit down for a few minutes, so we went to the seats where Mum and I often sat on the days when we came to the Cathedral for morning service. In a way you feel very humble when you look up to the high Norman arches in the oldest part of the building.

I knelt down to say a prayer to give thanks for meeting David. I wanted to keep him forever. I had never before prayed so fervently for anyone or anything. Then I felt him kneeling beside me. When I slipped back onto my chair he did likewise. When he turned towards me, our eyes met. I smiled. He said:

"I wanted to give thanks for meeting such a wonderful person. I am in a distant land, 5000 miles from home. I no longer feel alone. I feel I have known you all my life."

I knew that my prayers had been answered. I moved my hand in his direction. He immediately took it between both his hands, raised it to his lips and gently kissed it.

Some weeks later he said to me that, with this gesture, he had pledged his troth. I knew this.

As we walked out into Cathedral Close I took his arm. It was dusk. I told him that Mum would be home by now and would be most upset if he didn't have tea with us. We usually had a late high tea on Saturdays and a snack with cocoa before we went to bed.

I left David in the hall as I went to the kitchen to tell Mum we had a guest. Mum understood the importance of the occasion without my explaining and I went back to David. In later years Mum used to say how she had instantly understood the look in my eye and the intensity of my expression. She had the gift in any situation of immediately understanding what was important and acting accordingly When anyone complimented me in my later business career on my ability to do just this, I blessed Mum as the person from whom I must have inherited this gift. I bless her even more for manifesting it at this vitally important moment in my own life.

David was studying the photos of my grandfather and great-uncle William. Dad was not only proud of his father's and uncle's war record, but I remember in the pre-war years how he used to get angry when he had been having political arguments with some of his guests. He would wave his hand at these pictures as he showed his guests out, complaining that his father had not died in the campaign to capture Baghdad and his uncle at Jutland for a bunch of bumbling political idiots to lose the peace so that we would have to fight another war. I mentioned this to David as I explained who these people were. When we went into the drawing room and he saw the pictures of Dad and Jean, which Mum always kept on the mantelshelf, I likewise explained who they were. Dad, he had guessed straight away.

"He looks a very strong character. You're like him", he said. "So is your sister, but in a different way."

"It didn't do to get on the wrong side of Dad", I said. "Many was the time when Jean and I climbed into our beds and had to sleep on our tums after he had finished with us", and we both grinned.

"You're truly a patriotic family", he said. "I hope when my time comes to show my mettle I will prove worthy of the great traditions families like yours have set. It was a miracle that Dad survived at Vimy. He was nearly buried in a shellhole, but somehow they managed to dig him out after dark. There was a bullet mark on his tin hat and he still keeps this as a souvenir. He didn't want me to volunteer, neither did Mum, but they accepted that if Dad had felt it to be his duty that it was my duty too."

A shadow crept over my thoughts and it must have shown. Although I knew that I wouldn't have met David here in England if it hadn't been for the war, it was a jolt to be forced to remember that all the training and manoeuvres we saw going on were merely preparations for the 'Second Front' which everyone was expecting to happen any day. Some had expected it to happen in 1943, but as Autumn turned towards Winter, the general expectation was that it would be the Spring of 1944. As an officer, David would have to lead his men 'over the top'. In those days everyone thought in the military terms of the trench warfare of 1914-18 because, as children, we had been used to hearing our elders either speaking at first hand or talking about members of their families they had lost 'leading their men over the top'. I shuddered in anguish at the thought that 'my David' (and that was already how I was thinking of him) would soon be doing just this.

Mum cheered us up when she wheeled in the tea trolley. I could see that she immediately took to David. I know that she would have gone out of her way to be agreeable to anyone that she knew I liked (and she knew that I loved him) but on top of this I think she also felt motherly towards him. I sensed her wanting to sew on buttons for him and darn his socks. She wanted him to stay the night, telling him that Dad had always kept a spare pair of pyjamas, a spare razor and a new toothbrush to offer, in his territorial days, to any of his fellow army officers who might have missed his last bus or train home (usually after convivial festivities rather than manoeuvres). David hadn't got a sleeping out pass so couldn't stay, but promised to stay the next weekend or weekend after if he could get a 36 hour pass.

I insisted on going with him when he set off to walk to the pick-up point for the trucks that would take the Canadians back to camp. This was down near the ice-rink and he needed to be there a bit before 10 pm. He was worried about me having to walk back home alone in the dark. I said I was used to doing this. He was also worried that a lot of the troops would be rather the worse for drink. We compromised and I agreed to leave him before we got into the Rose and Crown/ice-rink area which had become a bit of a 'red lamp district'. We turned into a quiet road where there was no-one at that moment and he tentatively asked if I would allow him to kiss me goodnight. I sensed that he had been trying to pluck up courage from the moment we left our house. It is one of the ironies of life that the boys and men who care nothing for you will grab you and kiss you at the slightest opportunity, because they couldn't care less if you are annoyed. There are plenty more fish in the sea. But a man who loves you will worry and fret and possibly leave you without kissing you or daring to ask because he is frightened of upsetting you and because he values your good opinion of him more than anything else.

I threw my arms around his neck and we kissed as I had never kissed or been kissed before.

I had, of course, been kissed and fondled by hosts of College boys during the previous two and a half years, but it wasn't the same. The warmth and intensity of his feeling and the tenderness of the way he held me, were what counted and it was to these that my body and soul were responding and not just to the physical contact of lips, tongues, and the four hands that were joining the two bodies into one.

As I walked back home I felt lonely as I had never felt before. I was a different person. I knew it and so did Mum.

CHAPTER 16

MARRIAGE

I met David only three times before we were married. I have described the first meeting in the previous chapter. Most women have the opportunity to spend far more time with the men they decide to marry, or at any rate this is my impression in the England I have known for a substantial part of the 20th Century. Some people spend years courting. For me every meeting with David was significant and I, therefore, remember all the time we spent together as vividly as if it were yesterday but, of course, we spent remarkably little time together.

I have often reproached myself for my failure to take many of the practical steps that any woman with a bit of common sense should have taken. In the event, however, nothing that I might have done on the practical side during this period would have altered the end result.

You must accept that I am a fervent believer. My life would be a misery if I did not have the faith to believe that when I die I shall be re-united with David. But you must recognise that there are little voices within me, as there must be within you, that try to gnaw away my belief saying "What evidence do you possibly have for the existence of an after-life?" As often as I like I can say "Get thee behind me Satan", but this doesn't send the voices away.

So in the weeks after my first meeting with David I had to listen to voices saying "You're just dreaming, my girl. You are an infatuated schoolgirl who's lost her head to the first grown-up man who's made passes. Soldiers make similar passes to all the girls they meet."

I fought back, but I needed reassurance in a way the disciples needed reassurance. As someone accustomed to think in biblical terms from my early childhood, my mind is always drawn to biblical analogies when I have been contemplating my own situation.

When David succeeded in getting a 36 hour pass the following weekend I basked in the glory of his presence from 2 o'clock on Saturday 23rd October when he rang the doorbell until 9.30 pm on Sunday 24th October when I kissed him goodbye as he left to climb onto one of the 'passion wagons' (so called at the time) that would take him back to camp. There was no surplus mental energy left to consider and to start thinking of practical solutions to the problems that would have to be solved to enable us to get married before he would be posted away. Was he even going to propose?

During the next fortnight I had to start cranking round the wheels of my mind in the hope of getting to grips with a totally new set of practical problems, knowing that the outcome was going to be far more important than anything I had done in the past. In later life I have often had the impression that most other women have had the intuition or instincts to cope, whereas I have had to work everything out as if I were construing a Latin text. In later life this character trait has been helpful to me in building a career as a management consultant, but it left me bumbling along pretty hopelessly in my personal life in the Autumn of 1943.

I knew that when you dance with a man you don't push him around the floor in the direction you think you want to go. The intimate bodily contact enables you to anticipate his next movements so that you glide around the floor as one person. Or at least that used to be the case where most dances involved intimate bodily contact and where, incidentally, the music was usually quiet enough for you to hear what your partner said to you while you were dancing.

David did not succeed in getting another 36 hour pass until Saturday 6th November. The Indian Summer we had enjoyed for much of October had ended and the weather was now bitterly cold and we were waking most mornings to find the lawn covered in hoar frost. David had had an exhausting training spell and we both sat sleepily together on the settee in front of a warm fire for most of Saturday. It was perfect peace. Mum had planned a special dinner for us and offered us all sherry. It helped me to feel that she was now treating me as a grown-up and no longer a schoolgirl.

We livened up over dinner but when David started telling us about the passing-out parade two days earlier for the previous batch of officer cadets it set alarm bells ringing. They had already been posted away to other units. Where would David be posted after his passing-out parade, which was only a fortnight away, at most three weeks?

He wanted to kiss me goodnight on the landing before we went to bed, but I smiled and said I wanted to be kissed properly and would come to his room in a few minutes when we were both in our night things. He was in Jean's room and my room was next door. I left him a reasonable amount of time and then tapped very lightly on his door. Mum was in bed and I expected that she would already be asleep. Her natural tact would prevent her from doing anything that might embarrass us.

I was wearing a simple white cotton nightie. It was not transparent but would have been partly so if I stood in front of a reading lamp. I had arranged the way I wanted my hair to fall on my shoulders and I hoped he would approve.

I had given him a surprise that he hadn't expected and he immediately clasped me to him, letting his hand glide gently down my back until he held me firmly by the behind, which is what I wanted.

We had no central heating in those days. We had gas fires in the bedrooms but in those spartan days a bedroom gas fire was only lit if the bedroom occupant was ill with a temperature.

Either I shivered or said "It's cold", and David said:

"You'll be warmer in bed", and I think he meant in my own bed, but I was determined to interpret it as in his bed and said:

"If you faithfully promise, David, that it's only for a cuddle and nothing more" and he immediately nodded agreement. I don't think he could believe his luck as I climbed into bed and he followed me.

As our bodies came together and his erection pressed against me I sensed he was feeling awkward and embarrassed and he confusedly mumbled "Sorry".

I said "David, darling, you wouldn't be a man if you didn't feel that way and I'm feeling exactly the same way in a secret place that is as keen to welcome your 'gentleman' as he is to get into it, but I want our first time to be special for both of us. We are both tired, David. That's why I just want a cuddle."

My words must have been soothing balm, or at any rate they had that effect. It was the first time I had called him 'darling', and I made it clear that there was going to be a first time and also that I wanted it as much as he did. I suspect he had a Presbyterian conscience. He was getting it drilled into him day and night at the camp that as an officer he would be expected to behave as an officer and a gentleman and he was in the Mother Country which had high standards of behaviour. He had met an English girl who appeared to be from a traditional English family and he was concerned to be on his best behaviour with me, as he was in the army. I had to find a way of making him more relaxed and natural with me. We went to sleep in each other's arms and didn't wake until the early morning when I slipped quietly back to my bedroom. My bed was too cold to sleep in so I got dressed.

I had arranged that instead of going to the Cathedral we should go to St. David's church in Bishop Wantock. It meant a four mile cycle ride and David had said he didn't mind riding Mum's bicycle. In those days if it was too far to walk and when there wasn't a convenient bus we went everywhere by bicycle.

We used to go to Bishop Wantock by car with Dad before the war. Bishop Wantock is a tiny village near the castle which was the official residence of the Bishop but where there were very few inhabitants. The church, however, went back to Saxon times. You took a step down as you stepped through the door and the arches under the tower were pointed.

The person who would normally be called the vicar, was officially titled a "perpetual curate" or rather he had been granted the 'perpetual curacy' of Bishop Wantock. He was high church and everyone called him 'Father Wakehurst'. His name was Gerald Wakehurst and if he had been a Catholic he would have been called Father Gerald. To recap from Chapter 3, in the days when Uncle Henry had been a house master, Gerald Wakehurst had been one of his pupils. Gerald had been a chaplain in the first war and wanted to share the life of the front-line troops to whom he was ministering. As a result he had lost his left arm when a shell had exploded in the trench near to him. After the war Uncle Henry had found him the perpetual curacy and he was devoted to our family.

He had married Dad and Mum in Bishop Wantock church and he had christened both Jean and me. When we were small children, he used to tell Dad or Mum to give us picture books to look at. He had a play area at the back of the church. He was the most kindly, Christian priest that I have ever met and he made us feel we were being welcomed into the Kingdom of Heaven and we loved him. He was often a guest in our house. He used to amuse us, pretending to make our small teddy bears or dolls slide down the banisters.

Since Mum and I had been on our own and our car had been laid up for the duration of the war, and it meant a fairly hilly four mile cycle ride, it was only occasionally that Father Wakehurst saw us in his very small congregation. There was something about the warm, Christian humanity of Father Wakehurst and the intimacy of the small Bishop Wantock church that I had loved from my childhood days and I wanted to share it with David so I had arranged with Mum that he should borrow her bicycle. She would be independent. She had, in any case, been invited to lunch at the Squires'. So had I, but Mum had 'phoned to excuse my absence as soon as she knew that David was coming.

At breakfast, as soon as Mum had left us to starting clearing up, I sensed that David was much troubled.

"It all seemed so natural", he said eventually.

I thought I understood what must be going on in his mind, but I wasn't sure.

"But it is natural, David", I said. "If you'd told any of your friends that you had spent the night in bed with me and not done anything, they wouldn't believe you any more than my friends would believe me, but we're not going to tell them. How could anyone but you possibly understand what I mean when I say that I love you even more than I want you with my body, yet I want you with my body more than I have ever wanted anything else in my life."

I could tell by the more relaxed way he answered that I had put him at ease.

"Those are exactly my feelings, too, we are meant for each other."

After a pause I said, "I knew that from the moment you took my hand on the first day we met and, as you said, pledged your troth. I knew you were meant for me from the moment I first saw you in Market Square, but it was only when you took my hand and kissed it that I could know the way you felt."

In a few moments he said, "Would you be very angry with me if I were to ask whether you would marry me now and not wait until the end of the war?"

"I would be very angry", I started and then said "No, sad, not angry, if you hadn't asked me."

"Then you will?" He stood up from the table and held out his arms, so I got up and went to be held ecstatically in his grip, nodding my head. I was so overcome with emotion that I had difficulty in saying the words "Yes, darling."

It took some time before we would let each other go and I then said:

"It might be diplomatic, David, if you were to ask Mum. Tell her I have said yes subject to her consent and I know she won't refuse. I'll have a quick word first" and I went to the kitchen where she was preparing things for our lunch. I told her what had happened and she kissed me.

"I couldn't have wished for a better husband for you" she almost sobbed. "It brings back the day when Dad first asked me."

"Mum", I asked, "Do you remember when you once said I could have grandma's (i.e. her Dad's mother, Catherine) engagement ring because Dad had promised Jean his mother's engagement ring? Do you think I could be like the prodigal daughter and ask for it now so it can be my engagement ring?" Mum nodded and went upstairs to look for it. She came back with it in its case and I followed her into the breakfast room.

She let David say his piece and then she kissed him so he would know all was well. She then handed him the ring case and said that, although it was not a family heirloom, she would love to know that something that had strong sentimental value in the family would be worn for another generation and not merely kept as a relic. David then placed it on my finger, then took my hand and kissed it.

Mum was looking at her watch, knowing we would have to leave in about ten minutes, and said:

"I want a picture of you both while the sun is shining, so hurry up."

In those days people like us didn't have cameras with flash bulbs to take photos indoors. She took a number of photos of David and me in the front garden before we got on our bicycles to cycle to Bishop Wantock.

We didn't have the chance to speak to Father Wakehurst before morning service, but he gave us a welcoming smile when he saw us amongst his very small congregation and he invited us in for a coffee or tea (as we might prefer) in his cottage. I introduced David and said we had just got engaged, showing him my engagement ring. I said I hoped he would perform the wedding ceremony and he beamed with enthusiasm, telling us how he remembered marrying Dad and Mum and how Henry had said Mum was the most beautiful woman he had ever met and that he couldn't believe Dad's luck to marry a woman who was both beautiful and had a Cambridge degree in Mathematics as well. I had often heard how great-uncle Henry had a soft spot for Mum, but it is always nice to hear these stories told by someone else.

He turned to David and said:

"You see what a lucky fellow you are. Mavis is just like her mother was when I first met her" and added, patting me on the shoulder, "And I must congratulate you, my dear, on finding such a handsome young gentleman. I am sure you will make each other very happy indeed and Our Lord will bless you both." Then he added, turning to David, "She is a mischievous little girl. You'll need to keep her in order.

You'll need a good, stout hairbrush every now and again. This is the advice I give to all newlyweds."

When I told Mum about this afterwards, she laughed and said he had given the same advice to Dad 22 years previously.

"Did Dad take it?" I joked. "I thought Jean and I were the only sufferers. It used to hurt like hell even if it was nothing but his bare hand."

Mum smiled benignly. "You'll understand better when you are married", she said. The traditional ideas seem to be that if a husband spanked his wife when he was angry with her, his anger would quickly be replaced with ardent desire and in satisfying his ardent desire he would realise how much he loved her and the cause of his anger would quickly pass out of his mind. So far, so good. But Mum didn't answer my immediate, second question which was what a wife should do if she felt angry with her husband.

My prime purpose in seeking the advice of Father Wakehurst was to find out what we had to do if we wanted to get married before David was posted away. I knew that banns had to be called on three Sundays, but surely there were special rules for soldiers in wartime. What about going to Gretna Green? Was the proverbial blacksmith still waiting there to marry a couple within minutes of crossing the border? I knew, in fact, that it would not be practicable for David to get away from camp long enough to travel to Gretna Green, but as a schoolgirl ignorant on such practicalities, I was trotting out every idea that came into my head.

Father Wakehurst was sympathetic. He explained how we could apply for a special licence, but pointed out that as I was under 18 there were special procedures involving parental permission and Dad was in Ceylon. He said that in his army days an officer was supposed to get the permission of his commanding officer to marry, but things may have changed and it might be different in the Canadian army. I said:

"But, surely, if we are married in the sight of God... couldn't you marry us straight away?" I was desperately trying to seek a solution.

"When Henry the Eighth nationalised the Church of England he turned all us priests into acting, unpaid civil servants, so I am a civil servant, even if I may not look like one. If I marry you as a priest in church, we have to go into the vestry afterwards to sign the various bits of paper, one of which is your all important marriage certificate. It is my job as a civil servant to provide you with the marriage certificate which gives you certain legal rights, including the right to use your husband's name, which gives him what are called 'conjugal rights'. In a country like France you can go and get married one day in front of some civil servant, or whatever, who calls himself a mayor, or one of the mayor's odd-job men and that provides you with the legal paper and the next day you go to church to be married before God, which may be the only ceremony to which Christians attach any importance but, as a civil servant, I have to advise you of the requirements imposed by law before two people can be legally married.

"And don't think of going to Gretna Green. It would break your mother's heart if you ran away like that, I am sure she would do anything to help. You know when old Henry spent a weekend in Cambridge to see how your father was getting on and your father introduced him to the young lady he wanted to marry, old Henry was swept off his feet. When I saw him afterwards he said 'Young Bill must have some hidden talents that none of us has suspected. He seems to have persuaded the most beautiful woman I have ever met to marry him. And she is not only beautiful. She is a mathematician.' And old Henry was completely captivated. He was always saying that x or y couldn't add two and two together. He was also a ladies' man. As a young man he'd married the boss's daughter and she was a stunner. I knew he wanted to get young Bill to the altar as soon as he could in case your mother changed her mind. I am telling you a lot of family secrets." He turned to David.

Father Wakehurst promised to give us God's blessing on our engagement if we went back into the church and added that if there were an emergency one of us should telephone him and he would see what could be done. He asked David to go into the church and when we were alone and looked at me anxiously and said:

"Is this a shotgun wedding? If you are expecting a child, I'll do what is necessary."

I told him we hadn't yet done anything together and that if we had I wouldn't be ashamed to tell him. I added that I didn't want to feel virtuous because I had not, so far, had the chance to say no to any temptation, either from David or from anyone else, and he smiled.

"All right, my child, you know how Our Lord treated Mary Magdalene and the woman taken in adultery. These are not real sins. You know and I know that real sins are the horrendous things that men and women do to each other." He patted me gently on the shoulder and we went into the church to join David, where he blessed our engagement and forthcoming marriage. David and I then cycled home.

I knew that David's military instructors had daily been instilling into him an awareness of all the things that, as an officer and a gentleman, he must never do, particularly during his stay in the Mother Country. I suspected (and I think rightly) that they were not telling him that one of the important duties of an officer and a gentleman in England was to provide much appreciated bedroom services to the lady in his life (preferably the one he was with at this moment). I would therefore make it my delectable duty to fill this gap in his military education. Of course I was flattered at the high esteem in which he held me and my family, but I wanted to make him feel at home and relaxed with me so that he could laugh and joke, as I am sure he did with his friends in the army or back in Victoria. He was, of course, a person of the highest seriousness (and so was I) and this was one of the things I loved about him.

As soon as we got home I put the gas poker in the fire that Mum had prepared and asked David to keep an eye on it while I rushed upstairs to change. In a warm room I could dispense with stockings, and I did. I took off my formal church clothes and put on a sweater (the name we gave in those days to any pullover because the film star, Dorothy Lamour, had launched the smart term 'sweater girls') and I took off my bra. I didn't need one then and I am one of those fortunate people that still doesn't need one, although I tend to wear one from habit.

I put on a loose-fitting, beige cotton skirt and then, somewhat mischievously, I put on the most feminine piece of underwear that I had been able to find in my mother's chest of drawers. I imagine she bought them some years before the war in Paris. They were plain white cotton and much more voluminous than the sort of thing that has been fashionable in recent years, but they had lace round the legs, which were wide, instead of elastic. For many years afterwards if you wore that sort of thing it was assumed by any man who got his hands that far to be an open invitation to continue.

Mum had left the sherry bottle on a tray on the sideboard with two glasses. Having sherry two days running made me feel very adult. David and I clinked our glasses and drank to our forthcoming marriage. We sat down together on the settee and I said:

"If the commanding officer wishes to inspect his recently conquered territories that are now flying the white flag of surrender, the princess is ready for his inspection" and I flicked a corner of my skirt back far enough for him to glimpse just that little bit of white lace. His right hand immediately grasped my knee and edged tentatively towards the invisible barrier. The warmth of his hand matched my own bodily warmth and I knew we were right for each other, but of course I knew the night before, just as I knew when he first held my hand as we sat together in the Cathedral.

My mind kept saying that his gentle and tentative approach meant that this was probably the first time he had ventured thus far with any woman and kept vigorously pushing this thought out of my mind. I had made a vow on the day I had met him not to think about what David might or might not have done with other girls before he met me, because I didn't want him to be thinking about what I had done, or might have done. I was superstitious to the extent that I believed that if I kept such thoughts out of my mind, he would do the same. I thought that he might have had girls in his life who were the equivalent of Jacko. In all probability a serious and studious person such as David may have been too shy. By comparison it was easy for a girl like me. I didn't have to do anything except say no if I disliked a boy or felt he was going beyond acceptable limits. What was important for me at this point was that David and I meant everything to each other and that nothing that we might have done in the past had any significance.

I sensed that he was not only aroused, but also more relaxed and sure of himself. Although his fingers were still too timid to push their way inside the legs, a sudden impulse caused him to remove his hand to put it inside my sweater and as soon as he found I was not wearing a bra he had quickly lifted my sweater and was kissing the tips in a way that was sending me wild.

Fortunately by then our sherry glasses were empty and I stood up and put them back on the sideboard.

David was now coming into his own. He knew what he wanted.

"I now give permission for the garrison to lower the white flag of surrender", he said with a smile and I immediately responded.

"The commanding officer has the right to exercise his droits de seigneur in accordance with our surrender treaty and to lower the flag", which he immediately did. I slipped neatly out of them and he put the gusset to his lips before casting it aside on the settee and grasping my bare behind firmly while he kissed me.

"So this is what I am supposed to punish with the back of a hairbrush", he said and I bent obediently over his knee whilst he planted kisses on each hip before reaching his hand between my thighs in search of his number one objective.

I broke free, stood up and set myself down sideways across his legs, saying:

"The portcullis has been raised so that the commanding officer can approach the sacred wood through the main castle gate", which he did and if he had been in any doubt in his mind about the reception he would get (and I am sure there wasn't) such doubts could exist no longer. We were both ready for the real thing.

Over lunch I told David how desperately I wanted us to make love properly, but that I would prefer to wait until we were married, which might only be another week, but that as we were now at the 'everything but' stage I felt it unkind to force his 'little man' to spend a day of total frustration before he had to go back to camp.

To people who have grown up in the 70s, 80s and 90s, the idea of two grown-up people doing what we did must seem so ridiculous that you may have difficulty in believing that lovers such as David and I could have acted in this way. But my purpose in writing this book is to tell it like it was.

Whilst my body was crying out for David to make love to me, I had and still have a fervent belief in the mystical union of the bodies and minds of a husband and wife in Christian marriage and I wanted our first true union to take place after we had married. My idea for a dress rehearsal was to let David come to my bedroom, remove his tunic and trousers and lie on top of me, putting it between my legs, which were and are well-rounded enough to grip very tightly when they are shut. I insisted that he put on a French letter to avoid leaving any tell-tale evidence. This was a sensible precaution because I sensed he would need some relief after a few hours of continuous arousal and he did.

By the time Mum returned (she had a committee meeting after her lunch with the Squires) David and I were sitting holding hands in front of the fire in a relaxed harmonious state. I think our 'dress rehearsal' helped us both the following week. When we walked together in the direction of the ice rink for him to pick up his transport back to camp he insisted, as before, on my leaving him at the corner of the dark unlit street before we got near what we euphemistically called the 'red lamp district', although with the wartime black-out there were no street lamps of any kind, red or otherwise. David was no longer satisfied with a chaste kiss and a hug. Now he knew his way around, his hand was in a flash gripping my bare behind which he said was the best radiator he could possibly have found on a cold night.

As I walked back home I marvelled at what we had achieved in the few hours since I had slipped into his bed the previous night and tried to figure how long it might take normal courting couples to know each other in the way I now felt I knew David. I also thought about the steps I would need to take to get a special licence and about all the schoolwork I was supposed to be doing, remembering that on top of this I was supposed to be speaking at an inter-Sixth Form debate the following Saturday when the College was hosting the next Sixth Form conference. Ominously that was going to be Saturday the thirteenth.

Saturday 13th November 1943 was indeed a day which threw me into consternation. While Mum was shopping for the weekly meat ration and groceries David rang from a call box and asked if we would accept the charges, which was the arrangement I had made with him. Today was to be his passing-out parade. He had to attend a formal church parade the next morning at 10 o'clock, after which he could have time off until the evening. They had all received postings to different destinations, to which they were to travel on Monday 15th November.

I told him to telephone again in an hour and I immediately telephoned Father Wakehurst. He started to repeat everything he had told me the previous week about the differences between civil and church marriage and I interrupted. I knew this was impolite but he didn't seem to mind and I asked, with my voice almost breaking, whether he would bless our marriage in whatever form he might consider appropriate. I think he understood fairly clearly that David and I would be man and wife with our bodies by Sunday evening, whatever he might do. I had never spoken to an adult in this way and I felt guilty, but when I saw him the next day I knew he had understood and he didn't hold it against me.

My next problem was David. When he telephoned and I told him I had arranged for us to be married in church at 2.30 pm the next day and I wanted him to book a room for half an hour, an hour, two hours or whatever he could get at the Rose and Crown, he hummed and hawed about this not being the sort of place he would want to take me. I had to be blunt. I had to tell him I knew all about the Rose and Crown, that I would be prepared to sell my body on the street corners for him and that, in any case, once we were in a room with the door closed the outside world didn't matter. If we were to marry I wanted our marriage to be consummated. At the same time I was wanting to kick myself for failing to take the opportunity of letting him make love properly the previous Sunday.

With all this on my mind I was still able to get up in big school at the College later that afternoon and argue the case for the restoration of monarchies in the occupied countries, which was being opposed by the left-wing republicans. I cited the heroic role of the young King Peter of Yugoslavia in 1941. I pointed out how the existence of a monarchy in Italy had enabled a king to get rid of Mussolini, although the allies had been slow to follow up their advantage and how poor King Leopold of the Belgians, who had fought heroically for his country and was now virtually a prisoner, would not enjoy the popularity of returning home at the head of a victorious army and I succeeded in mustering a lot of votes, although the republicans won in spite of the fact that many of their speakers made it clear that they wanted to maintain the monarchy in Great Britain. How I kept my mind on the subject I still don't know.

Perhaps it helped me to detach myself from my immediate problems and, in fact, from my biggest problem.

This was whether to tell Mum. If I did and she said no I would be scuppered. I wasn't prepared to take even a 0.0001% chance, so I lied to her about my plans for Sunday, but it hurt. Neither she nor I were expecting David until the following weekend, which was what had been provisionally planned.

David did as I had suggested. He was able to get a taxi from outside the Rose and Crown straight to Bishop Wantock where I was waiting for him. Father Wakehurst conducted the proper marriage service. There was no bride's father to give the bride away and no best man. I had bought the simplest wedding ring I could find. I had in fact bought it in readiness during the week and had not waited until Saturday the thirteenth. While I was waiting for David, Father Wakehurst told me about some of the marriage ceremonies he had conducted in the first war between men about to go up the line and French girls from nearby villages who were already pregnant. This was not the sort of conversation that was good for my morale at that particular time, but I was so grateful to him. He was prepared to flout the law for my sake and there are not many people who would do such a thing then and there are probably fewer now. He was one of the most truly Christian men and certainly the most truly Christian priest whom I had ever known and I bless his memory every time I think of him. I always associate him with the lines which were written by Ezra Pound two years after these events and which I did not read until they were published four years later:

> And the greatest is charity
> To be found among those who have not observed
>
>   regulations

After the service, in which Father Wakehurst pronounced us man and wife, David and I walked slowly to the bus stop. He was now a Lieutenant and other soldiers were obliged to salute him and he was obliged to acknowledge their salutations. In Bishop Wantock that afternoon there were no other soldiers, English or Canadian.

He had managed to get a room, but only for one hour. He was fretting about how he would be able to smuggle me into this dreadful place and out again. He was more worried than I was. Now that we were married other problems seemed to me to be of secondary importance. I was confident that we could arrange a civil marriage in a registrar's office as soon as he was able to get any leave from his new unit. I didn't think I would get any problems from the school or College if someone reported me for visiting the Rose and Crown because I would be able to say that I had been there with my husband.

David, however, was worried. I knew he was worrying for my sake. I loved him for thinking about me in this way, but at that time my only concern was to ensure that we did have our brief hour together. It had a symbolic value for me that may be difficult for other people to understand at this distance in time, but I still remember it as vividly as if it were yesterday. I still think of the 14th November 1943, my wedding day, as the most important day of my life.

The Rose and Crown was not such a seedy place as I had been led to believe. The people in the lounge where we went for afternoon tea while waiting for our room time looked pleasant and respectable. The women, many of whom were wearing hats, were in the main much older than I had anticipated, many of them much older than Mum. There were some tables with three or four women sitting together having tea and apart from wearing a little more make-up than was normal amongst Mum's friends, this seemed no different from any other tea-room. I was, no doubt, doing my best to keep my left hand on the table so that anyone who looked could see my wedding and engagement rings, but in this I was no different from any other newlywed.

When the time came for us to take possession of room number 16 on the first floor I was already more relaxed. As soon as I turned down the bedclothes and saw a slightly crumpled sheet I inevitably started speculating on the amorous exploits of the previous occupants, but quickly put such thoughts out of my mind as I got undressed and saw David doing the same. As I lay completely naked on the bed and he came and stood beside me I saw that he had already covered the important place with the regulation protective clothing. He said:

"You're more beautiful than I could ever have imagined" and then he started kissing me all over. I began to worry in case he got too excited but he was quickly on top of me and I guided him in. I told him I wanted him to move gently and slowly and he did. I had expected it to hurt but it didn't. There were one or two twinges but nothing more. I had, no doubt, prepared the way pretty effectively.

It wasn't over as quickly as I had feared, but when I began to feel my muscles twitching a certain serenity came over me. I feared from what I had been told that it was too much to expect it the first time. Although he was ahead of me I was able to hold him firmly in place so that, like me, he was able to feel that our marriage had been truly consummated and that we had become one body.

We lay with very little movement. Even when he had slipped out I held him firmly over me until we heard the 10 minute warning bell. I thought I heard the muffled voice of a woman shouting out in ecstasy from the next room but it may have been imagination. We had washed, dressed and were out by the required time, remembering to turn right and go down the north stairs so that we wouldn't meet any of the next occupants of the rooms in our corridor as they came up the south stairs.

The Rose and Crown has remained in my memory as the place that provided a safe haven for David and me in our hour of need. In retrospect I'm glad that we had to go there because it taught me not to belittle such places, or the people who had to make use of them. The fact that I was fortunate enough to have a husband who loved me with his soul and mind, as well as with his body just as I loved him was not of my doing. I had no personal merit whatever. It was God who had treated me kindly. If other men and women who have been less kindly treated had to make do with the consolation prize of half an hour or an hour's bodily contact but without the rest, then surely I should be glad on their behalf that they had at least obtained some form of consolation and not begrudge them receiving far less than what had been bestowed on me.

When I had said goodbye to David at the place where the army trucks were parked I walked back home and started to focus on what I was going to say to Mum. I had had to concoct an impulse story about having to meet some of my school friends on a work matter, but the way I had dressed must have given me away.

The way she looked at me when I walked through the door made me feel guilty. The one thing I hadn't planned for in the hectic past day and a half was what I was going to say to Mum afterwards and now I really felt a worm. I burbled away and made the worst possible case for myself. Whilst I could make a good case on the podium for a cause that I believed was righteous, I proved to be pretty hopeless when the cause was mine. Mum burst into tears and wouldn't listen to me for the rest of the evening. It wasn't that I had got married. It was the fact that I had distrusted her to the point where she had been deprived of the right to attend one of the most important events in the life of any mother and that I had refused to bring my husband back to a home where he had been warmly received on the first day I had met him, that I had preferred to consummate my marriage in a seedy hotel room. Having later in life had the joy of being present at the weddings of my own four children, I can understand how these things must have hurt.

As I was leaving for school the next day Mum said to me, rather acidly, "And you'd better tell Miss Blantyre what you have done before anyone else does. I'm not going to go around apologising for you."

With a heavy heart I left a note that I wanted to see the Headmistress. When she sent for me I was surprised at her friendly manner and at being asked to sit down. Before I could say anything she congratulated me on my 'magnificent' performance at the debate on Saturday. She had been sitting in the gallery in the College hall. She said our side should have won hands down, but unfortunately so many Sixth Formers from other schools had been subjected to continuous republican propaganda.

When I told her why I had come to see her she looked at me intently and said nothing. I then went on to explain my sadness at the way I had upset Mum. She got up from her desk, walked over to me. I stood up and she shook my hand to congratulate me and wish me lifelong happiness. I sensed real warmth and affection. Inevitably I had grown up to think of her as a rather stern and forbidding figure, which she was, otherwise she wouldn't have been chosen for the job she was doing.

Then she went back to her chair and waved me to sit down.

"If you have a few minutes", she said, "I want to talk to you as a friend. One of the important things you have to learn in life is when to disobey orders, which also means knowing when to act without orders and when to avoid putting yourself in the position where you may be given orders that you will find impossible to carry out. We're all brought up with the example of Nelson putting his blind eye to the telescope."

"I know it can be heart-rending when it means doing as you did and not telling your mother in case she might say no. You were right. You passed the rest which I failed 27 years ago when I was your age and ever since I have bitterly regretted the worst mistake I ever made in my life."

Then she smiled and said "I told you I was talking to you as a friend and not as your Headmistress, which means this is a private conversation. I would never dream of repeating what you have just told me about yesterday and I am sure you will understand my reasons for not wanting my private life to be talked about."

She had correctly judged me although she would have known she was taking a risk. For me it was a wonderful experience to be treated as a responsible adult by a person of her age and position.

In the Spring of 1916 she had been secretly engaged to a young infantry officer, Edward Carstairs. He had wanted her to marry him before he went to France and had found a priest like Father Wakehurst who was willing to conduct the ceremony, but she had asked her mother who had said no. Her parents knew only too well that the life expectancy of a young infantry officer in that period of terrible slaughter might be weeks rather than months and they wanted to protect their daughter from the sorrow of bereavement. They had good intentions, but they were wrong because they had failed to understand their daughter the way, even at that age, I believe I had understood her.

Edward Carstairs was one of the 60,000 British soldiers whose lives were sacrificed in the suicidal attacks launched by incompetent Generals and politicians that we now remember as the Battle of the Somme.

By refusing to let her marry, her parents had not saved her from distress. Instead of bringing Edward happiness in the last few weeks of his life, she had said farewell to a man she had left bitter and disappointed. She had never married.

Having told me this she was anxious to provide reassurance by talking optimistically about the much greater competence so far manifested by our Generals than in 1914-18, but we both knew that although we had not so far suffered the mass slaughter of the 1914-18 trench warfare, the 'Second Front' was expected to start next Spring and that the Canadian army was building up its strength, together with the British and American armies, in readiness.

As I got up to leave she said "Mrs. Rainham has often praised you for your decisiveness and told me she hoped it wouldn't lead you into serious trouble. It's an admirable family trait. When your father was here to chair Council meetings everyone admired the quick way he summed up the case for or against doing anything and made instant decisions, which were nearly always right. We used to finish meetings in three-quarters of an hour and now they last for two or three hours, as your poor mother knows when she sits there trying to produce sensible minutes.

I will see if I can put in a good word for you when I see her this evening." She shook my hand again warmly and I left.

There was a Council meeting that evening and, whatever was said, I being an optimist, thought Mum's attitude to me had softened a little when she came home late that evening, but it may have been wishful thinking. It took at least a week before I felt we could talk normally and I could ask for her help in trying to sort out a civil marriage in the registrar's as soon as David could get some leave to visit us.

By Wednesday 17th November (wartime postal deliveries were remarkably good) I received the first of many letters addressed to Mrs. D. McBain and I immediately thought of the famous Wordsworth lines that have, for me, retained a sacred personal meaning:

>...we who were strong in love,
>Bliss was it that dawn to be alive

David, after spending all day Monday travelling, was in his new camp. For me it was reassurance. I had not been dreaming. I felt that even Mum was beginning to relent when she saw the joyous expression on my face as she handed me the envelope.

I hadn't even thought about my change of name. Intuitively I decided that I would be less of a problem for the school if I went on being called Mavis Fortingall. Some of the teachers, I feared, might feel embarrassed at having a Mrs. McBain sitting in front of them as a pupil and I didn't want that. I wanted to go to Oxford. I wanted good results in my Higher School Certificate. I believed that with an Oxford degree I could get a teaching job in Victoria or Vancouver or wherever David would be when the war was over. I knew that he would need to finish his studies as an architect, and I would have to be the breadwinner.

I should add that in those days it was not common practice, as it is now, for women to keep their maiden names. Both my daughters have done so. One is a doctor and the other is a barrister. My granddaughters look set to do the same. Having set the precedent with David, I found myself following it automatically when I married John. My married name is the name I use for family wining and dining and collecting children from school. I remained as Miss Fortingall, first as a teacher and later as a company director. I never took to Ms which became customary usage long after the practice I had adopted had been established and accepted by everyone with whom I had become associated.

CHAPTER 17

CHRISTMAS LEAVE 1943

God was truly kind to David and me that Christmas and we were blessed with ten heavenly days, the most wonderful ten days that I have ever enjoyed in my whole life or could possibly have imagined. I knew that David was trying to get Christmas leave. The army used to do its best to make Christmas special for troops who were staying in camp. Unless a Canadian or American had English friends or family to go to there was not the same competition for Christmas leave as amongst English troops, but it was touch and go until David 'phoned on Thursday to say his leave had been granted and he would be travelling on Friday, Christmas Eve. Even then there were doubts as to whether he could reach us by Christmas Day. He had to travel to London, find his way across London on the Underground (which he had never used before) and there catch a train to the north. Wartime trains were unreliable and heavily overcrowded in normal times, so the crush of service personnel trying to reach their families for Christmas was horrendous, but he made it just before midnight.

Mum was wonderful. She was now reconciled. I had helped her to put the embroidered sheets and pillowcases in the guest room which she called the bridal suite. She hugged her new son-in-law as soon as I had let him go. She loved him and was very proud of him. We had a simple cold meal which she had prepared hours ago and we went to bed.

We slept as if we had been married for years, luxuriating in the love and warmth of each other's presence. This was not the time for anything more.

We were determined to be in our places early for Christmas morning service in the Cathedral because we wanted to sit in the seats where we had, knelt and silently communed together on the day of our first meeting. We did so and he immediately took my hand in both his hands, raised it to his lips and kissed it. He had Mum on his right.

I have always loved Christmas Day, and I loved joining in the carols. Everyone was more homely and relaxed. The Cathedral atmosphere was less formal than on normal Sundays, but this Christmas Day was unique.

We all stood as the choir started to proceed up the aisle singing 'Once in Royal David's City'. I gripped his hand and sang with all the force my voice could muster.

This was my Royal David's city singing to welcome my King David into his domain. On our return home Mum announced that she had prepared a 'wedding breakfast' and produced a bottle of champagne which, unknown to us she had put in the 'fridge earlier that morning. Neither David nor I had tasted champagne properly. I had been allowed a few sips as a child before the war when the adults were celebrating some family occasion and when I was staying with Arrière. Mum was about to give David instructions on how to open the bottle when we heard a key turning in the front door latch and Jean burst in on us. She had got Christmas leave at the last minute but she had to be back by the 30th December to relieve all the Scots who wanted to go whoopee for Hogmanay. She had not been able to get on a train but had been driven down from Rosyth by a young Lieutenant Commander, Eric, who lived only a few miles away. He had only come in to be introduced but at the sight of champagne he had quickly been persuaded to telephone his parents to say he was on his way and he joined in the celebrations. Described by Jean as the expert, Eric quickly opened the bottle. Father Wakehurst toasted the health of the bride and bridegroom and David and I basked in the congratulatory aura.

Mum had decided some weeks earlier to invite Father Wakehurst to share our Christmas lunch to thank him for what he had done for David and me. About a week before Christmas he had asked one of his car-borne friends to deliver one of the treasures from his cellar, a 1926 Margaux. He told Mum that he had been given a case before the war by one of his first war comrades and kept it for special occasions. He had sent the bottle in advance so that it could rest for a week and then be decanted. He explained over lunch that 1926 was not such a good year for claret as 1927 and 1929 but it had been a vintage year for Mum and she was touched by his thoughtfulness. So was I.

Neither David nor I had had the chance to develop a taste for good claret. I had been used to drinking red wine and water (as most French children did at that time) on my long Summer visits to La Tour du Pin and probably had a small glass of good wine when we sat with the grown-ups on special occasions, but even in a home like ours where Mum had been a wine drinker in normal times, the fact that Dad was away, and that France was occupied so there was no current supply, meant that we normally drank water with our meals and cider on special occasions.

Father Wakehurst said grace and again gave his blessing to the married pair and we sat down to a wonderful feast. I felt at times as if Mum had killed the fatted calf for her prodigal daughter and I was a little worried that Jean might be thinking thoughts similar to those of the elder brother in that most moving of all parables. Fortunately, my mind was put at rest as she and I were carrying the plates through to the kitchen as Mum prepared the Christmas pudding.

"He's a lovely boy", she said, "And you're a very lucky girl. I hope you will have a wonderful life together when this wretched war is over." She was enjoying every minute of these unexpected festivities and so were Mum and Father Wakehurst, who as connoisseurs enjoyed most of the Margaux, a small reward for their role in our happiness.

To end in style Mum produced a bottle of Cognac which had been left to mature in the sideboard since Dad's last home leave in 1940. Father Wakehurst's friendly driver called to collect him and was offered a glass. Before Jean and I did the clearing up I popped upstairs to light the gas fire in our room and slip on the 'white flag of surrender' that David had remembered so vividly from the day on which we got engaged and had quietly mentioned in moments when we were alone. With the washing-up done, both Mum (who had been up most of the night preparing our Christmas festivities) and Jean (who had been travelling in a slow car on slow roads most of the night) wanted a nap and this would be a cue for David and me to start our honeymoon proper.

Now that he knew his way around he wanted to undress me and take down the white flag himself. I can best describe the wonderful two or three hours that followed by leaving it to women readers to remember the similarly wondrous moments in their own lives and to the men who have participated to recall the moments they have shared. If such moments have so far passed you by, then words are so inadequate that I shall merely express the hope that one day a similar experience will be yours.

We didn't have to worry about being too nervous with each other or about a bell ringing in the corridor that would require us to dress and leave. We had the warmth of each other and the warmth of a happy home and if I did express my response in audible noises as well as with my body, the only people to hear were David who loved it, and possibly Mum who was sleeping or resting in the next room. Jean's room was at the other end of the landing.

It was seven or eight in the evening before we were all downstairs together to find that Mum had organised another surprise. Instead of the normal Christmas cake she had prepared a wedding cake. Not only that, but she had arranged with a friend who lived a few hundred yards away, and who was a professional photographer, to join us for a sherry. He came a few minutes after Mum telephoned him and took a number of pictures of David and me together and David and me cutting the cake.

As a person with a business he was entitled to a petrol allocation and he had also promised to drive the four of us to Bishop Wantock for morning service on Boxing Day, which was Sunday, and then he would take some photos, both inside and outside the church, the photos he would have taken at our wedding on 14th November if it had not been held in secret.

I'm eternally grateful to Mum for her thoughtfulness in doing all this. Without the photos on these two days and at the ball I would have had no good photos of David, apart from the snapshots taken outside our house on the day we were engaged. I know his parents were also overjoyed when she sent them these photos. He looked very distinguished and smart in his Lieutenant's uniform. Wartime deliveries of transatlantic mail through U-boat infested waters meant that some mail never reached its destination and the first set of pictures were a bit crushed. They were nevertheless received with joy and were the only memento his parents had until Mum was able to send a better set of prints after the war.

Although the moments that David and I spent alone together were the most precious, it was wonderful for both David and me to feel the warmth and affection around us. The little church of Bishop Wantock was crowded. With so many troops building up in England for the second front, many families were fortunate at Christmas in having husbands, sons and daughters home on leave. I think church attendance was probably higher during the war years, at any rate amongst families such as ours. It was not so easy (as I think it is now) to be entirely materialistic in a world where you were constantly reminded of the transitory nature of life on earth.

In addition to all this, Father Wakehurst, who had been through it all in the first war, knew and loved not only his immediate parishioners, but all those of our family whom he treated as his 'adopted children'. He had probably baptised most of the younger generation who were now in uniforms, just as he had baptised Jean and me.

I do not know whether he had originally planned 'Once in Royal David's City' to be the opening hymn, or whether he had rearranged the order of carols after hearing what I had said at lunch, but this was what we sang. After this he opened with a few words of welcome to all those service men and women whom he had not had a chance to welcome on Christmas Day, and then added that he wished to extend a particular welcome to a new member of his family, a young Canadian service man who had volunteered to travel 5000 miles from Victoria, British Colombia to join in the defence of the Mother Country.

As he had only recently had the privilege of joining David McBain, this Canadian officer, and Mavis Fortingall in Holy Matrimony, he was sure that all present would wish to join him in wishing the young couple a long and happy life together. He asked David and me to stand up which we did, turning and bowing to the congregation. As this was the first public announcement anywhere of our marriage, it provided an opportunity for everyone who knew us to crowd round as we came out of church and offer congratulations, just as if this had been the wedding ceremony itself. Like any mother on such an occasion, Mum was weeping tears of joy. So was I for that matter. She was over the moon with all the compliments she received about her 'handsome young son-in-law'.

It was a sunny Boxing Day morning for our wedding photos outside the church door, but we were also photographed standing in front of the altar with Father Wakehurst.

After that our marriage was 'regularised' in an unconventional way. A day or two after our real marriage Mum had asked the partner in the firm who was the specialist in matrimonial matters (ironically he had to be so because he was a divorce lawyer) to sort out the question of a licence. Initially the idea was that we would have a second wedding in the registrar's office which would enable us to be provided with a marriage certificate. Then there was some idea of being able to do it by proxy on the 14th December. Then it was decided that Father Wakehurst could deal with the certificate once he had the relevant papers and he decided that no-one would notice if he put the date 14th November (the date we were actually married) instead of 14th December and if anyone subsequently picked it up the mistake it could be attributed to a superannuated cleric. In fact he had left a space for us before starting a new page. It wasn't the 14th December when we signed, but the 26th December.

As Mum said afterwards, the divorce partner would have done his nut if he had known the way that matters were finally arranged because if David or I had wanted at some later stage to pretend that our marriage had never taken place it could have been easy. Mum knew her lawyers as well as anyone and she had also decided that the present happiness of her daughter and son-in-law was much more important than the sort of considerations which a divorce partner in a law firm would regard as paramount. She was right.

The news of our marriage quickly spread and later that afternoon Mrs. Wilding rang Mum to say that she and Dr. Wilding (the Dean) hoped that she would bring both her daughters and her new son-in-law to the Dean's traditional Boxing Day sherry party for the 'workers', which this year was being held at 6pm on Monday. Mum's invitation card, addressed to 'Mrs. Fortingall and Family' had been on the mantelpiece since late November. Mum had in fact intended to take all her family, but Mum was the sort of person who was always charmed by these little personal attentions. She knew that the Dean and his wife had a soft spot for our family, particularly after Dad had departed on military service and people who may previously have taken Dad for granted, had come to realise how much unpaid work he had done on the various committees reporting to the Dean and Chapter. In those days, Sunday evenings were not good days for social functions, particularly in church circles where a number of the probable guests were responsible for Evensong, either in the Cathedral or in their respective churches. When Boxing Day fell on the Sunday, social events would automatically be transferred to the Monday, which was a Bank Holiday.

It may be worth explaining the ironic use of the term 'workers' in this context. As soon as the Germans attacked Russia in 1941 the British communists, who had been anti-war until then, launched a massive propaganda campaign to preach the virtues of our 'gallant Russian allies'. Every time the Russians had a military success it was heralded as a victory for a country run by the 'workers'.

With the coalition government and a political truce between Conservative, Labour and Liberal parties, the British communists and their sympathisers (and there were many crypto communists at the time) had the field to themselves. They were always shouting for a 'second front' not to help the British to win the war, but to take pressure off our 'gallant Russian allies'. Britain, it was claimed, would be a far more efficient country if, like Russia, it was also run by the 'workers', by which was usually meant men in blue overalls who continued (in spite of the needs of the war) to call strikes over trivial issues such as alterations in shift patterns for bus drivers, or a non-union RAF fitter being permitted to use a spanner on a newly developed aero engine when he was on an induction course at a factory where there was a closed shop.

Rather than divert their energies to countering this insidious communist propaganda most professional people contented themselves with debunking it by parody - hence the Dean's jocular use of the sherry party for his volunteers as a 'workers' party'.

In his younger days the Dean, as a History lecturer climbing the academic ladder, had written a history of the American war of independence, followed by a history of the development of the federal constitution for Canada. He had travelled widely on lecture tours, both in the United States and Canada, had met McKenzie King who was to become Canadian Prime Minster during the war and even visited the Parliament buildings of the province of British Columbia in Victoria, David's home town. He was, therefore, delighted when I introduced David to him and chatted enthusiastically about the wonderful welcome he had been given, adding: "...and I am one of the few English people who doesn't make the stupid mistake of referring to the Canadian provinces as states."

Afterwards, in his welcome speech to the guests, the Dean mentioned David and me and then went on to pay tribute to the Canadians who, unlike the USA, had not been attacked and who, with a population (at that time) of no more than 10 million, had made both a military and an economic contribution to the allied war effort in both wars out of all proportion to their population. He finished by congratulating David, not only for being prepared to give up his architectural studies and volunteer, and for being promoted from the ranks, but also for winning the affections of one of the loveliest English girls he could possibly have found on his visit to the Mother Country. Even I blushed as he proposed a toast to the recently married pair. Mum was over the moon and for the rest of the evening the three of us basked in the warmth of this accolade as everyone came to congratulate us.

Milly was absolutely charmed by David, but of course pulled my leg about the way I had been able to keep it secret for so long. Neither she nor anyone could have guessed that David and I had met for the first time on the 16th October and I had no wish to enlighten them. As we were leaving, however, and I was saying our goodbye thanks to the Dean and Mrs. Wilding I said how I had first seen David on a Saturday afternoon in Market Square looking at the old town hall and studying some notes and how I had offered to show him round the Cathedral and any other buildings he wanted to see.

"So your training as a Girl Guide wasn't wasted after all", he chuckled as we shook hands.

Although every moment when David and I were alone together was precious, these social occasions were also important, not only because I wanted my family friends to meet him, but also because I loved to see the way he was feted and welcomed. During the three weekends when we had met before our wedding I had sensed a certain shyness on David's part. Although I loved everything about his character I felt he was being boxed in, both by the necessity of complying with what was expected of an officer and a gentleman and by the fact that he was in a strange country. He had now had a few weeks of actually being an officer and this had made him more relaxed. Because I was in my own country, in my own home and amongst my own friends I felt I had a psychological advantage which was unfair. I knew that since the Sunday of our engagement when we had been left alone together that he was relaxed with me, but I felt it important for him to feel the respect as well as the warmth and affection of our family friends and I knew he was particularly touched by the way a senior public figure such as the Dean, who knew Canada, had spoken about the Canadian war effort and David's part in it.

Because I had felt guilty about the way in which I had treated Mum (however good my justification) I loved to see the happiness in her eyes at the joy these festivities were giving her. And on top of this there was, of course, my own little ego. I was only a schoolgirl. In those days we wore our regulation uniform right until the day we left. I knew I would be back in under a fortnight sitting at a desk again as I worked for Higher Cert. so I wouldn't have been human if I hadn't rejoiced in these few days at being treated as Cinderella at the ball.

In fact, the final big social event of David's home leave was the combined College and High School 'old girls and old boys' dance (and both schools had impressive names for their former pupil associations, as the Scots call them) held in big school on 29th December. As a member of the Upper Sixth this was my first opportunity to attend. Jean had never been home on leave at the right time, or if she had (which I think not) there hadn't been anyone with whom she wished to attend.

Jean planned to be driven back to Rosyth with Eric on the 30th when they both had to report by 23.59 to relieve the Scots so that they could start getting drunk for Hogmanay on New Year's Eve and start sobering up about five days late, or whenever. She had not shown much enthusiasm for the dance until Mum suggested she should ask Eric, which she did, and he accepted. Eric was the son of wealthy Catholic parents who had sent him to Ampleforth so he didn't have many school friends in his home district. No junior officer in those days could have afforded to run a car out of his pay unless his parents provided him with an allowance. He also needed ingenuity to get petrol. Eric had both.

He came to collect Jean, David and me in his 1931 Morris Minor which was a diminutive box on wheels, that required double de-clutching when he wanted to change down. He boasted glibly about this as the best excuse anyone could have dreamed up for getting his hand on his front seat passenger's knee, and a lot more.

Mum did her best to persuade Jean to put on a glamourous ball gown, but Jean, after some initial hesitation, preferred to go in uniform. I think she was right. She was very proud of the rank she had obtained and what's more she looked extremely smart and attractive. She was tall and fair-haired (she still is) and her uniform was immaculately tailored. Whether she had put the finishing touches herself, or found a superb dressmaker, is immaterial. It was the result that counted. In contrast I was (and still am) shorter, dark-haired with broad hips and well-rounded thighs - what some men call cuddly. I didn't have a big bust. In any case they were not fashionable when many women wore uniform.

My second husband's comment has always been that quality is more important than quantity and one of the men who enjoyed fondling me in later life came up with the delightful expression that I have just what it takes to fill the hand of a gentleman. Why this should be different from what it takes to fill the hand of a bounder is not the question that a lady would dream of asking a gentleman or a bounder who had her in his delectable grip (and by that stage in the proceedings she would be past caring to which species he might belong).

David helped Mum to dress me and was, obviously, more interested in what I wore underneath. If Mum hadn't been there he would no doubt have interrupted proceedings but my wifely services to my lord and master would have to wait until the ball was over. The only point on which Mum and I disagreed was whether I should wear make-up. I had plenty of colour in my cheeks and in my lips and good skin texture, so I was against. Make-up was forbidden at school. It was in any case in short supply during the war. Some girls used to put on lipstick for the College dances, but I never did. I was always kissed passionately when the lights went out and when the dance was over and I knew the boys didn't like being teased about having lipstick on their hankies.

David succeeded in convincing Mum that he preferred me in my natural state by telling her that she had done such a marvellous job in making me as I am (or rather as I then was) and that to start trying to improve me would be as big a sacrilege as trying to add finishing touches to the Mona Lisa. So off we went, pop, pop, pop, squeezed into the back seat of Eric's Morris Minor.

Everyone told me I was a princess, the belle of the ball. Whilst flattery and politeness may have accounted for a good part of this, I still believe that being loved in mind and body as I was during the most wonderful ten days of my life, would render a woman beautiful whatever she looked like in ordinary times, so I must have been at my best. When David danced with Jean, Eric was quick to step into his place. When I introduced David to the Headmistress and he dutifully invited her to dance, who should make a bee-line for me but old Jacko who was escorting Louise. Jacko looked a joke in the ill-fitting wing collar, white tie and tails that he had presumably borrowed from his father, and started off wryly:

"There's no chance for me any more with competition like this", he grinned as cheekily as ever, while his right hand was working its way down my left thigh, or as near as he could get to it through all the taffeta.

"Be honest with yourself, Jacko", I said. "You never really tried."

"I shall always remember you as you were on the day when you had just had three of the best from old Whackers", he went on, and his hand tried to give my behind a squeeze.

"Jacko, please, we're on the dance floor. If you want to have any success with Louise you should learn to say nice things to her, not remind her of painful moments as you have been trying to remind me."

I was thanking my lucky stars for Jacko's incompetence on that earlier occasion and for the fact that I hadn't done anything with him and that David had been my first true love in every sense.

There were many women in ATS, WAAF and Wren uniforms, who had been senior girls in the days when I was considered, if at all, merely as Jean's kid sister and my ego was clearly sensitive to the looks and words of approval that I got from many of them and when the Headmaster gallantly kissed my hand as I paid my respects to him and introduced David, I felt I was walking on air. I wondered how I would re-adapt to my role as a respectful pupil in school uniform, but I did.

For reasons which I shall recount in a later chapter, I was particularly grateful to Louise for introducing me to her older brother, Dick and his wife, Janet. Dick was nearly ten years older than Louise and a Captain in the parachute regiment. He had the charming demeanour of his father but, in addition, he was extremely good-looking. He had met Janet at Cambridge and she was now teaching. I had no doubt met him in the Squires' house on one of the occasions when I had been playing as a child with Louise, but I had not remembered him. In any case he had probably changed a great deal since his student days.

The photographer who had taken our wedding photos was busy for much of the evening taking photos of all the couples and groups that asked him to do so. Mum had told him to take as many good photos of David and me and also Jean as he possibly could and she would buy the lot. One photo in particular was to have lasting significance. It was of David and me as we were just finishing a dance and were still holding each other. Mum loved this photo for the loving tenderness in David's eyes. In later years we learnt that it had become the favourite picture in the home of his parents. Very many years later when I met his Mum and she thanked me for the happiness I had brought into the last few months of David's life, she said that it was this photo that told her more than any words any of us could have written.

When we eventually returned home (whether 2 am or 2.30 am I knew not and cared not) we left Jean and Eric on the sofa downstairs. Whether they spent most of the night there or in Jean's bed (a wide single bed where I had spent my first night with David) I cared not. He may even have left with no more than a fondle, although I think not. His fondness for Jean was apparent during most of the evening and as we drove home she put her head on his shoulder. As good sisters we never asked each other questions on such matters. I didn't even hear his car drive away. In any case it was Jean's room and my room that looked out onto the front garden. Mum's room and the guest room (where we were) looked onto the back garden.

David had, as I anticipated, started unzipping my dress as soon as I came through our bedroom door. He was already in his pyjamas with the all important protective item in place, although he stepped out of his pyjama trousers as soon as he had removed the 'white flag' and was immediately on top for me. For both of us it was as if foreplay had been going on all the evening and almost as soon as he entered me I was into a multiple (although at that time I didn't know what it was or the term for it) and was squirming in paroxysms of ecstasy and was making the fact known to anyone within hearing distance. Mum must have been a wonderful sleeper (and I suspect she may not have been) not to have heard, but if she did I am sure she shared something with me, as did David. I have been fortunate in having many wonderful moments in my later life but this has remained unique. David and I were made for each other in soul, mind and body.

The rest of his leave was over in a flash. We had a momentary panic on New Year's Eve because we had both grossly underestimated our likely consumption of Durex and the local chemist was out. He had probably underestimated the likely consumption of service personnel home on leave, but a walk to the chemist in what we termed our red lamp district solved the problem.

Although it may sound self-centred, one result of our time together was to put me at peace with myself. From the time my bodily desires started to manifest themselves I had been in a state of internal conflict between what I believed was my spiritual self and my body. Now they were in harmony. I guessed that David had a similar problem (perhaps exacerbated by the Presbyterian conscience inherited from his father). Like many men he appeared to have grown up with the belief that his bodily needs would prove an unwelcome imposition on any woman with whom he might fall in love. I like to hope that my straightforward and honest expression of my own bodily desires exorcised such inhibiting ideas. He was constantly saying that "I never realised that it would just be so natural" which it was.

Cynics may mock and say that our marriage might never have lasted if David had lived. I believe they are wrong. My second marriage to John has lasted over 50 years. Both of us had suffered emotional loss before we met, albeit of different kinds.

Although she was discreet enough never to ask me about the intimate side of my life with David, Mum had understood in a way that very few mothers do. Instead of feeling jealous or put out she seemed to share it in some indirect way and with her wonderful ability to find solutions to problems, she wrote to some cousins who lived in Ruislip and asked whether she and I could stay with them if we had the opportunity to come to London. In this way I had two more weekends with David when he was able to get to London on 48 hour passes, first in February 1944 and then in March, so we were able to enjoy four more wonderful nights together before the D-day landings. Like all daughters I owe a tremendous debt of gratitude to Mum. Her understanding and help for me during the most wonderful period of my life puts me in her debt to the extent that no words of praise or thanks would do justice.

Whenever I think of the miracle that changed my life and of those wonderful days spent with David, I am also grateful for the wise, practical philosophy that I had learned in Mrs. Rainham's Fifth Form English classes 'live the best moments in life to the full. God gives them to you to enjoy so that you can relive them in testing times of sadness and endurance.'

CHAPTER 18

MUM'S PROBLEM (AND MINE)

In the weeks following David's return to camp after his Christmas and New Year leave when I was dressed once more in my regulation High School uniform, I kept pinching myself (metaphorically speaking) to see if I was awake and this was the real world and to ask myself whether my life as the fairy princess married to David, the king of my heart, had just been a dream. I kept thinking of poor Cinderella back in her rags in the kitchen. I wasn't poor like Cinderella. I was in a happy home and a happy school and I was working hard for Higher Cert., being constantly reminded that if I got good results I would stand a chance of winning a scholarship to St. Hilda's. It was only David's letters to me and my letters to him that provided a life-line. I had inevitably become more self-absorbed and dreamy and this is no doubt why I failed to notice that Mum was somehow unsettled and not her normal self.

After supper, when she would normally settle down to read one of her favourite French authors or one of the historical biographies from Dad's library (that she had never had time to read when Dad was at home and all the family had to be looked after) she would now only read a few lines, close the book, walk through to the drawing room where we kept the radiogram and put on a record, probably a dance tune from the 1920s and then take it off and go and find a job to do in the kitchen.

She was a very attractive woman. We had celebrated her forty-third birthday the week after my first meeting with David and by present day standards she looked young for her age but a seventeen year old daughter could not be expected to be a good judge of such matters. In the pre-war days she had been Dad's princess, the belle of every ball to which he had taken her in London, Cambridge, Paris and even our home town Burns Night. Our Scots ancestry might have been remote, but with a name like Fortingall and Dad's skill in persuading Scots celebrities of the day to be guests of honour, he was always considered to be the pillar of the local Caledonian society.

But Mum had also devoted her life wholeheartedly to Dad and to her children. While he had been away she had effectively run what is nowadays referred to as the 'back office' of his law practice and provided a home for Jean and me. After Jean had joined the Wrens in 1941 Mum and I had developed a much closer relationship than that enjoyed by many mothers and daughters. We shared the housework and cooking and did everything together, but unlike an ordinary flatmate she could always be relied upon to sort out my problems, just as she had sorted out my discipline problems in the Lower Sixth and as she had sorted out my marriage certificate.

Masterminding the Christmas and New Year celebrations for her two daughters and new son-in-law, planning everything including the way I should dress for the ball, the photographer and the car journeys, stretched her to the full and when it was over something snapped. Like me, she was probably left wondering whether it had all been real. I suspect she had identified with me completely and had been enjoying everything I enjoyed as if it had been happening to her. Just as I was having to get used to sitting at a desk as an ordinary schoolgirl, so she was left to come to terms with the fact that her own future life was not mine and what did this future life hold in store for her?

If I had been less self-absorbed at that time I might have found a way of getting her to talk to me about such matters. I don't think she had yet reached the stage where she had begun to formulate her concerns in a way that she could express them in words. And whereas she had a vivid memory of her own courtship and marriage, was able to understand my feelings and aspirations at this critical stage of my own life, I could not be expected to be able to share Mum's experience of re-adaptation to normal life, when the years of mothering are over, until the early 1970s when my youngest child was well into her teens.

What I didn't know, although I was soon to learn, was that Mum and I had something else in common. We both had tremendous bodily appetites. For some reason this important fact of life has not been socially acceptable in many countries in many parts of the world, so we both grew up, and no doubt girls are still being taught this, that women have to pretend to be passive partners in such matters. In any case it is not the sort of subject that a mother would find easy to talk about to her daughter. But sleeping in a bedroom adjacent to the guest room where David and I were spending so many rapturous moments every evening, morning and afternoon (we took a siesta almost every day) she had ample opportunity to note that her daughter was anything but a passive participant.

If the 'enquiring mind' on which various teachers had complimented me in my school reports had been working properly on home matters it would have occurred to me to wonder why mum had bought herself such a vast collection of feminine underwear, nightwear, negligees, etc. We had been told so many times in our childhood by our French Grandmother and Arrière that English women didn't know how to dress elegantly that we regarded it as normal for a Mum with French family connections to stock up on her French holidays with clothes that she wouldn't expect to find in the local shops where we lived. In fact, most French women didn't dress like Mum.

I have never made any secret of the fact that I wear what I wear because of the effect that I think it will have on the men in my life. I don't think I have anything like as much choice in the 1990s as Mum had in the 1920s and 1930s, but this may be old age on my part. I have always assumed that other women wear what they wear for similar reasons. I have never had any reason for knowing so I have never attempted to pontificate. Every woman to her own.

Mum needed to talk to me but found it difficult to break the ice. A lady called Mrs. Jameson provided the catalyst. Mum must have been conscious of the fact that since Dad's departure in 1939 and Jean's in 1940 her life revolved around her work, her committees (which were in reality an extension of her work) and me. She had tended to lose touch with many other friends except when she bumped into them while shopping, and as I did a lot of the shopping, this was not very often. She had found herself standing at the same counter as Mrs. Jameson while shopping and on an impulse had invited her to tea on a weekday and had come home early from the office to be hostess. Mrs. Jameson was an attractive, slim lady who always looked sad, or that was my impression. When I came home from school to find home-made toasted teacakes and Mum with a guest I tucked in enthusiastically. Mrs. Jameson congratulated me on my marriage and it was clear that Mum had talked in glowing terms about David and me.

When she left Mum said:

"Poor woman, she misses Dad dreadfully."

I was puzzled. How could anyone miss Dad more than Mum, or more than me? Mum went on:

"She was his favourite mistress."

I took another bite of teacake and a gulp of tea because I needed time to think.

"And you didn't mind?" I asked.

"Now that you are a married woman, I don't have to hide these things from you", she said. "Dad with all his energy and enthusiasm has a voracious appetite for women."

"So that's where I get it from", I said "except that mine is not for women."

"And your poor old Mum counts for nothing in all this", she said plaintively, "and what about Arrière who went on bribing randy young conscripts from the local army depot to dance attendance in her bedchamber until a few months before she died at the age of ninety?"

"You never told me these interesting bits of family history, Mum", I added, "There are obviously serious gaps in my education."

Mum laughed, "What did you expect me to tell you? You got into enough hot water at school simply by reading French novels. If you started trotting out family history as well you'd have been really in the soup."

"But I did, Mum. I talked about Arrière in my lecture and that was what got old Rogers so steamed up."

"You only referred to her legendary youth", Mum went on, "If you had talked about her later life and old age, God knows what would have happened to you."

"But I didn't know anything about her later life or old age", I went on, "but I am all ears if you want to tell me.

Mum made it clear that this was not the moment when she wanted to start reminiscing about Arrière. Mum explained that she was the person who had found Mrs. Jameson for Dad. Apparently Mr. Jameson was peculiar, which I presumed meant PD, the term the French use for queers. When I asked why on earth he had married, she said that a man like that obviously needed a woman to cook his dinner and to darn his socks, as well as providing an alibi.

"What a rotten deal", I said, "I think she is very attractive."

"So did Dad", she said. Apparently the Jamesons had been sitting at Dad and Mum's table at Burns Night some years earlier. Dad had danced with her and she had 'melted in his arms'.

It seemed that Dad was quite accustomed to telling Mum all that he felt about any woman. She enjoyed these conversations and encouraged him. If they were in a restaurant together and they saw a waitress (if her skirt were short enough) bending over a table or side table and showing plump thighs and stocking-tops, Dad would take a sip of whatever he was drinking and say to Mum that he would love to mount that filly from behind, just where she stood. Mum knew that Dad wouldn't take risks. He didn't want to risk catching the pox. He would never do it with any of the maids we had because he knew the risks posed by unmarried servant girls trying to claim his paternity as a result of the carelessness of one of the other men that might have mounted her. He was, therefore, restricted to married women who were not too emotional or clinging.

Mum had apparently facilitated Dad's bedding of Mrs. Jameson by inviting her to complete a foursome when she had one of her unmarried male cousins staying and Mr. Jameson was in London on business. Dad had, presumably, consummated the affair in the Jamesons' house when he had driven Mrs. Jameson home, but after that it had been love in the afternoon in our house on weekdays when Mum had discreetly gone shopping. Mrs. Jameson knew that Mum knew and there was a bond between them. During the war years, however, Mum's full-time job combined with the fact that she had no maid at home (only an occasional morning cleaner) left virtually no time for keeping up with her other friends. Mrs. Jameson on her side had become active in the WVS and was also a volunteer in a YMCA canteen for service men from the nearby camp that was now occupied by the Canadians.

I asked Mum how she thought Dad had managed all these years in the Far East.

"I don't think you need to worry too much about your Dad", she laughed.

"If he had been a Private I would have worried about all the diseases he might catch from the native women, but as a Brigadier I don't think he is likely to suffer too much deprivation."

Senior Staff Officers were accustomed to being driven around by smart uniformed ladies who were appropriately known as FANYs, many of whom were no doubt virtuous virgins but some of whom were likely to have a temperament more akin to mine or Mum's and Dad was more likely to have one or more of the latter as his chauffeuse in Ceylon than one of the former.

"And what about you, Mum?" I asked.

"You've taken an awful long time to think about your poor old Mum and wonder what she has been doing for the last four years. In fact she has been doing nothing. It's not easy for a woman. Men are clubbable and cover each other up. When Dad went off for a fortnight's territorial camp it was an open secret that most of the officers installed their lady friends at a local hotel and spent the night with them, rather than sleeping on camp beds in their tents. But even if this were common knowledge, there was a general feeling of indulgence towards men who were prepared to do their bit and no officer would ever dream of talking to the wife of a fellow officer about her husband's exploits at camp. There is nothing like the same solidarity among women. Furthermore, men have the propensity to boast about their 'conquests'."

I understood how difficult it would be for someone like Mum, who valued the esteem in which she was held in a small town where a large part of the middle class population knew each other, to deviate from the straight and narrow, however many eligible men might be out there waiting to offer their services.

"Now that you're married", Mum said, "I can at last talk to you about such things and that's a relief in itself."

"But I would have understood, Mum", I tried to reassure her.

"How could I know that", she went on, "until I heard you with David. I wasn't eavesdropping. I loved every minute of it but at times I couldn't sleep. I was driven into a frenzy because I wasn't able to do the same thing. But at least it has enabled me to talk to you."

"Is there any sherry left, Mum?" I asked as I went to the sideboard and took out a bottle of Dry Sack and two glasses. "This is one of the bad habits I got into over Christmas. I may be dressed like a schoolgirl but I want something to turn me back into a married woman again. I need a potion like the one Dr. Jekyll drank to turn himself into Mr. Hyde and back again. I love when you treat me as an adult."

"But I always treat you as an adult", Mum protested. "Or at least I have done for a long time now."

"Not the way you've just treated me", I went on. "Here's to your next lover." I raised my glass and so did Mum. We both laughed.

I loved hearing about Dad. I was even more grateful in later life. My main memory of him had been as a stern father and although I loved him I would have felt guilty in later life at the idea of him looking down from Heaven at some of the disreputable things I was doing. What I had learned from Mum changed all this. Whenever I thought of him at such moments in later life I imagined him chuckling and saying "There's no prize for guessing that that girl has Fortingall blood coursing through her arteries." It's been marvellous for my peace of mind.

Mum, in fact, had what sounded like a sensible idea and this may have been why she broached the subject. She had recently met a young officer, Pierre, in the Free French forces, who had been given the job of lecturing on France after the war to various schools and civic bodies in the UK. It was part of a campaign by De Gaulle's Free French Government in London to counter the communist propaganda. Like all Frenchmen of his type, Pierre would pay court to any attractive woman whom he might meet and Mum was no exception. The Dean knew that Mum was a French speaker and had family in France. Mum was, of course, desperate for news of her family from whom we had been cut off since June 1940. The Dean had asked her to arrange for Pierre to give a public lecture in the town hall and talks at the College and High School and to various other bodies and she thought it might be a good idea for him to stay with us. I didn't mind in the least if he got into bed with Mum and the great advantage was that he would disappear off to London as soon as the lectures were over and after the war would disappear back to France, so there shouldn't be any gossip.

So, two weeks later Pierre came to stay with us and was installed in the guest room next to Mum. I was back in my own single room at the front of the house so I could be diplomatically ignorant of what might or might not have gone on during the night, or even in the afternoons when I was at school. Mum, however, seemed to be in a much happier mood so I assumed that Pierre was living up to her expectations and that this first experiment was working according to plan.

There was, however, a snag. Pierre was one of those Frenchmen who regard any woman as fair game, although he treated me dismissively as a 'gosse' or as the maid when I was waiting at table. There was something about his arrogant air that I disliked intensely, but Mum needed a break. Even if Pierre was not to my liking, the least I could do was to be co-operative and help as much about the house as I could, just as Mum had done for me at Christmas.

Disastrously, however (as it turned out) she had to go out for a few minutes on Saturday morning. Pierre sat at the breakfast table with his feet up on another chair, smoking one of his foul-smelling cigarettes (they may even have been Gauloises) and reading as I cleared the table and in a flash he had jumped up, grabbed me, kissed me and yanked my knickers down to my knees.

"Vite sors ta culotte avant que ta mere rentre."

"Non", I said, trying to push him away.

I have been fortunate in never having to deal with a situation like that ever again, but it has left me with an irrational aversion to Frenchmen. My heart went out to all those ladies' maids and farm servants about whom I had read in French novels and who had suffered this kind of treatment from the bewigged nincompoops who were filling in time as they awaited the pleasure of the lady of the chateau, or whoever they were courting. I had mistakenly imagined these sexy romps with the maids below stairs were pleasurable to both parties. What pleasure, I thought, could any girl have got from a smash and grab raid by someone like Pierre wanting to do no more than a quick in-and-out as part of an ego-boosting exercise to convince himself that he was irresistible to women.

Those poor girls had no chance and my chances were not much better. I was hoping desperately that if I could keep my cool until he had his trousers off I could then try to do that grabbing and twisting exercise that Peggy had recommended at the farm camp, but I wasn't sure if my nerve would hold. He might have some technique of holding both my hands behind my back. I knew that France, like Italy and Ireland, was a Catholic country where the church apparently turned a blind eye to girls being raped, but loudly condemned the use of contraceptives. I was also afraid that as Pierre was this sort of person he might give me syphilis.

"Si j'etais ton pere", he went on, "Je te ferai obeir."

"Tu n'es pas mon pere", I shouted, "si mon pere etait la il te tuera."

"Ne fais pas l'innocent", he mocked "tu n'es pas vierge - tu es mariée."

I was livid. Just because I was a married woman - this didn't mean I was an open road for any unclean syphilitic bastard like him and I used the most insulting French words I knew and added that he had been beaten by the Germans because he was a coward who was only capable of raping women and had escaped to England for a safe refuge.

I was lucky to escape physical injury. Fortunately he was still treating me like a kid, so I suffered nothing more than being held across his knee and spanked on the bare behind. He was vicious and it hurt like hell, but it bought time and the bell rang. I said it was Mum who had forgotten her keys and he let me go to run to the door. It wasn't Mum. It was our cleaning lady who, thank God, had forgotten that Mum had changed the day she was due to come. I almost bundled her inside, slammed the door and ran as fast as I could. To anyone who might have seen me I must have looked a dishevelled creature as I turned off our road into a side road and went into somebody's front garden to get my breath back, adjust my knickers and run my hands over my hair. I was in my housework clothes with an apron, which I took off and put over my arm. I was wondering whether to go into one of the nearby houses and telephone the police, but as I didn't see him or hear anyone running up our road I decided he may have given up the chase. It was one thing to try and grab me when I was on my own at home - another to try and grab me in a public road where I might scream, shout and struggle. At any rate that was what I hoped. It was a cold February day and I had no coat or thick pullover. I thought first of going to the Squires' but I decided the school library was much nearer and I could work there where it was warm while I planned my next move.

I had no money but one of the girls lent me 2d (tuppence) which I could use to 'phone Mum, but I didn't want to ring until there was a fair chance that she would be home and I hoped to God that Pierre wouldn't answer the 'phone.

It was nearly lunchtime and it was Mum who answered. She was desperately worried. All she knew was that our cleaning lady had told her than I had rushed past her in a state of semi-undress and disappeared down the road like a mad woman. When I said that Pierre had tried to rape me she was silent and I thought he must have told her a pack of lies. In fact, he had been in his room packing his bags and was no doubt trying to think of some reason for having to leave instead of staying for the rest of the weekend. I told Mum that I was afraid to come anywhere near our house as long as he was in the neighbourhood. I said he might try to kill me after what I had said to him. By then I think she had understood the seriousness of what had happened. It had not just been a playful attempt to steal a kiss. She asked me for the telephone number of the school call box and said she would ring back, which she did half an hour later.

After my first call she had immediately telephoned the police superintendent, whom she knew well because Dad's firm handled a lot of police prosecution work. A policeman, accompanied by a sergeant, was at our house in ten minutes with instructions to escort him to the first London bound train and threaten him with arrest if he ever reappeared. Mum told him that she would cancel his remaining talks to schools and other bodies and if he gave her any problems she would speak to his commanding officer and have him court marshalled. They got him to the station two minutes before the next London train pulled in and that was the end of him. The police car then drove to the school and took me home.

I was lucky. I doubt if many girls can now count on this type of support. Part of it was bluff. It is highly improbable that the French military authorities would ever have court marshalled one of their own merely for 'having a bit of fun' with a girl, but Pierre knew that Mum was someone to be reckoned with. Nowadays girls are left to make a case in court. Even rape is difficult to prove given that it is one person's word against another and attempted rape pretty well impossible.

A lot of women have made things even more difficult by bringing actions for rape when they have got into bed with a man (or the equivalent) and then changed their minds. Press and political attacks on police who take a tough line have undermined their authority. One should also remember that local control of police forces tended to make them more accountable and ready to take pre-emptive action, as happened in my case. I was, in any case, extremely grateful for the way the police responded to my predicament. I would add that far more people in those days, whether in police, in the courts or in public administration, were trained to exercise judgment and were able to form an instant view of who had a genuine grievance and who was the culprit, rather than being constrained to feel neutral.

Mum understood how shaken I had been and started apologising for bringing Pierre under our roof. I would have none of it. I said:

"I hope you don't think I am becoming an alcoholic but I could do with a glass of sherry, or something like that."

Mum smiled, "I think we both need a glass of Scotch."

I had never had whisky before and I didn't know whether I would like it, but it sounded a good idea. She prepared it the same way 'as Dad liked it' except with a bit more water. Mum said to sip slowly and I did. She was right. It was a good medicine to calm the nerves after a crisis and it certainly made me feel warm. I may not have evolved into a connoisseur of malt whiskies, but I am grateful to my remote Scots ancestors for inventing a potion that can help restore you to your equilibrium when things have gone awry. According to Mum, Dad used to say it was the finest drink in the world. He had clearly convinced her or we wouldn't have been drinking from a bottle that had been left to mature in the sideboard since his departure.

Once the danger was over I was almost apologising to Mum for depriving her of the man whom she had hoped would compensate for Dad's absence, but she would have none of it. She was so outraged that this little nobody from the back-streets of Lille of wherever, on whom she had been bestowing a tremendous favour, should show such ill manners and ingratitude as to insult and threaten her daughter and that the only fate good enough for him was to be hung, drawn and quartered, which is what I felt.

She clearly felt guilty and that she was being punished for wanting to have a flutter with a young man, which was unfair. If she had been an experienced amorist knowing all the ropes, she wouldn't have suffered in this way. It was only because she had been so loyal to Dad and to her family that she lacked the experience. But it wasn't simply a matter of experience. She knew she had a position to maintain and therefore didn't have the freedom that a lot of other women had and used. I may not have understood the position fully, but I had a gut feel for it. I wanted to help Mum. In spite of my frightening experience. I also felt a bit guilty because I had deprived her of whatever she was expecting from this man, Pierre.

I honestly don't know whether she managed to get into bed with the type of man she was likely to want during the next few months. She didn't bring anyone home, but she did leave me on my own to look after the house on two occasions and I presumed that she was spending each of the weekends in question with a man who would treat her in the way she would like.

Obviously, the early months of 1944 were months of tension for me. The words 'second front' were on everyone's lips. I had two wonderful weekends with David. The Headmistress would have allowed me to take any time off I wanted when all I asked was the Thursday when I would travel to London, the Friday when I hoped David would arrive and the Monday when I would travel back. Somehow I had won my spurs with Miss Blantyre by the way I had arranged my marriage with David and by the way I had continued to act as a normal Sixth Former. I suspect she may initially have worried about the problems of having a married woman in the school and been relieved to find that I had done my best to behave as an ordinary pupil and this may have helped me.

There were other joys. David's parents had written letters to Mum and me full of warmth and affection. We both felt it was from the heart and we knew in later years that it was. I had at first feared that they might have thought of me as a scheming woman who had hooked their son.

The warmth of Dad's congratulations, when they eventually arrived, elated me no end. I had always been afraid of Dad, so I had been apprehensive. Mum had sent the photographs she had taken on the day of our engagement and what had now become the famous ballroom photograph. Dad, who had last seen me just before my fourteenth birthday was also (he said) congratulating himself on having produced a girl who would turn all the men's heads. But it was wonderful the way he put it.

What made me particularly exalted was the fact that the Canadians in his mess had feted him, drunk his health and that of David and me because he had acquired a serving Canadian officer as a son-in-law. Speeches were made in his honour at a dinner where he had been congratulated on the fact that he had two daughters, one a serving Wren and the other married to a serving Canadian officer. If Dad in earlier days had been disappointed at not being able to have a son, I believe that any such disappointment had long since been forgotten and that in later life he was well content with his two daughters.

CHAPTER 19

IN MEMORIAM DAVID M^CBAIN AND DICK SQUIRES

A week or two before the first Higher Cert. exams came the D-day landings. I had been working very late the night before trying to memorise quotations from King Lear (one of the two set plays). There was no time to listen to the news before I cycled to school. At lunchtime I learnt that 'the second front had started' and I said a silent prayer for David. The Allies had been successful in keeping the Germans guessing as to where it would be and when. This meant that the civilian population, as well as most of those in the armed forces, knew nothing. I had no means of knowing whether David's unit would be involved, but there was a reasonable expectation that it would. We all knew that the big build-up of Allied troops in the south of England was intended for this purpose. David mightn't be amongst the first to land, but something inside me told me that he would and I was tense.

I had no letters from him during the next few weeks and I, therefore, assumed that he was in France and in the front line and would have no opportunity to write. The families of two of my friends had received the fatal official telegrams and on two days the school stood in silence before morning prayers, after the Headmistress had announced the deaths of the fathers of two girls. I began to feel that no news was good news and I completed all the Higher Cert. papers, which lasted for a number of weeks. History, for example, as a main subject, required three three-hour papers, one for American history, one for English history and one for the special period. There were as many papers for each main subject and even the subsidiary subjects required two papers each. I had never worked so hard and I was exhausted.

Although term wasn't over, the Headmistress allowed us to take some unofficial holiday when we had finished all the papers. On the first such day I slept late and Mum brought me breakfast in bed. The postman had been and there was one letter from Dad and an air letter from Canada, but Mum left them downstairs. Without my knowledge she had telephoned her office to say she wouldn't be in. She had a premonition and wanted me to eat something. She had been worried about my eating too little during the tense examination period and she was right.

It was only when I was dressed and came downstairs that she came to meet me with these letters, unopened, in her hand as if they had just arrived. She opened Dad's and passed me the other. I recognised the handwriting of David's father. When I opened it I could hardly read more than the first few lines. It was the end of my world. I couldn't read any more. I couldn't speak, but Mum understood. I managed to hold on to the back of a chair and then sat down at the kitchen table, with my head in my hands. Mum kissed the top of my head and sat down beside me and knew there was nothing she could say or do, except to remain with me in silence.

Meeting David had not only changed my life. It had changed me. All my spiritual and bodily yearnings of previous years had been transformed into a love for someone else. I no longer existed for myself or to satisfy ambitions. David's death changed me in a different way. It brought on what I can best describe as a spiritual crisis.

I had been brought up as a Christian. In those days this meant a lot, apart from going to church every Sunday, learning to say our prayers with our parents every night and every morning, studying scripture in school so that we had an extensive knowledge of a great deal in both the Old Testament and the New Testament, and having attended confirmation classes at a senior level and studied comparative religion, I had an extensive knowledge framework. Furthermore, my father and his uncle had, for much of their lives, been closely involved in the affairs of the Church of England. My first moments of true exchange with David had been while I was kneeling in the Cathedral. I had been married in St. David's by one of the most wonderful and understanding Christian priests, who had broken all the rules for me.

But I must now beg the forgiveness of any Christian whom I may offend and think what I have to say is blasphemous. It isn't meant to be and I don't think it is. On receipt of the news of David's death I kept thinking of the eleven remaining apostles on Good Friday, and of Our Lord's Mother and Mary Magdalene and many others. The man in whom they had believed had been taken from them, just as David had been taken from me. I think that at that moment I understood how they must have felt. Was it the end?

Then in the midst of my memory I seemed to hear the voice of Father Wakehurst reading the Lesson when I was a child - I don't know when - "I am the Resurrection and the Life" and I said to Mum:

"I would like to go to Bishop Wantock. Don't bother with a taxi, I'll cycle."

Mum, of course, telephoned Father Wakehurst and told him the news. He had both experience and understanding and remained out of sight when we arrived. I was, therefore, able to slip into the church unnoticed, to kneel down and to pray that David had not suffered too much agony in the hours or minutes preceding his death. Father Wakehurst must have quietly slipped into the church from a rear door and knelt down a few rows behind me. When I eventually stood up he came slowly towards me and I could see the tears in his eyes as he took both my hands in his and said a short blessing. I had thought that he would have been hardened to such situations, but he was not.

"David is with you in spirit and you with him", he said. And somehow I felt that David was present with us.

In later life I have often sensed that David was beside me, just as he was in those moments when we walked, sat or prayed together and didn't need to say anything. These are moments of peace. Every year I try to make a pilgrimage to the Normandy beaches on or about 6th June. It was not possible when I was teaching, or about to give birth, or when I was on standby for the expected birth of a grandchild. I had to rearrange my plans in 1994 when the D-day veterans and their families from all corners of the earth came to join me and I was able to join a large gathering of Canadian families at the Canadian memorial cemetery near Bayeux where we sang Abide With Me.

Right up to the year before she died, Mum used to join me.

You can now go as a foot passenger on the Brittany Ferries' boat from Portsmouth to Ouistram and you are already at Sword Beach where the English troops landed. You walk along the coast past Lion sur Plage, Luc sur Plage, St. Aubin then Courseulles and between St. Aubin and Courseulles is Juno Beach where the Canadian forces landed and where we stop to pray in silence for a few moments, looking out to sea and then looking at the land as it would have appeared to David on 6th June 1944. It has, of course, changed because it is full of seaside houses. Out of season it is peaceful.

The Canadian Scottish companies in which David served were allocated to the St. Aubin sector (the eastern end) and had one of the worst ordeals. The change (for the worse) in the weather had delayed the first landings sufficiently for the tide to be further in than had been allowed for in the plan and hence covered many of the undersea booby-traps. As a result, many of the troops were killed while they were wading ashore and still waist-high in water. When they got ashore many of the houses had been booby-trapped and the naval bombardment which preceded the landing had failed to knock out the large concrete gun shelter which protected this part of the coast. Overall, the Canadians had won an important victory by the end of the first day of the landings (6th June) and their forward elements had penetrated deeper into France than the British troops to the left and the right of them and by the US troops further west. The Canadians had suffered a total of 1000 casualties (in fact nearly 2000 had been expected) which included 335 dead. There were, therefore, 354 other Canadian families that suffered a loss on the same day comparable to my loss of David and this is something I always bear in mind when I pray for David. And this leaves out of account the losses of the British and US families whose armies were landing in larger numbers.

I am grateful to Sir John Keegan who (at the time of writing) is the defence editor of the Daily Telegraph for the clear picture he presents of the D-day battles in his excellent book, Six Armies in Normandy.

One year John's father asked if he could come with me. At first he was concerned that I might regard him as intruding. On my part I was unsure how he felt, as the father of my second husband, about the important place I had always made in my life for my first husband. I need not have worried.

As we walked along the shore he talked about the weeks and months of anxiety he had suffered when he had news that John's plane had been reported missing. It was a miracle that John had been able to make a safe parachute landing and survive the war as a PoW. If, as he put it, John had been killed and David had survived the war and John had been my first husband, he knew that I would have done for John what I do for David and that John, like David, would have wanted me to remarry and have a family. If John's father had not joined me on the pilgrimage we might never have had that conversation which was important to me.

The tragedy of David's death did, however, torture me in my beliefs for many months to come. Whilst I could sense David's presence, and I felt my belief in the Resurrection strengthened as I was kneeling beside Father Wakehurst, there were days when the Doubting Thomas voices in my mind kept repeating the fact that I had no proof and that I had to believe that I would be reunited with David, because that was what I wanted to believe, but I know this is what all believers suffer from time to time and it is one of the reasons why I was so determined to give David the opportunity to be with me, whether by making these pilgrimage walks, or kneeling down in church or at home and praying that one day we shall be reunited.

Mum, as ever, did all the practical things such as telling the Headmistress and writing to the Canadian military authorities that had failed to include me as one of David's next of kin. In fact it was probably fortunate that my first news had come from David's parents rather than in the form of an official telegram.

Term had not finished. I didn't know how I could bear up if I went back to school the last day or two, but it was agreed with the Headmistress that I should try. She announced David's death at the start of prayers and the school stood for a minute in silence. For the first time in my life I remember feeling faint and putting my hand on somebody's shoulder to steady myself.

I realised that I wasn't up to it. There were no more classes and there would only be the end of term euphoria, in which I was in no state to participate, and so I contented myself with saying goodbye to the people whom I knew were leaving, collected my belongings and went home.

It was the only time in my life that I can remember going completely to pieces. I am not proud of myself. At that time a lot of other women were suffering the loss of their husbands, fathers, brothers and sons and they were able to keep going. In many cases they had jobs where they were working flat out and they had to come home and cook for their children and themselves, do all the normal housework and so on and keep up the morale of their families. They have my undying respect. I knew what they went through but they made a much better job of coping than I felt capable of doing.

During the school Summer holiday in 1944 I felt for a lot of the time as if I were sleep-walking. I had intended to do a lot of reading in preparation for the scholarship paper that would be my next hurdle if I had succeeded in getting good results in Higher Cert., but I couldn't concentrate. In peacetime we would have had a holiday and I was probably getting stale after the work for Higher Cert. I had been promised a visit to Oxford with Mum and her friend, Alice Draper, and an introduction either to the Principal or the Senior English Tutor at St. Hilda's, but this would be in September just before the start of the term. I had to do something, so I wrote to Peggy to see whether it was too late to sign up for the farm camp. It wasn't.

Peggy was wonderful. Although she had been a severe task-master and we all remembered her as someone who put the fear of God into us a year earlier, we respected her and had come to like her. What's more, she had proved her point that the girls could work as hard as the boys (in fact we achieved more per girl hour) and there had been no scandals. As a result she had been able to organise two teams for 1944, the second team joining when the first left. I joined the first team and stayed on for the second, so I did a total of four weeks farm work which is all I was capable of doing at that time, but it enabled me to feel I was doing something for the war effort and not being a parasite. I could think about David, meditate if you like, and try to rethink what I was going to do with my life.

On this occasion Peggy treated me as a 'mate', the word we all used extensively in those days in this type of situation. I knew that she, herself, had suffered a tragic loss early in the war. She didn't like to talk about the past and had clearly pulled herself together and succeeded in losing herself in her work. She knew that I was trying to do the same. From time to time we relaxed a bit and she would tell me what a frightful worry it was being in charge of "all these kids".

In her period in the ATS she had seen many girls from sheltered family backgrounds who had not been able to cope with the men, who were all too ready to take advantage of their inexperience and who were too careless to take the proper precautions. She had been given the task of accompanying a number of these girls home to their parents, either in the latter stages of pregnancy or after they had given birth. In those days many people (often the girls' own parents) treated these poor girls as lepers and Peggy knew that they faced the prospect of a wretched existence. "So you can see", she said, "why I was worried stiff about having you lot in my charge. You're no longer a kid, thank God, but I'll be scared until at least three months after this year's second lot have gone home. The trouble is that neither parents nor school give these girls proper advice. They talk in highfalutin terms about morality and that isn't what is needed when it comes to real life."

She was, of course, absolutely right, but I had agreed with everything she had said and done the previous year, except that I had then been anxious to avoid the attentions of Fred, although there was no risk of my receiving his attention this year.

When I returned home I was physically exhausted but beginning to get my mind back into shape. A lot had happened. From being penned into a corner of Normandy our armies had advanced across France, Paris had been liberated and we had landed on the Mediterranean coast of France and quickly advanced up the Rhone, so that most of France had been freed from the German occupation. Mum was doing her best to re-establish contact with the French side of our family, but the country was still in a state of chaos. Marauding bands who were calling themselves resistance groups were going around killing all the people they disliked, claiming that their victims had been "collaborators" when many of the members of the so-called resistance groups had been collaborators themselves when they thought the Germans were going to win, including the communists who had been against the war until Russia was attacked a year after the fall of France. It was some months before Mum heard from Tante Nicole that Grandmaman (Mum's mother) had died in May, only a month before the liberating armies had landed in Normandy.

When term started I was just beginning to focus my mind on the work plan for the scholarship exam. It was a total change from the fairly narrow concentration on set texts that had been necessary for Higher Cert. Although the scholarship exam was to enable me to read for an Honours Degree in English Language and Literature, it contained a general paper where I could use my knowledge of history. In the event I was fortunate in being at a school which had opted for American history where the syllabus included a lot of constitutional history. In the scholarship exam I got a question citing the famous Jefferson quotation from the Declaration of Independence "We hold these truths to be self-evident..." and so was able to write a three hour essay contrasting British and American constitutional practice, with a few comments on the failed attempts to introduce democracy in most European countries. I might not have had good marks if I had had a left-wing tutor marking the paper, but in the event it was a paper on which I was told I had done well.

But before I started at Oxford in October 1945 a number of tragic events occurred, including the news of Dad's death which didn't reach us until after VJ day, 15th August 1945. First came the death of Dick Squires, Louise's eldest brother, at Arnhem.

Dick was an officer in the parachute regiment who had been given the job of seizing the key bridges for the allied armies to advance through Holland into Germany at a time when we all thought the war in Europe would be over by Christmas 1944. The episode has become legendary in the film "A Bridge Too Far". From what I have read in later years, my own view is that the Allies made the mistake of taking the Dutch resistance into their confidence in the hope of enlisting their co-operation and it was these so-called resistance people who betrayed the Allied plans to the Germans.

One has to remember that lot of the resistance movements in Western Europe had been penetrated and taken over by communists, whose prime objective was to take over these various countries in the chaos following the collapse of Germany. The communists had wanted an Allied invasion in the west as a means of diverting German arms away from the eastern front, thus making it easier for the Russians to advance. The sudden breakthrough of the western allied armies in France and Belgium in the Summer of 1944 was not what the communists wanted. If the war had been finished

IN MEMORIAM DAVID McBAIN AND DICK SQUIRES

in 1944 the Russian armies would not have had the opportunity to occupy Poland, Hungary, Romania, Bulgaria, etc. as they were able to do in the Autumn of 1944 and early part of 1945, leaving the peoples of these countries to suffer nearly half a century of Russian dominated repression, from which they have still not recovered.

My heart went out to Janet, Dick's lovely wife, whom I had met for the first time at the school Christmas/New Year ball and I immediately wrote to her. There was a lovely photo of Dick, Janet, David and me standing together as a group at the Christmas ball which Mum's photographer had taken. It had been given a place of honour on our dining room mantelpiece and the print she had given to Milly was framed on the desk in her study. I still treasure this photo.

Walford and Milly were devastated, as I would have been if I had lost my eldest son, William. There is something sacred in the first born child of any marriage. It doesn't mean that one loves one's other children any less. Walford, whom I had always seen as an unflappable person with a benign smile who had never let anything get him down, was no longer the same. The tragedy in his life and in mine somehow created a bond between us and made me ready to forget and forgive. I had never objected to his punishing me the way he had done in March 1942, but his manner and attitude at the time of that confrontation had taken away the high esteem in which I had once held him. No doubt this would have happened in any event as part of the growing-up process in which one reassesses a lot of older people as one begins to look at them on one's own level. But now we were just two ordinary human beings and we had each suffered a tragic loss.

Father Wakehurst, who had married Dick and Janet in Bishop Wantock church, as he had married David and me, suggested to the Headmaster that a memorial service in the College chapel would be appropriate. Dick was not only an old boy of the school but also the son of the second master. He then suggested to Walford and Milly the idea of a combined memorial service for Dick and David, which was agreed. I still have a copy of the order of service which was printed for the occasion showing the In Memoriam dedication on the front page to Richard John Squires and David McBain and a brief note about Juno Beach and the Arnhem landings.

Although Father Wakehurst gave the address he asked me if I would read the first Lesson and whether I would like to choose a suitable passage from the Old Testament. Walford would read the second Lesson.

This was a challenge, but I was grateful to Father Wakehurst for suggesting it. It compelled me to take a firm grip on myself. I could so easily have stood behind the lectern and collapsed in a flood of tears. It is this memory that makes me so angry when I hear people berate the English as lacking in emotion and feeling because they have learned to master themselves.

I searched through the First Book of Samuel in the hope of finding a suitable passage in the battle of young David, the shepherd boy, against mighty Goliath of the

Philistines. This was a story I had loved as a child, long before I knew my David. I told Father Wakehurst I wanted to compare my David, an architectural student who had gone out to fight the mighty Goliath, the most powerful army of our time, with David the shepherd boy. But David the shepherd boy had won, whereas my David had fallen in battle. But then he said to me the British, Canadians and Americans had in fact thrown the mighty Goliath of the German army out of France and it was thanks to the millions of young boys like David and Dick who had, like David the shepherd, left their peaceful occupations in order to gain this victory.

"Why don't you say this in your own words as an introduction to the Lesson", he said.

And that's what I did. I finished by saying that rather than choose a passage from the battle scene, I had chosen the most famous Psalm that David the shepherd boy had bequeathed to us and was known and loved by all "The Lord is My Shepherd". I said that I had never felt more in need of the Lord as my shepherd than I had since the death of David, my husband.

I managed to get through without my voice giving, as I feared. I did not burst into tears but I was told afterwards that it would have been difficult to find a dry eye in the chapel, that was packed to capacity with people standing at the back and in the aisles. Although the words were not written until over a year later by the poet Ezra Pound, when he was in the death cells near Pisa, and I didn't read his Pisan Cantos until they were published in Britain in 1948: "First master thyself then others shall thee beare", these words describe something of the way I was coming to terms with my loss.

When I sat down (I was between Janet and Mum) Janet took my hand and held it for a moment. She was shaking and I knew that she was fighting the same battle to keep control. She did.

The second Lesson, which was read by Walford, was taken from St. John's Gospel. It had been chosen by Father Wakehurst and told how at Bethany, Our Lord raised the brother of Martha and Mary, Lazarus, from the dead after he had been in the tomb for four days. It finishes with the passage where Jesus says to Martha "Thy brother will rise again" and she replies:

"I know well enough that he will rise again at the resurrection, when the last day comes."

"Jesus said to her 'I am the resurrection and the life, he that believeth in me, yea although he were dead, yet shall he live. And whosoever liveth and believeth in me to all eternity cannot die.'"

Father Wakehurst had clearly chosen this most appropriate second Lesson to provide the theme for his address, which opened with the words "I am the resurrection and the life". He then spoke first about the young Canadian student who had travelled 5000 miles and who was a volunteer, in order to help in the defence of Mother

Country, which was where his father had been born. He then spoke about Dick's brilliant career at the College and then at Cambridge and about the various other theatres of war where he had served with distinction before being gunned down at Arnhem. The address continued with a comparison of Martha and Mary's sufferings to those of Janet and me and the sufferings of Dick's family, and then to his concluding reaffirmation of belief in the resurrection as one of the cornerstones of Christian theology. What, he asked in so many words, would all those who had suffered bereavement in this war, the first war, and from a thousand and one other causes, have to comfort us in our difficult lives ahead if we did not have the hope of one day being reunited with our loved ones.

Throughout history it has been people like Father Wakehurst who have brought Christianity into the lives of all of us and not the organisations and church groupings that can attract good, mediocre or bad people to represent them. Father Wakehurst lived the Christian Gospel and my faith owes more to him than anyone else although I would not have been brought up as a Christian had it not been for my parents.

Plenty of people, however, are brought up as Christians but it is easy to fall away in later years unless someone like Father Wakehurst takes care of you at a critical moment in your life. He was loved and respected by everyone with whom he came into contact. He was not a misery person, a hot gospeller or a brimstone and hellfire merchant. He behaved naturally as a friend and although he lived frugally he was at heart a bon viveur as he showed when he brought his 1926 vintage Margaux to the wedding breakfast that Mum had organised for David and me on Christmas Day 1943.

Apart from the Headmaster and Headmistress there were a number of important people at the service, including the Dean (as chairman of the governors), Mrs. Wilding and most of the governing body and the mayor. The Dean invited Mum and me, together with the Squires family, the Headmaster, the Headmistress and a number of other people to a small reception to honour the memory of Dick Squires and David McBain. I still have the invitation letter.

When Mum and I arrived, Dr. Wilding said, as he shook my hand, "Thank you for reading the first Lesson and for what you said. You have a beautiful voice and you spoke with clarity, dignity and authority. I shall know who to call on to read on important occasions in the future."

Sadly the occasion on which he did call upon me was for the memorial service in the Cathedral for Dad, nearly a year later. It wasn't, in fact, usual for women to read the Lessons in Cathedral services or in any Church of England services in those days and so, in spite of my strong emotions at the time - or possibly because of them - I must have put up a creditable performance.

The church fathers, or whoever, in Christian history were responsible for the way in which we formalise and externalise our deeply felt need to honour the dead and to enable us to express our grief in a manner which teaches us to learn to control it, had an insight into a fundamental psychological truth. When Mum died at the age of eighty-seven this took the form of the normal funeral service. But for David, who died on one of the battle fields of Normandy, the memorial service was the only way in which I could have received this spiritual consolation and I am sure he would have appreciated the honour accorded to his memory by some of the people in the country he had come to defend.

Although a great distance separated his parents and us, and the war made it impossible for them to attend (and the postal system at that time would not have enabled them to know in time anyway) I know that they were very moved indeed when they received copies of the order of service. The service was a watershed for me in my spiritual and mental recovery and I am eternally grateful to Father Wakehurst for suggesting it in the first place and for the way he planned and directed it.

As a postscript to this sad period in my life, I think my vivid memory of it helped, two years ago, to bring consolation to my granddaughter, Jennie. I have been very attached to her from the time she was a small child when she stayed with us quite a lot when her mother (my daughter-in-law, Sue, William's wife) had a long spell in hospital. I knew Jennie tended to be headstrong but she is a loving and giving person and I always feared that sooner or later she would get hurt. At seventeen, while she was still at her Sixth Form College in Leicester, she had left home to live in a small flat (part of a converted terrace house) with her twenty-one year old boyfriend, Mike, who was training to be an accountant.

When I was doing my usual Sunday evening 'ring round' to see how all the family were I learnt from Sue that Jennie 'was in a dreadful state' because Mike had left her. What worried me most was her mother's comment.

"She'll soon get over it. It will serve the poor kid right and teach her a lesson."

Mother clearly did not understand daughter. Jennie was no more a kid at seventeen than I was when I married David.

I rang Jennie and asked if she could spare a few hours with her old gran who had a problem and would be with her in two to three hours, depending on traffic, if she could give me exact directions as to her whereabouts, which she did.

We talked into the early hours of Monday morning, sharing a pizza and a bottle of wine which I had brought with me and I told her about another headstrong girl of seventeen who had married a Canadian soldier. Although all my family knew that I had been married at seventeen to my first husband and that I made an annual pilgrimage to Juno Beach, I had never described it in detail to any of them (apart from John) and it was the experience of telling Jennie that gave me the idea of putting it in a book.

"But Gran, you make this sound as if it all happened in the last few months and you talk as if you are still seventeen. Why have you come to tell me all this now?"

"Because you are the only member of the family old enough and mature enough to understand", I said.

"But Mike's still alive and in good health, thank God", she went on. "I haven't suffered as you suffered. You can't really compare us."

In spite of what had happened she clearly still loved Mike and hadn't allowed herself to become vindictive. The reality of the situation is that she had a maturity of spirit far beyond her years and a sense of responsibility, while Mike was not much more than an overgrown schoolboy who was happy to have someone who would give him sex on demand and mollycoddle him, but that was where his interest in Jennie stopped. Some men remain like this all their lives.

It is ironic that when, as a fifteen year old Sixth Former in 1942, I had read one of Bertrand Russell's books advocating temporary childless marriages for students, the idea seemed eminently sensible. I was desperately longing for a lover who would satisfy my bodily needs, as well as satisfying his own and the Bertrand Russell solution seemed more efficient (i.e. you could get what you wanted more often) and less risky (in terms of catching VD) than the alternative of what is now called casual sex, which is less efficient in the sense that you can't get it all the time as in a single relationship.

The Bertrand Russell idea is now, of course, widely practised although I doubt if many of its practitioners have ever heard of him. The sad story of Jennie illustrates the downside of the idea. There is always a risk that one partner will be much more involved than the other and get badly hurt when the relationship ends. Another downside is that it gets more people accustomed to the idea that they can start and stop relationships when they want and this can be disastrous for family life once there are children.

I don't want to moralise. Most of my professional life has been one of telling people that wherever there is a problem, there must be a solution and so whenever I reflect upon the basic problems of human existence I always think that there ought to be a solution, but in most cases, there isn't. The solution of wanting and waiting until Mr. Right was old enough to have a proper job had disadvantages that were self-evident to all of us. The solution adopted by many of Jennie's generation has its cost in terms of human unhappiness. In an earlier chapter I have floated off the idea of legal, customer friendly and staff friendly brothels and it wasn't meant to be tongue in cheek. I have to confess, therefore, that whilst I may have been competent at solving business problems I wouldn't have got far as a consultant in solving these basic problems of mankind, but then who has?

I went on to tell Jennie the sad story of John's (her grandpa's) fiancée who had abandoned him for dead when his plane was reported missing and the suffering of

John when he learnt that she had married someone else. I added that I had always put John's loss of his first love on a par with my own and that, in one sense, his was greater. Throughout my life I have been able to honour the memory of David as my war hero. To lose faith in someone whom you have honoured and trusted is a devastating experience and I wanted Jennie to feel some of the support that I had been given, both from Mum and from Father Wakehurst. We cuddled up beside each other, as we used to do when she was a very small child and unable to sleep. I stayed with her for a few days and I think I helped her to get back in control of her mind and emotions.

But she also helped me. In recent years the memory of my early life has come back to me much more vividly than in earlier days. I have a visual memory and I tend to see things happening as I would if I were to re-run an old video that we had taken of some family event. I realised that, like the ancient mariner, I needed to tell my story to someone who could understand, and I knew that Jennie could and would. She gave up her flat and returned home. She got herself a university place and is now staying with John and me. She has been the person who has been most persistent in persuading me to write my life story, or at any rate that part of it when all of these important events took place.

CHAPTER 20

DAD'S PLANE IS REPORTED MISSING

The Winter of 1944-45 was a period in which I was fortunate in being able to re-focus my mental energies on scholarship work and come to terms with the need to rebuild my life without David until I could be re-united with him in the hereafter. I had my ups and downs, but so had everyone else who had suffered in like manner, as does all humankind at all times.

I didn't gain a scholarship but I did sufficiently well to gain a place at St. Hilda's in October 1945. One of the lessons I was later to learn at Oxford is that however good a candidate may have been by the standards of his or her own school, one was now competing with the most able candidates from all the other schools and one would be competing with them in university life.

The victory celebrations in May 1945 following the unconditional surrender of the Germans involved great jollification for both College and High School. We had a day's holiday, but for the boarders who remained at school it was simply a day of no class work during which everyone was officially allowed to smoke and drink without fear of retribution. Large numbers of the High School girls flocked to the College to participate in the unconstrained orgy of eating (whatever goodies could be produced), smoking and drinking and many were incapable of walking, even if they were not drunk. Memoir writers in recent times tend to talk about the day as one when large numbers of girls lost their virginity. I don't think this applied to our High School lot. Even though many may have been incapable of resisting, an even larger number of College boys were incapable of doing anything had they been so minded, and for all the high jinks I don't think there were many College boys at that time who would knowingly have taken advantage of the girls who had become their work companions. Whether this was because they were basically honourable or afraid of the consequences, no matter.

As a war widow I think I enjoyed something of the respect that would normally be accorded to masters' wives and to women teachers. I participated in the evening celebrations when we burnt Adolf Hitler in effigy at the top of a massive bonfire, but the day's events kept reminding me of the cost in human life that had been needed to achieve that victory. I spent a lot of the day at home listening to the radio, to Churchill's speech, and to descriptions of the crowds outside Buckingham Palace.

For Mum and me a far more important day was VJ day, the 15th August 1945. The war in Japan had been expected to last another three years, but with the dropping of two atomic bombs on Japan leading to the unconditional surrender by the Japanese, we knew that Dad would no longer be at risk and we hoped he might be home by Christmas. The Squires invited Mum and me to a sherry party that evening and we all spoke enthusiastically about the future in spite of our respective family losses.

Most of us were disappointed at the victory of the Labour party in the elections. We were shattered that Churchill had not won, but we had all been preaching the virtues of democratic government throughout the war and we believed he was right to accept the victory of the other side in an election with the same spirit as the losing side would accept the victory of the winners in a cricket or rugger match. What made us feel uneasy was that during the electoral truce of the war we were all aware that the left wing propaganda machine had been working full-time, or that was our impression.

There were no VJ day celebrations at the College because it was in the middle of the school Summer holiday. I still feel angry when I read revisionist historians and would be humanitarians condemning the Allies for dropping atomic bombs on Japan. Whilst the atrocities committed by the Germans against the Jews and many others in Europe are still remembered, little attention is now paid to the appalling atrocities committed on a large scale by the Japs against the Europeans. The evidence we have today comes from those prisoners who survived. Many men who would normally weigh twelve or thirteen stone were found as skeletons weighing six stone or less when they were released and a very high proportion of the British forces taken prisoner died in prisoner of war camps.

In later years I met a nurse who had survived after being taken prisoner in Singapore in 1941. She told me that many of the nurses were subjected to gang rapes and then brutally ill-treated and then bayoneted by the Japs for the amusement of the onlookers. The Japs at the time, no doubt, resented what they construed to be the superior attitudes of the Europeans, but by the same token they were showing themselves to be the most savage barbarians we had read about in the Dark Ages. Those of us who knew about these things wouldn't have minded if we had dropped enough atomic bombs on Japan to exterminate the whole Japanese population, even if it had only shortened the war by only one week.

Informed military opinion at the time was taking the view that two to three years would be required to win the war conclusively in the Far East, a war that would be fought on an island-by-island basis in the Pacific with large numbers of casualties, not only at the hands of the Japs but also because of the exposure to tropical diseases in an extremely unhealthy part of the world. On top of this most of the prisoners who were released and recovered would not have survived.

However many bad things the Germans did, one has to be fair to them about matters in which they acted reasonably. For example, when John's plane was shot down when he was on fighter escort duty on one of the large bombing raids over the German industrial towns on the Ruhr, and was fortunate enough to bail out, he was taken prisoner and given reasonable prisoner of war treatment until he was released by the Allied advance in the Spring of 1945. It would have been understandable if the German population, that was at that time suffering nightly from thousand bomber raids, was so incensed against the perpetrators, that the civilian who found John might well have been tempted to kill him in cold blood, but he didn't. Conditions in the German prisoner of war camp were spartan, but John survived to bring happiness into the lives of his parents who had feared him lost when his plane was reported missing and to bring over fifty years of happiness into my life, as well as making a wonderful father and grandfather for the family that would never have existed had he not returned.

But first I must deal with the saddest event of all.

On Wednesday 22nd August, a week after VJ day, I received a telephone call from a Colonel Widdowson who said he had just returned from Colombo and wondered if it would be convenient for him to call on Mrs. Fortingall. I suggested 6pm when I knew Mum would be at home and told him how to find our house. I then rang Mum at the office to warn her because I knew she would want to get home early to get changed and smartened up. I sensed straight away that she didn't share my enthusiasm. The combination of her intuitive feel for any situation and her experience of the ways of humankind had immediately sent warning signals to her brain, but she kept her own counsel. Fortunately we had a reserve of whisky, gin and sherry which we hardly ever touched. These were not rationed items during the war, but they were scarce and we were not regular customers. Dad, however, had done a good job in sorting out some court case in the late 1930s for our local wine and spirit merchant who was still in business as the proprietor.

I vacuumed the drawing room, dusted and smartened up the glasses with a drying towel and was ready to do duty as bar-girl.

Colonel Widdowson arrived promptly on time in a staff car driven by an ATS chauffeuse with a neat haircut - the style of the times was straight hair which was neatly curled inwards at collar level. I opened the door and asked whether he would like me to look after his driver in another room while he spoke to Mum, but he waved his hand in a way that suggested that this was not necessary. When I served the drinks I was surprised that Mum asked for whisky, and more surprised when she didn't say 'when' until after I had half filled her glass.

Colonel Widdowson quickly came to the point. The plane in which Dad had been travelling three weeks ago had gone missing. There were no traces of wreckage nor any survivors and it was his sad duty to tell us. Presumably the end of the war had meant that senior officers now had the time for such delicate tasks and hence we had not received the usual telegram. Dad also held a senior position as a Staff Officer in

Mountbatten's headquarters. I knew nothing of the protocol of such matters. I had lost David. I had now lost Dad, but the only thing that concerned me was how Mum would take it. I watched her as she gripped her glass tightly and noticed it was empty, so I filled it up before I walked over to top up Colonel Widdowson whose glass was nearly as full as I had left it. Mum's instincts had been right and I had been living in cloud-cuckoo-land. Colonel Widdowson left shortly afterwards, making the usual offers to do anything he could to help and leaving us the telephone number where he could be contacted.

Mum held up for the rest of the evening. We went out and sat together in the garden. She may have drunk two or three more large whiskies and I began to be worried because she was not a drinker, at any rate not during the war years, but her mind kept racing away at high speed on all the problems we would have to deal with. If Dad's share in the partnership was to be worth anything it would have to be merged with a bigger firm, possibly a London firm, and this would take time. None of the present partners had the money or was capable of generating the money needed to buy him out on reasonable terms. There might in future be profitable business that could be generated by big property deals, but which of the present partners was capable of landing them. There were one or two partners who might make a useful contribution but they were still in the forces and it might be a year or two before they were demobilised and back at work.

She had money tied up in trusts, some of it in the US which she didn't think she could get out until exchange controls came off because at the outbreak of war all individual US shareholdings of UK citizens had been 'nationalised' but her money wasn't individual money. It was her grandmother's (Arrière) inheritance. She had been paying minimal fees at the High School and was working out how to pay the £250 a year anticipated costs of my Oxford education. She had it all in her head and I had difficulty in keeping up with her.

Then, as it got dark, we began to talk about the future in wider and more general terms, and she was very pessimistic. With a Labour government we were unlikely to get back to normal and high taxes would continue. The Russians had finished the war with the largest armed forces in a Europe that had been destroyed and once the Americans pulled out Great Britain could be reduced to the squalor and misery of a communist satellite state.

Mum didn't normally talk in this way. She read a lot and knew a lot, but when she spoke it was nearly always to tell somebody what to do today or tomorrow, or the next day, whether at home or in the office.

I thought of Aldous Huxley's 'Brave New World' which I had read as a Fifth-Former, feeling rather arrogant in the way I had talked about it to my classmates, as I did whenever I talked about avant garde writing, but with the recent release of two atomic bombs, the end of our preoccupation with the German and Japanese menace and the way Mum was talking nineteen to the dozen about future practical problems, I began to see some of these fictional nightmares as getting too close to reality for comfort.

But then, after I had kissed Mum goodnight and heard her close her bedroom door, as I went to clean my teeth, I heard Mum burst into tears. She had cracked. She wasn't quietly sobbing to herself. She was crying in a loud, almost hysterical voice and it didn't stop. There was a bitterness and hopelessness in her voice that made this the worst and saddest time in the whole of my life. It made me think of Our Lord on the cross crying out to God "Why hast thou forsaken me!" Like many people of my age and upbringing I had been nurtured from childhood on the authorised version of the Bible and the familiar words and phrases would automatically come to mind in a crisis and I was facing the worst crisis in my life.

Mum never recovered her old self. After a difficult spiritual odyssey I was able to build a new life. My loss of David had strengthened my faith and I have always lived with the firm belief that I shall be reunited with David, with Dad and Mum and all the people I love, in the world to come. Although Dad and David had suffered death in the war I believed that their suffering was over, whereas Mum lived for another forty-two years as a shadow of her former self.

This didn't mean to say that she wasn't a wonderful mother and a wonderful grandmother to my children and didn't rejoice at the birth of each grandchild and each great-grandchild, but I knew there was something missing. Even when I stood at her bedside in her last moments and I said:

"But you'll be reunited with Dad", all she could say was:

"We'll see."

I knew many people who had suffered bodily injury as a result of the war, whom we would describe as war wounded. This was not Mum's case, but it was injury in the mind.

It had been love at first sight for both Dad and Mum when they had first seen each other at the beginning of 1920. In 1945 they were two years short of their silver wedding, although Mum had been left to live in hope without him for the five years since he had been posted overseas in 1940. She had suffered a double blow, losing her own mother, from whom she had likewise been separated as a result of the German occupation of France since 1940 and who had died just a few weeks before the allied liberation of France. Now she had lost her husband, whom fate had snatched away a week after her hopes had been buoyed up by the unconditional surrender of Japan.

She had had reason to be confident that Dad, as a senior staff officer at SEAC headquarters in Colombo would not be in the firing line unless a disaster happened.

She had, therefore, lived through most of the war in the confident expectation that he would return and, apart from looking after me, all her mental energies were expended in "looking after the shop" (as she put it) in the hope that the firm's finances would not be in too much of a mess when Dad returned. Of course the fee-earners were the lawyers and Dad was the biggest fee-earner of all, as well as being the dynamo that inspired, bullied, or both, the other partners and assistants to maximum effort.

Mum was a person who was always in command of every situation. I never remembered seeing her in a flap or giving way to emotional outbursts at home. Although she appeared to be a quiet, amenable person as compared with someone of Dad's forceful personality, no one would dare argue with her. I had only known her get really upset on one occasion. That was when I came home and told her I had married David without taking her into my confidence. Even then she didn't say much to express annoyance, but I knew she felt hurt that I had not considered her worthy of my trust, although as I have recounted, she forgave me. But now the Spring, which appeared to have unlimited resilience in almost every human situation, had broken and I always think of Mum as one of the saddest and most heart-rending casualties of the war - at least among all the people I have known.

CHAPTER 21
OXFORD - MICHAELMAS 1945

With Mum weeping bitterly and loudly throughout the night I felt helpless and useless. Whenever I went to her room she would shout "Leave me". I should have had the presence of mind to telephone our doctor, but I had grown so used to Mum taking charge on all such matters that it didn't occur to me. I waited until late in the morning before I dared telephone Milly. I had assumed that Mum would want to break the sad news herself and certainly wouldn't want the office to know, or anyone, else, but I knew Mum trusted Milly, so I explained the situation. Fortunately she understood. She promised not to tell anyone, even Walford, and came herself within half an hour. She called the doctor and, without giving the reason, explained that Mum was in a state of severe shock and needed something to calm her down and get her to sleep. I'm sure he understood the real reason, but he was an old family friend and he wouldn't have said anything. Milly wanted me to get some sleep, but I was past it, so she insisted that I ate a proper breakfast, which I did.

During the next few days she took charge. I had merely 'phoned the office to say Mum was seriously ill, so no one as yet knew. Milly and Louise moved in so we could take turns to keep an eye on Mum, sleep and do the necessary shopping. I had always had a high respect for Milly's integrity and capability. If a job had to be done, she would do it. I had not, however, fully appreciated the extent of her love and respect for Mum until that week which she spent with us. I had always regarded Milly as the most intelligent and capable member of the Squires family, to whom Walford owed everything, but she was much more than that. I think Louise, although she has totally different talents, has a lot of Milly's character and this may be one of the reasons why I intuitively liked Louise at the time when we were both very small children, and why Louise and I have remained such mutually supportive friends for the whole of our lives.

It took the best part of a week to get Mum back into a state where she could cope. I had sent a telegram to Jean in the hope that she could get some leave and she did. Mum telephoned Dr. Wilding and asked if she could see him urgently, because she wanted to break the news in person and not by letter or by telephone. After that she called a meeting of the senior partners in the firm and then we put a notice in the Times and started writing to all the relatives whose addresses we still had.

We decided that it would be good for Mum to have a change of scene and I wrote to the cousins in Ruislip who had been so kind to us in early 1944, enabling me to spend those last two weekends with David before he went to his death on the Normandy beaches. They wanted Mum to stay as long as she liked, but we postponed departure until the end of September when Dr. Wilding planned to hold the memorial service for Dad in the Cathedral.

As I have already mentioned, he asked me to read the first Lesson. It was, of course, a much grander occasion that the memorial service for David and Dick the previous year, with tributes by many speakers to Dad's life and work. For me, however, it was not as intimate, as personal and as moving as the service in memory of my own David. I was now much more conscious of the need to try and do for Mum what she had done for me. I think I succeeded. At any rate, no-one could have been kinder and more complimentary than Dr. and Mrs. Wilding.

At the reception afterwards, my Headmistress took me aside. She had tears in her eyes.

"I never thought on the day when you came to see me to say that you had married, that you would suffer both the loss of your husband and your father."

We chatted for some time and I told her about the Fortingalls who had lost their lives in the first war. I told her that I was worried about Mum being on her own and that, apart from her work, the office, her committee work and her friendship with the Squires, she had virtually no social life since Dad had left. I wanted her to get out and about a bit more. Miss Blantyre promised to do what she could to help and she did help.

I travelled with Mum to Ruislip, complete with my trunk of clothes ready to leave for the start of my first term at Oxford.

While we were in Ruislip, we managed to get seats for Lawrence Olivier's Old Vic production of King Lear, which was the start of a brilliant season at the New Theatre in St. Martin's Lane. Apart from Sir Lawrence, I was impressed by the actor who played the part of the fool. It was Alec Guinness who was later to become famous. My arrival at St. Hilda's was the start of my rehabilitation, the word that was being used everywhere to describe the adjustment process of people trying to rebuild their lives after the war.

I had lived all my life in the same house, and all my school life had been spent with the same group of people, or at least the same group had formed a nucleus with whom I had moved up from the junior school to the senior school, my circle being steadily widened as we became integrated with the College. Now I was adapting to a totally different world. St. Hilda's is a beautiful College in a lovely setting and extremely well placed for getting to lectures in the Schools and for Professor Tolkien's language classes (Old English) which were held in the Hall of Merton.

I was impressed by the deference shown to us by the tutors and lecturers. The women students came from a wide range of backgrounds. I was initially intimidated by some of the remarkably well-dressed and self-assured women who looked more like my idea of pre-war debs than students. There were others who dressed and behaved very much like Fifth Formers, but who were obviously intelligent, otherwise they wouldn't be there. Although I was not old enough to be ex-service, I found myself more relaxed and at ease amongst the women who had served in the Wrens, WAAF or ATS and, although I was younger, I seemed to be accepted very easily by them, particularly when they knew about my sad loss of David.

There were a lot of older men at the lectures, but 1945 was still early days for the demobilisation process. Everyone had a demob number which was based on age and length of service, so it was the oldest people who were demobbed first. There was, however, a special category known as Class B where you could be demobbed quicker to return to work of national importance and some students were able to get Class B releases in time to start the academic year 1945-6. The main bulk of the ex-servicemen didn't appear on the scene until 1946.

There was considerable amusement at the pep talks/warning lectures given in many women's colleges about returning ex-servicemen. We were warned that we were no longer dealing with boys from school, but with men who might be six or seven years older than us, who had lots of experience not only in the arts of war, but also in the arts of Venus. Like all warnings of this sort, they had the opposite effect of what was intended and got many of the girls into a frenzy of excitement. I would, no doubt, have been as frenzied as the others if I hadn't lived through the sad period which I have described.

Margaret Thatcher also started her first term in October 1945. She was in Somerville and reading Chemistry, so our paths wouldn't normally have crossed unless we had been active in the same social circles. She was then Margaret Roberts and probably active in the university Conservative Association. I paid my half-crown for membership in my first term in order to get the opportunity of hearing a number of the leading political figures of the day who came to speak. I was disappointed. I was expecting a much higher level of intellectual content in talks to an undergraduate audience, when in fact we tended to get little more than the platitudinous political comment that one was accustomed to hearing in talks on the BBC. I no doubt grossly overestimated the level of political understanding amongst undergraduates. I was expecting to hear the sort of arguments that I was accustomed to hear in the years before the war when Dad was holding forth. After my first term I would only buy termly the membership for any political club (of whichever party) if I particularly wanted to see and hear what some well-known figure actually looked like in the flesh. I was usually disappointed.

The one undergraduate of my era who achieved widespread recognition (some would say notoriety) was Ken Tynan, who was something of an enfant terrible. He was an actor and a showman determined to make his mark. His biggest coup was when, as editor of the Cherwell, he sent out a questionnaire to women undergraduates on their sex lives. This would be old hat today, but at the time it created an uproar. He was fined £50. The Cherwell was banned for the rest of that term and he was lucky not to be sent down.

The social side of Oxford life did not mean that we didn't have a lot of work to do. During the short eight-week terms we lived very much a hot-house existence where we were stretched to the limit on the workfront, as well as being stimulated on the cultural and other fronts by the people with whom we were mixing. My experience may have been unusual in some respects. Firstly, I had the good fortune, in fact I would say the privilege, to have Helen Gardner as my tutor. I shall say more about her in a moment, but at this point I shall merely make the point that she was devoted to her students. She had been a St. Hilda's student herself in the 1920s. She was a superb judge of each student's capability and woe betide you if you didn't live up to her expectations.

But first, a word about the most important person in the Oxford English faculty at that time and for some years to come, Professor J. R. R. Tolkien. He is now known to many readers, young and old, all over the world for his 'Lord of the Rings' and 'The Hobbit', but the Lord of the Rings was only published after he had retired as Merton Professor. English students of my generation knew him mainly for his language classes, his periodic lectures on one of our difficult set texts, Sir Gawain and the Grene Kniht, and also for his British Academy lecture 'Beowulf - the Monsters and the Critics'. We knew, of course, about The Hobbit, which was supposed to be one of the legendary fairy tales that he used to tell his children and which they had persuaded him to publish.

I should, perhaps, mention that out of the nine papers that constituted the syllabus, three were language papers. The first involved the study of Anglo Saxon (which we were informed at an early stage that we should refer to as 'Old English'). This meant learning a complex set of grammatical rules and then we had to study a number of set texts such as the first part of Beowulf, The Wanderer, The Dream of the Rood, etc. I found this more difficult than Latin.

Our next language paper was Middle English, which involved the study of another set of texts such as Gawain and Havelock The Dane. This was English literature before Chaucer because we then did another paper on Chaucer and his contemporaries. The third language paper involved the study of sound changes, spelling changes and changes in the meaning of words between 1400 and 1700.

I mention the syllabus to show why language teaching played such an important part in our curriculum and why the way in which this abstruse and difficult subject was taught was so important. There were a number of other lecturers and we had text books full of notes giving different interpretations of the way in which a phrase might be construed, given the corruption of many of the manuscripts or where it was assumed that the text had been miscopied.

What Professor Tolkien did, for me and for many other students, was to bring to life a subject that I initially found baffling and depressing. For one thing he had a dominant and radiant presence. His mind worked at great speed and most of his lectures took the form of inspired, spontaneous conversation. I found it easy to remember what he said. I also learnt a tremendous amount from his throwaway lines on things that had nothing to do with the syllabus.

His opening remark at the first class I attended was:

"I'm not here to explain what you can find in your text books. I'm here to try and help you to see a pattern in a set of blobs on old parchments, which are the only evidence we possess about the way people thought in the period we are studying.

This was precisely what I needed. I have a poor memory for isolated and unconnected bits of information. The moment I can understand a connection between something I am told and a wider picture which I hold in my mind, it sticks fairly effortlessly.

A lot of the things he used to tell us were never (to my knowledge) published or even common knowledge and in later years I found that even people who were specialists in the pre-Norman period appeared to be unaware of some of the things he used to talk about.

My favourite example is the history of the names we give to days of the week. Professor Tolkien used this to illustrate the commercial links between the Romans and the Angles, Saxons and other northern peoples going back to the pre-Christian period. The fact that the English use the word 'wine' for 'vinum' indicated to him that the word had been taken on board in north west Europe in a period when the Romans still pronounced their 'v' as 'w'.

For days of the week he showed that the northern peoples had adapted the Roman system, but substituted their names. Thus the Lord's day, Dominus Daeg, had been translated as 'Sun day' at a period when the sun was worshiped as the sun God.

Likewise, lune-daeg, the moon's day, was translated as Mon day. Marte-daeg, the day of Mars, the war God, was translated as Tiwes-daeg, Tiw being the Nordic God that equated with Mars.

Mercury-daeg, the French Mercredi, was given the name Woden's day, or Wednesday. Although Woden was the equivalent of Jupiter, the boss God, Professor Tolkien explained that Mercury had held this position in earlier Mediterranean hierarchies before Jupiter had ousted him.

Jupiter, or Jove's day, familiar to many of us in the French form Jeudi, was easy to equate with Thor who gave us Thursday. Both were the Gods of thunder (James Joyce in Finnegan's Wake refers to Thunder's day).

The only goddess in the Mediterranean hierarchy was Venus, who gave us both venery and Venus day, or in modern French, Vendredi. The equivalent Nordic Goddess was Frea. Frea-daeg survives in German Freitag and in English, Friday.

There was no Nordic God equivalent to Saturn, whose name has been corrupted into Samedi in modern French and Saturday in English. The Finns appropriately refer to it as bath night.

I have quoted this example in full to illustrate the wealth of fascinating information that used to flow from Professor Tolkien, almost as asides in the course of his language classes. It is a sad fact of modern life that academic promotion no longer seems to depend upon gifted individuals devoting their lives to their students, their subject and (in Professor Tolkien's case his family and his many friends). In the present era a high proportion of academics seem to believe that the way to get on is to get mentioned in the popular press, or television, or to write/be interviewed in respect of some gimmicky presentation of research. During the period of my university education such external distractions and irrelevant considerations did not exist. A professor or lecturer was judged by his students and his peers.

This applies with even greater force to my own St. Hilda's tutor, Helen Gardner, who unlike Tolkien never became a widely read author outside her subject area. In the 1960s she became Merton professor of English at Oxford (the post that Tolkien had held). I think she was the first woman to hold such a post, or in fact any comparable, senior academic post in a classical subject at Oxford and this says a great deal for the esteem in which she was held, both by her students and her peers, although she was the sort of person who would have been very angry if anyone had suggested that her appointment, or any position she held, should depend on any factor apart from the expectation that she would do a good job. In fact she was widely recognised in later life as one of those people who could and would do a good job, no matter what it was. She was appointed to the Robbins committee on university education, made a Dame of the British Empire and acquired a number of other awards and distinctions, but in the period when she was my tutor she was still relatively junior in the Oxford hierarchy, having been appointed tutor at St. Hilda's in 1941 and then made a Fellow in 1942. Her first major publication on T.S. Eliot didn't appear until 1949, a year after I had taken my degree and had, therefore, ceased to be one of her students.

It was thanks to Mum's College friend, Alice Draper (who stayed with us in the Summer of 1943), that I set my sights on getting a place at St. Hilda's. Alice had, in earlier days, hoped to find a university teaching post, ideally at an Oxford or Cambridge women's college and this had, no doubt, been one of her reasons for keeping abreast of all the positions that were likely to fall vacant when the present incumbent reached retirement age. As a conscientious head of the English department in a leading girls' school, she had kept up her reading of most of the learned journals such as 'The Year's Work in English Studies' and being unmarried she had been able to spend more time during the 1920s and 30s attending meetings of various literary and academic societies and socialising. This helped her to build up a good rapport with the colleges and universities, where she thought her able Sixth Formers would best succeed in getting places. In the course of this she had built a solid reputation for fair and objective assessments of the candidates she was recommending, conscientiously resisting the temptation to which some teachers are subject, of exaggerating the merits of their own pupils. In this context she had known the then Principal of St. Hilda's and had known, probably in 1941, how enthusiastic the College was to welcome one of its own members back as English tutor.

Although Mrs. Rainham, with a family to bring up single-handed in addition to her job, had not kept up links in this academic network, she had in fact met and liked Helen Gardner in her totally different network. Helen Gardner's first academic post was as a lecturer at Royal Holloway College, London. She was an all-rounder and keen to meet contemporary poets and writers. When I told Mrs. Rainham that she was to be my tutor, Mrs. Rainham told me that I was unlikely to find any women's college in the country where I could have enjoyed the personal attention of someone of Helen Gardner's range of skills and commitment to her students.

As for the latter day educationalists who criticise the tutorial system as 'wasteful'. Poppycock. The one-to-one relationship that you build up at a key period in your intellectual, moral and social development can be the most important influence in your life, after that of your parents and of vital importance, not only to you but to all the people for whom you will ultimately have responsibility.

If you accept that it is natural for many of the ablest and most ambitious people in the country to strive for places at Oxford or Cambridge, there is a fair probability that a substantial proportion of these people will in due course be promoted to leading positions in government, public administration, the professions (including education) and business.

One of my regrets has been that I did not live up to Helen Gardner's original expectations of what I could achieve. She clearly thought I was capable of getting a First and I didn't. I think she was reasonably satisfied with my performance during my first year, but after I met John towards the end of Michaelmas term in 1946, he became the centre of my life and, if I hadn't spent so much time at the weekends and in vacations charging around the country for his old RAF comrades' gatherings (which I shall describe more fully in Chapter 23), I might have done enough extra work to get a First, but who knows? To Helen Gardner's credit she never criticised me on this score. Although she could be a martinet, she was deep down a person with a wonderful warmth of human understanding. She knew of my tragic loss of David and she understood that, for a person of my character and temperament, it was vital that I should achieve a secure, loving and long-lasting marriage, which I did.

Some academics can be very good lecturers and can write excellent books, but not be good as tutors, often because they find the tutorial job a bore. Not so Helen Gardner - she was so thorough in the way she commented on your essays, questioning you about what you had read and whether or not you had followed up some of her reading suggestions that, if you'd had a bad week, you felt pretty miserable in her presence. You certainly couldn't flannel your way through.

I often regretted that I had told her more than I need about my family background and, in particular, that Catherine Johnston was one of my great-grandmothers. 'Catherine the Great' as she called her, was one of her heroines as a pioneer reformer who had enabled so many women to benefit from a university education. She also considered Catherine to be a very competent and able writer. Although Catherine's style of novel writing had been out of fashion for some years, she told me that her plots were well constructed and that her style was impeccable.

But woe-betide me if I produced an essay that was below Miss Gardner's expectations of what I could do:

"Catherine is not amused" delivered in a manner that made me truly ashamed and contrite. It is possibly for this reason that I have always thought of my ancestors (particularly my two renowned great-grandmothers) keeping a watchful eye and being ready to tell me to pull my socks up.

No tribute to Helen Gardner as a tutor would be complete without mention of her encyclopaedic knowledge of, and interest in, both major and minor writers over the very extensive period covered by our syllabus and many other subjects outside it. Friends in other Colleges used to speak of some of the tutors who might have become big names in the academic world in a particular period such as the 14th Century or 18th Century, but who showed very little interest in studies that had taken place since their own student days in other periods. Helen Gardner was always full of witty and knowledgeable comments on any subject on which she would ask me to write an essay. I have mentioned her book on T.S. Eliot. Some years after I left Oxford she published a number of authoritative studies of Donne and the Metaphysicals.

Our syllabus finished at 1820, but it was assumed that we would already have an extensive knowledge of anything written after that date. During my period she gave a number of popular and well-attended lectures (attendance at lectures was voluntary and so a lecturer either had to be very good, or famous, or both to get a large attendance) on Dryden as a satirist and, another term, on Dr. Johnson.

One of my favourite quotes that I must have trotted out hundreds of times in later life to show how dependent our thought processes are on vocabulary and use of words, was taken from Boswell. When Dr. Johnson is reputed to have said to Mrs. Thrale.

"Think before you speak, woman."

Boswell quotes her as replying:

"But how can I know what I think till I see what I say."

Apart from having to work damned hard, learning to find my way round the English reading room in the Radcliffe Camera, the English School's library, and College Library, I managed to find the extra curricular activities that suited my interests and temperament. Apart from activities, such as the Poetry Society, I was able to enjoy dancing again. A number of clubs held a dance each term. For some reason they were always called 'socials' and typically cost 2s 6d for admission. In those days there were roughly ten times as many men students as women students, so it was easy to get dancing partners. Many of the men used to bring nurses from the Radcliffe Infirmary, or trainees from Dorset House as their guests. The French club had the reputation for organising the best socials, which meant it was usually difficult to get in, but I seemed to manage and it was thanks to my persistence in getting hold of tickets that I first met John a year later at the French club social, but more of this anon.

It was in dancing slow fox-trots to sentimental tunes with men who had, no doubt, been in a similar rehabilitation phase that I came to terms with the fact that I would marry again and that David would want me to marry again and build a new life. I had learnt in my life with David, that I was not just a person with a higher than average (or so it seemed) sex drive, but also a person with a very strong need for emotional support. I may be an active, hard-boiled, argumentative person in some aspects of my life, but I am also a romantic and loving person. I danced cheek to cheek with many men and let my head rest on their shoulders. This was very much the wartime spirit that I have described earlier in this book, a spirit that still lived on. Nowadays we might describe the effects as therapeutic, which they clearly were. None of my dancing partners at the time nor I would have wanted to use such terms.

By the time I returned home in early December 1945 for my first Christmas vacation, I felt different, more enthusiastic and above all refreshed, even though I was physically and mentally tired after the intense hot-house life that one used to lead in a short eight week Oxford term. I was well on my way to rehabilitation.

CHAPTER 22

REHABILITATION

Whilst my first term at Oxford played a key part in my rehabilitation, it was my first home vacation in December 1945/January 1946 that I now think of as the watershed between my old life and my new.

Oxford terms are short, but fairly intense. I was home more than a week before the High School end of term so I was able to go and see Mrs. Rainham, the Headmistress, and some of my other teachers and talk excitedly about what I was doing. I then realised there were hardly any girls left that I knew. Most of my Sixth Form friends had in fact left in the Summer of 1944, after Higher Cert. I had already been something of an oldie in my last year, but I had hardly noticed because, apart from work, I had been something of a recluse after David's death and had not attended any social functions such as College dances. I began to realise that I had very few friends in my home town, at any rate at that time. I would, of course, meet many of them at church services over Christmas. Other universities had longer terms, so Louise for example, who was studying medicine at Edinburgh, only arrived shortly before Christmas.

Believe it or not, the College and High School were still doing a combined performance of Gilbert and Sullivan in the old town hall - in 1945 it was the Mikado. I suppose that with Japan defeated we could now go back to treating the Japanese as figures of fun.

I got myself a ticket for the first night in the hope that I might meet a few more old friends, including some of the College masters such as Mr. Ferrers, who was there with his wife. I am afraid I could only laugh when I heard there had been a re-run of the December 1941 saga. The Sixth Form girls to whom I chatted before the performance started, and during the interval, had no other subject of conversation. Mildred had swooped and a lot of girls were in fear and trembling and if they were sitting in the audience they were not sitting as comfortably as they otherwise might, not because they had suffered any punishment, but because of the thought of what lay ahead.

Louise confirmed, when I saw her over Christmas, that her Dad had had a busy last Saturday of term and I'm afraid I thought the whole saga rather amusing. I was quoting to myself the famous Hegel dictum that the only thing men learn from history is that they learn nothing from history, but then I remembered in fairness that these girls, who had no doubt spent an uncomfortable Saturday afternoon and evening, had only been kids of 11 or 12 at the time of the 1941 saga and would have had no interest in, and possibly no knowledge of, the way their seniors had suffered at the receiving end of Walford's cane. I began to understand why Mum had found my particular experience so amusing. I was now taking precisely the same view and thinking "that'll teach the stupid kids a lesson", not in a sense that it would teach them not too smoke, but not to be stupid enough to get caught.

I was amused to find that Louise had reacted in the same way. She had arrived home from Edinburgh late on the Friday evening and intended to sleep late on the Saturday morning, but was woken by the familiar sound of girls yelling and shouting "Please sir, no more" only to be followed by the next resounding whack and another yell.

She got up, made herself a coffee and offered to do front door duty so that Milly could get on with Christmas preparations. The nervous and apprehensive expressions as she took the girls' coats to hang on the row of pegs said everything and when Walford had finished with them and she silently handed them back their coats, she knew it would be unfair to speak to any of them, knowing that even the bravest were struggling hard not to burst into tears.

"The world of home and school hasn't changed one bit", she said, "but I am damned glad those days are over."

But the world did change. In the Summer of 1946 Mildred met a recently demobilised senior officer whose first wife had been killed in the blitz and who, like many people at that time, was trying to build a new life, trying like me to be 'rehabilitated'. Mildred was half his age and he no doubt found her enthusiasm for the sports of Venus helped him to feel young again, although for how long I know not. Her bossy sergeant major-ish manner didn't seem to worry him. No doubt she cuckolded him a great deal in his later life, but he would have had to be far more stupid than I think he was, not to anticipate this when he married her.

With Mildred gone and the High School trying to return to peacetime normality, Saturday morning punishment sessions at the Squires' disappeared into history. It was left to the returning Dads to deal with any daughters who might prove troublesome.

Even when I met a number of my old school friends over Christmas, I began to realise that I was no longer living in quite the same world. Although I was not yet 20, I felt much older and found it difficult to get enthused by the small talk, mainly about schoolgirl crushes on the various male students or lecturers that had come into their lives. I was, no doubt, feeling a bit pretentious, but so be it.

I had only been home for a few days and was buying some bread and cakes when a familiar voice shouted "Boadie!" and I turned and saw Jacko. He was wearing a suit and looked much smarter than in his College days, but he still had the same cheeky, saucy look. In that strange lottery of the time he had been granted exemption from military service on medical grounds (I think he had flat feet or something equally absurd), and had a proper job in the family firm. He was, of course, older than me and had left school in the Summer of 1943. He was at the stage of learning the job in the office in the centre of town and, no doubt, studying for professional qualifications. That was not the side of his life that interested me.

He had just come out of his own bachelor flat, which was above the cake shop and small café. It had belonged to one of his uncles who had died a few months earlier and, in those days of protected tenancies, the family didn't want to let it to an outsider, so young Jacko had a place of his own. I followed him up the steep and narrow stairway to have a look. It was fairly basic but would have been the dream home of hundreds of thousands of young marrieds who were at that time, crowded in with their in-laws. What is more, Jacko had a proper job and a proper salary, at a time when most men between 20 and 40 were still in uniform, awaiting demobilisation and unsure of their job prospects in an economy that had been dislocated by the war and was now being dislocated further by a socialist government hell-bent on nationalising everything.

I couldn't imagine Jacko leading a celibate existence and I quickly sensed the recent presence of another person, who I assumed to be the current lady in his life. This is an area where a woman's antennae are much more attuned than a man's. If you sit opposite a man in a train or anywhere, you quickly sense he is no longer concentrating on his book or paper, but watching like a hawk in the hope of getting a glimpse of knicker when you cross or uncross your legs. If you are a sporting type you are deliberately careless on a number of occasions and make him happy as a sand-boy, smiling conspiratorially, so that he knows you know and you then have a pleasant travelling companion for the rest of the journey, who will do anything (such as get coffee or sandwiches) for you. Modern trains unfortunately (no matter whether you are travelling first or second class) have removed this old world pleasure by boxing you into open plan compartments with diminutive tables, so that when you lean forward you bump your head against the head of the facing passenger, who is probably yelling his head off into a mobile phone as if it were a speaking tube.

Women have different priorities in the way in which they direct their sense of observation. The first thing I noticed about Jacko's flat was that the bed was unmade. He had just told me that he had a woman who came in every morning to Hoover, wash his dishes and tidy up. There was a fresh aroma of perfume when I opened his bathroom door and when I looked behind the door I saw an attractive nightie that looked as though it had been made out of parachute nylon, which was the most fashionable thing a girl could wear in bed those days.

When we were back together in his sitting room he asked, as I hoped he would:

"May I kiss you, Boadie, for old time's sake?"

"What if your mistress comes back and sees us?" I said. "Will she shoot us?"

Jacko looked sheepish. "Oh, June, she works in Wilsons (our main market square drapers/clothes shop) and doesn't usually finish until after five. What made you think I had a mistress?"

I can't imagine you in a monastery, Jacko, any more than you can imagine me in a nunnery and I can hardly imagine you spending your nights alone, wearing that pretty little nightie."

So I took my coat and jacket off and we kissed, as we had done when I was a Fifth Former and his hands quickly discovered the old territories they had once known so well.

It was a release. I had made up my mind some weeks before that David would want me to re-marry, but I had a morbid fear that if I did fall in love that I would burst into hysterical tears when we got to the intimate stages. With Jacko this wouldn't matter because I didn't love him and he knew that, or must have known. Anyway he was the sort of person I could talk to in plain, homespun terms. Nowadays I would probably have said I needed his services as a sex therapist, but in the 1940s we didn't try to kid ourselves or anyone else with pretentious jargon of this kind. He knew straight away that I was just as randy (perhaps more so) as he had found me on the first night he had taken me home after a dancing lesson and the occasional use of his cod-piece might be appreciated, so long as it didn't involve any commitment on my part, or any social complications. Could he be trusted to keep his mouth shut? I think he knew which side his bread was buttered. Above all I didn't want to foul up his relations with any of his other mistresses, or get into any conflict situations.

According to Jacko there was only June and she didn't live with him. She was 30, about ten years older than me and eight years older than Jacko, married to a staff sergeant in the Ack-Ack who was currently in Germany with BAFO (British Armed Forces of Occupation). She was living with inhospitable in-laws. The only time she could spend with Jacko was during the lunch hour and from 5.30 to 6.30 before a half-hour bus ride to the small town where her in-laws ran a profitable fish and chip shop and provided hot suppers for one or two works canteens. She probably needed someone like Jacko in the way I needed him and couldn't risk getting involved with a man who might become persistent or want anything more. I am sure Jacko wasn't the marrying type, at any rate not at that time, and he was shrewd enough to know that a married woman was a safer bet as a mistress. He would have been too good a catch (given his relative affluence and possession of a flat) for most young, single girls to let go lightly.

I told Jacko that if we were to do anything together I would prefer the night shift. I am a cuddly, romantic person who likes to fall asleep afterwards. I don't think he could believe his luck. I said I still wasn't sure, but would ring him, and so we left it.

The treatment did work. I am sure most women readers can recollect plenty of occasions when they welcomed such moments, even if they are not in the same realm as the mountain top exultation that I had experienced with David. It was an important step in my rehabilitation.

One of the most unlikely results of this encounter with Jacko was a long-lasting friendship with a woman who was older and wiser, or at any rate who had the maturity of outlook that I then found lacking in so many of my former school friends. I knew I was taking a risk by trying to meet June and see what she was like, but I think my curiosity is readily understandable. Just as many men are said to choose second wives who closely resemble their first, they may well choose similar women for their mistresses, although I have no first hand knowledge on which to base a general theory, apart from the fact that June and I had a lot in common. Sadly, though, she was not well treated by the lottery of life apart from being born with remarkably good looks, a good brain, tremendous determination and staying power and a lovely personality.

As a woman I suppose I should have been jealous. Perhaps I would have been if she had been David's mistress, but I wasn't in love with Jacko. The fact that he had a mistress would (I hoped) reduce the risk of his becoming too attached to me, which I didn't want. I was nevertheless curious to meet the woman who took the trouble to undress and put on a nightie for her short lunchtime sessions with Jacko. I understood why as soon as I saw her. She was immaculately groomed, had naturally wavy, fair hair, moved very elegantly and was meticulous in the way in which she did things.

I had no difficulty in spotting the person who must be June when I walked around Wilsons and saw her in the ladies hosiery and underwear department. In fact I recognised her distinctive perfume before I stopped to ask her if the nylons had come in. This was what every girl asked in every shop and the answer was usually no. They were like gold dust.

My left hand was conspicuously on the counter and she asked:

"Will you have your husband home for Christmas?"

So I told her why not and she apologised for asking and I said I was doing my best to rehabilitate myself, but at times it was hard. I then asked if her husband had been demobbed or whether he was due home for Christmas and she shook her head. I put my hand on hers and our eyes met.

I continued the conversation and quickly found out that she was from Sidcup in Kent and, as I had suspected, lonely. It was obvious that she had needed someone like Jacko, not only for relief but as a human contact. Her in-laws, no doubt, resented her as a 'stook oop' southerner. It was one of the odd quirks of those days that, whilst most middle class English parents wanted their children to move up the social scale and marry someone a rung or two up the ladder (and so did most of the Scots and the Welsh of any class) there were obstinate pockets of lower class Englishmen who had emotional hang-ups at the idea of one of their sons or daughters becoming 'one of them'.

Again, I had grown up accustomed to the prevailing view of my parents' friends that the man who married a pretty woman was to be respected for his success in the marriage market. It was assumed that he must have something positive in him, even if nobody else could see what it was. But there were clusters of people in underclass England who seemed to nurse a seething resentment against the better things of life. If they heard the start of a Mozart piano concerto on the radio they would turn the knob angrily in search of another station. They resented people who spoke good King's English and they likewise resented well-dressed, well spoken people. Presumably an attractive woman was regarded as someone dangerous who might go over to the enemy (i.e. the upper classes) or in some other respect prove to be 'unreliable'. No doubt she might not prove as easy to control.

Although I had grown up in an area where lots of people like this existed I had never had reason to notice them. Dad and Mum, like all our friends and the teachers at both the College and High School spoke good King's English and so did all my friends. In those days BBC newsreaders were supposed to be model speakers of educated English. If there were High School girls who spoke with a local accent their parents would have them sent to elocution lessons. In later life when someone commented that I didn't speak like a northerner my puzzled response was to say "and you don't speak like a Cockney". The "ee bah goom" and "shan't be rehn termorrer" stereotypes of radio humour no doubt existed, but we didn't expect to have serious conversations with people who spoke like that.

June's in-laws were not poor or downtrodden. It used to be said that the locals in many of the towns in our part of the world lived on fish and chips. It used to be said that the King Edward potato which quickly goes mushy when it is boiled, owed its popularity to the fact that it was good for chipping. People living near the breadline were said to queue up every night to collect their fish and chips (often more chips than fish), the fat from which would be absorbed into the old newspapers in which this food was wrapped, to be carried home or to wherever it was eaten.

The increased wartime earnings of fish and chip shop customers had made June's in-laws wealthy and they had expanded their business by taking over another fish and chip shop in a nearby town and by getting contracts to provide hot suppers to a number of works canteens where overtime was the order of the day. For a short time after the war the business continued to boom, but by the early 1950s when consumer tastes were changing, her father-in-law had become bankrupt.

In her school years June had had similar aspirations to mine. She wanted to be a teacher, but her father had an estate agency in Sidcup. He believed higher education for women was a waste of money because they would get married, and anyway he needed her to work for a pittance in his firm, which she did. This would have been around 1932. He had been badly gassed in the first war and died suddenly in 1935, so she had to find another job. She had always wanted to wear nice clothes and the idea of working in a smart West End shop had appealed. After various attempts she had a break by getting into Dickins and Jones in Regent Street, where she had been given the chance to do a bit of everything including window dressing and stock control, as well as serving customers, where she had a successful sales record in the underwear and nightwear departments.

With men she had had a number of false starts, which I can well understand. If you are not particularly keen on going to the altar with any old Tom, Dick or Harry, but nevertheless feel tempted by a night or two in the Strand palace with one of the men who happens to be sweet on you, then you spend as many nights as you are invited in the Strand Palace or wherever else he is prepared to take you. When war came the West End was full of service officers hoping to spot pretty girls in the lounge of the Regent Palace, Strand Palace or wherever. In 1943 she fell head-over-heels for Jack, whom she had met, while sheltering during an air-raid in her home town of Sidcup.

Jack was a staff sergeant from an anti-aircraft unit which played an important part in the defence of London. There were many such units on the Kentish approaches to London. They had quite advanced predictor equipment which was supposed to predict the flight path of German bombers, so that anti-aircraft shells would burst at the point the plane was supposed to reach. Jack owed his promotion to his technical capability in operating these early versions of computers. He had never been out with a girl like June and he likewise fell head-over-heels.

When the V1s started there was virtually no warning and anyone's number could be up at any time. Jack was keen to marry and get his wife safely away from the dangerous area where she lived and so she came north to live with inhospitable in-laws who wanted her to work for a pittance in one of their two fish and chip shops. With her Dickins and Jones training she was able to get a job in Wilsons, which paid her modestly but enabled her to have some independence and get away from her in-laws during the daytime. Jacko, with an eye to the main chance, had been quick to spot a pretty girl waiting at a bus stop and had given her a lift in the car he had as a perk to his job and the rest is history.

Before I left Wilsons on the day of our first meeting, June had gone and found me some nylons, put them in a bag and told me not to breathe a word or she would have a queue all around the shop. In those days people used to talk about having such things 'under the counter' for favoured customers.

I said "If you are a Londoner living up here with in-laws you must feel lonely. I have my Mum and a lot of old friends. Would you like to come for tea one day?" And she nodded yes and that is how our dialogue started.

If he had known, Jacko needn't have worried. He probably panicked when he saw June and me talking when I came out of the bread shop one day late morning as she was, no doubt, preparing to get her latch key to open the street door to Jacko's flat. It was merely hello and farewell for me, as I didn't want to embarrass her, but Jacko arrived and proceeded to introduce me as the pin-up girl from the College in days gone by, who was always getting up to mischief and being punished by old Whackers. I turned with a shake of the head to June and said, "All this incorrigible boy ever does is to remind me of painful moments I would rather forget. This is all he could say to me when we met two years ago on the dance floor. See you in two years' time, Jacko, for your next reminder. I've got to get lunch for Mum." And I left them.

That, no doubt, gave Jacko a cue for telling June his version of my life story. June did take up my invitation and we had a long heart to heart, but not about Jacko. She also asked me to have tea with her at her in-laws.

In the normal course I might have been as suspect as a southerner, but luck was on my side (and June's also).

June had already spoken about me as a young widow, whose husband had been killed in the D-day landings. I was telling them how Mum was trying to cope following Dad's death only four months ago and (in my view) still doing the work of two or three men 'looking after the shop' as she used to describe her work in Dad's office. In those days an 'upper class' (as she would have been perceived by June's in-laws) woman who worked was the exception, although in reality this gives a false picture when one remembers all the women, like Milly, doing vital jobs but not being on anyone's payroll. Mum's metaphor about 'minding the shop' was well chosen, because this was largely Mrs. Barnes's (June's mother-in-law) job. She was the person who kept her eye on the till. I was, therefore, almost 'one of them'.

When I talked about most of the lawyers being pretty useless when it came to money, I saw Mr. Barnes looking at me intently. I had noticed when I arrived that he looked preoccupied and, in fact, was paying very little attention to the small-talk until he heard the word 'lawyers' out of the corner of his ear.

In those days fish and chip shops could be dangerous places to work, or at any rate more dangerous than working in most other shops. At peak times, with staff rushing around and getting in each others' way and with the frying process taking place behind the counter, there was always the risk of an employee getting his hand burned by the fat or more seriously burned if the fat caught fire. There had been a serious case in one of Mr. Barnes' fish and chip shops where burns had gone septic and there was a risk that the employee's right arm might have to be amputated. The insurance company, to whom Mr. Barnes had paid premiums for employer's liability cover, had threatened to void his policy because of non-disclosure by Mr. Barnes of what was considered to be a material fact. In those days there was no insurance ombudsman.

Even if he had used an insurance broker, the probability was that it would only be a small tin-pot outfit that collected his premiums and drew its commission - given the very modest level of turnover in such a business and the relatively low level of premium payable. Mr. Barnes had not incorporated his business as a limited company (very few businesses of this kind had anyone on hand to advise them to do this). He knew he didn't have the resource to take on an insurance company by going to court. He feared that anything appearing in the local papers about a court case in which he was involved would be bad for his business. Even if paying the compensation out of his own pocket may not, at that stage, have threatened him with personal bankruptcy, it would mean serious embarrassment for him and his business, which was already suffering because there was less overtime (in many cases none at all) at the factories where he supplied hot suppers. Until the insurance company agreed to reinstate his policy he was, strictly speaking, acting illegally by trading at all.

As luck would have it, one of the commercial partners in Dad's firm (I never called it anything else, even though Dad was no longer around to run it) had persuaded a client in a similar situation to take the insurance company to court and had won. What's more, the judge had been very forthright in his criticism of the insurance company in question for misleading the public and attempting to escape its liabilities on the grounds of a minor technicality, stating that it was up to the insurer to prove that the fact which had not been disclosed in the proposal form, or at the time of renewal, was a material fact.

Insurance companies have never been popular and with Hitler out of the way, the court case in November 1945 in which the insurance company was the villain of the piece made a good story in the national, as well as the local, press. Dad's firm was able to get a lot of kudos. The case had been one of the main talking points when I came home for the vacation. I didn't need to know the details of the case, but I was able to sow the idea that the same partner was probably in a good position to write a stroppy letter and either force the insurer to climb down, or agree an out of court settlement. I took the details and passed them on to Mum when I got home.

In fact, the partner concerned got the insurer to pay in full and resume cover without further ado. In retrospect I should perhaps say that, in those days, there were large numbers of insurance companies with names like Atlas, Beacon, Sea and heavens know what, who were all taken over by the 1960s, if not earlier, and whose names have disappeared from view. This was long before the recent mammoth mergers and take-overs.

For me, the important result was that it established my credibility, and Mum's credibility, with the Barnes family as useful people for them to know. In fact we were seen as white knights. It also helped June because she was indirectly seen to be helping the business by having the right sort of friends, so when I pointedly asked her, in front of the Barnes family (as I was leaving), whether she would care to come as a guest to a get-together with my old school friends (I didn't describe it as a dance with men) and, as it would finish late, to stay the night with Mum and me, it was smiles all round.

This meant that June could have her night with Jacko and no questions asked. Not only this, she stayed with us (ostensibly that is) on many more nights during the Christmas, Easter and Summer vacations, until Jack was demobbed and she had him home. In fact by Easter 1946 when all the paperwork on the case had been finalised and the claim paid, i.e. Mum and I had shown we were capable of delivering and not just promising, I could do no wrong and June was encouraged to spend as many evenings as she could spare (naturally followed by overnight stays) helping to cheer up her lonely war-widow friend. I have to confess I derived a certain amount of sensual enjoyment as I lay in bed and imagined what was likely to be going on in Jacko's flat. I was beginning to recognise the old self that I had been before David had changed my life.

The lovely thing about my friendship with June was that we didn't have to explain things to each other. Just as I had instantly understood the nature of her relationship with Jacko and its whys and wherefores, and had stage-managed her invitation to spend the night of the College and High School ball with Mum and me (and many other nights thereafter), she likewise understood my need. She had, of course, assumed that my rapid departure on the day of our first tripartite meeting was a sign of my displeasure and that Jacko had been a long-term lover from days of yore, but when I explained my fear and the fact that I didn't want relations with Jacko to become too serious, she understood and, also, why I was relaxed with him in a way I wouldn't be with anyone new.

We didn't discuss intimate details. There was no need to. There was a certain camaraderie in the knowledge that we were sharing the same lover, but, as she pointed out, if you added together the nights in the typical months that he would spend with both of us, it would still leave him with a lot less work to do between the sheets than if he had had either of us as a wife or full-time mistress. And we hoped that he wouldn't complicate things by finding a third woman who mightn't be as discreet, which could have been embarrassing for June.

We needn't have worried. I met Jacko about ten years ago at a reunion dinner dance for the wartime veterans of the High School and College. Poor Jacko had not worn well. He was white-haired and stooping and a bit vague in the way he spoke. My impression was that he had in due course matured, had married and had children, but we didn't get onto his later life. However, when I reminded him of the days when he was being shared by June and me, his eyes lit up and he said he had never in his life enjoyed such a wonderful period of intense amorous activity.

Jack was demobbed in 1947. He was still desperately in love with June and they had a happy life together. When I met him I was able to drop a few hints about the difficulties that any young wife has when she is left living alone with in-laws. Jack wasn't happy with the idea of spending his life in the family business and when it went bust he decided that job opportunities were better in the London area, so they moved south and June was able to get a job again at Dickens and Jones, where she was eventually promoted to buyer. She has not only remained a life-long friend, but has been my wardrobe mistress. I like wearing attractive clothes, but I have always hated spending time shopping around. June has done that for me.

Of course, the nights I spent in bed with Jacko did a lot for my rehabilitation. I took my amorous farewell of him at the beginning of October 1946, before returning to start the Autumn Term, in the course of which I met John, starting a new phase of my life which has not yet finished and I hope will last a few years more, but this is the subject of my next chapter.

CHAPTER 23

MY NEW LIFE - AN EMOTIONAL AND SPIRITUAL ODYSSEY

1946 was an important year for me and for many other people. It was like Spring after Winter, albeit a cold Spring. A former Chancellor of the Exchequer, Norman Lamont, would no doubt have referred to it as a year of 'green shoots' for the British economy which was to suffer a serious setback in the long, cold Winter of 1946-7. We were still living in an age of food rationing, clothes rationing and austerity. Our Chancellor at the time was a man called Hugh Dalton who went around saying he had a 'song in his heart'. One of the few readable right-wing weeklies at the time 'Truth' published a jingle:

> Dalton is smart
> With a song in his heart
> And I've pondered a long time upon it
> Now I know he is wrong
> What he thinks is a song
> Is the sound of the bees in his bonnet

Thanks to Jacko I had started the year feeling less beleaguered and lonely. In reading what I have written I may have given a misleading impression of my relationship with Jacko. There was an emotional bond between us which went back to the Winter of 1941-2 when he had cycled home with me after a mixed dancing lesson in the College and had given me my first passionate kiss as we stood in our driveway. Most women must have vivid memories of such moments which remain for the rest of their lives. I knew in my bones that he was not the man I wanted as a husband and I am sure he recognised this. We understood each other in many important ways. We were completely relaxed in each other's presence and didn't need to hide things. A lot of marriages never achieve as much. The loving moments that I spent with Jacko during the Christmas vacation and then at Easter 1946 and again in the Summer of 1946 meant a lot more to both of us than if they had been sexual encounters and no more.

The next big family event was the announcement of Jean's engagement to Angus. As I have already explained, Angus was a career naval officer who had been educated at the Royal Naval College in Dartmouth and achieved the rank of Captain by the end of the war. Jean was 23 and Angus was 48 when they married. His first wife had been killed in one of the bad bombing raids on Plymouth. He had a daughter of 14 and a son of 12. Jean was worried at first that they would look on her as a wicked stepmother, because as children we had grown up with the stories of Cinderella, Snow White, etc. which, no doubt, reflected the high level of mortality of women in childbirth in previous generations, and where the father's second marriage had brought unhappiness to the children of the first marriage.

It would be difficult to imagine anyone who looked less like the stereotype of the wicked stepmother than Jean. More important than this was the fact that Jean was determined to be a good mother to her husband's children and when Jean is determined to do something, she usually succeeds. She never had any children of her own. She never talked to me about the subject and I never asked. If she and Angus were disappointed, they never showed it. They were both people who had developed skills in the art of putting on a public face.

I don't know when Jean and Angus first met, nor do I know whether or when they first became lovers. They were both discreet people. They came to stay with us for a few days during the Easter vacation and I immediately liked him. Not only that, I felt he was the right man for Jean and so did Mum.

When Jean showed him the pictures of Dad, our grandfather and great uncle William, he shook his head sadly at the losses our family had had to bear in two World Wars and when he eventually looked at the beautiful photo of David and me at the Christmas ball, he stood silently for a few moments before turning and taking my hand in his. I could sense his emotion, although he was more skilled than most of us in keeping a stiff upper lip. Then he said:

"Like me, you're trying to build a new life. I hope you're as fortunate as I am" and he turned and kissed Jean on the forehead.

It was decided that the wedding should be held at the end of June at St. Margaret's Westminster. It was a very public affair, with pictures in the Tatler and there were a number of distinguished guests. Jean was given away by Uncle Charles (Aunt Beatrice's husband, Dad's brother-in-law, the family we used to stay with in Putney) and I was one of the bridesmaids. The wedding was one of the best things that could have happened for Mum. It took her away from the recent past, back to her memories of her youthful days when she lived in Kensington. The announcements of the engagement in the Times and the Telegraph enabled us to re-establish contact with many of our relatives who had moved during the war, and who wrote to congratulate Mum and Jean. Mum had managed to re-establish contact with Tante Nicole, who was able to put us in touch with a number of our French relatives.

There were many elegantly dressed women with decorative hats, mostly Angus' relatives and friends. In spite of post-war austerity, the older generation who (like Mum) had succeeded in preserving much of their pre-war finery, were able to bring it out and give it an airing. Angus and Jean were, of course, in uniform and so were most of Angus' friends.

Mum and I stayed in London for ten days after the wedding. Covent Garden had just re-opened and we saw the Sadlers Wells ballet. Mum took me on an educational tour of such places as the National Gallery, the Victoria and Albert, Westminster Abbey. We walked around the roads north of Kensington High Street where she had lived as a girl and she had decided that when she had succeeded in negotiating the sale of Dad's partnership share she would like to buy a house in Hornton Street.

This was, in fact, the first of a number of business trips that Mum made. Dad had built up a number of links with London law firms that would refer local business to him. She decided to make a systematic approach to a number of them, but she didn't want the wrong sort of rumours to get out amongst the other partners. She, therefore, persuaded Aunt Bea to accept a contribution to the housekeeping if she could stay with her on a number of weekly visits and to arrange for a part-time secretary who would type all her letters. With the aid of a telephone directory I helped to build up a list of the current addresses of the likely firms (many of which had been bombed during the war and had to move).

Mum knew that she could only leave the firm for a week or so at a time, because she didn't want to see it turn into a wasting asset. Some of the partners were returning from the forces and property transactions were helping to increase fee income, but she had to keep a close watch on the finances to see that bills were issued promptly and clients chased for payment.

In retrospect, Mum proved herself to be an extremely able business woman at the most difficult time in her life. She was, as I have already noted, a very able and determined person. Once she had put her mind to something she pulled out all the stops and wasn't going to take no for an answer. She must have arranged meetings with sixty or seventy firms. At that time there were not many women in the legal profession and very few indeed who combined her intellectual capacity, experience in handling people, business acumen, imposing elegance and great personal charm. It was late 1947 before she decided that she had got the deal that she wanted, and then she had to set about selling it to the other partners and staff.

She salvaged more from Dad's share of the partnership than she dared hope for when she first started, but part of the deal was that Mum had to say in post for a five year period. It wasn't her original intention, but it proved a blessing in disguise. She needed something that was going to keep her mind and energies fully utilised, even if she didn't know it at the time. Furthermore, it enabled her to remain where she was known and respected.

It also enabled her to remain active in the various finance and other committees of the Dean and Chapter, the College and the High School, where she was now a Governor in her own right and had handed over the job of secretary to someone else. I don't envy the person who had to take over her job as secretary, when there was someone like Mum who knew it all backwards, keeping an eye on her.

Even at the end of the five year period, Mum found herself doing a similar job in the London office of the expanded firm, which by then had absorbed two other partnerships and desperately needed someone of Mum's calibre who could pull the whole organisation together. This enabled Mum to buy a house in the part of Kensington to which she dreamed of returning, fortunately before the big hike in central London house prices.

Michaelmas term 1946 was enjoyable for a number of reasons, but memorable above all for my first meeting with John. Starting at the beginning of one's second year is always more enjoyable. You know your way around. You've made a lot of friends. You know which lectures are any good, so you don't waste time taking notes and kidding yourself you're working, when you'd get much more information for your essay by reading the right books in the library. The star performer at that time was said to be Lord David Cecil. He was full of mannerisms and you could hardly hear what he said unless you went to the lecture before in order to get near the front. When I could hear I wasn't impressed. He made the same corny joke about three times and it wasn't even his own.

"As Doctor Johnson said, you could be as happy in the arms of a chambermaid as of a Duchess, if it weren't for imagination". Ha, ha.

Apart from Professor Tolkien who could tell you more in his throwaway lines:

"It isn't an infinitive - so how can it be split" - than most lecturers could tell you during the fifty minutes or so in which they performed, I learnt a lot from Professor Wrenn (on Beowulf), F. P. Wilson ("Bacon was a Scholar") and C. S. Lewis ("Prolegomena to Renaissance Poetry") and, of course, from Helen Gardner, my tutor.

One of the people to whom I am eternally indebted was the late Clifford Dobb. He was another English student and not a lecturer, but he was much older. He had spent a year reading English from 1938-39 and then been away in the army for the whole of the war, returning in 1946. We met in Professor Tolkien's language class and then as I was going into Bodley. He was very studious and afterwards, like John, did a B.Litt. He was one of those shy men (at any rate with women) who probably took a liking to me and found I was an easy person to talk to. We were both studious and systematic in the way we worked. He showed me how to find my way around the Cambridge Bibliography of English literature so that whenever I had an essay to write I could find the books that had been written on the subject. He showed me that, instead of relying on the books on the open shelves in the Radcliffe Camera, I could use the main Bodley catalogue, order the books and have them sent to a table in Duke Humfrey's which was a wonderful library in which to work. It had an atmosphere which I found suited my temperament. It made me feel quite donnish and started stimulating ambitions about an academic career. I was astonished by the end of my third year to find how few of my colleagues had ever bothered to use the Bodley catalogue or had done anything more than just take the books from the open shelves from the Radcliffe Camera.

As Clifford and I would often see each other in the afternoons in Duke Humfrey's, he used to come and tap me on the shoulder about 4 pm, raise an imaginary cup of tea to his lips and point with his thumb and I would follow to join him for tea and toasted teacake at the Kemp nearby. I insisted on paying every alternate time we came together. He was on an ex-service (FETS - further education and training scheme) grant which, at that time, was probably about £260 p.a. I remember him jocularly asking me if I were one of the 'nuns of St. Hilda's' and when I replied that I would hardly be a fit person to become a nun, he roared with laughter. Apparently there was a bawdy song which they used to sing in his College called 'The Nuns of St. Hilda's. He never felt he knew me well enough to tell me the words, but it was clear that the so-called nuns in the song were anything but chaste.

He noticed my wedding ring and asked if my husband would object to me having tea with other men so I told him about myself and he said that he ought, perhaps, to call me 'the merry widow'. He saw immediately that I didn't like this description. I may have recovered my good humour, but I was the opposite of merry about being a widow.

October 1946 saw a very large influx of ex-servicemen and women. Either their demob numbers had come up or they had succeeded in getting a class B release. One has to remember that when the war in Japan finished in mid August 1945 there were vast numbers of British troops getting ready for what was expected to be a three year slog against the Japanese and there were vast numbers of troops in Germany, Austria and Italy. There was tremendous uncertainty about the intentions of the Russians, who had by far the largest number of troops on the ground in Europe and who were beginning to cause trouble all over the place. I had no doubt about their intentions and neither did most of the people who shared my political views, but we were in a small minority. The UK seemed to be full of communists, or at any rate the people we refer to as 'fellow travellers' for whom the Russians could do no wrong. Even if there hadn't been the threat of Russia it would have been impossible to organise mass demobilisation sooner than we did. The home economy was dislocated and there simply were not the jobs ready and waiting for returning ex-servicemen.

By 1946 the men's Colleges in the university were overcrowded. A much higher proportion of students than normal had to live in digs and tutorials were often shared instead of being one-to-one. Quite a number of the men had married and were able to get grants to support their wives and children. Accommodation was extremely scarce and many of them had to cycle in every day from some distance out. One of our married friends lived in Boars Hill and another in some outbuildings of a vicarage or old vicarage near Nuneham Courtney.

The famous French club social took place mid to late November and by a stroke of good fortune I managed to get a ticket and so did John. Chance brought us face to face when the music stopped and I knew as soon as our bodies touched as we started dancing. I had a few anxious moments before I felt him press me tightly against him and I sensed that we were at one. In later years I often pulled his leg in front of friends about him needing twenty seconds when I needed ten and there used to jokes about how well I might have done as a fighter pilot, but I don't have John's rapid response in other domains. Even now when he is driving his eyes spot potential hazards long before any normal person and he seems to take in everything to the left and right of him in a flash. One of our friends said that he had more confidence when he sat in the front seat beside John than with any other driver. John is a fast driver when traffic conditions are right, but you sense his foot easing up slightly on the accelerator when he spots something miles away - and I'm talking about doing speeds of up to 120 mph on the German autobahn.

We were inseparable for the rest of the evening, but I knew nothing about his background. Even if it was only to be a short passionate affair I was determined to live every moment of it to the full. He was in civilian clothes. I knew nothing about his service background. I knew he was older. I was twenty. He was not yet twenty-five, but looked older, with receding hair. With my wedding ring I might well have been married to someone else, but he was likewise prepared to live for the moment. He took me back to St. Hilda's and we kissed passionately before I had to leave him.

He was not normally a churchgoer, but when I told him I would be at St. Mary's (the university church) the next morning, he said he would be there and he was. His College was BNC, which was only a stone's throw away. He took me to lunch at the Mitre and we spent all afternoon talking in his room at BNC. He heard my story and I heard his. He still loved Cynthia, his home town fiancée to whom he remained devoted throughout his service career. He said that she had had every reason to believe that he was dead when his plane was reported missing and so he didn't hold her hasty marriage against her, although John's parents would never forgive her. John's father, however, used to say in later years that her marriage was a blessing in disguise because he didn't think she was well suited to him in the way I was. Whether he said this to please me I know not and I care not. I told John that I still loved David. I believe his own experience enabled him to understand how I thought and felt, just as the personal tragedy in my life no doubt enabled me to feel much more at ease with John's emotional position. If I had been an insecure, virginal school leaver I might have started worrying in case Cynthia got fed up with her present husband and came back to grab John. I was prepared to live with that situation should it ever occur. Such spectres weren't going to cast shadows over my life with a man with whom I had fallen desperately in love.

A lot of things are different the second time round. Neither of us was shy or inhibited. I had not only been married, but had had Jacko as a lover. I managed to get permission to be absent from St. Hilda's the following weekend. I probably said I was visiting Mum. John took me to a lovely country hotel, Weston Manor. To me it was like a second short honeymoon and I must have given John such a wonderful time that in later years we have often been back and every time the memory stirs his ardour and mine, too.

We could have got married, but there were a lot of reasons for waiting until I had taken my degree. Living accommodation for married couples was pretty abysmal. We both had pleasant accommodation in our Colleges. Many people had to live out in digs for one year out of three, possibly two. If you acquired a position of secretary of one of your College associations, you might well be able to have a room in College when others of the same year were having to live out in digs.

John had different career aspirations from most of his RAF colleagues. He had always dreamed of being an Oxford professor, whereas most of his colleagues who had trained as pilots wanted to remain as pilots. Although only a small number were able to make long-term careers in the RAF, many of them were successful in obtaining extended service commission, which might enable them to keep body and soul together for another eighteen months or two years in the hope that civil aviation would be sufficiently developed for them to find jobs as pilots in what became British Overseas Aircraft Corporation (BOAC) and British European Airways (BEA) which were later amalgamated to form British Airways.

There were many people like John, in the sense that they had adapted successfully from essentially peace-time roles to playing an important part in the war effort. David, as an architectural student, was in the same category. People who think of Oxford dons as impractical thinkers with their heads in the clouds know nothing about the people inside the caricatures they claim to be describing. One of our language lecturers (old and middle English) had been one of the first people to be parachuted into Yugoslavia to link up with Tito's partisans. Another student reading for the Honours School of English Language Literature had risen to the rank of Colonel during the war and was, subsequently, to become the senior Fellow in English in his College, a role which he doubled up with that of Investment Bursar. It was worth pointing out in this context that, whilst professors are two a penny in many modern universities and business schools, the title denotes a very senior position indeed in the hierarchy of a subject faculty at Oxford. Before the days of mass university expansion you held a much coveted and very senior position in your College if you were a Fellow and Senior Tutor in your subject.

Once I had met John we spent most of our free time together, both during term and vacations. Mum accepted that we lived as man and wife when John stayed with us. She didn't ask any questions. She didn't even comment. Fortunately she liked John and was so overjoyed that I was rebuilding my life that she, no doubt, kept her fingers crossed and hoped for the best. It was the same when we stayed with his parents. Sadly, his mother was already suffering from terminal cancer and I think she knew it, although everyone tried to buoy up her hopes. His father and I had an instant rapport which lasted as long as he lived. His home was in Warwickshire, which was not much more than an hour's drive in John's souped-up old Alvis, which he drove at frightening speeds when there was still relatively little traffic on the roads and my first visit to his home was unannounced. He hadn't yet told his parents of my existence.

A lovely photo of John in uniform standing with Cynthia had pride of place on the mantelpiece. She had beautifully sculptured features, but there was a hardness in her expression, or that's what I saw and I immediately read her character as that of an egotistical person who was happy to wear her RAF Squadron Leader fiancé as a trophy in the days when they were the heroes of the hour, but would be quick to discard him when he could no longer be of service. John, like many men, would endow a woman of this kind with the characteristics of his imaginary ideal wife and see her the way he imagined her and not as she was. I was obviously reading my own knowledge of what had happened into the photo, so that what I knew and what I saw instantly fitted into what was, for me, an easily recognisable pattern.

John had been talking to his parents in the kitchen while I had been alone in the lounge looking at the photos. When John's father came into the lounge and saw me looking at the photo he immediately started to apologise.

"I'm afraid we're not a very tactful family. If we'd known you were coming we would...". Before he could continue I told him I knew all the background and if John was still desperately in love with Cynthia, I was still desperately in love with the husband I had lost on the Normandy beaches.

"John needs time to pick up the pieces and decide where he wants to go. I've been struggling along the same stony path for two and half years. John's been giving me a helping hand, I hope I'm doing the same for him. What the future holds, time alone will tell."

Obviously I hoped for a lot more, but understatement was the only sensible approach in conversations of this kind.

John's father (Hugh) was a successful Midlands business man and was at that time having to cope with a Labour government that was in the throes of nationalising every business it could lay its hands on. Nowadays people only think of such industries as mining and the railways, but in those days when the Labour MPs had sung the Red Flag in the House of Commons after their 1945 victory, they were hell-bent on the Marxist objective of taking over the means of production so that control would be 'in the hands of the workers', just like Russia.

It took a long time for the message to sink in to the public at large that nationalised industries were monopolies run by remote oligarchies and that Russia wasn't a workers' paradise, but a brutal dictatorship that inflicted far more misery and massacred many millions more people than the Germans had done during the war.

Hugh had had a successful road haulage business that had been started by his grandfather. It was nationalised and he received a pittance in the form of government paper for his shares. Cheap money meant that government stock was being issued with a coupon of 2%, which meant it would fall in value as soon as interest rates started to rise. Hugh was nearly fifty. On the one hand he was working flat out negotiating terms for compensation and trying to save the ancillary operations of his business that were not covered by the relevant nationalisation legislation. On the other hand he was trying to plan the sort of business that he thought he could run profitably under a Labour government. He wanted to provide for John, so that John could pursue an academic career, even though it would offer little financial reward. He had investments in shares as well as a number of properties, but share prices didn't take off until the mid 1950s and the combination of controlled rents and protected tenancies meant that he would have to wait until the late 1950s before he could get rid of some of his residential tenants and sell at more realistic values. And at that time the Conservative party looked as though it was unelectable and the Socialists were here to stay. On top of this he had an ailing wife. Somehow I must have given him the impression of being a matter of fact, down to earth person with both feet on the ground with whom he could discuss these problems.

I was, in fact, more interested in talking to him about his current problems than John had been. Hugh had a lot of views that reminded me of the comments that Dad used to make. He was accustomed to dealing with large numbers of youngsters who had no first hand knowledge of business or politics, and who were repeating parrot fashion the left-wing clichés that were so frequently heard on the BBC, from left-wing teachers and ABCA (Army Bureau of Current Affairs), the sort of outfit which, predictably, attracted lefties who were able to use their positions to spread their propaganda.

By temperament I have usually tended to react against such people, whatever garbage they may be spouting. I still do. In more recent years I have recognised the same kind of people campaigning against fur coats, fox hunting and the export of calves for veal. I have never owned a fur coat and I have never wanted John to buy me one. I have always been a practical person in the clothes I buy myself and I have never seen the point in spending a few thousand pounds for something to keep you warm in Winter, when all I usually need is a raincoat to get from heated car to heated house or office, or an anorak to wear on country walks. What I object to is the dictatorial attitudes of these interfering busy-bodies and I've often said that if someone cared to lend me a fur coat I would deliberately wear it to visit people I knew were anti-furs and I would spit in their faces if they made derogatory comments.

Likewise, I've never tried to sit on a horse and I obviously wouldn't get any pleasure from hunting, but a hunt is a nice piece of old English pageantry to which I enjoy taking overseas visitors who come to England at the appropriate time of year. If I sense that I am amongst people who sympathise with the anti-hunt saboteurs, one of the advantages of being a septuagenarian is that I can treat people in their thirties, forties and fifties as kids when I argue with them. I remember John telling me that he felt almost sorry for the wretched female who was sitting opposite when I was saying that the anti-hunt saboteurs ought to be treated as criminals and locked up in Wormwood Scrubs with a few hungry foxes. I had, obviously, had a few whiskies and I told the stupid creature that the only reason she was against fur coats and hunting was that she was a proletarian slut with an inferiority complex, who resented people who were superior to her because they could afford fur coats and resented fox hunting because it was a traditional upper and middle class sport and that it was the negative attitudes of people like her who had lost us the British Empire - and I probably said a lot more.

I was, obviously, much more polite and tactful when I was in my twenties and dealing with people who held different opinions, but you'll have no difficulty in seeing why Hugh and I quickly found we had a lot of opinions in common. He had a vast amount of first hand knowledge on industrial matters which I did not have, but I had inherited the type of enquiring mind that led Dad to seek the views of people who had first hand knowledge of what they were talking about, rather than relying on what he read in the newspapers and it's easy to see why Hugh found me, a mere twenty year old at the time, refreshing to talk to and, no doubt, why he considered me a safe pair of hands if my relationship with John were to become permanent.

John's rehabilitation process for the next year or two took the form of clutching at his remaining links with his RAF comrades. Some were people with whom he had trained. Others had been in the same fighter squadron. Others had been in the same PoW camp. Quite a number, as I have mentioned, had remained in the service on extended service commissions. Apart from work and participation in cultural activities, all my social life for the rest of my time at university was one and the same as John's social life. I was not only his mistress, or fiancée (no-one worried about the words - I was just his woman and I wouldn't have wanted to be anything else), but also his mate, a very important term in those days.

We travelled all over the place, mainly in vacations, but sometimes during weekends in term time. I met so many people that I couldn't possibly keep up with who was who. At that time most servicemen and women had taken to wearing civvies when they were off duty, so I never knew who was still in the RAF or WAAF and who had been demobbed. My health was drunk when I was his guest at a Ladies' Night in the mess at his old squadron, but most of our get-togethers were informal, boozy and uproarious. Even for a person like me some of the songs they used to sing (Salome for example) were nauseating and uncouth rather than saucy. It was, as I have described in Chapter 12, a case of men who had carried tremendous responsibility reverting to the state of College boys, but without any of the constraints and inhibitions which school life imposes.

It didn't matter what you wore for these occasions because the only thing the boys were interested in was turning the women upside down (literally on some occasions - I remember a dance where there was a competition for the first man to touch the lamp with his partner's feet) and the best way to make yourself popular and attract a

MY NEW LIFE - AN EMOTIONAL AND SPIRITUAL ODYSSEY

few more wolf-whistles was to wear provocative pants. As John is the sort of person who has always been turned on by that sort of thing (and by sexy nighties) I rarely let him down on such occasions.

Some women would, no doubt, have hated this childish fooling about. For example, the prize for a man who might win one of their silly games might be to kiss the girl of his choice, which meant that not only did he kiss you, but the lights were turned out long enough for his hands to get into your pants. He might be a repulsive, half-drunk creature with bad breath, but if you were the unlucky girl (as I often was) you had to learn to laugh it off as a joke. The booby prize for a girl, which she could get for almost anything, was to be held over someone's knee and spanked. The spanks were intended to be playful because the main attraction for the onlookers was the sight of a sexy be-knickered bottom. There were always shouts of "get them off" but I never saw that happening. On one or two occasions I found myself over the knee of a man who couldn't resist the chance to give me a few smacks that were far from playful, but some of the other girls had to endure more than I did and none of them complained.

I got to know a number of the women. Some were still WAAFs. Others had been demobilised, but had formed attachments or were married. Others were life and soul of the party people who might sleep with anyone, or no-one, and there were women who were just wheeled in to make up numbers from whatever location we happened to be in. Nobody seemed to be the least interested in who you were, or where you came from. I did, however, get to know a number of WAAFs or ex-WAAFs who had been at the same station as John when he was on ops (operations) before he was shot down. From what I could gather he had been far more restrained in those days. One girl said to me:

"He never used to let his hair down like this. If it's thanks to you, good show. I'm sure he's told you about the way that rotten bitch treated him."

I said, "He did, but we're all trying to put the past behind us", I pointedly thrust my left hand in front of her so that she couldn't help seeing my wedding ring.

"My husband was killed on the Normandy beaches. We're all trying to build our new lives. I want you to succeed. I want John to succeed. There are certain things that it's better not to speak about", and I think the message got through.

John would have been angry if I had told him about that girl's remark and I didn't. In fact, it's one of those things I've always liked about John. He doesn't get angry with people. It's one of his strengths. His patience is much greater than mine. The chivalrous attitude he took to Cynthia after she left him is something I respect and admire. He didn't hate his German opponents. He respected their skills as pilots. He had the intelligence, as did most of his colleagues, to recognise that the men in the German forces had no option, and in any case they were patriots, just as our troops were patriots. We both get very annoyed at attempts in recent years to blacken individual Germans because they had joined the Nazi party before the war. Someone even tried to criticise the famous opera singer, Elizabeth Schwarzkopf, for being a member of the Nazi party before the war. To most young Germans it would have looked like the party of the future and the way to get on, just as most young Russians had to try and join the communist party if they wanted to get on.

The people that John and I have always regarded as unspeakable lepers are the traitors. There were infinitely more British traitors willing to sell the security of their country to Soviet Russia than to Germany. We now know that there were many more cases than the high profile figures such as Blunt, Burgess, Philby and McClean.

In the Summer vacation 1947 John accompanied Mum and me on our first visit to France after the war had ended. It was something of an adventure because there was a lot of uncertainty about such things as train services, food supply, etc. We were each restricted to £50 foreign currency per annum, most of which had to be taken in travellers' cheques. Civilised methods of payments such as credit cards didn't come into existence until many years after the war. The newspapers were running stories about the starving peoples of Europe. One had difficulty in believing that a rich agricultural country such as France, which was more than self-sufficient in its food supply, could have suffered such privation during the war, but France had been split into two. There was a German occupying army in the north and west and the armistice terms of 1940 required an enormous daily "reparations" payment to the Germans of food and manufactured goods. The normal country to town distribution system had broken down. The rationing system was not respected as it was in Britain. It was the people living in towns who suffered most, particularly if they didn't have money to buy things on the black market. Although a black market in food and other commodities existed in Britain, it was frowned upon and few people would dare admit to their friends that they had bought anything on the black market, whereas in France it was accepted as the normal method of getting supplies if one had the money to do so.

As Tante Nicole wanted to spend a few weeks in England she promised to look after us as well as she could if we stayed with her when we were in Paris, which we did, and we would reciprocate when she came to us.

John had never been to Paris before the war and so he wanted to see round, but Mum's main agenda, and mine, was to get to La Tour du Pin.

We were able to get a train to Lyon. A lot of bridges over rivers such as the Rhone had not been rebuilt and we saw many temporary bailey bridges.

We stayed for two nights at a small hotel in Lyon and looked around. We were astonished at the large number of American cars. Most were, no doubt, travelling south to the Riviera. There were a lot with Belgian number plates. It was said that the Belgians had done well out of the large American presence in their country at the end of the war and although their country might be poor and dislocated, the people who had done well were spending their money in flamboyant style.

We were able to find our way by bus and train out to the chateau. Grandmaman who had survived until late 1944 had managed to remain in occupation without the building being commandeered. The Germans had only occupied the 'unoccupied' part of France (i.e. what had previously been under control of the Vichy government) in December 1942 when the Allies landed in Morocco and Algeria, by which time the Germans had few troops to spare in country areas that had no strategic significance and they were driven out eighteen months later.

Grandmaman had, in fact, been providing a refuge for quite a lot of people from her extended family. A number were trying to escape from the occupied zone. If a prisoner of war escaped from Germany he would try to get false identity papers and escape from occupied to unoccupied France. There was no revenue from Arrière's foreign investments coming in, so they had to try to be self-sufficient. The family owned the farm, but much of the land was tenanted. Any able-bodied person in the family had to become an agricultural labourer on a farm where there might be tractors, but no fuel to make them work.

By 1947 the food supply in this country district was back to normal. In fact, things had been normal by 1946. There was plenty of fresh fruit. It was lovely and sunny and John and I became enthusiastic wine drinkers. There was plenty of cheap red. Even quite respectable Côte du Rhone was remarkably cheap, but neither of our palates had yet acquired much skill in discriminating. It was just the lovely warm feeling we got polishing off a litre bottle between the two of us over lunch (Mum preferred something better) and another bottle over dinner. At the end of our meals we had Eau de Vie, which was a plentiful white spirit drink which French country people seemed to consume in vast quantities. Compared with the food we had in our Colleges and the measly meat rations we had during the war and early post-war years, here we were tucking into large rump steaks such as neither of us could remember. It's not surprising we didn't do much except laze in the sun and pass many loving and intimate moments together, which we still cherish in our memories 55 years later. It is shared memories such as these which form an important part in the bonds that bind husband and wife together in later years, when events and people may be trying to pull you apart.

Mum, however, worked like a beaver. She knew there was a vast sum of money tucked away in trusts in the US. Grandmaman had never been much of a business woman and in any case there was probably not much she could have done in the period between the death of Arrière in December 1938 and her own death. Mum spent most of the time working through the vast quantities of papers that had been left virtually untouched since Arrière's death. She was looking for such things as names and account numbers. I offered to help, but she said there was little point as no-one else would know for what she was looking.

We were there for four or five weeks. She wrote a number of letters to people in Geneva and got replies, on the basis of which she decided we would try to make a detour via Geneva on the way back to Paris.

We hadn't spent much currency because we had been able to buy our tickets to Lyon in England without using our allowance of French currency. Tante Nicole had looked after us in Paris and the only money we had spent was getting around sightseeing. Mum worked out a train route to Geneva and we paid the extra, but third class French train fares were cheap by English standards. The compartments were pretty uncomfortable, with nowhere to rest your back. They usually stank of second-hand garlic. Most of the Frenchmen seemed to spend their time eating sandwiches stuffed with garlic sausage and smoking Gauloises.

In Geneva Mum found us a cheap hotel. We didn't stay at the Hotel Les Bergues. Switzerland was expensive compared to France, but the exchange rate at that time was 12 Swiss francs to the pound. David and I loved Geneva. We took a boat trip to Vevey and back and it brought back wonderful memories of my childhood. Mum spent most of the time seeing the various people she had written to, but on our last day she had a big smile on her face, opened her handbag and waved a wadge of crisp Swiss franc notes at us. We could have a bean-feast, which we did and we could get as much money as we wanted whenever we decided to come to Switzerland. It was no good taking Swiss money back to England because the law at the time required you to change foreign notes back into sterling, but if we wanted to come to La Tour du Pin or go down to the Riviera, all we had to do was to go to Geneva first and pick up some cash.

I learnt afterwards that she had gone to the bank armed with Arrière's death certificate, Grandmaman's death certificate and copies of their respective French wills which set out all the inheritors. French law gave parents virtually no discretion in how they willed their money. Everything had to be equally divided between children. Proof of identity and a French will were satisfactory evidence for the Swiss bank with which she was dealing.

As soon as we were home Mum started writing to the various US addresses. She wasn't able to travel to the US until she had finished negotiations for the merger of Dad's firm, but then she took two months leave. She travelled the old-fashioned way by boat. At that time you had to wait months to get a passage.

All the money I have, all my financial independence until I was able (quite late in life) to earn a good salary, all the money to pay for our children's education and to get them launched in their professional careers, all the wonderful holidays that John and I were able to take with our growing family, our ability to pay for a nanny when the children were small, even John's freedom to spend his life in a career that he enjoyed, but paid very little, all this was thanks to Mum's efforts on our behalf during that critical period yet she didn't even drop a hint as to what she was really doing. She had a Sherlock Holmes type skill in following up leads and if it meant taking a ship to New York and travelling on to Chicago on her own, she did so. Her mind was working on this all the time she was sorting out the partnership merger.

Many people, as they grow older, find that their parents are not quite the brilliant people that they thought in their early days. My respect for Mum has steadily increased throughout my life. Even after she died I discovered lots of things she had done without saying a word. She was the opposite of a flamboyant person. She had suffered an unbearable loss in Dad's death and yet she never let up when it came to doing something that she knew was for Jean and me, and in due course this meant for her four grandchildren and the great-grandchildren she had the joy of seeing before she died. To quote that wonderful phrase coined by Sir Gordon Newton in his tribute to Harold Wincott, she was 'a peer without equal'.

Our long Summer holiday in France worked wonders for John. For me, it had been a marvellous opportunity to revisit part of the fairy tale world I had known as a child. For John, it was the first real opportunity to relax. The war years had been tense and so had the re-adaptation to university life, but above all, the loss of his first true love. Although he had loved me from the moment we first met, I sensed that he now felt at peace with me. I had become more than the object of a passionate love affair. I had become his mate and he realised he could take me for granted. Many women may not have liked this, but to me it's an important part of a stable relationship. You don't have to keep worrying about what your other half is going to think when you do this, that or the other. He or she will always give you the benefit of the doubt. I'm not saying this happens in every marriage, although I suspect a lot of the problems that arise between couples stem from the fact that this state of mind does not exist in such marriages.

It would never have worried me in the least that John had slept with someone else, whether he told me himself or someone else did, and I've always been confident that he would react in a similar way. That doesn't mean I wouldn't have been dreadfully worried if I thought I was going to lose him, but that's totally different. I didn't in fact sleep with anyone else until I was nearly fifty and I don't think John did until approximately the same period. I was twenty when I met John, twenty-one when we got engaged and twenty-two when we got married. What one does in relative old age is governed by different rules.

John proposed formally when he was staying with Mum and me in September 1947, just before the start of term. Mum was delighted. We went to Bishop Wantock for Father Wakehurst to bless our engagement. We agreed that I should continue to wear the engagement ring that David had put on my finger and in due course the same wedding ring. We would marry after I had taken Schools in 1948, although my plan was to stay on for another year and do a Dip.Ed. I would no longer be living in College and John and I hoped to rent a flat.

I got a second. I was told it was a good one. I didn't expect to get a first. There were, in fact, remarkably few in English that year. I would have liked to do a B.Litt. but with a

Dip.Ed. I knew I could get a job teaching. There was still a considerable teacher shortage at that period, although teacher's salaries were abysmally low. Even with a degree and a Dip.Ed. you could only expect to earn between £300 and £400 p.a. Soon after Christmas 1948 I knew I was pregnant and my first child, William, was born in August 1949, so I didn't start teaching until the Autumn Term of 1950 and then not for long.

We were married by Father Wakehurst in Bishop Wantock church at the end of June 1948. I had Louise as one of my bridesmaids. Jean and Angus were in Washington at the time (the first of Angus' overseas liaison posts) and were unable to attend, but June was over the moon when I asked her. Not only that, but she dressed me for the occasion as well as organising dresses for Louise and herself.

In fact, she continued to choose all my clothes until she retired from Dickins and Jones many years later. Although she was only responsible for the underwear and nightwear department in Wilson's, she knew all the buyers and had her London contacts and no matter whether it was suits, overcoats, dresses or blouses, she had an unerring sense of what would look right on me. It isn't that I'm not interested in wearing lovely clothes. I've simply never been the kind of person who's prepared to spend the time going round shops, trying on things I don't like. What June would do would be to ring me up and say I've got something that will look absolutely right on you, and it always did. She's always recognised the constraints imposed by my character, i.e. that I refuse to wear anything in which I feel uncomfortable, or where movement is restricted.

How we got everybody into the church, Heaven knows. Apart from my family and John's family and many friends, we had all sorts of well-wishers. We were back to peacetime hired morning wear from Moss Bros. and all the paraphernalia of a peacetime wedding.

Mum, who had planned the guest list for the reception with her usual meticulous care, had invited my Headmistress and Mrs. Rainham, who came with her husband. It was a wonderful day and yet I kept seeing in my mind's eye the church as it has been four and a half years before, when only David and I were standing before the altar with Father Wakehurst, and there was no-one else in the church. I kept repeating to myself:

"The only thing that matters is that you are married in the sight of God."

John understood when he saw there were tears in my eyes, as we were standing together in the final stages of the ceremony, and gave my hand a squeeze. He said later that he understood. Father Wakehurst also noticed and he, certainly, understood. When we were in the vestry signing the register he said he had been worried all along on my account and had wondered if it was wise for me to return to Bishop Wantock for my second wedding. I said that it wouldn't have been a real wedding for me to be married by anyone else but him. He had been the priest who had helped me in my hour of need.

I have often thought of how pig-headed and stupid we are to run weddings the way we do, with all their clutter and paraphernalia. For many people it's just a bit of theatre. I know it's a big day for the parents and grandparents and Uncle Tom Cobblies and I suppose that, traditionally, they are the people who pay for it all and have, therefore, called the shots, but it's perverse and misconceived. For days and weeks before the most important day in her life, a woman is forced to listen to continuous tittle-tattle about what hats and gloves who is going to wear and with what, who mustn't be seated anywhere near whom at the reception and so on.

For a man it's not so bad. All he seems to have to worry about is whether he has chosen a Tom Fool idiot as his best man, who can't be relied upon to be on time, or find the ring. Fortunately, John decided not to have a stag party the night before. As he put it, he had spent so much of his mis-spent youth going to the equivalent of stag parties, that getting married was a time to sober up and be serious. So he didn't have a hangover. He noticed the tears in my eyes and his mind was sufficiently alert to understand why.

Some people, no doubt, regard marriage as the equivalent of putting a collar and a lead around a dog's neck so that the husband or wife can't run away, or as a means of ensuring that the children are born legitimate, and that the other person will be required to contribute a fair share to the cost of running a home and bringing up a family. For them the junketing is, no doubt, acceptable as good, clean fun. They get a lot of presents and their pictures in the paper, but if we really believe in Christian marriage as a sacrament, the mystical union of two human beings who are solemnly committing themselves, each to the other, until all eternity, then we should think of arranging matters differently.

I suppose my experience of the solemn ceremony in which I married David is unusual. I would have preferred Dad and Mum to be there, because I know they would each have understood what I wanted and would have approved. We would all have dressed in our normal church clothes, so that there would have been no fuss and palaver beforehand to take our minds off what was important. If David's parents had been with us I am sure they would, also, have understood and joined unobtrusively and fervently in prayer that our marriage would receive God's grace in abundance and be long-lasting.

The festivities could take place two or three days later, as when you invite your friends to come and rejoice in the birth of a child a few days after the event.

I am perhaps being unrealistic in trying to base a general theory on my own experience. All I know is, hasty though it was, and makeshift as the arrangements had to be before and after, the actual marriage ceremony when David and I knelt before Father Wakehurst alone in the little church of Bishop Wantock, when we both felt that we had become one mystical body in the presence of God, was the most moving and memorable moment in my life. We had nothing to distract us. I wanted it to be the same in my marriage to John and it wasn't, and I kept thinking of my earlier ceremony with David, which is why there were tears in my eyes.

But I pulled myself together and smiled at all the photographers and the guests and I chatted to everyone as if I were a first time bride looking forward to her honeymoon. I did, however, have the opportunity for a long chat with Father Wakehurst and I told him the thoughts that had been going through my mind over champagne and lunch about the way marriages should be organised. I have, in fact, talked to quite a number of women who have thought, more or less, the same. Admittedly, I have only talked to the sort of people who I felt were of like mind and we are, no doubt, an infinitesimally small minority. I do think that in a period where so many marriages end in divorce, that it might help if more thought were given to ways in which couples could be helped to focus more clearly on the spiritual side of the marriage ceremony, instead of being caught up in the task of coping with an exhausting schedule of trivial pursuits.

Father Wakehurst smiled, "You're absolutely right, but like so many people who are right, you would be branded as a heretic, or in present-day parlance, a nut-case. The only criticism that could be made of your proposals is that a marriage ceremony can be uplifting for many of those who attend, and I am sure a lot of your true friends today would much rather (if they had to choose) have had the chance to be with you in spirit at the religious ceremony than coming here to drink your mother's champagne and join in the jollification."

He did, however, suggest that if we went to early morning communion the next day and remained behind for a few minutes, he would conduct a short service in which he would ask for God's special blessing on our future lives together and the grace to rebuild our lives after the tragedies that we had both suffered (I had told him about John's broken engagement with Cynthia). We had no plans to go away for a short honeymoon. We had been living together and we were shortly to depart for our second post-war holiday in France.

For me it was a very moving service, and I think it was for John. Father Wakehurst put his right hand (his only hand) first on my head, then on John's. He prayed for us both and his prayers and our prayers were answered, because our marriage has lasted for over fifty years and our children were all born sound in mind and body.

Sadly, that was the last time we saw Father Wakehurst. He died while we were in France. We only learnt of his death on our return, so we were unable to attend his funeral. Dr. Wilding conducted a memorial service in the Cathedral at the beginning of October. I had never seen so many people at such an event, but it was not just the numbers that caught my attention. It was the devotion and love so manifest in those that came from all over the country. Some came in wheelchairs. Some were managing to walk on crutches. There were the blind, and those with only one arm. Dr. Wilding had suggested to the British Legion, who had publicised the event, that he hoped those with campaign medals would wear them, and they did. In addition there were those of the younger generation, such as Louise, her surviving brother and sister and myself, who had been baptised by him during the years of his perpetual curacy at Bishop Wantock.

MY NEW LIFE - AN EMOTIONAL AND SPIRITUAL ODYSSEY

For a man who had managed in the course of his life to bring comfort and consolation to so many, it made me feel extremely humble at the thought that he had been able to find so much time to give me help and guidance at two critical moments in my life. I have said it before and I say it again, the true strength of the Christian church throughout its existence has lain in the lives and characters of people like Father Wakehurst, rather than in institutions, but I accept that without the church organisation, be it Anglican, Catholic, Methodist or whatever, a person like Father Wakehurst would not have been able to exercise his ministry in the way he did.

As, in the Summer of 1947, we spent some six weeks in France. We were a little more adventurous now that we knew that if we travelled from Paris to Geneva Mum could pick up Swiss francs for our living expenses and that we could, no doubt, find someone to drive us from Geneva direct to the chateau. But before that we decided to see if we could find Juno beach. We went to Paris on the Newhaven Dieppe ferry instead of on the train via Boulogne. We had found an agency in London that claimed to provide local guides, so we were able to break our journey in Dieppe where a driver took us in a somewhat battered old Simca on what seemed a roundabout route to the St. Aubin coast near Courseulles and I was able to walk on the beach. I had feared that there might still be mines, but our driver claimed they had all been cleared and that holidaymakers were back.

I knew far less about the actual battle areas at that time than I subsequently read up, but for me it was enough to conjure up the picture of David coming ashore in a landing barge, with his infantry men and at some point during the day, falling to the ground as a result of machine gun fire, or shell fire. I knelt down on the sand and I wept bitterly. John and Mum were kneeling beside me. Whether it was David's presence that I felt, or for some other reason, the storm in my mind began to abate and I experienced a wonderful feeling of serenity. It was as if David were saying to me that I had done the right thing and then as if he were saying to John:

"Look after her and she will look after you."

I felt that I had reached, in Churchill's phrase, 'the end of the beginning'. The rest of my life has not been so turbulent. It has been more conventional, more like any other person's life. I have brought up a family and run a business. If I were to write about my business life it would be a business book, which is not what I have set out to write here. I have mentioned later events in my own life and in the lives of my children and grandchildren where they have been relevant, but apart from the epilogue which follows, this, for the time being at any rate, is the appropriate place to end what I hope will be a chronicle of wider public interest of a life lived in the turbulent days of World War II and of how those of us who survived had to struggle hard to rebuild our lives at the end of the war, so that our children, grandchildren and future generations should be able to live in peace and enjoy the fruits of the earth and the abundance of riches with which God has endowed this great country of ours - and if we only knew it He has also endowed us with the grace and wisdom to use our inheritance in the way He intended when He gave us our life and being.

CHAPTER 24

EPILOGUE

THE TESTAMENT OF BOADIE
(with apologies to François Villon)

I am indebted to John (who has produced some excellent verse translations and 'imitations' of his favourite Villon masterpiece) for the title of my epilogue. For example, one of his more quotable 'imitations' begins:

> Where are the belles and beauties of Babylon?
> Where are the lips that died with a kiss?
> Tell me Prince, yes tell me this
> Where is last year's snow?
>
> Marie d'Ecosse and Antoinette
> That the guillotine's sharp knife cut off.....

Instead of continuing my narrative to cover the 54 years of my life since 1948, I can make (I think) a more useful contribution to your education (as well as tying up a few loose ends) by using this chapter to survey what later generations have made of the country that so many of my contemporaries gave their lives for you to inherit. Part of me still stands on the high moral ground which so many of us did our best to hold in the war years. As I have tried to show, this was not a pretentious, self-righteous period, a description attributed (unfairly) to the second half of the 19th Century by people who use the term 'Victorian values'. We were not collectivists, so my views differ from those of many of my contemporaries, but we encouraged each other to think independently about important constitutional matters.

I often have to read garbage by newspaper columnists, many of whom write as if they had suffered education (if that is the right word) in one of the poorer comprehensives during the 1990s. If their patronising articles about people in my era lump the whole British population of the 1930s into a Stanley Baldwin mindset, I have no intention of lumping all those alive and kicking at the start of the 21st Century into a collective mish-mash. I have given many examples of the men who volunteered for service in the territorials and in the auxiliary air-force in the 1930s because they had the capability of seeing where Britain was heading, even if the Baldwin administration had its head in ministerial sand. And I have given the example of David, who could see what was happening from as far away as Western Canada and for whom England mattered.

Most of my grandchildren and those of their friends whom I have known have the same high seriousness and concern as my contemporaries for matters of fundamental importance to all of us, but I think my grandchildren's generation suffers much more from high pressure propaganda through press and television. The malign spirit of Dr. Goebbels lives on and it is more important than ever that those of us who have been granted length of days should do what we can to establish meaningful dialogue to provide a lifeline to those of independent spirit who are impatient and uneasy under the pressure of currently popular dogmas by which they are deafened, as they are deafened by the noisy beat of some of the tribal music (so called) to which it is impossible to dance and which makes conversation impossible.

From the comments of my grandchildren and friends my vivid memories of life growing up in the thirties, the war years and the post-war 'rehabilitation' period when so many people were trying to rebuild their lives, provide a historical record which is worth preserving and my personal tragedy has so many parallels in the lives of other families that survived, that in a sense it is more than just my story.

My later life story cannot have the same general interests, I therefore, leave it to others to chronicle the way the changes of the half century since 1950 have affected the lives, thoughts and aspirations of another family who loves this country as I do.

The lens, however, through which I now see my memories of the period covered by this book is inevitably that of a mind which has been conditioned by my life and experience in the ensuing half century. I have inserted explanations of words and attitudes current in the 1940s in answer to questions posed by those of my granddaughters, who have given the impression of being intensely interested in my subject matter and I am sure this interest is genuine and on a par with the interest of my sister and I when Dad used to talk to us about great-uncle William's sea stories set in the late nineteenth and early twentieth centuries - before his ship went down at the Battle of Jutland.

At various points in this narrative I have, therefore, almost without thinking, inserted a reference to an episode in my later life to illustrate the relevance of the event I was describing to the life experience of people born in later years, so there are a number of loose ends to tie up. As one of my academic friends put it "you need to understand the future in order to understand the past".

My job has also influenced the way I write. If I had been a professional writer, or I wanted to become one, I might have taken time to revise a lot of my homespun expressions. In the job I have done for over forty years (which I shall explain more fully in a moment) there has been only one test of whether I have got the language right - it has been whether the person to whom I was writing or speaking understood when I was telling him or her what to do and did it. There are only so many hours in a day and if the letter or memo is clear enough you don't spend time rewriting it in order to impress people who wouldn't have come to you in the first place unless they thought you could do what they wanted.

One of my proof readers has told me she wouldn't have expected an Oxford English graduate to use an expression such as "Mum was over the moon" to describe the way my mother felt after church on Boxing Day 1943 when she was basking in the congratulations of so many of her friends following the announcement of my marriage to David. Surely these words adequately describe the joy a mother would normally be expected to share with her daughter and son-in-law on such an occasion. Everyone in my generation understood what this commonly used expression meant and none of my grandchildren has had any difficulty in understanding, so why say more? As a postscript I would, however, say that the professors of the Oxford English faculty in my days as an undergraduate (and I have mentioned Tolkien and Helen Gardner at a number of points in my story) were the opposite of pretentious and pompous and in their lectures and tutorials used the plain, homespun English which I have always regarded as a natural mode of speech.

When I have used quotations it is because the poet or writer in question has encapsulated an important idea or observation in a phrase, or in a few lines that are infinitely superior to anything I could dream up and common decency obligates any normal person to acknowledge the author of the lines you are quoting, as opposed to paraphrasing them and attempting to pass off the idea as if it were your own. I defy anyone to sum up the tragic loss inflicted by World War I on the families of so many of my fellow countrymen and women so effectively and succinctly as the eight lines from Wilfred Owen's Anthem for Doomed Youth which I have quoted in Chapter 3.

If this were a business report my first chapter would have been headed Executive Summary and this final chapter would be called the Appendix, but this isn't a business report, it is the story of that part of my early life which may now be of wider historical interest. It is also my personal story, so I, therefore, prefer to retain the classical terms of prologue and epilogue that were current in my school days and in my time at university.

BUSINESS LIFE

I have referred at various points in my narrative to my job in later life as a 'management consultant'. Unfortunately the term has been devalued in recent decades and now tends to conjure up a spectre of a pretentious business school graduate, stringing together cliché-ridden reports full of dreadful words like 'prioritisation' for the benefit of in-house executives in large corporations, who haven't much of a clue as to what they are supposed to be doing and want to cover their backsides by demonstrating to their superiors that they have taken advice from all the acknowledged experts, who can in due course be blamed if the recommended course of action proves to be disastrous. This was not the business I was in.

My business was started by Hugh, John's father, when a large part of his livelihood was taken away from him in the stampede by the post-war Labour government to nationalise everything that ran on wheels and to turn a lot of small, manageable units into a large unmanageable mess.

In the period when John and I were pre-occupied with getting married, starting our new life together and (in 1949), having our first child, Hugh was wonderfully supportive yet he, himself, was in the throes of a crisis. He was 52. He had lost his wife, who had been terminally ill for some years. His only son now had his own home and own family and the company to which he had devoted the whole of his working life had been taken away, in exchange for a pittance in the form of government paper, which inflation would soon devalue. Worse than this the low coupon government bonds being issued in those days suffered a dramatic fall in terms of market value as soon as interest rates started to rise in the early 1950s.

Those of you with memories of the 1970s will, no doubt, recall the days when 3.5% War Loan fell below twenty pounds and at one stage the yield was equal to the price. And yet, in the Labour government's post-war heyday of cheap money, War Loan was standing above par. This was a period when owners of businesses were robbed, just as doctors and dentists who had paid real money to buy their shares of their professional practices were compulsorily bought out for 'compensation', much of which was only paid in devalued pounds many years later.

All this compulsory acquisition took place at the time when ordinary share prices remained low, because the economy was still in the doldrums as a result of war-time dislocation, compounded by the fact that Britain had locked itself into a straight-jacket exchange rate mechanism (the Bretton Woods formula) so that for the thirty years, 1945-1975 or thereabouts, of post-war history we kept having a sterling crisis which would have been avoided if the sterling exchange rate had been left to move in line with the market. Every time the economy started to buzz and our traditional manufacturing companies increased their imports of raw materials in order to meet increased demand for their products and increase their exports, our dollar reserves would go down, so our recovery would be cut short by a series of government 'crisis measures'.

By 1949 Hugh (as I shall refer to him in this chapter, although it was not my practice or the general practice in those days to call one's in-laws by their first names) had made up his mind to continue in business, even if it meant starting again. A number of his friends used metaphors like 're-learning to live', normally after having had an arm or a leg amputated, but Hugh would have found such terms distasteful. He had been too close to personal tragedy in his own life, first with the life and death struggle of his wife, and then with the news that his son's plane had been reported missing, for him to put lesser considerations on the same level. He used to say that as long as he could wake up in the morning knowing that he had both arms and both legs, a mind that worked and that his son's family were alive and well, he wasn't going to let anything else get him down. I think the perspective helped him enormously and may have been the key to his assessment of the business opportunities that he could grasp and turn to his advantage. Many people in his situation could do little more than wring their hands, forecast doom and spend all their mental energies (usually with a glass in one hand and the other elbow supported by the bar) forecasting the disastrous results of government policy.

What Hugh understood was that genuine business enterprise could survive and often thrive in chaotic periods of dislocation and there were plenty of historical parallels. In the post-war years people who were nicknamed 'spivs' were able to make a living selling articles in short supply. In many cases they were not doing anything illegal.

A lot of government surplus stock was sold off cheap. Clothing was still rationed until 1949. Nylons were scarce. In an earlier chapter I have mentioned how vast quantities of nylon parachutes produced during the war were sold off to people who knew how to organise teams of women (many of them working at home with sewing machines) to produce the glamourous nightwear and underwear for which women were crying out. Much of it may not have been glamourous by present day standards, but after wartime austerity it was manna from heaven. These are just examples. What many of us understood was that most politicians were at least a generation behind the times in their approach to current business problems.

In the 1940s and 1950s, when there were chronic labour shortages, these politicians were pre-occupied with the task of solving the unemployment problems of the 1930s. They would only think of nationalising traditional industries (what we now refer to as 'smoke stack') that had been around when they were boys learning their political rhetoric.

Hugh understood that a customer's needs would generate business opportunities, which traditional and nationalised companies would fail to understand and exploit. As organisations got bigger (and certainly when they got nationalised) an increasing proportion of the decision making jobs would go to unimaginative bureaucrats. Further down the ladder there were, of course, large numbers of one-man bands who might be spivs, moonlighting builders and so on, but there were substantial opportunities in the middle where some capital, combined with business organisation and experience were needed.

Hugh started with some capital and a lot of business experience. He also had a heterogeneous collection of little businesses that had evolved as appendages to his mainstream haulage business, which he had been able to uncouple and keep when the haulage business was nationalised. They posed problems of control and co-ordination and this was a challenge to Hugh. It did, however, mean that he had a reasonable number of people working for him whom he knew and trusted and various business premises.

His key decision was to dig out enterprising men or women, many of them recently demobbed and even if they were lucky, (i.e. in getting back into employment) stuck in frustrating jobs in big organisations that were as bureaucratically run as parts of the army or civil service. Such people were unlikely to have money to start a business and they didn't have much of a clue on the financial side.

Hugh had spotted the appalling service given by travel agents in his area that appeared when demand for foreign travel was growing. Bookings were not made and there was a nine-to-five lackadaisical air in all the places with which he had dealt that were staffed with people to whom customers were a nuisance. He found one bright guy who sorted out our travel to La Tour du Pin and asked him whether he would like to run his own travel agency. Hugh had the premises. He also knew a young journalist from the local paper that ran a competition for the family that could produce the worst story of incompetence in the way other travel agents had made a mess of things. His best coup was when one of the agents sued the paper for defamation. The resulting court case received widespread publicity for the string of horror stories from the witnesses for the defence. The complaining travel agent lost his case and had costs awarded against him, so he went bust.

Two other successful areas of operation were shoe repairing and watch and clock repairing. This was not a priority for the shoe shops who made money by selling shoes, nor for the jewellers and watch shops. As a result, these repair businesses were badly handled. Customers had to wait weeks for shoe repairs and sometimes months for watch repairs. In those days we walked more and shoe leather was always wearing out. Old fashioned watches with springs were always in need of repair. You needed a new spring every time you dropped a watch and a new watch could be expensive. The people who did the repairs often worked from home, were treated as poor relations and paid a pittance.

One of John's friends had been a radar mechanic in the RAF. His father had been a watch repairer and he reckoned the job could be properly organised, given a bit of capital and the right publicity. It was. So was a properly organised shoe repair business.

These businesses are just examples. We now take such services for granted, but at the time they were light years ahead of current practice. It should be noted that these business activities were carried out on a local basis and they could be under the tight control of one individual. What Hugh quickly saw was that, no matter which business he might be backing, there were certain common support services where Hugh's business experience was essential to success. For example, a travel agent who knew what his customers wanted and where to find it and how to twist the arms of his suppliers (usually not easy) wouldn't necessarily have any skill in cash management or accounting. Neither would the sort of person who could exercise what to control in watch repairs and shoe repairs. None of these people would necessarily have the skill in recruiting support staff, knowing what to pay them and when to fire them. So this is how Hugh's central service organisation developed. It is also how he developed his formula for charging for the provision of these central services and getting a fee based on turnover. Obviously a member of the accounts team could be used more productively in a central office, otherwise you might have a chronic shortage during a peak time in, say, the travel business, while accounts staff were sitting idle (but no doubt pretending to be busy) in the repair services sector.

What I have just described was the formula that got Hugh's post-nationalisation business concept off the ground. Obviously, there were companies in which Hugh's company had a worthwhile share that grew at a phenomenal rate and were sold at a substantial profit. Other companies, as one might expect, bit the dust. Overall, however, the success ratio was good because (in my view) Hugh had a good nose for picking people, as well as a good nose for recognising a good idea when he saw it.

In broad terms, Hugh had recognised that it was the service industry, rather than 'smoke stack' product manufacturing wherein lay the future potential for British business and secondly that if he restricted his involvement to small companies operating on a regional basis, trade union involvement could be minimal.

My involvement in the business was fortuitous. I had been trained as a teacher. I was already walking awkwardly as a pregnant Mum to be in the final term of my Dip.Ed. in 1949 and so there was no question of my having a teaching job until some time after William's birth. I then did a year as an English mistress in a school where I considered the pupils as a pretty below average bunch, although this was in fact a Grammar School. It was then that I realised how much I owed to the teachers in my own school. I also became disillusioned about the potential career path (teaching English) that lay ahead, given the attitudes of the school concerned.

Not long after Catherine was born I began to recognise the importance for a woman of 'getting back in'. The teaching post I had left had been filled by someone else and the only alternatives at the time were grotty, unless I was prepared to move to some other part of the country, which I was not.

At that time Hugh was complaining of staff shortages and the general lack of ability of people who were prepared to do a 'proper job'. I asked him if there were any odd jobs that I could do. I wanted to get back to doing something. In addition, Hugh's company had something of a fascination for me. I suppose that somewhere in my Fortingall bloodstream there was a recognition that Hugh was doing what my Fortingall ancestors had done so successfully and I sensed a need to be a part of it. On top of this I had the need of any mother to want to do something for her children. Hugh's business was highly personal. It had depended for its success upon his unique personality and flair, combined with his ability to judge people and situations. The business might or might not have a future when he ceased to be part of it. I had an intuitive feel that it might conceivably be a goldmine (which it has proved to be) if someone else in the family would, in due course, be able to take over where Hugh left off.

You might say it was Joe Muggins volunteering. In fact, I started at the most junior level as an odd-job girl. I don't think anyone in the company knew I was one of Hugh's relations. On Hugh's advice I had set up my own company, so I wasn't even an employee, I was simply charging for my services as a credit controller. In blunt terminology I was there to make the buggers pay or else, but not to lose the business in the process. I succeeded, but there was a lot to learn and in the process I learnt a lot about the company's business and the more I learnt, the more I liked it.

My break came in a flu epidemic when a client turned up for a meeting. No-one else was around, so I sat down with him and talked through his business project, making copious notes. Apparently he liked me and my hunch (although I could not at that time boast any experience in such matters) was that he had it in him to make a success and he did. Afterwards he said such nice things about me on the telephone to Hugh, that Hugh began to sit up and take notice. There might have been an element of sex in the mutual attraction, but I don't think it was significant. In any case, nothing developed in that direction. The important thing was that Hugh ceased to regard me as an English graduate who was willing to turn her hand to anything to earn an honest crust, but as someone with a bit more potential. He started to look at me a bit more in the way he looked at the protégés that he had been so successful in identifying and from then on my progress was in leaps and bounds.

Hugh's enthusiasm was enormous because he had, obviously, been worried subconsciously about where the company would go when he was no longer able to run it. None of his then support staff was of the calibre to run the show and the sort of people who buy businesses rarely have the understanding to recognise the potential of a business like Hugh's. I like to think that I did, although I have to admit that my understanding initially was more intuitive than conceptual.

My progress was slower in the initial years because I took two more short career breaks when my other two children were born, but by the mid 1960s I was fast becoming what Hugh described as the 'dynamo' of the business. What is more, I realised I had found my vocation and found it exhilarating.

The job also gave me scope for exercising the crusading zeal which I like to feel I inherited from Mum's 'grandma' (Catherine Johnston). Whilst I have felt good reason to be proud of my Fortingall ancestors, who built their family inheritance on the back of what we would now refer to as a small entrepreneurial business, I have felt strongly since my school days that the commercial strength and hence the political strength of our country was based on our versatility and operational capability as free market traders. We may not have had much political skill (until Ralph Harris and Margaret Thatcher came along) in arguing the theoretical case for what we were doing, but we were just damn good at doing it and we still are when we set our minds to it. We were at the opposite end of the spectrum to countries like France, where Colbert under Louis XIV defined the basis for centralised governmental control of all his country's economic activity and did his best to put it into practice. He was operating in a dictatorial regime which Napoleon, another dictator, did his best to consolidate. The French still think this way and so do the Germans who came to modern statehood under Bismarck and the Italians under Mussolini, two other dictatorial regimes.

Since Britain joined what we originally described as the 'common market' (now the EU), I have been conscious of the fact that our free market business sector has been constantly under attack. The big three European powers that have dominated the Brussels bureaucracy are totally unfriendly and, although British governments may have been strong on rhetoric, the ability of an Englishman to run his own business in a way he thinks fit has been continuously eroded. There are, of course, a lot of fifth columnists in Britain who have never made any secret of their pathological hatred of the free market tradition and, even when Margaret Thatcher was Prime Minister, a number of her underlings were pretty useless in controlling their civil service departments, so as to reverse the trend towards what many of us referred to as the dumbhead dirigiste mentality of the Frog, Wop and Kraut Europrats in Brussels.

Employment law has been my main battleground. EU thinking is based on the medieval feudal system, where everyone is an employee of big brother and so such things as hours of work, who does what, when and how, should all (in the Europrat view) be regulated in minute detail. We are not talking about the basic matters such as the employer's liability for accidents and injury at work and so on, but about absolutely outrageous interference in normal employer discipline.

It has been known for years that those large organisations which had been dominated by powerful blue collar unions had been crippled in their ability to deploy their workforce by trade union agreements that prevented anyone using a screwdriver unless he has spent five years qualifying and belongs to the screwdrivers' union and likewise, only a qualified member of the spanner users' union is permitted to use a spanner to replace a nut. That is why so many of our 'smoke stack' industries were forced to bite the dust in the era where our blue collar unions were doing their best to sabotage our industrial strength.

One of the main advantages of operating in the small business sector was that you could select the people you employed on an individual basis and you didn't have to deal with unions. But to be successful in running a small business you have to be in sole charge. If you employ somebody you are the customer. You are buying that person's services. If that person's services don't measure up to your requirements, or are no longer needed, then you should be free to terminate that person's contract of employment in accordance with whatever notice period you may have agreed. If one of your employees finds what he thinks is a better job and he is on a notice period of one week or one month or whatever, he will give you that notice and can leave. For the employer, however, employment protection legislation now overrides whatever terms you may have put in the contract, so you are no longer free to terminate it.

Worse still, if you find an employee has his fingers in the till, call him into your office and ask him to explain what you have found and he resigns on the spot, he is then likely to take you to an industrial tribunal for 'constructive dismissal'. You then have to take valuable time away from your business and pay lawyer's fees which are likely to finish well above the maximum payment you could be forced to make of £15,000, so many employers pay the maximum award without fighting the claim. If they do fight they are likely to find themselves at the receiving end of all sorts of totally untrue allegations by the said ex-employees which are reported freely in the national press where the papers are unlikely to report the final outcome of the case.

Industrial tribunals have become kangaroo courts. People of normal, balanced judgment rarely seem to be selected for service on such tribunals. Possibly they have too much else to do. As a result ex-employees who have stolen vast sums of money from their former employers (and I am talking about sums that are often in excess of £50,000) find themselves accused of constructive dismissal. If they take legal action in the High Court they are likely to spend more money than they will recover and find that employees who have been earning vast salaries have been able to claim legal aid. Normal sized small businesses cannot stand this burden. Where the employer uses a lawyer, the average large law firm is so disorganised and useless when it comes to litigation that it will probably consume vast amounts in fees and then louse up the case by some silly mistake. If the employer goes to the police and the Crown Prosecution Service is involved, its reputation has likewise been tarnished by catalogues of silly mistakes resulting from the incompetence of the people it employs.

On a wider front, it has never ceased to astonish me that while quality control in any business depends in the last resort on the ability of the employer to say "do as you are bloody well told or you're fired" and mean it, our recent EU inspired labour laws prevent this. What's more the penalty for being fired needs to be pretty draconian. Traditional discipline in schools and in the forces has been based on similar sanctions such as "if you don't you'll get six of the best" or "I'll put you on jankers".

At the time of writing, the plethora of outrageous judgments from some of our industrial tribunals has become more than a sick joke. A silly woman in Birmingham, or wherever, wins a claim against her employer because he tells her to dress smartly in a skirt for work. If she had applied for a job at the Windmill her terms of contract would have required her to take off her clothes, but the requirement to be smart in the traditionally accepted sense is ruled out of order.

In my book, it is not a question of what an individual thinks is normal or reasonable to wear for work. It's the question of the employer as the man who pays the salary being able to specify what he gets for his money. This should outweigh all other considerations.

We also had a man who wore his hair in a ponytail being refused an interview for a job in a pub and getting compensation. As a customer, I prefer to be served by a man with a proper haircut. As an employer I would never consider recruiting a man with a ring in his nose or in his ear, or a woman with a ring in her nose. People with the type of minds to attire themselves as primitive savages are not the sort of people I would wish to employ. If I am the customer I believe firmly that it is my prerogative to specify the criteria that I apply to the people I choose to hire.

While I was active in my business I did everything to support the body that I referred to as my 'trade union', the Institute of Directors, which, as far as I can see, has been the only body that has been actively representing employers' interests on such matters. The CBI in my book has, in the main, been represented by big company wets who like to cosy up to trade unions. I have often employed in-house lawyers to develop a standard drill for a low cost and efficient procedure for dealing with dismissal cases. Much of this is concerned with building up the paper trail and also applying the right psychological pressure. I have not yet found a firm of solicitors that has organised itself to handle this type of business on a production line basis. I know that this is what Dad would have done, but his firm has long since been absorbed into a mammoth 'conglomerate'.

The merger of law firms into ever larger groups (some with hundreds of partners) means that most of these so-called "partners" have a pretty lowly status. They are scared of taking pre-emptive action on behalf of the client in the fear of putting a foot wrong vis-à-vis their mammoth employing organisations which (in my view) it is totally inappropriate to describe as "partnerships" in the way that Dad's firm was a partnership of independent professionals choosing to work together as a team.

The two other plagues affecting employers in recent years have been so-called race and sex legislation. It would be unusual for anyone to admit to himself, let alone to anyone else, that he is incompetent. The first straw at which he will clutch is to claim that he is being dismissed, or has not been recruited, because he is black, yellow, brown, Italian, Greek, Irish or whatever. Predictably every woman who is dismissed for being incompetent, dishonest or generally stroppy and unpleasant will claim that she was being sexually harassed and men will now do the same if there happens to be a woman in the firm that he can name. I have never quite worked out how a man can be sexually harassed by a woman, but given the perverted dimwits that seem to get appointed to industrial tribunals and who appear to swallow this type of clap-trap, I am not surprised that people try it on.

So, as you can see, I am still a crusader and perfectly willing to champion causes that are, no doubt, as unpopular amongst the general run of employees today as grandma's championship of free advice and free provision of contraceptives for women in the early decades of the 20th Century.

Another area of my crusading zeal in the small company sector has been pensions finance. It has always irritated me that the bulk of the retirement savings generated by small companies, partners in professional practice and sole traders gets siphoned off in the form of premiums to insurance companies, where it tends to get invested in FTSE 100 companies, handed to the government (which is what happens when you buy Government Bonds/Gilts) or in purchase of city centre, skyscraper blocks - instead of being recycled in the small company sector, or in small properties rented to professional firms. Furthermore, many of the insurance companies take a large cut for themselves - sometimes 80% of the first two years' premiums. As a result, small entrepreneurial companies find it desperately difficult to raise capital for what has always been one of the most important sectors in the UK economy, while a continuing flow of pension money has grossly inflated the price of FTSE 100 shares and UK Government Bonds, to produce ridiculously low yields.

I have always had the devil's own job persuading banks and even venture capital companies to invest in the client companies that I have been helping to build, the companies on which the traditional strength of the UK economy has been built and, in many cases, my company has been the sole source of finance. The traditional merchants banks have had it so good in recent years that they are only looking for easy money with big, well established companies and their venture capital arms tend to be staffed by young men who are learning their trade and often behave as if they have just started to wear their first pair of long trousers.

I was fortunate enough to read an article in the Financial Times in 1974 by Dryden Gilling-Smith the managing director of a small, entrepreneurial company of actuaries and consultants in the City of London, who had pioneered the concept of the small self-administered pension scheme where the directors are trustees of their own fund and invest their own money, so I had one of these schemes at an early stage for my company and I persuaded many of my clients to do the same.

EBS Management plc, who pioneered what is known as the SSAS has now got Revenue approval for their SIPP, a similar investment vehicle for partners in professional firms and other self-employed people who often use it to buy their own office buildings, but again the pig-headed Inland Revenue put an embargo on investing in unquoted companies, and yet it is precisely the people who run small businesses who are more likely than anyone else to have a good nose for sniffing out a new business opportunity and who are likely to be good judges of whether the people running the company in which they intend to invest are good, or not - far better judges, in fact, than today's typical bank manager, who seems to be little more than an insurance salesman, or any of the larger venture capital companies.

Unfortunately, the insurance companies fought back to protect their pitch, and, in many cases, have been fobbing clients off with their own brands of SSASs and SIPPs, which are really bogus imitations aimed at siphoning off as much of the money as possible into their own coffers. So you still have to be discriminating and highly sceptical with people who try to persuade you to have one of these schemes to be sure that you have the genuine article, and not a bogus imitation.

ON LOVERS AND MISTRESSES

John feared that I would use this section to treat you to the equivalent of Molly Bloom's monologue at the end of Ulysses. No such luck - for you. Had we been living in the 18th Century what I am going to say would have seemed so self-evident and obvious to most of the people who could read in those days that it would have been unnecessary to write it. Sadly, although we have progressed in the past two hundred years in some spheres of human endeavour so that intelligent teenage girls can look forward to professional careers, combined with the ability to control whether or when they have their children (and I'm including the phenomenal progress made on the treatment of infertility and not just to the invention of the Pill) we have regressed horribly in other areas, so that teenagers are drip-fed pernicious misinformation that can only result in misery and unhappiness in many families whose material comforts otherwise leave little to be desired.

Even if some of my grandchildren's generation may be fortunate enough to have teachers like Mrs. Rainham and Captain Ferrers, who considered the development of a child's critical faculty as the important part of the curriculum, so that we were encouraged never to take anything we might read in a newspaper, hear on the wireless or read in a history book on trust, but always to question the motives of the person who said it, who on earth can aid the development of such critical awareness on sensitive subjects such as love, marriage, extra-marital affairs, etc. except parents if our descendants are not to be left to the mercy of the guidelines they derive from television soaps and agony aunt columns?

Two much publicised newspaper topics are the use of slimline models to sell clothes and the nonsense about the 'glass ceiling'. In my school days when food was in short supply and rationed, no-one talked about slimming. As a well-rounded 'buxom wench', I had plenty of opportunity to observe, or rather feel, the effect I had on most boys who came into orbit, so I would never have had a hang-up about not being slim. When I read reports about unfair dismissal claims by women earning salaries of over £100,000 making themselves miserable because someone has sown in their stupid heads the idea that they are suffering from 'glass ceiling' treatment because they are not earning as much as some of their male colleagues, my only thought is that I'm glad these women were not working for me because if they had been they wouldn't have been working for me for long. Few of us are worth anything near as much as we like to think we are, but if we allow ourselves to think that we're undervalued or underpaid because we are women, then the only harm we do is to ourselves.

Much more pernicious mis-information takes the form of widely publicised results of so-called questionnaires, which the poor girls believe and which anyone who takes the trouble to fill in one knows, are a joke. If bank and insurance employees are asked to fill in questionnaires about salaries they'll all gross up what they get in the hope that a result will show they're horrendously underpaid. When it comes to sex, everyone has a field day. It's an open invitation to indulge one's fantasies. How many times did you do it before you were eighteen? And the results will prove that the underage population of the country was never doing anything else. If some stupid survey asked me to tell them my favourite position I'll answer 'standing up in a hammock' and I'm sure most of the other people who bother to reply treat the whole stupid charade in a similar manner. But the impressionable youngsters who get fed the results of such garbage are easily brain-washed into feeling they are being left on the shelf, and as a result they risk getting hooked up with boys they would never want to know if they were left to follow their own common-sense judgment. It is to give younger readers a meaningful basis of comparison that I've included all the episodes about my teenage fumblings with Jacko.

I've found my openness in discussing such matters, first with my daughters and then with my granddaughters has helped them to talk more freely about their worries without feeling guilty. Once they could get it into their minds that their old gran had once been a lecherous, impish teenager and hasn't changed much since, I think they've been more ready to take on board some of my practical tips, which is as much as any parent or grandparent could hope for. At the younger ages it is usually no more than a simplistic "Don't do it unless you desperately want to i.e. not just to please him. If that's all he wants let him take a running jump... there are lots more where that one came from and, if you do, insist he uses a Frenchie, even if you're on the Pill... he might look innocent but that doesn't mean he may not be infected."

If a few more mothers, grandmothers and women teachers spoke in this kind of hardboiled language and started to do so early enough, they might stand a better chance of being taken seriously. I may not be in the same league as Peggy, but she has always been my model of how to put it across.

An even more difficult task faces you mums, grans and supposedly more experienced women friends once the girls you are trying to help are married, or have otherwise set up home with a man. The temptation is to stoke the flames of righteous indignation if the man in question hasn't lived up to expectations, rather than trying to get your listener to come to terms with the way of the world. I have to thank Mum for getting me to understand, at an early age, that however much a man loves you, he will, after the first few months or years, inevitably get hooked by the prospect of a bit on the side and the real skill in running your marriage is in preventing the bit on the side getting ideas above her station, or at any rate putting them into practice. Part of the art of managing a successful marriage is knowing when to turn a blind eye, knowing how to give your man an honourable line of retreat so that if one of his floozies starts a bit of blackmail, you can laugh the whole thing off together and give him the confidence to follow the Duke of Wellington's example and say 'publish and be damned', or words to that effect.

One of the most tragic and all too frequent occurrences in the lives of the men and women I meet in my business and social life has been the unnecessary destruction of an apparently secure and stable family routine, by either a husband or wife suffering from a surfeit of righteous indignation at the peccadilloes of the other and living miserably ever after, whilst never wishing to admit it either to themselves or anyone else. What they all needed was someone to take them by the scruff of the collar and teach them the importance of fitting shock absorbers and also telling them something of gentle art of damage limitation. Just as our troops during the war were sent over assault courses to help them face the realities of their first battle, someone ought to devise a suitable training plan for wives who will, sooner or later, have to cope with scheming women who want to nick their husbands for keeps.

EPILOGUE - THE TESTAMENT OF BOADIE

As you can see, my own brand of reforming ardour is aimed at increasing the sum of human happiness, not only for the many husbands and wives who suffer unnecessary misery as a result of a failure to come to terms with the way of the world, but also for the far larger number of children who suffer the consequences of broken homes as they grow up and are deprived of helpful role models when their turn comes to lay the foundations of a successful family life for themselves and their children. Like anyone who indulges in polemic, I am guilty of exaggeration. In the hope of being taken more seriously in the debate, I have hinted on one or two occasions about my extra-marital dalliance and this may have led some of you to expect that my next volume will be something akin to the adventures of a latter-day Fanny Hill. No such luck - for you. There won't be another volume.

Nevertheless, I have to come clean, even if this means disappointing you by explaining that I only departed from the straight and narrow on two occasions, in what I thought was a modest and harmless way. What is more, most of this happened after the age at which the Inland Revenue permit you to take early retirement, but more of the circumstances anon. Nevertheless, I have always been mindful of the fact that, had I lived in certain countries in the past, or even today, even in the United States, in the period described by Nathaniel Hawthorne, I could have been made to stand in the pillory with a large A for adulteress hung around my neck - as the poor girl in the Scarlet Letter accused of doing far less than I did, and from all accounts she was innocent.

Since my days as a High School Sixth Former I have always felt it relevant to see my own life and doings in the context of a historical backcloth and this has helped me to gain a perspective which has stood me in good stead in understanding the world as I think it is seen by my grandchildren's generation.

One of my other pet irritations in recent years has been the apparent failure of many of my grandchildren's generation and of High Court judges to understand the value of what we used to refer to as 'slap and tickle' as a safety valve for dealing with men on heat. I've given plenty of examples, both in Chapter 12 and Chapter 23, of the sort of high jinks our boys used to get up to and how some of them were pretty unpleasant if you were one of the girls paying a forfeit in some of their silly games, or being pawed in the dark by a drunken oaf with bad breath, but we never seemed to have the cases of rape or serious assault such as now seem to fill many of our newspapers.

We didn't have all the nonsense of women getting up in the law courts claiming harassment for happenings that we regarded as part of the normal give and take. As Mum used to say, you can't expect to have men who will act like Lotharios in the bedchamber and spend the rest of the time behaving like eunuchs. Even Jean, who seldom expresses strong opinions on anything, can get very angry when she reads press accounts of young naval officers being court-martialled for behaving in the traditional manner with some of the Wrens who volunteered to serve at sea.

"Do we no longer want to recruit sailors who will win battles? With this sort of regime we would have court-martialled Nelson for larking about before he had the chance to fire any shots at the French in the Battle of the Nile, let alone Trafalgar. If they want to take girls to sea, they should make sure they recruit a sprinkling of randy minxes who know what to expect from a sailor and are unlikely to object."

I've had a number of reasons for wanting to bang the drum on this somewhat hobby-horse-ical topic of mine. To start with, I have always believed that the ideal to which every husband and wife should aspire is lifelong faithfulness. What has always got me angry in the extreme has been the holier than thou posturing, whether it be of politicians, the press, television or of anybody else.

There are a lot of things that I shouldn't do. I drink too much. I eat too much. I exceed the speed limits. I never seem to stop having lecherous thoughts. In this I don't think I differ significantly from most other human beings. I like to think that if my failings in this direction have not caused serious hurt to anyone else, that they are minor peccadilloes and would be absolved for minimal penance if I were a Catholic and went to confession.

I share what I understood at the time to be Father Wakehurst's view that the real sins that afflict the world are the evil that men and women do to each other out of hatred, or for other reasons. In my own work experience the most common and detestable evil that I had to cope with almost every day of the week was character assassination. In virtually every business in which I have been involved there have been people ready to stick the knife into their colleagues, either because they want their jobs or they are jealous because the other person is more intelligent, more hard-working, more attractive, etc. I am usually quick to sense the drip, drip, drip of the poison (in some cases great subtlety and sophistication is used - in other cases none).

I like to think that I have been gifted with a sixth sense in enabling me to identify the poisoner for what he or she is, but I can't be sure. What I do know is that the number of careers that I have seen blighted, often accompanied by soul-destroying breakdown in morale of the victim, having disastrous consequences on his or her marriage and family life and my blood really boils when I hear this sort of poisoner (and there is no other word for it) criticising an honest, hard-working minister (as he then was) such as Cecil Parkinson because he had the misfortune to spend a few moments in bed with someone other than his wife and this fact was publicised in the newspapers. I hold similar views of assassins, muggers and burglars. Fortunately (for me that is) I have lived in a safer world, but my experience of poisoners has been enough and, fortunately, I have survived, although my company has no doubt lost a number of worthwhile clients who did not have the perspicacity to recognise the poisoners amongst my would-be competitors.

A fact that I have often remarked in my study of history is that some of our best monarchs have also been some of the least inhibited when it comes to dalliance in female company. There may be no correlation, but if we take Henry I, Charles II and Edward VII, the evidence is interesting. Henry I was, from all accounts, the king who knocked England into shape after the Norman Conquest. He appeared to be successful in establishing the rule of law, respect for authority and having married a native of these islands, achieved a remarkable reconciliation between the natives and the Norman invaders. From all accounts he had twelve illegitimate children by different women and acknowledged them all, which suggests that he probably passed agreeable moments with other women who were either married or who didn't give birth as a result of his dalliance.

Everyone knows about Charles II's many mistresses and those of you who remember any of the history you learnt at school, probably know he was the only Stewart monarch who knew how to run the country, minimise civil strife, provide conditions which enabled the economy to recover after a disastrous civil war and move to what we would now call boom times. We, likewise, know about the diplomatic skills of Edward the Caresser and how everyone generally believed that World War I would have been avoided had he still been around in 1914.

My favourite example is my own biblical hero from childhood days, King David the shepherd boy. He was born hundreds of years after Moses had given the Jews the Ten Commandments, which included "Thou shalt not commit adultery" and yet he had vast numbers of wives and hundreds of mistresses which the Bible refers to as concubines. We never read about God being angry with him for any of this. We read that God was angry with him because he took a fancy to Bathsheba and deliberately sent her husband on a dangerous military escapade where there was a high risk of his being killed (as he was). It was the abuse of the kingly power to cause the unnecessary death of a loyal servant of the crown so that David could thereby profit, that was the reason that God was angry with him, but even so David was forgiven to the point where Solomon, the son born to him by Bathsheba, succeeded to the throne and, as king, received God's blessing.

Whether it is my historical perspective, or the way I was brought up, I have always found it difficult to come to terms with the holier than thou attitudes of so many of my contemporaries towards occasional lapses of marital fidelity. Mum's attitude towards Dad's occasional philandering (I can't believe it amounted to much) was the attitude that (in my view) any sensible wife ought to adopt - or sensible husband for that matter. I keep coming back to my favourite metaphor that however well you eat at home, you occasionally like a meal out and the important thing is not to get food poisoning.

If I think back to my childhood days when I watched Marianne, a matronly grandmother who was probably not far short of sixty, enjoying siesta time sex each afternoon with Georges, who may have been fifteen to twenty years younger, and remember what a lovely woman she was in every way and how well disposed she was towards all the children and adults with whom she came into contact, I am sure there must be a correlation between these different sides of her life. I'm sure her husband, the postman, never suffered as a result of her extra-marital enjoyment. I'm sure she would have been more than enthusiastic to do the same with him whenever he wanted as she did with Georges and that he benefited from her lovely disposition towards all humankind.

Our Lord's treatment of the poor woman taken in adultery who was being made a scapegoat by that bunch of lecherous, old hypocrites is one of the most moving passages in the New Testament and I have loved it for as long as I understood what it was all about. Even when I didn't understand the nature of her supposed "transgression" I loved it for its compassion - how could a woman like that have done anything wicked in the real sense of the word!

What is so galling in our present Godless world is the spectacle of any irreligious Tom, Dick or Harry, be it in the popular press or television, talking in the name of a public morality that can have no validity unless it is placed in a clearly defined religious context. People who deny that England is a Christian country anymore are, nevertheless, ready to apply moral condemnation to someone who has not broken any civil laws. Adultery and fornication are not civil crimes. Even the Victorians, who were much more broadminded than many people now care to admit, applied practical good sense to the way they behaved in a number of ways. For example, it was unforgivable for a gentleman to 'trifle with' an unmarried lady (because she might produce a child that would not have a father), whereas married ladies were considered capable of deciding for themselves whether or not they were happy to be 'trifled with', as many of them were, and hence the Lily Langtrys and vast numbers of others who were neither literally nor socially stoned to death but were, on the contrary, publicly admired.

Having beaten the drum fairly loudly on one of my favourite themes, I will revert to the small world of my own private life. I have told you what I got up to with Jacko eighteen months after David's death, in fact during the three university vacations that I spent at home before I met John. After John and I married I don't think either of us trifled with anyone else for the next twenty-six years, by which time the youngest of our four children was over sixteen and was more precocious and liberated in such matters than I had been.

The catalyst (in my view) in our lives came when Wendy, a scheming young lecturer in John's department, began to see her professional boss (John) as a potentially useful stepping stone and got to work on him. Like many men in their fifties, John no doubt found the admiration of a young female exhilarating. Illusions of recovering his long-lost youth were, no doubt, filling his imagination. John could have spent as many nights and afternoons in bed with Wendy as he liked without giving me the least cause for concern, but my antennae told me that that wasn't what she wanted. She was, nevertheless, too stupid to realise that if she had destroyed John's marriage she would have destroyed him, destroyed his position and probably her own into the bargain. I loved and love John too much to sit back and let this happen.

I'm not exaggerating. John and I are people who would give our lives for each other as we both would for any of our children. I've always found it difficult to comprehend the apparent failure on the part of many people to distinguish between the way you view a husband or wife for whom you are prepared to die and the way you view someone with whom you would enjoy the prospect of a few hours amorous dalliance between the sheets, assuming of course that there would be no adverse physical or social consequences.

Fortunately, my sixth sense and other powers of observation enabled me to spot and take pre-emptive action before John could do anything silly. I did what I am sure Mum would have done and found him a much more attractive mistress. Obviously, I took a risk in trusting Myra, but it was a case of nothing ventured, nothing gained and she turned up trumps. I knew her reputation as a vampish female, but I had done her the odd good turn so I told her what I wanted her to do and invited her for the weekend. I don't think many men of John's temperament could have resisted all those glimpses of black, lacy underwear as she kept throwing herself back on to the settee and she was probably less inhibited than normal, knowing that I had given her the green light. This experience (and that of Mum) has formed the basis of the view that every wife should make it her job to find a suitable mistress for her husband if she is to keep him out of the clutches of something worse, but mistresses should not be allowed to get ideas above their station.

The experience, however, did take its toll in terms of my own adrenalin, involved a lot of play-acting on my part and I, no doubt, convinced myself in the process that the odd bit on the side was a normal and natural feature of a successful, long-term marriage. As a result I was presumably much more conditioned to opportunities that might come my way than might otherwise have been the case, a feeble excuse but I can't think of a better one. As the pert Isabella put it (talking about a husband she had not yet married) in John Dryden's 1670s comedy 'The Wild Gallant': "Why, if he play truant with the sword, I can play truant with the scabbard."

My opportunity took the form of an urbane and amiable finance director, Douglas, of a company that was planning to make a take-over offer to one of my client companies (in which I had a substantial investment). I thought the offer was fair, but I was obviously hoping to push it up a bit more and so I was being given the red carpet treatment at their corporate headquarters, which involved an overnight stay in a luxury country house hotel that they used for much of their corporate hospitality.

Douglas was my host for dinner at a time when his wife was enjoying the Summer in their holiday home near Cannes. There was a small dance floor and unobtrusive, romantic music and when another couple took to the floor we joined them.
When he escorted me to my room we could have kissed goodnight in the corridor and he would have been too polite to come in unless I had made an appropriate gesture, but as soon as the door was closed I was the one who was rediscovering my distant youth.

For any woman knocking on fifty, this type of experience can work wonders as long as it doesn't have any adverse consequences. Douglas was not a young man - in fact three years older than I. It was the delicacy of his touch as he undressed me and kissed me all over my body that worked wonders. No matter how often your husband does it, you are subconsciously unsure of whether it is part habit or whether he is seeing you as you once were and not as you are, but when it is someone new coming to you for the first time - need I say more?

Douglas and I had a number of similar trysts over the next twelve years, not very often and, fortunately, with no adverse consequences on his family life or on mine. I've mentioned in an earlier chapter how I came to cater regularly for his particular fetish based on his imagined, or real, wartime affair with a Wren by putting on black stockings, etc. when we were due to meet, but over and above the question of having an affair we each had a lot to offer and I am sure we benefited and were pleasanter to people in our dealings with our respective families. I always think of Marianne when I remember these moments in my own life and I hope you can understand why I have never felt guilty and why I hope St. Peter will not treat such departures from the straight and narrow as a reason for refusing me admittance to the Kingdom of Heaven.

My other departure from the straight and narrow was of a similar kind, except that Roger (the gentleman in question) was a widower and the affair ceased when he remarried. I did, in fact, do my best to persuade him not to put his second marriage at risk and he accepted my view that prudence was of the essence at this critical period in his adjustment to a new life.

In due course John found he couldn't keep what he felt was his guilty secret about Myra, so we had a heart to heart. I told John what I have just told you. Charles and Roger are, of course, fictitious names for people totally outside our family circle, and it would have been surprising if John had met either of them. I could not have included the previous paragraphs if I had not first had the opportunity to be open on the subject with John.

What I have tried to explain in this sub-section of my epilogue is that a life-long intensity of feeling for one person can co-exist, and I am sure does co-exist in many other people apart from me, with everyday lecherous appetites. Men have traditionally been less inhibited in admitting this, whether they queue up at the Windmill or the Folies Bergere or are (according to Mum) like Dad, always on the watch for a glimpse of stocking top (and sometimes more) on a windy day. With me it has always been much more tactile (one of the reasons why I am so fond of the dance floor), but also unplanned and spontaneous.

Although you may think this is a special pleading on the part of a woman in her mid-seventies, I would like to repeat my plea for greater tolerance of the odd bit on the side by those oldies who have the good sense to try and keep their marriages intact. Potency and desires can, and often do, decline much more rapidly in one or other party to a marriage. Above all we should not deprive ourselves of the services of able people in public positions by forcing cabinet ministers, Bank of England directors, senior staff officers, etc. to resign because the press has published the story of his dalliance with a woman who had taken his fancy. Jean's example of Nelson is as good as any and I'm sure Arrière would have been most upset if good King Edward the Caresser had been forced to abdicate or denied the throne in the first place because of his string of mistresses. There's nothing wrong with a man having a mistress, as long as he doesn't leave his wife to marry her.

DISTORTION OF HISTORY

Among the everyday irritations suffered by those of us who lived through the war years and knew what was going on, are the many and varied attempts to distort, in fact to change out of all recognition, the chronicle of what took place from 1939-45. I've already mentioned the way in which the brutal and barbaric treatment which the Japanese meted out to Europeans has been 'forgotten' and replaced by unwarranted criticism of the allies for dropping atomic bombs on Japan, but there are many other ways in which the events of those years are constantly misrepresented.

English men and women (at least I assume they were) have ignominiously attacked the memory of 'Bomber' Harris, the head of bomber command, for the mass destruction of certain German cities, involving the death of many innocent German civilians for which he was responsible. None of us at the time (at least in my recollection) hated Germans as individuals and had any wish to see innocent German women and children killed. We recognised that most of the German soldiers were conscripts who had no choice but to fight wherever they were sent and we had no wish to see them killed or maimed.

But we were fighting a war for our survival. The Germans had bombed London, Plymouth, Coventry and vast numbers of other cities. Military leaders had to make decisions in the heat of the moment and a lot of those decisions may have been wrong ones in the light of what we now know and understand, but we all make mistakes. I have never berated anyone working for me who had to act quickly in a crisis and got it wrong, as long as I had confidence that he was acting according to his best judgment in the light of his knowledge at the time. Even if I might have acted differently I've always known damned well that there are plenty of other ways in which I could have got it wrong.

Bomber Harris didn't know that his thousand bomber raids were having far less effect in damaging the German war machine than he believed. The Germans clearly believed that they could knock us out by bombing and it was not unreasonable for us to believe that we could shorten the war significantly by our raids on Germany, otherwise there would not have been a bomber command and we would not have bombed anything. Harris was appointed to make a thorough job of organising the bombing and people are now attacking him and throwing paint on his statue precisely because he did make a thorough job of it.

I've heard a great deal of first hand testimony from people who were trembling in cellars and air-raid shelters in occupied Europe to the effect that the RAF was remarkably accurate in its attacks on many military targets, such as port installations used by the Germans as pens for their U-boats. Of course, a lot of bombs fell wide of the mark and, of course, we missed a lot of targets, but we were fighting a war where there is bound to be a tremendous amount of hit and miss. If you are flying in the dark over a strange country which you have never known by day, where you are constantly at risk from anti-aircraft fire and enemy fighters, I challenge you to get it right every time.

I have already made the point that the Germans behaved honourably in many respects, notably in their treatment of prisoners of war. Of course there were exceptions. Prisoners were shot in cold blood without provocation, but if the Germans hadn't observed the Geneva Convention for much of the time John would never have survived the war. Among the military professionals on both sides there was mutual respect. In later life John and I have met some of his captors. It is probably fair to say that the professional soldiers on the German side who were serving their country in what they believed to be a patriotic war, behaved correctly. I have even been told by people living in occupied France, who had every reason to hate the Germans who were occupying their country, that in 1940 they were well disciplined and there was no looting or attacks on individuals. Even the women were not forced to have sex with their captors, although many in fact did so voluntarily or for money. It was in the later years, when most of the German fighting forces that were any good had been transferred to the Russian front, that most of the atrocities were committed by the riff raff. It was as if the Germans had been emptying their prisons and recruiting the gangsters from their equivalent of the Gorbels that most of the atrocities took place.

It is not the professional historians with whom I take issue. I have, in fact, been extremely grateful to historians such as Sir John Keegan for his Histories of World War I and World War II, in addition to his Six Armies in Normandy and to Peter Padfield for his War Under The Sea. For obvious reasons, we knew nothing at the time about our breaking of the enigma code. We had no means of knowing the way the Germans were planning their strategy and their points of weakness. We did not know at the time how we nearly lost the war as a result of the success of German U-boat strategy and that the German failure to win resulted much more from the crass stupidity of their high command in the pre-war days in building what were considered to be prestigious battleships instead of building more U-boats and training more U-boat crews, when they already knew from World War I that the U-boat had proved to be their most powerful naval weapon.

One historian to whom I am particularly grateful is the former Chancellor of the Exchequer, Roy Jenkins. In his book on The Chancellors he has published the evidence to show that Churchill was far less to blame for putting Britain onto the gold standard when he was Chancellor of the Exchequer in 1925 than was previously known. Churchill was, of course, ultimately responsible and in the 'Gathering Storm' in which he describes the various factors that resulted in World War II, he showed himself a big enough man to apologise for the biggest mistake he ever made. Imposition of a fixed gold parity impoverished British public finances so much that we had to cut our defence forces to the point where we ceased to be an effective world power. We could no longer be the commercial dynamo of Europe and the resulting mass poverty and starvation made it much easier for political gangsters (of whatever label) to gather support and seize power.

What the chapter on Churchill in Roy Jenkins' book shows is that Churchill was not as stupid and ignorant about financial matters as he later pretended.

He pursued the case against the gold standard with great vigour and determination. He had the Treasury mandarins and Montague Norman, the then governor of the Bank of England, against him and when he tried to drum up support from the supposed financial guru of the day, John Maynard Keynes, it was Keynes who let him down, proving to be something of a wet reed who was good at telling people after the event where he thought they had gone wrong, but was not the sort of person to put in any top job where decisions have to be made on the hoof. There are plenty of people like that and the only thing they can be guaranteed to do is to let you down at the critical moment.

Before we leave distortions in what is (for me) recent history, I must include some reference to the way World War II has been, and is often caricatured (and there is no other word for it) as a private feud between a criminal lunatic (Adolf Hitler) and the Jews. Adolf Hitler on his own could have done nothing much to harm either the Jews or anybody else. I believe that, sadly, there are numbers of people in the world today and always have been, like Adolf Hitler. It doesn't matter what political creed they claim to subscribe to. If they are clever they'll make it sound plausible. In essence they are people who have caused a lot of unnecessary suffering in the world.

Adolf Hitler could have done no great harm unless he had been sufficiently talented in his own perverse way to become head of state in a country with a strong military tradition and to enable that state to assemble, mobilise and motivate one of the most powerful armies that has ever existed in recorded history. In the end the Allies beat the Germans because we were able to mobilise millions more men and have the economic resources to manufacture and put into the field vastly superior numbers of tanks and aircraft, so we should not be complacent in terms of thinking that we were better fighters. Our own front-line people knew this and made no bones about it.

In essence it was the British Empire fighting the German Empire and we were fortunate in having the United States and Russia (both of whom had been attacked whilst we had not) fighting on our side. The Germans only turned against Hitler once they realised the tide had turned and they were going to lose the war.

The Jews suffered, but so did vast numbers of other people. What all of us, of whatever nation or creed, find horrendous is the idea of large numbers of innocent people being murdered en-masse and I distinguish here between the killing of innocent people which may be a consequence of a military operation (as when an enemy city is bombed to knock out its manufacturing capacity) and mass murder for its own sake.

In moral terms, whether the numbers killed this way were a hundred, a thousand, a million or six million, this type of mass murder horrifies every normal person. So does the cold blooded murder by the Russians of the Poles at Katyn. What annoyed me and many others was the cowardly and dishonest way successive British governments (everyone blames the Foreign Office) refused to admit that the Russians were guilty of the Katyn massacre, in spite of all the available evidence. Arguments about how many people were killed in these various massacres have always seemed to me as disrespectful and unpleasant as a family that bursts into loud-mouthed disputes where one of their own nearest and dearest is being lowered into the grave.

Professor Bullock's monumental book, Hitler and Stalin, has given me a better perspective than any other history of the period showing that these two were ordinary people and that, sadly, there are lots more like them in the world. He also shows that the destruction that each of them wreaked on vast numbers of their fellow human beings was based on their ability to harness modern technology in aid. Modern technology in the hands of criminal lunatics is the main problem with which we now have to deal and we should be concentrating our energies on the current perpetrators and potential perpetrators of destruction, people like the IRA, Animal Rights fanatics and some of the Islamic bomb throwers and assassins to name but a few.

We shouldn't be wasting our time putting octogenarians on show trials for things that happened over fifty-five years ago where we are merely likely to come unstuck and make the process of justice ridiculous. All I am concerned to do as regards the past is to ensure that future generations have a record that gives them a correct perspective on the most significant world shake-up since the French Revolution.

I pin the blame for many of the distortions (some of which I would call perversions) of our historical record on the way our academic system has evolved. In days gone by, university lecturers were assessed in large measure by their peers on whether they did a good job teaching undergraduates. If they produced one or two good research papers, well and good. If they had the gift of narrative and could pull together the relevant research covering a whole period they would become household names in schools and universities for many years to come. I have mentioned Professor Bullock's magnum opus on Hitler and Stalin. In my school days one of the big names was H.A.L. Fisher whose History of Europe was a must for all Sixth Form historians. Academic promotion now seems to depend much more on the ability of a young lecturer to 'fly a kite'. He feels impelled to produce some revolutionary interpretation in a book that will get him noticed in the popular press. Such people have nothing in common with the great academic names of my own period at university, who were in the main modest and humble men with a sense of responsibility towards their students. They were there to serve and not mere operators using public relations techniques to get themselves known by using their subject as a footstool to promote some new, gimmicky and no doubt shocking, interpretation of the past, which they know will be out of date within a few months when it is overtaken by the next operator keen to promote the idea that a great general or statesman of the past was, in reality, a 'no-gooder', was either a queer or beat his wife or did something unsavoury in his private life.

These operators not only confuse the public who may have minimal knowledge of the subject in question, but can also have serious negative effects on their students. As an example I quote one of William's business friends who studied history at a new provincial university, where the professor was a communist and made his students spend virtually all their time on the French and Russian revolutions and the only way they could hope to get good marks was to churn out his opinions, however much they might disagree with them. I would have disapproved of this professor whatever his particular politics. My complaint was that he was using his subject as a footstool, if not for his own personal advancement, then for the advancement of something with which he had identified. He did not see himself as a man whose integrity depended on his ability to help his students towards a genuine understanding of the events of the past.

THE SPIRITUAL/RELIGIOUS DIMENSION OF MY LIFE

If this sub-title sounds pretentious then I apologise. As I hope I have shown at each point in my life story where it has been relevant, I have always felt my Christian beliefs to be a natural part of me, although my understanding of what I have believed has evolved, as I have evolved. I used to think of myself as a conventional member of the Church of England, as it was in my childhood days and I was probably not very different from Mum and Dad and their friends, but with the passage of time I have become increasingly aware of the fact that I am no longer typical of anything. Nobody is.

For one thing, few people now seem to come out of school with much biblical knowledge. On top of this, I am the kind of person who thinks for much of the time about why I am on earth and I am probably more articulate and forthright than many in what I say about this part of my life, as I have been in other areas of intense personal feeling.

If I had a spiritual crisis in my life it was in the period following David's death. The belief that I shall one day be reunited with David has held me together for the rest of my life. I was particularly fortunate in having the wonderful support of Father Wakehurst, in addition to Mum and those friends who were close to me. I have said on many occasions that the church is only as good as the priest or minister who is the first point of contact of any member of his flock.

This brings me to my next point. I never felt myself as being denominational. I tended to regard Catholics, Methodists, Baptists, etc. as no different from those who went to any other Anglican church. Since my school days, I have recognised that if you don't have institutional continuity there would be no-one to train the priesthood. As a Sixth Form historian I had to write the standard essay on the theme that the Church of England under Henry VIII was "Catholic without the Pope" and I believed this until I had closer contact with a number of Catholic priests and theologians and learnt more about the differences. Nevertheless, I have seen the Catholic church change enormously in England in the last fifty years, just as the Anglican church has changed. It is easy, therefore, to see how any organisation that sub-divided nearly five hundred years ago will see different bits going different ways.

I have become much closer to the Catholic church following the conversion of both my sons when they married Catholic wives. I believe that most of the problems of religious feuding in the past stem not from religion but from power. If any institution, including a church, acquires too much power, it attracts the wrong sort of people. I still sense (but I may be wrong) part of this power syndrome in countries like Italy and Ireland, but I am only talking about individuals whom I have met and not about the general run of priests.

In one sense I would like to see the Christian churches in England moving back together. In theory, it is better to have a church independent of the state, so that we don't have bishops nominated by whichever prime minister happens to be in power but, as the Catholic historian Lord Acton stated, "All power tends to corrupt and absolute power corrupts absolutely."

This is what I think happened to the Catholic church just prior to the Reformation when people like the Borgias and an illegitimate Medici were becoming Popes. I am still horrified when I think of the Inquisition, as I always do when I listen to one of my favourite operas, Don Carlos.

In the present world I think the biggest mistake of a succession of recent Popes has been to become involved in the question of contraception. What on earth has this topic to do with the Christian religion? The only explanation I have ever been able to give myself is that unmarried male clergy in countries where the Church has too much power tend to think they know everything in areas where they may have no special competence. Perhaps some unmarried clergy resent the joys of married life from which they are excluded. This would not happen if they were allowed to marry, as they were during the first eleven hundred years of the Christian era. I put the Church's attitude to contraception on a part with the Church's condemnation in days gone by of people like Galileo and Copernicus and I believe even Harvey was condemned for propounding his thesis on the circulation of blood. Priests had no business to start pontificating on astronomy or the understanding of medical diagnoses and I can see no reason why they should start interfering with what husbands and wives do together in bed. M.Y.O.B.

Fortunately, the Catholic church, like the Church of England, has its share of humane and enlightened priests who will not follow the party line if their conscience and intelligent judgment tells them it is wrong. When my daughter-in-law, Sue (William's wife), was an undergraduate at Cambridge 1968-71, she (as a Catholic from childhood) regularly attended Mass and other functions at the Catholic chaplaincy. The priest in charge was quite open in advising his student parishioners that birth control was a matter for individual judgment and that the doctrine of papal infallibility was restricted to matters of theological belief. He went on to say that it is important for Christian parents to limit the size of their families if this enables them to bring up their children properly. I think he also had a letter published in the Times to this effect.

Churches, however, can only be expected to recruit priests with similar education backgrounds and independent powers of judgment to the people whom they serve. English priests, of whatever Christian denomination, who enjoyed the benefits or the type of education that I enjoyed, where you were taught to think for yourself and apply independent judgment, and English parishioners of a similar ilk, will have the ability to see what is important, without feeling the need to take on board the unnecessary baggage that inevitably creeps in to what people believe. Unfortunately, the inhabitants of primitive countries served by a priesthood drawn from people of their own kind, are more likely to have the presentation of Christian religion absorbed into an amalgam of autocratic prohibitions. In fact, I have known places where the priest has been perceived as something of a witchdoctor who can put a curse on people. This means that the minority who succeed in acquiring financial independence with the aid of a western education will tend to look down on Christianity as a primitive superstition.

My concern about the state of religious affairs in England today is that many intelligent children are being unnecessarily deprived of a major source of spiritual strength, on which I have depended throughout my life and which has kept me from going under at certain critical moments, as when I received the news of David's death. Even with my limited knowledge of Latin I was able to understand that the word 're-ligio' means to bind back. Instead of your mind being pulled apart by a lot of unrelated, stand-alone (and sometimes fanatical) beliefs, you have a system to pull everything together, to bind all your beliefs back to a single underlying concept of reality.

It used to be said in the American prohibition period of the 1920s that if you pushed Bacchus out through the front door he will come back in by breaking the window and cause havoc, which is what happened. Likewise, if the population at large rejects formal Christian religion it quickly becomes a prey to every charlatan who tries his hand at conning Joe Public. I remember Dad and Mum talking (in the 1930s) about one of their friends (who should have known better) who apparently played a key role in the local Theosophist lodge and who spoke in hushed tones about Madame Blavatsky's Secret Doctrine, prominently displayed in a locked, glass-fronted bookcase in his lounge. T. S. Eliot wrote a wonderful book about the modern heresies of the period "After Strange Gods" which ought to be reprinted in paperback and widely read. The prize, however, has to go to Noel Coward for his marvellous film, Blithe Spirit.

In later years Mum used to tell me how she was once invited to a house where her hosts were planning to sit round the table in the dark with a medium who would produce one knock for yes, two knocks for no, etc., etc. Mum, to her credit, got up and left as soon as she saw what they intended, not because she regarded them as stupid kids, but because she firmly believed it was morally wrong and dangerous to dabble in such matters.

Today, Joe Public is subjected to a different menace. It is the promotion of so-called "moral imperatives" that are not bound back to any underlying Christian belief. The religious fervour of the anti-hunting lobby, or the anti-fur coat lobby and some of the so-called anti-discrimination lobbies shares some of the fanaticism implicit in the way the communists would harness 'moral fervour' to mount attacks on minority groups as 'enemies of the people', and likewise the way the nazis operated. I tend to see all attempts to mobilise moral fervour without the essential discipline and control of a properly constituted Christian Church as Gadarene swine movements. The devil will take possession and ultimately drive them to self-destruction, but in the meantime they will have destroyed all the people who have been unfortunate enough to be trodden under foot in one of their periodic stampedes. Examples in our own time of the innocent victims who have been unfortunate enough to be identified in some demon dogma as public enemies were the Kulaks in Stalin's Russia and the Jews in Hitler's 'greater Germany'.

INSIDIOUS COLLECTIVISM

The defeat of Hitler's Germany and the collapse of communist Russia have not liberated us from the threats of various forms of dictatorship which have, no doubt, existed throughout history. I do, however, discern in many aspects of our present national and international life, a menacing, anti-democratic tendency which, in my mind, contrasts sharply with the fervent belief that most of us shared during the war years, that if you had to have a government to provide an army to defend your homeland, a police force, a fair legal system, roads, etc. (things which we all knew we needed - except of course the genuine anarchists, of whom there were few) then the democratic system for all its faults, was a lesser evil, or potential evil, than all the other systems of government that had ever been tried and that we knew about.

In Sixth Form History we all had to write essays about benevolent, rational absolutism when we were studying 18th Century European history and they nearly always finished with the view that people like Frederick the Great were not, in fact, all that benevolent, nor particularly rational, although there was no doubt about their possessing absolute power in their own kingdoms by the standards of the time. Given that the machinery by which they could control their subjects was primitive and amateurish when compared with the mechanism and control that could be exercised by the proverbial 'big brother' in George Orwell's 1984, we have a lot more to fear from present day absolutism.

By democracy we didn't mean simplistic ballot box totalitarianism, but the sort of constitution we had in England where there was a balance of power between kings, lords and commons. One of the positive side effects of the war was that schools of the type I went to devoted a lot more time, both in history and in current affairs period, to constitutional matters and I don't think any of my grandchildren (even those who have attended good, Independent Schools) have had anything like this grounding. We learned that there was trouble whenever one leg of this three-legged stool got too big and powerful and Joe Public would not have a comfortable seat. In the Wars of the Roses it was the over-mighty lords or barons with their armies of retainers that had become too powerful. Then it was the king. Now it is the commons, but in practice the clique that controls the party currently controls the commons. I'm, therefore, concerned whenever attacks are made on the diminishing prerogatives of the crown and when even Prince Philip and Prince Charles are attacked for voicing basic common-sense opinions which are, in fact, shared by a large number of Englishmen and women. I was particularly annoyed at the abolition of the right of hereditary peers to vote in the House of Lords because, as I have said in an earlier chapter, it is ridiculous in a country that puts a high value on the hereditary principle when it comes to breeding horses and dogs to pretend that it is unimportant when it comes to human beings.

Collectivism has always been a mechanism used by those seeking to gain power over other people. It is perfectly harmless and normal in many areas of life. We need each other and in a normal family a father and mother will exercise power over their children, but this is usually blended in an amalgam of power and love and as the children grow up, parental power will virtually disappear. I am, of course, talking about family life in England as I have known it and not that in more primitive parts of the world where children are forced into loveless marriages. Headmasters and Headmistresses exercise power in schools, but it is only for a short period of time and, to the extent that parents are customers who pay fees and have a choice, this power is limited to what is reasonable. I have already mentioned the constraints that operate on the exercise of power by government because we are born as subjects of the king or queen of our country.

In addition to the normal family, school, work and national loyalties which bind us together, most of us can be classified like products in a supermarket in a host of different ways, according to the nature of the department store in which we are on display. I am, for example, a semi-retired English business woman in her seventies, who also happens to be a grandmother, a motorist, who is no doubt overweight, has highbrow tastes in music and literature, goes to church (C of E) and so on. All these things are useful bits of information for someone deciding whether to include me in a mail shot in the hope that he might be able to sell me something that I want to buy, but that's where the uses of such classification should end.

It is the politically intrusive and not the normal uses of such classifications to which I object. For example, if I recruit someone to work for me, the fact that the candidate may be a he or a she is of minimal importance in comparison with my assessment of that person's character, integrity and a whole lot of other personal characteristics, which your sixth sense (if you've got one) takes in when you speak to, listen to or just sit with a person. You are trying to identify what the Greeks referred to as the God in that person.

I would be extremely angry if someone tried to tell me I should employ a given quota of men and women, which is what I get when I read reports of a political party saying it wants x-percent of its MPs to be women. There are, of course, many jobs where there is the probability that a man or woman will be better suited to a particular job, but there will always be exceptions. For example, the daughter of one of my friends recently employed a man as a child nanny, but this is beside the point.

My objection is to outside governmental or quasi governmental bodies interfering in the selection process. This is what is happening when the nutters in the Brussels commission and the Luxembourg court are allowed to get involved. I cite the case of a woman who was turned down when she applied for a job because she was four months pregnant. I can't think of any normal employer who would want her, except for temporary work, until she had had her child, but she succeeded in finding some lunatic fringe lobby to pay for her case to be taken to the European court which rules (and I'm being dead serious) that the employer was guilty of sex discrimination unless he could prove that he would have rejected a male applicant in similar circumstances. As Alexander Pope said:

> "And who'll wage war with Bedlam or the Mint?"

The other running sore of creeping collectivism is the way in which people of different national origins are classified and the 'discrimination' racket that has been foisted on us by would-be do-gooders who are, in fact, do-badders.

They will insist on using the dreadful word 'race' that in my school days was a low key, neutral term that was used pretty loosely, but which became endowed with emotional overtones in the Hitler era.

The traditional gift of the English was in being able to assimilate people of different national origins who chose to live here because they wanted to be English, as people who emigrated to the US wanted to be Americans. You can go back to the French Huguenot, German, Polish, Russian immigrants of the nineteenth and early 20th Century. If some of them happened to be Jewish, this was their religion and not an ethnic classification. The problem in recent years has been the counter-productive, political lobbying to treat African, Asian, Caribbean Africans and so on as 'ethnic minorities', in other words to discourage them from assimilating and to condition them to permanent imprisonment in ghettoes of the mind. As for the totally outrageous idea that recruitment or admission to schools or colleges should be on a quota basis, as opposed to normal selection based on individual capability, we are back in the world of Bedlam. Even more perverse, is the claim by some black law students that the Bar exams are discriminatory because English men and women with the traditional English education are more likely to pass. We are into a Kafka nightmare. We are in England, God damn it and if anyone wants to come and live here, then he or she should do so on our terms.

Whilst it is in our power as a democracy (or ought to be) to remedy matters when the law (as a result of a tom fool court decision) turns out to be an ass, such amendment doesn't help the large numbers of people who are permanently injured (even though the injury is usually mental) by the combination of perverse, single issue, fanatic propaganda and misguided attempts to legislate against 'discrimination'.

The technique used to recruit agents by the Russian government, which was uncovered at the end of the war when a Russian spy sought asylum in Canada, was fairly elementary. The Russians didn't look for Canadian communists. There weren't many. They targeted ethnic and occupational groups. If you could sow in the mind of a Ukranian working in Alberta the idea that if his girlfriend threw him out, or he lost his job, it was because he was a Ukranian, it was not a difficult task to convince him. Very few people are prepared to admit the role of their own shortcomings in any such situation. Once you could sow in his mind the idea that he was being discriminated against, it was not difficult to convince him that the country in which he lived was evil and the only way to get rid of this evil was to overturn it by revolution. Such ideas are like drugs - only they operate in the mind. People like Goebbels and his Soviet equivalents understood this perfectly well.

I was grateful to Hugh, John's father, for pointing out this technique at around the time John and I were getting married. Hugh had brought the full report of the Royal Canadian commission into espionage. It was one of the subjects that interested him.

In England we now have an underclass within which many of the immigrants who would traditionally have been motivated and encouraged to try for assimilation in the hope that their children would move up the social scale - many of these people are now having propaganda thrust at them, aimed at convincing them that every time they fail to get a job, a house or whatever they are seeking, that the other person must be a 'racist'. What better way could be devised for turning such people into resentful troublemakers, revolutionaries, criminals or what have you.

One can have a go at trying to control most things in one's environment, but you have no control whatever over whether you were born male or female, or whether your skin is dark brown, light brown, pink or white. If you drum into people from an early age that the only thing that matters in life is their sex or colour, you are condemning them to a soul-destroying fatalism, which makes it virtually impossible for friends or teachers at a later date to urge them to improve themselves and to believe that the only thing that matters in life is one's own immortal soul and not the collectivist classification which treats you like a butterfly pressed in blotting paper between the pages of a heavy book.

My best analogy is that of the ancient Greeks. They believed that when you captured a man in battle and made him a slave, you took away what they called his arêté - you were taking away half his mind. I believe that a similar process occurs when you succeed in brainwashing or conditioning a person into believing that the only part of him that matters is the bits that can be labelled as man, woman, dog or some ethnic nomenclature. It used to be the proletariat.

A lot of English people who went on believing in Russia as a workers' paradise long after they had ample evidence that it wasn't were, in my view, motivated by some kind of pathological hatred of the traditional English world in which I grew up and most of you did. Other countries have had their quislings, so there is no reason to be unduly surprised that we harbour our own variety who will, no doubt, latch on to any lobby or cause that they believe will be detrimental to the future survival and prosperity of the country that we know and love and which, in spite of its faults has contributed so much to the happiness of so many of us, whether native born or those who have come to our shores because they want to share our way of life with us.

ENVOI

Even if the testament of Boadie, as John has called this chapter, has been a less exciting read than some of the chapters describing my escapades and tense moments in days gone by, I hope you will nevertheless consider it worthy of inclusion in my life story. I am not a young, aspiring politician or hot gospeller out to sell a particular view of the world as a panacea to its many problems. On the contrary, I am an old age pensioner who has been privileged to live a varied and interesting life that has given me a first hand knowledge of many human situations that have caused me to reflect on some of the issues on which people tend to pontificate and also on issues on which no-one is currently expressing interest (at any rate in public). I'm sure that most of you do the same.

I would have loved if Dad had lived long enough and had put down his thoughts on paper or if Mum had done the same, on the subjects that I have attempted to cover in this epilogue. Dad was a fund of level-headed common-sense on most of the issues on which he touched and I still marvel at how right he was in so many of his judgments on the politicians of the 1930s, in spite of the fact that he didn't have access to much of the information that I have only gleaned from reading later historical works.

If my testament falls far short of what you expected when I mentioned François Villon as my model, then I apologise. I hope in my prayers that St. Peter will, in due course, allow me to enter the Kingdom of Heaven, where I will be reunited with David. It has never worried me that I have had two husbands and I hope in due course to be reunited

EPILOGUE - THE TESTAMENT OF BOADIE

with both. I believe that, as Our Lord said to the woman who had had seven husbands, that they order such matters differently in Heaven. I have merely to give thanks for having had two such wonderful men in my life and such a wonderful family.

I tend to think of St. Peter as someone like Dad. If my straying from the straight and narrow merits punishment, then I tend to think this is the spiritual equivalent of what happened when Dad put me over his knee as a small child. I will be the equivalent of a small child when I start my new life.

It may, or may not, be heresy, but in my own mind I have never really believed that the odd night spent in bed with someone like Douglas, or Roger, or Jacko for that matter, would matter in the least to St. Peter. What I regret most in my own life are the areas where I could have taken the initiative and achieved a worthwhile result and where I didn't do so either through inertia or because I allowed the job to get crowded out by less important things.

There are, of course, times where I have gone in like a bull in a china shop, thrown down the gauntlet and made provocative statements, as I have in this chapter, in the belief that they are right and in the process I may have upset people unnecessarily. My favourite poet, Ezra Pound, did the same and I can think of no better words to bid you, patient reader, farewell than by quoting his famous lines from the Pisan Cantos:

> *What thou lovest well remains,*
>   *the rest is dross.*
> *What thou lovest well shall not be reft from thee*
> *What thou lovest well is thy true heritage...*
>
> *Pull down thy vanity, it is not man*
> *Made courage, or made order, or made grace...*
>
> *'Master thyself, then others shall thee beare'...*
>
> *But to have done instead of not doing*
>   *this is not vanity....*
>
> *Here error is all in the not done,*
>   *all in the diffidence that faltered.*